Women
of Spirit

WOMEN OF SPIRIT

Female Leadership
in the Jewish and
Christian Traditions

Edited by
ROSEMARY RUETHER AND
ELEANOR McLAUGHLIN

Simon and Schuster
NEW YORK

Published by Simon and Schuster
A Division of Gulf & Western Corporation
Simon & Schuster Building
Rockefeller Center
1230 Avenue of the Americas
New York, New York 10020

Designed by Clint Anglin
Manufactured in the United States of America

1 2 3 4 5 6 7 8 9 10
1 2 3 4 5 6 7 8 9 10 Pbk.
Library of Congress Cataloging in Publication Data
Main entry under title:
Women of spirit.
Includes bibliographical references and index.
1. Women in Christianity—Addresses, essays,
lectures.   2. Women in Judaism—Addresses, essays,
lectures.   3. Women (Theology)—Addresses, essays,
lectures.   I. Ruether, Rosemary Radford.   II. Mc-
Laughlin, Eleanor.
BV639.W7W62   261.8′34′12   78-11995
ISBN   0-671-22843-9
ISBN   0-671-24805-7   Pbk.

Contents

Contents

Women
of Spirit

INTRODUCTION

Women's Leadership in the Jewish and Christian Traditions: Continuity and Change

ROSEMARY RUETHER AND
ELEANOR McLAUGHLIN

In this collection of essays on leadership roles of women in the Jewish and Christian traditions, we hope to make a contribution both toward the recovery of important chapters of women's history and toward the charting of the paradigms of female leadership possible within successive theological world views. These are both difficult problems. We do not hope to do more than make a beginning in these studies of women's leadership in different historical periods and traditions.

The chief problem in charting any history of women is the recovery and use of sources. The marginality of women in the Jewish and Christian religious traditions means that few sources exist for judging their roles. Those that can be found were generally recorded by males and display a male bias. Even those sources written by women were preserved by a male cultural system. They have to be looked at from the perspective of the woman's internalization of patriarchal ideologies or the editing of her views to make them acceptable to the official models of women's "nature" and prescribed roles. Material about women that does not fit these prescriptions is likely to be edited out, if the woman is to be held up as a "good" model, or turned into a polemic, if the woman is regarded as a "bad example" to be avoided. Women have seldom controlled the processes of the cultural interpretation of their actions.

This question of sources is directly related to whether women are regarded as Teachers—that is, shapers and transmitters of tradition. In Rabbinic Judaism the role of rabbinic student equipped each generation, in turn, to produce its rabbis, or teachers, who transmitted the tradition. Women were eliminated from these roles for the community as a whole, although occasionally a rabbi would flout this proscription by teaching his daughter Torah. A few teachings come down under the name of Beruria, but this is an exception to the rule.

In Christianity originally women seem to have been incorporated into the teaching role, but were eliminated early enough that the Church Fathers took for granted that women might never act as public teachers. The Middle Ages modified this where saints and holy women were concerned, but women were kept from the universities. There were women writers of spirituality, but no women scholastic theologians. The Protestant focus of theological training in the academic milieu and the abolition of monasteries eliminated such of the female teaching tradition as had been possible in the medieval world. Women teachers who arose were regarded as heretics (Anne Hutchinson) and/or appeared in the left-wing Protestant traditions, such as Quakers. An individualistic mysticism also appeared in Protestantism, but as a distinctly marginal phenomenon.

Even in the nineteenth century women predominated as teachers primarily in the sectarian traditions. Some liberal churches began the process of incorporating women into the official ministry. A group of women, many of them ordained ministers, gathered in the 1890s to make a commentary on the Bible, under the direction of feminist Elizabeth Cady Stanton. But the idea of women exercising such a role was still sufficiently scandalous that it was attacked by the male ministry as a collaboration between "women and the Devil."

Women scholars today who seek to recover role models

from the past also need to recognize their own subjective relation to the process. Much of the culture into which women were incorporated in the past may be experienced today as so demeaning that it may be difficult to cut through our way of experiencing it to discern the empowerment that women then may have found in it. A contemporary nun, looking for role models for her life in the foundresses of the past, may have a difficult time making such women come alive, both because they have been shrouded in pious hagiography and because she herself is too much a psychological prisoner of this piety to see the full dimensions of their activity. Those who stand at a certain distance from these traditions may be able to bring such figures alive more easily than those working their way out of particular heritages. Yet, in spite of these problems of sources and methodology, it is possible to see that women have played surprisingly varied and authoritative roles in Western religion. It is our hope to bring to light a fuller picture of these roles.

Since women until recently were barred as teachers and ministers in the orthodox or mainstream traditions, it is easy to assume that women moved to find roles in heretical movements. One might think that the more strongly a group rejected normative Christianity or Judaism, the more easily women might find a place in it. It is true that sectarian movements and those defined as heretical, such as Gnostics and Montanists, seem to have constructed theological systems that allowed a larger place for women. Moreover, the mainstream church could link the two to the denigration of both, under the assumption that woman's incapacity to teach or understand theology disposed her particularly to heresy, thus reinforcing the suppression of women in the mainstream. The question of sources also arises here. In order to obtain a just picture of the actual role of women in a particular period, it is necessary to overcome the later definition of normative and "heretical" sources and use all the sources of a particular period. Quite often the sharp division between the two is imposed by later judgment and does not reflect the actual sociological overlap of these groups at the time. Elisabeth Fiorenza, in her chapter on the New Testament, has particularly demonstrated this point.

Feminists today are apt to be especially attracted to rejected groups—heretics and even witches—expecting to find among them subversive views expressing feminist rejection of patriarchal religion. But in our opinion much of this search is mistaken. It is difficult in any period, but especially in an authoritarian culture, for persons to remain sane and mature from a stance of radical rejection of and by the normative culture. Important women do appear as leaders in marginal movements, but they are not more important than women leaders who arise at the center. Orthodox theology is appropriated by such women with a radicality and depth of insight that transforms it into an expression of the full personhood of women. Moreover, women themselves, already suspect by male leaders, are more likely to be scrupulous of their orthodoxy than otherwise.

It is women operating from a stance of "radical obedience" rather than dissent who are likely to make the greater impact on their male colleagues, for their claims cannot be so easily rejected. The positions taken toward authority by the Roman Catholic nuns of the Leadership Conference of Women Religious (discussed in the final chapter of this volume) are examples of this type of "radical obedience." Such loyal dissent typically takes its stand on a vision of the "true meaning" of the Gospel or of Judaism that, at the same time, rejects its patriarchal deformations.

It is characteristic of the leadership roles in Christianity claimed by women that they derive their authority from personal charism rather than from office. This is so, not because, as men have supposed, women are more disposed toward the emotive and intuitive, but because it reflects the sociological fact that women for the most part were not allowed to claim authority of office. So it was in those areas where roles based on "gifts of the Spirit" were recognized that there was likely to be space for women. There re-

mained, in Christianity especially, a heritage from its sectarian, apocalyptic origins that created an uneasy tension between the authority of spiritual gifts and institutionalization.
The Holy Spirit, unlike the institution, was recognized, even
by the official tradition, as no respecter of persons. The
Spirit might endow women or other marginal persons with
spiritual gifts. The Scriptural pentecostal tradition of Acts
2:17 declares that the prophetic spirit was poured out on the
"maidservants" as well as the "menservants."

Martyrdom too was seen as abolishing sex roles and distinctions and embuing women with a "manly spirit" to fight
side by side with their brothers. Moreover, in the early centuries of the church, the one who had suffered for Christ
was believed to be endowed with sacramental powers that
rivaled those of the episcopal leadership. Prophetic gifts
were seen as giving power to preach and to bestow the blessing over the Lord's Supper. Thus women, in maintaining
their roles in charismatic ministry, were also maintaining a
type of authority based on direct spiritual gifts which the
mainstream church later sought to define as marginal or
heretical.

Religious orders gave an institutional space to women's
spiritual gifts as seekers of sanctity, mystics and teachers of
holiness. Although mainstream Protestantism abolished this
option, sectarian Protestantism took up the tradition that
gave women authority through direct spiritual gifts. Particularly in those branches of Protestantism for which the minister was definitively a prophetic preacher who spoke the
Word of God directly out of spiritual gifts, we find the appearance of women as preachers and congregational leaders.
Among seventeenth-century Baptists in England women
who were recognized as spiritually endowed were allowed to
preach. Nor was it an accident that the Quaker doctrine of
Inner Light also moved toward abolition of sex roles and
sanctioning of female leadership.

When the question of the ordination of women first made

headway in the nineteenth century, this occurred among those groups whose evangelical understanding of preaching as prophetic ministry led them to affirm women's equal right to be a vehicle of the Spirit. At the first ordination of a woman, that of Congregationalist Antoinette Brown in 1853, we find this view of ministry. The evangelist Luther Lee, who preached her ordination sermon, justified the break with tradition by declaring that "every Gospel minister is a prophet, and every prophet under the new dispensation is a Gospel minister."

Women also tend to find greater space for leadership in the founding or renewal movements of Christianity. Such renewal movements tend to restore the crisis sociology of a charismatic movement. This is particularly true when church renewal is linked to a millennialist view of the present age. Millennial expectations make relative or set aside the authority of traditional institutions of family, synagogue, church and government. Those who have the gifts and the commitment are validated by the community as leaders. Such millennial expectation places the church in a "liminal" relation to normative society and allows it to set aside social distinctions. The greater possibility of leadership roles for women in Christianity than in Judaism doubtless has something to do with these millennialist origins and the continuing receptivity to eschatological renewal. The authority of prophetic and charismatic leadership is directly linked to both the crisis sociology and the apocalyptic mood of such religious movements.

Women's leadership also appears where lay leadership is stressed. Various renewal movements in left-wing Protestantism, as well as Catholicism, have been marked by an anticlericalism that validated the authority of the entire community to teach, interpret the Bible and evangelize. Those who have the gifts, rather than those authorized by the traditional institution, are acclaimed as leaders. In this situation women too can emerge as leaders. However, in the next generation, as renewal movements settle down and begin themselves to institutionalize, there is a loss of this early freedom. Institutionalized leadership again reverts to the patriarchal pattern, and women are eliminated. One can find this phenomenon recurring again and again in the history of Christianity.

On the other hand, in mainstream Christianity important leadership exercised by women is often linked to their class status. The relation of sex and class modifies the marginality of women. Although women are a subordinate "caste" within every class, they belong to all classes. So a woman who belongs to the leadership class may exercise power that derives, in part, from her social position. The striking role played by some women in fourth-century Christian asceticism undoubtedly had much to do with their status as wealthy, well-connected women. In the Middle Ages also, roles played by abbesses and queens reflected their social position. During the Reformation and on into later centuries of Protestantism, women leaders were likely to be related to leading families. The role played by nineteenth-century American women reformers was closely related to their social class. Leadership in Catholic religious orders also was linked to wealth and class connections (often a condition for entering an order). On the other hand, these women themselves often experienced their marginality within their own class in such a way as to wish to dissolve their prejudice and to reach across class lines to associate themselves with women of lower classes and different races.

But, for the abbess as much as for the sectarian preacher, it was the authority of holiness, the authority of direct charism, that was most important in compensating for their lack of recognized capacity for "headship" in patriarchal society. This possibility is linked in Christianity with a specific theology of the transcendent or the eschatological. Until the rise of modern liberalism, women's subordination in the "order of nature" was the accepted theological view. Female leadership was seen as forbidden by nature, if not originally, at least as a characteristic of present, fallen nature. In any case, female leadership was understood as contrary to "nature."

However, through holiness and ecstasy a woman transcends "nature" and participates in the eschatological sphere. She anticipates the order of salvation of heaven. In this eschatological order, sex hierarchy is abolished for that asexual personhood in which there is "neither male nor female." Holiness or rising to the transcendent, therefore, can be a way for women to claim an equality with men. For most of Christianity this eschatological dissolution of sex hierarchy was linked with celibacy. It is through directly renouncing their sexual role and function that women (and men) attain that neutral personhood which is neither male nor female. Protestantism, in abolishing the institutionalized sphere of monasticism, also rejected the idea that some persons already transcend nature and anticipate the equality of heaven.

Yet, in sectarian Protestantism, claims of mystic or ecstatic holiness that sanction sexual equality often were characterized by the reappearance of celibacy (as in the Shakers). Again, we find married women in the nineteenth-century Holiness movement also claiming that "going on to perfection" may give them a right to preach and teach that transcends or overcomes sex roles.

Theological images of the feminine—in God, in the relation between Christ and the church (or the soul), and in the anthropology of the self—also play an important role. Some sectarian groups, such as Gnostics and nineteenth-century Protestant sectarians, believed in the androgyny of God. The typology of Christ and the church as a nuptial image appears in the New Testament and continually reappears in Christian symbolism. The soul may be seen as female in relation to God but male (rational) in relation to the body. These symbolic typologies of the self and God are generally constructed on complementary lines that suggest that the male stands for the more active side of the relationship, the female for the more passive or receptive.

However, we should not therefore suppose that this symbolism always reinforced patriarchal subjugation of women, socially. It makes a great deal of difference in what context these symbols operate. A millennialist, eschatological Christianity, with a celibate spirituality, can appropriate these androgynous symbols to suggest that the redeemed person overcomes sexual dualism and experiences the reunion of maleness and femaleness in him or herself and in God. A spiritually androgynous self rises above the sexual dualism of physical bisexuality, an idea found in Gnosticism and again among the Shakers. Medieval monasticism continually suggested that the bridal relation to Christ allows a woman to reject her physical subordination to sexual roles in society. On the other hand, where the symbolism of Christ and the church as male and female operates in a church where marriage is the norm (as in Puritanism) it is more likely to reinforce the hierarchy of sexual roles.

Celibacy is important, sociologically, for women. Traditionally it mandated the creation of a separate space for women where they founded and ran their own institutions. The patriarchal church often struggled to maintain power over these female institutions, but the women themselves continually asserted an autonomy in their own sphere. Although Protestantism abolished the separate space of female celibacy for women, powerful separate female organizations grew up in missionary societies and other female-run institutions. Separate female ministries, such as deaconesses, were forerunners of the ordination of women in Protestant denominations. Again and again women have found that when their separate institutional base has been dissolved in the name of "integration," they have lost as well as gained power through being forced to give up organizational autonomy.

The nineteenth century is an important watershed in the

history of these traditional models of women's leadership derived from personal charism or holiness, and often expressed in sectarian or in monastic form. Traditionally the "neither male nor female" of the New Testament has been seen as an eschatological, not a historical, possibility. It might be expressed in personal or even institutional forms that transcended "nature," but not translated back into accepted social institutions of the state, the family or the church. Here "nature" *qua* patriarchy must reign.

However, the influence of nineteenth-century liberalism helped to create a new theology of the relation between history and transcendent possibility. Liberalism challenged the identification of normative social patterns with "nature." History had corrupted nature. Liberalism preached a doctrine of "original nature" that was egalitarian. Social reform, in the name of the law of nature, must restore this original egalitarian state. Now the ideals of "neither male nor female" of the New Testament ceased to be seen as beyond nature and became a goal of social reform. Eschatology was, so to speak, brought down from heaven and located in the future, as the goal of a historical process of evolution and amelioration of unjust social conditions. It was this revised theology of history that, for the first time, translated the concept of spiritual equality of Christianity into a demand for institutional reform that included women in the institutional, ordained ministry.

The impact of liberalism had a somewhat parallel effect on Judaism. Judaism lacked the eschatological traditions of celibate equality. For Jews, a patriarchal Law that interpreted the male as the normative Jew for religious initiation and observance was not susceptible to the same kind of apocalyptic subversion as in Christianity. But Jews too responded to a secularized millennialism that made social justice (*qua* social equality) the goal of reform. Moreover, liberalism had the effect of dissolving the ghetto walls that kept Judaism a separate enclave under religious law. Now Judaism became, like Christianity, a private dimension of life. But, unlike the

Christian, the "secular" society into which the Jew was thrust in public life was the secular expression of a rival religion and society. Jewish women, excluded from most religious expressions of Judaism, relegated even to learning their prayers in Yiddish rather than in Hebrew, had fewer barriers against this secularly Christian world, once the ghetto walls were down. Reform Jews, who sought to adapt but also to protect Judaism in this new situation, recognized the need to incorporate women into leadership roles and religious observance in order to make them religiously more Jewish. Orthodox Jews, on the other hand, saw the preservation of the unchanged Judaism of the ghetto as including the customs that excluded women. Judaism today continues to oscillate between these two impulses, as Ellen Umansky's chapter shows.

But the nineteenth century not only was characterized by rationalist, egalitarian liberalism but was also swayed by Romanticism, which renewed the complementary opposition of masculinity and femininity as dualisms that divided the sexes, society and the cosmos. Liberalism continued the reform impulse of Puritanism, which regarded the principles of religion as a mandate to reform the entire society into a pattern of righteousness. Romanticism, on the other hand, incorporated the growing split between the public and the private spheres fostered by industrialization and secularization. Religion, privatized in the domestic sphere, comes to be seen as peculiarly "feminine." The clergy too come to be seen as exercising a less than "masculine" profession. This relation between women, religion and the clergy fostered a newly ambivalent relation between the clergy and women. Clergymen often accepted the idea that women's nature incarnates particular aptitude for religiosity, and "goodness." Women and the Home can then be seen as a kind of launching pad for social reforms, looked upon as moral crusades, such as temperance. But this same identification fosters an unwillingness to see women themselves exercise roles "outside the home."

The "femininization" of religion also reinforced the fear of a male clergy of the women's entrance into the ministry. Medieval Christianity had seen the church and the soul as feminine in relation to God and Christ. But these were feminine elements that could be appropriated by men as well. God was seen as expressing all human characteristics, not merely those of males. But nineteenth-century thought tended to make the "feminine" element in religion much more exclusively a special endowment of women and to suggest a radically different piety and spirituality of women as such. Both the conservative concepts of "Total Womanhood" and radical feminist theories of female spirituality still exhibit the legacies of this nineteenth-century split between masculinity and femininity as particular endowments of males and females.

The twentieth century has seen a gradual change in the historical exclusion of women from the ministry and the rabbinate. More recently, the barriers against women in the ordained ministry of the Catholic traditions have also been challenged. Episcopalianism has been the pioneer in incorporating women into that ministry defined as priesthood. In so doing it has had to deal with a host of psychological and symbolic problems not faced by Protestants who come from a nonpriestly prophetic tradition. Deeply ingrained ideas of cultic purity, defined over against female "impurity," have surfaced. The symbolic image of Christ as bridegroom and the church as bride has been interpreted sacramentally to exclude women.

One question that women particularly need to ask about the religious tradition is why the priestly, cultic line seems so much more antagonistic to women than the prophetic preaching line of leadership. In many ways the sacramental tradition would seem to be receptive to women, with its bodily and nurturing characteristics, while the teaching tradition is more abstract and "asexual." Certainly women have been as firmly excluded from the Judaic rabbinate as they have from priesthood in Christianity, but Judaism has not had to deal with the question of priesthood since the fall of the temple cultus in A.D. 70. The medieval church spent more time polemicizing against women as teachers than against women as priests, but that may have been because women were more likely to appear in the guise of teachers, while their role as cultic ministers was out of the question. The linking of the preaching tradition with nineteenth-century liberalism and the sacramental tradition with Romanticism has undoubtedly much to do with reinforcing disparate patterns toward women that have appeared in the last hundred years.

In any case, women today have the possibility of playing roles in the institutional and ordained leadership of more and more branches of Western religion. No longer do they have to validate the possibility of leadership through roles marginal and subversive to the institution. Women must therefore ask themselves not only what they gain by these new developments but also what they may lose. Is it enough simply to be incorporated into paradigms of ordained ministry shaped by males for many hundreds of years in hierarchical molds intended to exclude women? Or must women, by their very presence, reshape the ministry into forms that are more open, pluralistic and dialogic? In gaining the leadership of office, will they abandon the insights gained through the authority of holiness and charism? Women, excluded from the institutional church leadership, have continued to represent forms of leadership that derive from a church shaped by direct religious experience, millennial hope and marginality within established social forms. They have represented the lay voice as well, united with the ministry of the people. Women should appropriate their history, not merely to deplore their past exclusion but to vindicate the insights of this alternative tradition and use it to reshape and enlarge the vision and life of the church today.

ONE

Word, Spirit and Power: Women in Early Christian Communities

ELISABETH SCHÜSSLER FIORENZA

Studies of the role of women in early Christianity generally conclude that women were marginal figures in the early Christian movement. Our sources scarcely mention women and refer to them only in passing. They do no more than transmit the names of some early Christian women, providing very little information about them. If we assume that these sources are objective reports of the crucial events and leading persons in early Christianity, we would have to conclude that this scanty information reflects the actual role women held in the early Christian church.

Academic and popular discussions of discipleship, church order, worship or mission have generally taken for granted that the early Christian communities had an all-male leadership. Scholars have believed that the structures of the early Christian communities reflected the structures and values of contemporary patriarchal Jewish or Greco-Roman society. Thus, by definition, women would have been relegated to marginal roles in early Christianity. This reconstruction of early church history from the point of view of male dominance functions today as a social and theological mythology that determines our self-understanding and justifies the present ecclesial structures of male power.[1] New analyses of the social world of early Christianity which show it, not as a culturally well-adapted, monolithic group, but as an egalitarian, countercultural, multifaceted movement suggest an alternative view.[2] This view becomes clear when all the early sources, apocryphal and heterodox as well as canonical and orthodox, are examined. Membership in this egalitarian, pluriform movement was not defined by gender roles, but by faith commitment to the Christian community. Women, in this egalitarian movement, were not marginal figures but exercised responsible leadership.

During the early missionary period, leadership roles were diversified and based on actual function and service. Gradually these became institutionalized, and a patriarchalization of the Christian community, offices and theology took place, as the early Christians adopted the institutional forms of the surrounding patriarchal culture. Charismatic leadership rooted in the experience of and in the obedience to the Spirit was gradually replaced by patriarchal office[3] and cultic ministry.[4] This development was not the same in all places, but followed different patterns in various Christian groups. The patriarchal line of early Christian development played down women's role or made it marginal. But the earlier countercultural and later extraecclesial groups accepted women as equal members with equal responsibility and leadership.[5]

The earliest Christians understood themselves as freed by the Spirit to a new life of egalitarian discipleship. This theological understanding is expressed in the pre-Pauline baptismal formula (Galatians 3:27ff.).[6] Newly baptized Christians affirmed that in this new community there was no longer any distinction between Jew and Gentile, free and slave, male and female, but that all were united in Christ Jesus. It was a commonplace among Jews as well as Greeks to be thankful that they were humans and not beasts, Greeks and not barbarians, Jews and not Gentiles, free-born and not slaves, men and not women. The Christian egalitarian creed was formulated over and against this commonly accepted ratification of social discrimination in Judaism and Hellenism.

This confrontation of the Christian affirmation with those of the surrounding cultures shows that the new vision of community was not just a heavenly ideal, but was accepted as a historical reality. Over against the patriarchal pattern of the "world," Christians understood themselves as a new community, in which all members shared equally in the freedom of the children of God [7] and in which privileged religious, class and gender roles were abolished. The patriarchal cultural paradigm was replaced by the vision of a community where people lived together in love and service. [8] Not only Gentiles and slaves but also women could be full and equal members of this community.

Women as Founders and Leaders of Congregations*

Historians of early Christianity generally fail to notice the important role women played in founding and promoting house churches. Since the house church was a decisive factor in early Christian development, [9] it provided the leadership and determined the form of church life. In the house church the early Christians celebrated the Eucharist (Acts 2:46; 20:7) and preached the Gospel (Acts 5:42). The assembly was called the "house of God," the new "temple," because the Spirit dwelt in it. [10]

Wealthy women converts (cf. Acts 17:4,12) exercised decisive influence on these gatherings. Acts 12:12 refers to a specific prayer meeting in the house of Mary, the mother of John Mark. Paul greets Apphia, "our sister," who together with Philemon and Archippus was a leader of a house church in Colossae (Philemon 2). The church in Philippi was founded with the conversion of the businesswoman Lydia from Thyatira (Acts 16:14). The author of Colossians refers to Nympha of Laodicea and the "church in her house" (Co-

* Throughout the chapter, references and spellings, etc., are to and from the Revised Standard Version of the Bible.

lossians 4:15). Paul twice mentions the missionary couple Prisca (Priscilla) and Aquila and "the church in their house" (1 Corinthians 16:19; Romans 16:3–5). He wrote the first letter to the Corinthians in response to a report made by slaves who belonged to the household of a woman Chloe (1 Corinthians 1:11).[11]

We have no reason to assume that women were excluded from the leadership of the house churches or from presiding at worship. The "household codes"[12] probably are a later patriarchal reaction to this leadership of women within the house churches.[13] This assumption is supported by 1 Timothy 2, where the injunctions that women should be submissive and not teach are given in the context of regulations for worship.

Paul explicitly mentions women as his missionary co-workers. The texts give no indication that these women were dependent on or subordinate to Paul. Only five of Paul's co-workers (Erastus, Mark, Timothy, Titus and Tychicus) "stand in an explicit subordination to Paul, serving him or being subject to his instructions."[14] The most common terms, e.g., "co-worker" (Prisca), "brother/sister" (Apphia), "*diakonos*" (Phoebe), and "apostle" (Junia), are also found in reference to women. The authentic Pauline letters equate co-workers and "those who toil." In 1 Corinthians 16:16ff. Paul admonishes the addressees to be "subject to every co-worker and laborer" and to give recognition to such persons. First Thessalonians 5:12 exhorts the Thessalonian Christians "to respect those who labor among you, and are over you in the Lord and admonish you." Paul uses the same Greek verb, "to labor" or "to toil," not only for his own missionary evangelizing and teaching but also for that of women. In Romans 16:6,12 he commends Mary, Tryphena, Tryphosa and Persis: they have "labored" hard in the Lord.

Paul affirms that women have worked with him on an equal basis. Philippians 4:2f. explicitly states that Euodia and Syntyche have "contended" side by side with him. As in an athletic competition, these women have competed with

Paul, Clemens and the rest of Paul's co-missionaries in the cause of the Gospel. Paul considers the authority of both women in the community at Philippi so great that their dissensions might be a serious threat to the existence of this community.[15] The texts indicate that these women missionaries commanded the same authority, esteem and respect as their male co-workers in the missionary communities.

One of Paul's most prominent co-workers is Prisca,[16] together with her husband, Aquila; like Barnabas or Apollos, she worked independently of Paul and was not under his authority. Paul declares that all the churches of the Gentiles have reason to be grateful to this missionary couple. They founded and led house churches in Corinth, Ephesus and Rome (if Romans 16 is addressed to that community). First Corinthians 16:19 has greetings from Aquila and Prisca. When Paul sends greetings to the couple (Romans 16:3f.) he addresses Prisca first, indicating that she is the leading figure (cf. also 2 Timothy 4:19).

In Acts, Prisca is also mentioned first. The references to her and Aquila (Acts 18:2ff.; 18:18,26) correspond with the information of the Pauline letters. Luke shows the importance of the couple and suggests that they were well known. They were by trade tentmakers and supported their missionary endeavor through their own work, which, like Paul's, made them independent of the churches that they served. They were expelled from Rome when Claudius banished the Jews from there. In Ephesus they converted Apollos, who would become one of the leading apostles alongside Paul (18:26).[17] Since Prisca is mentioned first in Acts 18:26, it was probably she who was primarily responsible for Apollos' conversion. Under her leadership Apollos learned "the way of God more accurately." The text clearly assumes that Prisca was the catechist and teacher of Apollos.

Whereas Prisca and Aquila are not directly called apostles, another couple, Andronicus and Junia, receives this title in Romans 16:7. There is no reason to interpret the name Junia as a short form of the male name Junianus, since Junia was a well-known name for women at the time.[18] Andronicus and Junia are a missionary couple who had converted to Christianity before Paul. At the time of the writing of Romans 16, they are fellow prisoners of Paul and outstanding among the apostles. We know from 1 Corinthians 9:5 that Andronicus and Junia were not an exception, since the "other apostles" also had a "sister" with them as a "wife" (literally, a woman) on their missionary journeys. If the term "brother" denotes a particular group of missionary co-workers (cf. Philippians 4:21f.), there is no reason not to assume that these "sisters" were co-workers. Very likely many workers in the early Christian mission were couples.[19] When Paul stresses celibacy as the best precondition for missionary work (1 Corinthians 7:23ff.), he is expressing his own opinion, not the practice of the early missionary church.

Romans 16:1f. mentions another important woman, Phoebe. She receives two titles: *diakonos* of the church at Cenchreae and *prostatis* "of many and of myself as well." Exegetes have downplayed the significance of these titles when they refer to her. Wherever Paul uses the title *diakonos* for himself or another male leader, scholars translate it as "minister," "missionary" or "servant," whereas in the case of Phoebe they render it as "deaconess." After characterizing Phoebe as an "obviously well-to-do and philanthropic lady" Lietzmann goes on to say: "Even at that time there had long been women deacons in the Christian church who, when *their sex made them specially suitable*, came forward and gave signal help in caring for the poor and sick, and at the baptism of women"[20] (emphasis mine). Unconsciously Lietzmann here projects back into the first century the duties of the deaconess of a later period whose service was limited to the "ministry to women." Yet the text does not indicate any limitations of the office of Phoebe by prescribed gender roles. She is not the deacon of the "women" in the church at Cenchreae, but of the whole church.

Paul uses the term *diakonos* together with *synergos* (co-worker), as can be seen in 1 Corinthians 3:5,9 and 2 Corinthians 6:1,4. According to 1 Corinthians 16:15 the co-workers and laborers are those who "have devoted themselves to the *diakonia* of the saints." The *diakonoi* appear to be not only itinerant missionaries but leaders in local congregations.[21] The term is used in the New Testament and also in secular sources to refer to preaching and teaching. Thus, the *diakonoi* served in a recognized official capacity as teachers and preachers in the Christian community.

The second title of Phoebe, *prostatis*, is usually translated as "helper" or "patroness," even though in the literature of the time it has the connotation of leading officer, president, governor or superintendent.[22] In 1 Thessalonians 5:12 the verb characterizes persons with authority in the community, and in 1 Timothy 3:4f. and 5:17 it designates the functions of the bishop, deacon or elder. Phoebe thus had a designated role of leadership and teaching in the community of Cenchreae. She was a person with great authority for many and for Paul himself. Like other missionaries, Phoebe received a letter of recommendation. It is possible that, as the *patrona*[23] of the church at Cenchreae, Phoebe, like other *patroni* of collegia (or clubs), traveled to Rome to defend there the interests of her community.

Paul's letters indicate that women were among the prominent and leading missionaries in the early Christian movement. They were co-workers with Paul but did not depend on him or stand under his authority. They were not excluded from any missionary function. They were preachers, teachers and leaders of the community. If we compare their ministry with those of the later deaconesses we have to stress that their ministry was not limited to the ministry to women nor to specific gender roles and functions. The prominence of women in the early Christian movement is confirmed by examining the list of names in Romans 16. Of the thirty-six persons mentioned, sixteen are women and eighteen men. The Pauline letters thus give us a glimpse of the egalitarian early Christian missionary movement.

The writings of the Pauline school, however, also transmit

the injunctions of a patriarchal reaction which, on theological grounds, decree the subordinate role of women. Whether or not Paul himself initiated this reaction is disputed.[24] Certainly, however, those who produced the justifications for the patriarchalization of Christian leadership were able to claim the authority of Paul without being challenged. Even though 1 Corinthians 11:2–16 concedes to women the gift of prophecy and liturgical functions, the passage nevertheless demands that women adapt to the role definition of their society. This demand is theologically justified by regarding the headship of God over Christ, Christ over man, and man over woman as a revealed hierarchy: God–Christ–man–woman.[25] For the sake of order the church order in 1 Corinthians 14:33b–36 forbids women to speak in the assembly and directs them to their husbands for religious instruction.[26]

The so-called household codes of the Deutero-Pauline literature uphold the patriarchal order of the family. These rules of conduct were universally accepted in Judaism and Hellenism and soon became a part of Christian theology.[27] According to them, women express and practice their Christian faith by observing the social-patriarchal order. In 1 Timothy 2:9–15 women are both commanded to keep silent and behave modestly, and explicitly forbidden to teach or to have any authority over men.[28] This ruling bases itself upon Genesis 2 and 3: Eve is second in the order of creation, and first in the order of sin. The author formulates this patriarchal theology for his community against a rival Christian group which had great success among women (2 Timothy 3:6) and probably accorded women teaching and leadership functions.[29]

The Acts of Paul and Thecla is a second-century writing devoted entirely to the story of a woman missionary.[30] In many regions this book was regarded as canonical in the first three centuries. It mentions a great number of women, besides the apostle Thecla. Thecla is converted by Paul. She takes a vow of continence and is persecuted for this by her

fiancé and her family. Condemned to death, she is saved by
a miracle and goes with Paul to Antioch. A Syrian falls in
love with Thecla, is rejected and takes revenge. When Thecla is condemned to fight with wild beasts, she baptizes herself in a pit full of water, whereupon, since the beasts do not
harm her, she is set free. Her protectress, Tryphena, together with a part of her household, is converted to Christianity. Thecla proclaims the Word of God in the house of
Tryphena, then follows Paul to Myra. After only a short
while with him, she receives the commission "to teach the
word of God" and goes to Iconium and from there to Seleu-
cia, where she enlightens many with the Gospel.

Since Paul does not stand in the foreground of the narrative, the author of *The Acts of Paul and Thecla* appears to
have incorporated independent traditions about Thecla.
The image of the woman missionary depicted here is striking.[31] Thecla is commissioned by Paul to "go and teach the
word of God." Women in Carthage at the beginning of the
third century still could appeal to the apostle Thecla for
women's authority to teach and to baptize.[32]

In other ways the picture of Thecla reflects typical feminine stereotypes. She falls in love with Paul, follows him and
is dependent on him. On the other hand, her rejection of
marriage brings her into conflict with the patriarchal values
of her society. Motifs of the Hellenistic novel or romance
are here taken over for missionary purposes.[33] We find the
motif of "love at first sight," the separation motif, the theme
of the "devoted couple," and faithfulness despite great pressures. Of course, in the Christian work the apostle and the
woman are not sexual lovers but live in absolute continence.[34] Obviously these legends and stories could imagine
women as preachers and missionaries only in romantic
terms. Women renounce the old family and kinship ties, not
for independent values of the faith but for a spiritual love
relationship to the apostle. In the genre of romantic love,
the woman is infatuated, follows the apostle, and remains
faithful to him under the greatest pressures. Nevertheless,

the picture of Thecla retains elements of the authority of early Christian women missionaries.

Women Prophets in Early Christianity

Prophets played an eminent role within the early Christian community. From the very beginning they functioned as inspired oracles of the resurrected Lord, their authority based on divine revelation communicated by the Spirit. Paul regards prophets as second only to apostles in the leadership of the church, and they were still regarded as the normative church leaders in some Christian communities in the mid-second century.[35] Paul takes for granted that women also act as prophets in the Christian assembly. He insists, however, that they do it in a proper way and do not overstep the gender differences between women and men (1 Corinthians 12:2–16).

In Luke it is declared that the Spirit is given to all Christians, to women as well as men (Acts 2:17f.).[36] In the infancy narrative Anna and Mary function as prophets.[37] He also refers to the four prophetess daughters of Philip (Acts 21:9). Eusebius tells us their fame was so great in the early church that the provinces of Asia argue for their apostolic origin by referring to the burial place of one of them in Asia Minor.[38] Papias of Hierapolis claims to have known them personally.[39]

In the second century the Montanists attempted to legitimate their prophecy by establishing a prophetic line of succession. They referred to an Asiatic prophet called Amnia, whose name was still highly respected at the end of the second century.[40] The anti-Montanist writer does not deny her prophetic ministry but claims her for the Catholics. He lists in his succession of recognized prophets Agabus, Judas, Silas, the daughters of Philip, Amnia in Philadelphia, Quadratus and some others.[41] At the beginning of the second century Justin affirms that Christian men and women have charisms from the Spirit of God.[42] Irenaeus argued against the Alogoi, who denied the validity of prophecy, that Paul acknowledged prophetic women and men in the community.[43]

The Acts of Paul and Thecla mentions women prophets, like Theonoe, Stratonike, Eubulla, Phila, Artemilla and Numpha. At Corinth a prophet Myrta encouraged Paul and the community not to lose heart because Paul has to go to Rome. "The Spirit came upon Myrta, so that she said: . . . Paul the servant of the Lord will save many in Rome and will nourish many with the word . . . so that there will be great grace in Rome."[44] The references to the worship service show that she spoke in the Eucharistic assembly. Early Christian prophecy was liturgical prophecy. Paul's remarks in 1 Corinthians also suggest this. In the *Didache* the prophets are likened to the high priests and have the right to say the Eucharistic prayer. They are, as Spirit-filled persons, not bound to a liturgical formula, but can give thanksgiving freely as much as they want. Only if no prophets and apostles were present were the local ministers, bishops, presbyters and deacons entitled to take their place.[45] The author of the Apocalypse likewise understands himself as a prophet and insists that his "words of prophecy" be read aloud in the liturgical assembly.[46]

The author of the Apocalypse directs his criticism against a rival group of prophets (22:16). The opponents of the author seem also to have been organized in a school.[47] At the end of the first century a prophet-teacher whom the author calls "Jezebel" was the head of such a school in Thyatira. Her followers are characterized as disciples with the technical term "her children."[48] The same expression is used in 2 John 1, 4 and 13 to characterize the followers of the "elect lady" to whom the elder writes.[49] The Apocalypse characterizes "Jezebel" and her activity in language taken from the Old Testament prophets, which called the lapses of Israel into idolatry "adultery and whoredom."[50] In labeling the teacher-prophet "Jezebel" he insinuates that, like the Old

Testament queen, the prophet promoted idolatry and achieved her goals through seductive power and malevolent scheming.

The authority of this prophet and her "school," however, must have been well established in the community in which the author of the Apocalypse also had some followers (2:24). Despite the earlier warnings of John, the "school" of "Jezebel" continued to be a part of the community at Thyatira, and we can therefore assume that the school of this woman prophet was able to withstand the influence of John. Despite this attack on a particular school headed by a woman prophet, John did not discredit female prophecy as such. Asia Minor continued to recognize women as prophets even in the second and third centuries. The impact of the prophet-teacher "Jezebel" may be reflected in the fact that Thyatira later became a center of the Montanist movement, in which women prophets were prominent.[51]

Together with Montanus, Maximilla and Priscilla (or Prisca) were the leading prophets in Montanism.[52] They were not just his companions and followers, but enjoyed equal spiritual gifts and leadership in the Montanist movement. Like Montanus, the women prophets claimed that the Paraclete, or Holy Spirit, spoke directly to them, basing this claim on faith in revelations by the Holy Spirit given to women and men in prophetic ecstasy. The Montanists expected a speedy coming of the Lord and showed a passionate contempt for this world by advocating sexual asceticism, fasting, and martyrdom. The pronouncements of the first three prophets, Priscilla, Maximilla and Montanus, were written down and gathered as sacred documents similar to the words of the Old Testament prophets, the sayings of Jesus and the letters of the apostles.

The two best-known oracles of Priscilla and Maximilla are significant. When Prisca was asleep, Christ, in the form of a *female figure*, appeared to her saying that this was a holy place and here would Jerusalem descend out of heaven.[53] After the death of Montanus, Maximilla became the leader of the movement. She was persecuted, and commissions were sent out in order to expose her as a fraud.[54] Her opponents attempted to raise doubts about the genuineness of the movement by testing her spirits. Maximilla complained bitterly: "I am pursued like a wolf out of the sheep fold; I am no wolf: I am word and spirit and power." Since the Montanist opponents could not refute the movement on doctrinal grounds, they attacked it by slandering its leading prophets. Charges of immorality and the abandonment of their husbands were brought against the women. It was claimed that Montanist leaders committed suicide and that in their mysteries they slaughtered children, whose blood was mingled in their sacrifices, a charge originally made by the pagans against all Christians.[55] Thus, despite their basic doctrinal orthodoxy, the Montanists were reviled and finally driven out of the mainstream church.[56]

The considerable literature against the Montanists focused its attack especially on the leadership of women. Since Maximilla and Priscilla were proof that the Holy Spirit spoke through the female sex, the Montanists admitted women to church "offices." Didymus maintains that the women prophets in Montanism taught and prophesied in the assembly of the community.[57] Firmilian knows of a Montanist prophetess in Asia Minor who, in A.D. 235, converted many lay people and clerics, and who also baptized and celebrated the Eucharist.[58] Montanists appealed to Galatians 3:28[59] and to the women prophets in Scripture to justify these practices. According to Origen, "those disciples of women, who chose as their master Priscilla and Maximilla, not Christ, the spouse of the Bride, appeal to the following women prophets: the daughters of Philip, Deborah, Mary the sister of Aaron, Hulda, and Anna the daughter of Panuel."[60] Origen refutes this tradition by arguing that these women prophets did not speak in public or in the assemblies.

Scriptural texts cited against the leadership of women by Church Fathers are especially 1 Corinthians 14:34f., 1 Timothy 2:12ff. and 1 Corinthians 11:3,5. The argument against the prophetic leadership of women is summarized in the comments of Didymus the Blind on 1 Timothy 2:14:

Scripture recognizes as prophetesses the four daughters of Philip, Deborah, Mary, the sister of Aaron, and Mary, the mother of God, who said as recorded in the Gospel: "Henceforth all *women* [emphasis mine] and all generations shall call me blessed." But in Scripture there are no books written in their name. On the contrary, the Apostle says in First Timothy: "I do not permit women to teach," and again in First Corinthians: "Every woman who prays or prophesies with uncovered head dishonors her head." He means that he does not permit a woman to write books impudently on her own authority, nor to teach in the assemblies, because by doing so, she offends her head man; for "the head of woman is man and the head of man is Christ." The reason for this silence imposed on women is obvious: woman's teaching in the beginning caused considerable havoc to the human race; for the Apostle writes: "It is not the man who deceived, but the woman." [61]

Yet the mainstream church also appealed to the women prophets of Scripture to justify the minor role which they accorded women. The *Apostolic Constitutions* of the fourth century categorically declared: "We do not permit our women to teach in the Church, but only to pray and hear those that teach," and they limit the liturgical ministry of the deaconess to the functions of keeping the doors and assisting the "presbyters in the baptism of women for reasons of decency." [62] The prayer of ordination of women to these minor roles reads:

O Eternal God, the Father of our Lord Jesus Christ, the Creator of man and woman, who replenished with the Spirit Miriam and Deborah and Anna, and Hulda; who did not disdain that Thy only begotten Son should be born of a woman; who also in the tabernacle of the testimony and in the temple, did ordain women to be keepers of Thy holy gates . . . [63]

This church order thus accepts the Montanist appeal to the women prophets of Scripture, but uses their argument to justify a secondary role for women in the church.[64]

Women and the Divine Female Principle in Gnostic Communities[65]

Despite the standard complaint of the Church Fathers that women were prominent in Gnostic groups, we have very little information about the actual status and role of women in such communities.[66] We can attempt here only a sketch of the images of male and female in Gnosticism and the roles accorded women in these groups.

Whether or not Marcion [67] be called a Gnostic is disputed. He distinguished the alien God of Goodness, the Father of Jesus Christ, from the World God of Justice, who is the antithesis of the Good God. The Demiurge, or World God, created the cosmos and humankind, but the Good God is absolutely alien to all created things. Human creatures belong bodily and psychically to the World God. Christ came to save them from the World God and to make them children of the alien Good God. Since the Marcionites rejected the created world, they were devoted to rigorous asceticism, and by protesting against flesh and matter they demonstrated that they did not owe allegiance to the World God. Because procreation strengthens the sphere of the Demiurge, they did not marry and have children.

Severus, an associate of Marcion, taught "that woman is the work of Satan. . . . Hence those who consort in marriage fulfill the work of Satan." [68] Marcionism belongs to the type of Gnosticism that starts from a dualism of two opposed principles.[69] In this system femaleness belongs to the sphere of creation, whereas maleness stands for heavenly transcendent realities. In *The Gospel of the Egyptians* a saying of the Savior is quoted: "I am come to destroy the works of the female, by the 'female' meaning lust, and by the 'works' birth and decay." [70]

The classic expression of this dualism of two opposed principles or pairs of opposites is found in terms of male and female in the Pseudo-Clementines: "The present world is female, as the mother bringing forth the souls of the children, but the world to come is male, as a father receiving his children." [71] Therefore, of the two types of prophets in the world, one type is the female, whose words accord entirely with the created world, and the other type is the male prophet who speaks for the coming, higher world. [72] In the encratite *Acts of Thomas* the "communion of the male" is a parallel expression to the "highest gift of grace," "Holy Spirit" or "the power of the Most High." [73] The categories "female and male," therefore, do not so much characterize actual women or men as denote opposite types of dualistic principles.

The Marcionites were well organized, with a hierarchy of bishops and priests. We do not know much about the actual role of women in Marcion's church, but he is said to have appointed women to all church offices on an equal basis with men. [74] A saying of *The Gospel of Thomas* about Mary Magdalene could be applied to these women. In *The Gospel of Thomas* Simon Peter demands that Mary Magdalene leave the circle of disciples, "because women are not worthy of life." Jesus responds, "See, I shall lead her, so that I make her a man. That she too may become a living spirit, who is like you men. For every woman who makes herself a man shall enter the kingdom of heaven." [75]

Apelles, another member of the school of Marcion, revised his teacher's radical dualism. He was influenced by Philumene, an ascetic virgin and prophet at Rome, who supposedly encouraged Apelles to found a new sect. [76] Tertullian therefore calls her not only prophet but also the "*praeceptrix* and *magistra*" of Apelles. [77] Philumene taught and also accompanied Apelles on his various trips, and in the communities of Apelles her writings were acknowledged as "Holy Scripture." [78]

Like the Marcionites, the Carpocratians distinguish between the unbegotten Father and the God who gave the Law. [79] Since they believe in the migration of the soul, they hold that they can be liberated from the body and from reincarnation not through asceticism but through libertinism. All things are indifferent, and nothing in the world is by nature evil. Not through obedience to laws, however, but only through faith and love are persons saved. [80] The Carpocratians appeal to Salome, Mary Magdalene and Martha as the source and guarantors of their traditions. One of their teachers, Marcellina, represented their teaching in Rome in the middle of the second century and acquired many followers there.

The son of Carpocrates, Epiphanes, taught that the "righteousness of God is communion with equality." [81] Since God provided for all beings equally, no distinction should be made between "rich and poor, people and ruler, foolish and wise, female and male, free and slave." [82] Epiphanes thus espouses the same ideal as Paul (Galatians 3:27f.), but argues the fundamental equality of all, not on the basis of baptism, but on the basis of creation. Therefore his "fellowship with equality" extends not only to gender roles in the Christian community but also to sexuality and marriage. "In that God made all things in common for man and brought together the female with the male in common and united all the animals likewise, he declared righteousness to be fellowship with equality." [83]

It was the evil Lawgiver God who introduced "mine and thine" and so promulgated private property rights and the institution of marriage. Since his law destroyed the fellowship of the Divine Law, in their liturgies the Carpocratians attempt to restore the Divine Law by uniting "as they will and with whom they will." [84] However, we do not know if this "love feast" of the Carpocratians was a ritual celebration of the basic equality between the sexes or whether they prac-

ticed intercourse indiscriminately, since the charge of forni-
cation was a standard polemic of various religious groups
against each other.[85]

Valentinianism belongs to a different type of Gnostic dualism. It holds that maleness and femaleness are not antagonistic opposites, but complementary.[86] This group places the
origin of darkness, evil and dualism within the godhead itself
"by means of a genealogy of personified divine states evolving from another, which describe the progressive darkening
of the original Light in categories of guilt, error and
failure."[87] Thus "the Valentinians did not identify the female with any absolute principle of evil, but rather with the
fallible part of God, which became involved in the material
world."[88] The Valentinian system begins with the Dyad By-
thos=Primal Cause and Sige=Silence, who bring forth a
couple, Nous and Truth. Though the primal Tetrad appears
to consist of four different hypostases, Bythos and Sige as
well as Nous and Truth form one single male-female substance or entity. The second Tetrad, Logos and Life and
Man and Church, comes from the first Tetrad and brings
forth in turn ten and twelve aeons. The ten aeons in the
female series have names which allude to the union between
man and woman, whereas the names of the twelve aeons in
the male series recall the Christian virtues. The divine Pleroma thus consists of a series of male-female aeons. The last
aeon, Sophia, plays the role of Cosmic Eve. Because of her
ignorance and her desire to know the incomprehensible Father, she initiates a Fall in the Divine World that is the origin
of the evil, visible world. Sophia is restored to the Pleroma,
but her "abortion" cannot remain in the Pleroma. It is given
form by Christ and the Holy Spirit and called Achamoth.
Since Achamoth cannot enter the Pleroma, she falls into all
sorts of distress. At her request the Savior, Jesus, is sent to
give the "formation according to knowledge" and to release
her from her passions. Achamoth can now give form to the
Demiurge, who in due course fashions everything else. The
Demiurge creates the human body first as incorporeal and

later puts a skin over it, but without his knowledge Achamoth introduces spiritual "seeds" in some humans. Humanity, therefore, consists of three classes of beings: the hylics,
or "fleshly" ones; the psychics, who have souls; and the pneu-
matics, who have the spiritual seed from the Mother or
Achamoth. The female and the male element were originally united. They are reunited when the female element
becomes male, and are then united with the angels and enter
into the Pleroma. "Therefore it is said that the woman is
changed into a man and the Church here below into angels."[89] It is clear that "male and female" are not simple
gender distinctions, but characterize mythological, arche-
typal realities.[90]

The Gnosticism of Marcus, a disciple of Valentinus, is
distinguished by the fact that he places another Tetrad,
called Unity, Oneness, Monad and One, before the thirty
aeons. This first Tetrad is also called "the inconceivable and
nonmaterial Father, who is without paternity and who is
neither male nor female."[91] He claims that the "spiritual
man," formed in the image and likeness of God, was mas-
culine-feminine.[92] The Marcosians seem to have celebrated
the sacraments of the "bridal chamber" and of baptism.
They baptized into "the name of the unknown Father of all
things, into Truth, the mother of all, into him who descended on Jesus, into union, into redemption, into the
communion of the powers."[93]

The rite of the "bridal chamber" is related to the New
Testament bridal and marriage imagery.[94] The celebration
of the "spiritual marriage" in the Marcosian rite was a pre-
figuration of the perfect eschatological marriage union. At
the end of the world-process, Achamoth will enter the Pleroma and receive the Savior as her bridegroom. The per-
fected "spiritual seed" will then be given as brides to the
angels. The "spiritual marriage after the image of the unions
above"[95] expresses in different terms what is meant by "becoming male." Thus the Valentinians had a very positive
image of the marriage union and took it as a symbol and type

for salvation that restores the original androgynous unity of humanity. According to *The Gospel of Philip*,[96] a book which shows close affinities with the Marcosian teachings, when Eve was separated from Adam "death arose. When they reunite and he receives her to himself, death will be no more."[97] Christ came in order to remove the separation and unite the male and female.[98]

Marcus is reported to have had great success with women, which his opponents ascribed to his sorcery and love potions.[99] Yet it appears that his teaching was congenial to men as well as to women. He asked women at the Eucharistic *epiclesis* to speak the thanksgiving over the cup of mixed wine. Mixing the contents of the woman's cup with that of his own, he prayed: "May 'Grace' (*Charis*) who is before all things, who is beyond thought and description, fill thine inner being and multiply in thee her knowledge, sowing the mustard seed in good soil."[100] He understood himself to be a prophet, upon whom the first Tetrad had descended in female form,[101] and he ordained women as prophets with the following words:

I desire to make thee a partaker of my Grace (*Charis*), since the Father of all doth continually behold thy angel before his face (Matt. 18:10). The place of thy greatness (angel) is ever in us: we must come together. First, receive from me and through me Grace. Adorn thyself as a bride who expects her bridegroom, that thou mayest be what I am, and I what thou art. Receive in thy bride-chamber the seed of light. Receive from me the bridegroom, and give him a place, and have a place in him. Behold Grace has descended upon thee; open thy mouth and prophesy.[102]

Irenaeus claims that Marcus especially deceived wealthy women of high rank in order to obtain their property and abuse them physically. Such a woman was prepared "to be united with him in everything, in order that she, with him, might enter into the One . . ."[103] It is apparent that Ire-

naeus no longer understood "the mystery of union" and the
rite of the "bridal chamber" which was an "anticipation of
the eschatological union between the spiritual gnostics and
the angels." Such a misunderstanding was easily possible,
since according to *The Gospel of Philip* the "holy kiss" was
the center of the rite: "For the perfect conceive through a
kiss and give birth. Because of this we also kiss another. We
receive conception from the Grace (*Charis*) which is among
us." [104] In the same Gospel Mary Magdalene is called the
"consort of Christ" whom he loved "more than the disciples,
and kissed her on her [mouth] often." [105] Since the Valentinian system knew three Christs and perceived the divine
and the world in *syzygies* (couples), it is possible that Mary
Magdalene was thought of as consort of the earthly Jesus, as
the Holy Spirit was the consort of the aeon Christ in the Pleroma and Sophia was the consort of the Savior.

Gnosticism, we may conclude, employed the categories of
"male" and "female," not to designate real women and men,
but to name cosmic-religious principles or archetypes. Salvation in the radically dualistic Gnostic systems requires the
annihilation and destruction of the female or the "feminine
principle." In the moderately dualistic systems, salvation
means the reunification of the male and female principle to
an androgynous or asexual unity. In Gnosticism, the pneu-
matics, men and women, represent the female principle,
while the male principle stands for the heavenly realm:
Christ, God and the Spirit. The female principle is secondary, since it stands for the part of the divine that became
involved in the created world and history. Gnostic dualism
shares in the patriarchal paradigm of Western culture. It
makes the first principle male and defines femaleness relative
to maleness. [106] Maleness is the subject, the divine, the absolute; femaleness is the opposite or the complementary
"other." [107] Gnostic dualism reflects the chasm between the
world and the divine, the body and the spiritual self. We do
not know whether this dualism also divided men from
women and whether, in the rite of "the bridal chamber,"

men represented the male and women the female archetype. Since all Gnostics understand themselves as "female," it is possible that the ritual signifies overcoming this dualism for both men and women.

The Theological Justification for Rejection of Women's Leadership

Women were prominent in the church even after the middle of the second century. They participated in church leadership, not only as widows and deaconesses, but also as prophets and teachers. Women actually dared "to teach, to debate, to exorcise, to promise cures, probably even to baptize." [108] Their leadership and initiative were, however, more and more rejected by the patriarchal church: "No woman is allowed to speak in church, or even to teach, to baptize, or to discharge any man's function, much less to take upon herself the priestly office." [109]

Montanism, Gnosticism and the mainstream church all appealed to apostolic revelation and tradition to justify their own church order and theology. [110] Since the formation of the canon was still in flux, [111] certain groups considered so-called apocryphal writings as "Holy Scripture," whereas other groups rejected some of the Scriptural writings which were later acknowledged as canonical. To justify prophecy by women, the Montanists appealed to the succession of women prophets in the Scriptures, whereas some Gnostic groups rejected the Old Testament and part of our New Testament. Yet writings like *The Acts of Thecla* were long considered canonical, even by the mainstream church.

The canonical Gospels mention women, such as Mary Magdalene and Salome, as disciples of Christ. Gnostics built on these traditions to give the women disciples a special role in the reception of revelation and secret teaching. Mainstream Christianity, on the other hand, attempted to play down the significance of the women disciples and concentrated on figures like Peter and Paul and the Twelve. The debate between patriarchal and egalitarian Christian groups is reflected in various Gnostic texts which relate the competition between Peter and Mary Magdalene.[112]

Mary Magdalene is mentioned in all four canonical Gospels as the primary witness to the Easter faith event. She and the other women, whose names vary, were disciples of Jesus during his ministry and witnessed his death, burial and resurrection.[113] Yet Luke's Gospel already attempts to play down the role of women as proclaimers of the Easter kerygma, by stressing "that the words of the women seemed to the eleven an idle tale and they did not believe them" (Luke 24:11).[114] The motif of the apostles' skepticism toward the message of the women is even further developed in the *Epistula Apostolorum*, an apocryphal document of the second century. According to this account Mary Magdalene and Sarah (in the Coptic version it is Martha and Mary) are sent to announce to the apostles that Jesus had risen. But the apostles did not believe them. Finally, the Lord himself goes with Mary and her sisters to them, but they still do not believe. Only after they touch him do they know "that he has truly risen in the flesh."[115]

According to the *Sophia Jesu Christi*, the Redeemer appears after the resurrection to the twelve disciples and tó the seven women who had followed him into Galilee.[116] Of the women disciples, only Mary Magdalene is expressly mentioned. The Redeemer teaches the male and female disciples about the "perfect one" and of "the will of the holy angels and of the Mother that the manly host may here be made perfect . . ."[117] The "manly host," in this text, are the Gnostics. Their salvation is willed by the angels, who represent the male principle in Valentinian Gnosticism. The Mother is Sophia, as can be seen in this text: "The Son of Man agreed with Sophia, his consort, and revealed himself in a [great light] as bisexual. His male nature is called the 'Savior,' the begetter of all things, but his female 'Sophia,' 'mother of all,' whom some call Pistis."[118] The conclusion is typical of the Gnostic Gospels: "From that day on his disciples began to preach the Gospel of God, the eternal Father . . ."[119] It is apparent that women here are counted among the disciples who preach the Gospel.

Mary Magdalene, together with two other Marys, is mentioned in *The Gospel of Philip* (32) and in *The Dialogue of the Redeemer*,[120] whereas in *The Gospel of the Egyptians* Salome has a prominent role. In *The Great Questions of Mary* Christ gives revelation and secret teaching to his privileged disciple Mary Magdalene.[121] The vision reveals to Mary the prototype of the mystery rite of union practiced by various Gnostic groups. *The Gospel of Thomas* alludes to the antagonism between Peter and Mary Magdalene,[122] a theme more fully developed in the *Pistis Sophia* and in *The Gospel of Mary* (Magdalene).

In the *Pistis Sophia*[123] (third century) Mary Magdalene and John have a prominent place among the group of disciples.[124] Jesus stresses their outstanding role: "Mary Magdalene and John, the virgin,[125] will surpass all my disciples and all who shall receive mysteries in the Ineffable, they will be on my right and on my left and I am they and they are I."[126] Here we have the same formula as in the prayer of Marcus for the authority of women prophets. The other women disciples mentioned are Mary the mother of Jesus, Salome and Martha. Mary Magdalene asks most of the questions (thirty-nine out of forty-six) and plays a major role in giving interpretations. Peter's hostility toward her is apparent throughout the whole work. He objects: "My Lord, we shall not be able to endure this woman, for she takes our opportunity, and has not let any of us speak, but talks all the time herself."[127] Mary in turn complains that she hardly dares to interpret what has been said by the First Mystery. Peter intimidates her so much because "he hates the female race." Yet she is told that whoever receives gnosis and revelation is commanded to speak. It does not matter whether it is a man or a woman. The argument between Peter and Mary Magdalene clearly reflects the debate between the mainstream church and Gnosticism on whether or not women have received apostolic revelation and are the legitimate transmitters of the apostolic tradition.

The controversy between Peter, the opponent of gnosis, and Mary Magdalene, the authority within gnosis, is even more pronounced in *The Gospel of Mary* [128] (second century). The first part of the work ends with the exhortation of the disciples by Mary Magdalene. After the departure of Jesus the disciples do not proclaim the Gospel because they fear they might suffer the same fate as did their Lord. Mary Magdalene then promises them that the Savior's "Grace" *(Charis)* will protect them and that they should not be afraid, because he has made them "to be men."

The second part begins with Peter asking Mary to share with them the revelations she has received from the Savior "who loved her above all women." But after Mary has told them of a vision, Andrew and Peter react in unbelief. Peter objects: "Did he then speak privily with a woman rather than with us and not openly? Shall we turn about and all harken to her? He has preferred her over against us?" Mary is offended by the reaction of Andrew and Peter to her revelation. She weeps and insists that she has not invented the visions and lied about the Savior. Levi comes to the defense of Mary Magdalene and rebukes Peter:

"Peter, thou hast ever been of a hasty temper. Now I see thou dost exercise thyself against the woman like the adversaries. But if the Savior hath made her worthy, who then art thou to reject her? Certainly the Savior knows her surely enough. Therefore did he love her more than us. Let us rather be ashamed, put on the perfect Man, as he has charged us, and proclaim the Gospel . . ." [129]

This polemical dialogue reflects the opposition that Gnostics encountered when they appealed to Scriptural precedents, especially Mary Magdalene, as female transmitters and interpreters of the apostolic tradition. *The Gospel of*

Mary, in turn, declares that whoever rejects the revelations and traditions transmitted under the name of a woman rejects the true revelation of the Savior himself and does not do the work of proclamation he has commanded. The followers of Andrew and Peter, who argue against the authority of women because of their contempt for "the female race," distort the true Christian message.

Various third- and fourth-century church orders reflect the patriarchal reaction against female leadership. The *Didascalia Apostolorum* maintains that women are not appointed by Jesus to teach and to proclaim Christ. The *Didascalia* does acknowledge that women were disciples and refers to three of them by the name Mary (Mary Magdalene, Mary the daughter of James, and the other Mary). The text, however, insists that the Lord "did not send them to instruct the people with us. For if it were required that women should teach, our Master Himself would have commanded these to give instruction with us." [130]The *Didascalia*, however, appeals to the women disciples when arguing for the ministry of deaconesses.

The *Apostolic Church Order* transmits a dialogue between the male and the female disciples on whether or not women can celebrate the Eucharist. [131] The dialogue is very similar to that between Peter, Andrew, Levi and Mary in *The Gospel of Mary*. Yet the tone is quite different. It is not just Peter and Andrew but also John, James and Mary herself who object to the Eucharistic ministry of women. Andrew introduces the question as to whether the apostles should organize a ministry for women. Peter acknowledges that some steps have been taken, but then poses the question of the Eucharistic ministry for women. John points out that at the Last Supper Jesus did not permit women to stand with the apostles, an argument already reflecting the priestly character of the minister of the Eucharist. (According to the New Testament Jesus "lay down at table" with his disciples.) Martha objects that this is not an argument against women, for Jesus did not let women stand beside the men because Mary (who is early identified with Mary Magdalene) laughed. However, Mary rejects this argument of Martha. She argues against the Eucharistic ministry of women by quoting Jesus as saying, "The weak shall be saved through the strong," i.e., women through men and not vice versa. A woman herself is made to provide the theological argument against women's Eucharistic ministry.

Similarly, in *The Questions of Bartholomew*, Mary, the mother of Jesus, argues that women should pray standing behind men, because the Lord (actually Paul) said that the head of man is Christ, but the head of woman is man.[132] Later it appears that Mary herself is the sole exception to this, because she stands up and lifts up her hands in prayer to heaven.

Thus it appears that in the second and third centuries the leadership of women within the Christian community is still a very live and controversial issue.[133] Both parties, the opponents as well as the advocates of women's leadership roles, appeal to the apostolic tradition to make their point. The advocates refer to significant women, e.g., Mary Magdalene, Salome or Martha, and to passages such as Galatians 3:28 or Romans 16 to prove that Christian truth is based also on the apostolic authority of women. The patriarchal opposition cites the injunctions of 1 Corinthians 14:33b–36 and 1 Timothy 2:9–15 or the "household codes" for their view that women can occupy only subordinate positions limited to the care of women.

Those women whom the patriarchal writers could not erase from historical consciousness they declared frauds or heretics or interpreted from a patriarchal perspective. Origen, for example, acknowledges Phoebe, but reduces her to an assistant and servant of Paul and argues that women who do good works can be accepted as deaconesses.[134] Chrysostom affirms that women had leadership roles in the nascent Christian church, but maintains that only when the "angelic condition" existed could women travel in the service of the Gospel, prophesy and be called disciples or apostles.[135] But these privileges applied solely in the primitive Christian communities.

Historical studies have demonstrated that the early Christian writers did not include all the extant materials in their writings, but selected and rewrote early Christian traditions that were important for their theological argument. Since the opponents of women's leadership in the church wrote from a patriarchal point of view, we can assume that they transmitted only a fraction of the rich traditions about significant women and their contributions in early Christianity. Most of the egalitarian traditions of primitive Christianity are probably lost. The few references to women's leadership that survived in patriarchal records are like the tip of an iceberg indicating the wealth of information that has vanished from historical consciousness.

Early Christian writings were shaped by a struggle between opposing groups over the equality of women. They cannot be taken as a complete history of the actual condition of women in the early church. The texts written to justify male leadership record the sad demise of the original Christian vision of oneness in Christ. Those that transmit remnants of the egalitarian tradition remind the mainstream church that the community founded by Jesus was meant to be one of mutual service of brother and sister, not one made in the image of the society where some "lord it over" others.

NOTES

1. Cf. the Biblical arguments of the *Declaration on the Question of the Admission of Women to the Ministerial Priesthood* and the Vatican's official press *Commentary* which were issued simultaneously by the Vatican Sacred Congregation for the Doctrine of the Faith (Jan. 27, 1977). For theological evaluations, cf. among others K. Rahner, "Priestertum der Frau?," *Stimmen der Zeit*, vol. CXII (1977), pp. 291–301, and J. R. Donahue, "Women, Priesthood and the Vatican," *America*, April 2, 1977, pp. 285–89, who points out: "The declaration correctly states that equality can coexist with

differentiation. But is there not a danger that differentiation may meld into discrimination when one group in the church (male ecclesiastics) tells the other group (women) exactly what their rights and roles are?" Cf. also the commentary edited by Arlene and Leonard Swidler, *Women Priests: A Catholic Commentary on the Vatican Declaration* (New York: Paulist Press, 1977). For the patriarchal stance of other Vatican documents, cf. the excellent review by Nadine Foley, "Woman in Vatican Documents, 1960 to the Present," in J. Coriden, *Sexism & Church Law: Equal Rights and Affirmative Action* (New York: Paulist Press, 1977), pp. 82–108.

2. Cf. J. G. Gager, *Kingdom and Community: The Social World of Early Christianity* (Englewood Cliffs, N.J.: Prentice-Hall, 1975); G. Theissen, "Itinerant Radicalism: The Tradition of Jesus Sayings from the Perspective of the Sociology of Literature," *Radical Religion: The Bible and Liberation* (Community for Religious Research and Education, 1976), pp. 84–93; *idem*, *Soziologie der Jesus bewegung* (ThExH. 144; Munich: Kaiser, 1977); *idem*, "Soziale Schichtung in der korinthischen Gemeinde: Ein Beitrag zur Soziologie des hellenistischen Urchristentums," *Zeitschrift für Neutestamentliche Wissenschaft*, vol. LXV (1974), pp. 232–72; R. Scroggs, "The Earliest Christian Communities as Sectarian Movement," in J. Neusner (ed.), *Christianity, Judaism and Other Greco-Roman Cults*, vol. II (Leiden: Brill, 1975), pp. 1–23.

3. Cf. the "list of duties" for the office of bishop: he should be "one who governs his own house well and keeps his children in respectful obedience—for whoever does not know how to govern his own house, how can he take care of the church of God?" (1 Tim. 3:4–5). The patriarchal family is here the model for church structure.

4. H. v. Campenhausen, *Kirchliches Amt und geistliche Vollmacht in den ersten drei Jahrhunderten* (Tübingen: Mohr, 1963); *idem*, "The Origins of the Idea of the Priesthood in the Early Church," in *Tradition and Life in the Church* (Philadelphia: Fortress, 1968), pp. 217–30; G. Dix, "The Ministry in the Early Church, c. A.D. 90–140," in K. Kirk (ed.), *The Apostolic Ministry* (London, 1964), pp. 183–303; J. L. Mohler, *The Origins and Evolution of the Priesthood* (New York, 1970); E. Schüssler Fiorenza, *Priester für Gott* (Münster: Aschendorff, 1972); A. E. Carr, "The Church in Process: Engendering the Future," in A. M. Gardiner

(ed.), *Women and Catholic Priesthood: An Expanded Vision* (New York: Paulist Press, 1976), pp. 66–88, and the excellent research review by A. Lemaire, "The Ministries in the New Testament: Recent Research," *Biblical Theology Bulletin* 3 (1973), pp. 133–66.

5. For a fuller development of this perspective, cf. my articles "Die Rolle der Frau in der urchristlichen Bewegung," *Concilium*, vol. VII (1976), pp. 3–9; "Interpreting Patriarchal Traditions," in L. Russell (ed.), *The Liberating Word: A Guide to Nonsexist Interpretation of the Bible* (Philadelphia: Westminster, 1976), pp. 39–61; and "The Study of Women in Early Christianity. Some Methodological Considerations" (forthcoming).

6. Cf. R. Scroggs, "Paul and the Eschatological Woman: Revisited," *Journal of the American Academy of Religion*, vol. XLII (1974), p. 536; W. A. Meeks, "The Image of the Androgyne," *History of Religion*, vol. XIII (1974), pp. 165–208; H. D. Betz, "Spirit, Freedom and Law: Paul's Message to the Galatian Churches," *Svensk Exeg. Arsbok*, vol. XXXIX (1974), pp. 145–60; M. Bouttier, "Complexio Oppositorum: Sur les Formules de I Cor xii.13; Gal iii.26–8; Col iii.10, 11," *New Testament Studies*, vol. XXIII (1976), pp. 1–19.

7. R. Scroggs, "Paul and the Eschatological Woman," *loc. cit.*, has suggested that the opponents of Paul held that the baptismal formula eliminated the distinctions between the sexes, whereas Paul wants to eliminate the inequality between the sexes but not the distinctions (cf. 1 Cor. 7 and 11). However, Gal. 3:27f. does not eliminate sexual distinctions on the basis of creation, but eliminates specific gender roles within the community. Therefore it is not likely that the text is to be understood within the context of the Gnostic myth of the reunification of male and female, since "male and female" are here clearly parallel expressions to "Jew and Greek," "slave and free"; i.e., social relationships are meant. As the elimination of the societal religious distinctions between Jew and Greek becomes reality within the community of the baptized and is not just an eschatological hope, so is the elimination of specific gender roles a reality in the Christian community. Gal. 3:27f. therefore does not mean an eschatological utopian or an individualized and spiritualized Gnostic declaration but speaks about relationships within the Christian community.

8. For the connection of the *diakonein* motif with the Eucha-

ristic tablefellowship, cf. W. Brandt, *Dienst und Dienen im Neuen Testament* (Gütersloh: Mohn, 1931), p. 69; J. Roloff, "Die Deutung des Todes Jesu," *New Testament Studies*, vol. XIX (1972), pp. 38–64, 51–62.

9. F. V. Filson, "The Significance of the Early House Churches," *Journal of Biblical Literature*, vol. LVIII (1939), pp. 105–12.

10. B. Gärtner, *The Temple and Community in Qumran and in the New Testament* (Cambridge: Cambridge University, 1965); R. J. M. Kelvey, *The New Temple: The Church in the New Testament* (Oxford: Oxford University, 1969); and my article "Cultic Language in Qumran and in the New Testament," *Catholic Biblical Quarterly*, vol. XXXVIII (1976), pp. 159–77.

11. Cf., however, the derogatory remark of W. A. Meeks (ed.), *The Writings of St. Paul* (New York: Norton, 1972), p. 23: "It is a response to reports which have come to Paul by . . . *gossip* from 'Chloe's people' (1:11), otherwise unknown" (emphasis mine).

12. Cf. J. E. Crouch, *The Origin and Intention of the Colossian Haustafel* (Göttingen: Vandenhoeck & Ruprecht, 1972); D. Balch, "*Let wives be submissive . . .*": *The Origin, Form and Apologetic Function of the Household Duty Code in 1 Peter* (Ann Arbor: University of Michigan Microfilm, 1974).

13. G. Theissen, "Itinerant Radicalism . . . ," *loc. cit.*, p. 91, has suggested that the urban Hellenistic congregations "represented a family-style love-patriarchalism, in which the social distinctions survived in a softened, milder form. Characteristic of this ethos were the early Christian instructions to household members . . ." Cf. also his "Soziale Schichtung in der korinthischen Gemeinde," *Zeitschrift für Neutestamentliche Wissenschaft* vol. LXV (1974), pp. 232–72. However, Gal. 3:28 and the leadership of women in early Christian house churches speaks against such a "love-patriarchalism" in the earliest missionary communities.

14. Cf. E. E. Ellis, "Paul and His Co-Workers," *New Testament Studies*, vol. XVII (1970–71), pp. 437–52, especially 439.

15. Cf. W. E. Thomas, "The Place of Women in the Church at Philippi, *Expository Times*, vol. LXXXIII (1972), pp. 117–20; cf. also R. W. Graham, "Women in the Pauline Churches: A Review Article," *Lexington Theological Quarterly*, vol. XI (1976), pp. 25–33, especially 29f.

16. Cf. A. Harnack, "Probabilia über die Addresse und den Ver-

fasser des Hebräerbriefes," *Zeitschrift für Neutestamentliche Wissenschaft*, vol. I (1900), pp. 16–41, especially 33ff.

17. The writer of *Codex Bezae* (D) (parchment manuscript of the fifth/sixth centuries which probably represents a second-century text) places the name of Priscilla (Prisca) in second place in Acts 18:26. He not only makes Aquila the subject of the sentence in 18:2 by writing "Aquila with his wife Priscilla," but also plays down the leadership of Priscilla insofar as he mentions Aquila three times in Acts 18 (3, 7, 22) without referring to Priscilla. On the whole, Codex D has a tendency to minimize the references to women in Acts. In Acts 1:14 he adds "children" and thus makes the women disciples into wives of the apostles. In Acts 17:34 he omits "and a woman by the name of Damatis," and in 17:12 he writes "men and women" instead of "women and men." Cf. E. J. Epp, *The Theological Tendency of Codex Bezae Cantabrigensis in Acts* (Cambridge: Cambridge University, 1966), pp. 74f.

18. Cf. M. J. Lagrange, *Saint Paul: Épitre aux Romains* (Paris, 1916), p. 366. Some manuscripts read "Julia." ▬

19. See my forthcoming articles "The Twelve" and "The Apostleship of Women in Early Christianity," in Arlene and Leonard Swidler (eds.), *Women Priests*, pp. 114–22 and 135–40. Cf. B. Bauer, "Uxores Circumducere (1 Kor 9:5)," *Biblische Zeitschrift*, vol. III (1959), pp. 94–102. Cf. also the interpretation of Clement of Alexandria, who likens their missionary ministry to that of the deaconess and limits it to women: ". . . and took their wives with them, not as women with whom they had marriage relations, but as sisters, that they might be their fellow ministers [*syndiakonous*] in dealing with housewives. It was through them that the Lord's teaching penetrated also the women's quarters without any scandal being aroused" (Clement of Alexandria, *Stromateis*, III, 6:53,3f.). Clement understands "sister" here in an encratite sense, even though the text does not give any indication of encratite tendencies, since "brother" never has encratite overtones.

20. H. Lietzmann, *The History of the Early Church*, vol. I (London: Lutterworth Press, 1963), p. 146. For a similar patriarchal interpretation, cf. E. A. Judge, "St. Paul and Classical Society," *Jahrbuch für Antike und Christentum*, vol. XV (1972), p. 28: "The status of women who patronized St. Paul would particularly repay attention. They are clearly persons of some independence and

eminence in their own circles, *used to entertaining and running their salons*, if that is what Paul's meetings were, as they saw best" (emphasis mine).

21. K. H. Schelkle, "Ministry and Ministers in the New Testament Church," *Concilium*, vol. XI (1969), pp. 5–11; A. Lemaire, "From Services to Ministries: Diakonia in the First Two Centuries," *Concilium*, vol. XIV (1972), pp. 35–49; J. Gnilka, *Der Philipperbrief* (Freiburg: Herder, 1968), pp. 35f.

22. The verb as well as the substantive "have the twofold sense of leadership and care." In the First Epistle of Clement of Rome, 36:1; 61:3 the substantive is used with reference to Christ, the High Priest. (B. Reicke, *"prohistemi,"* *TDNT*, vol. VI, p. 703.)

23. Cf. "Patronage and Patronus," in *The Oxford Classical Dictionary*, 2nd ed. (Oxford: Clarendon Press, 1970), pp. 790f.

24. The judgment depends on the decision whether or not 1 Cor. 11:2–16 is genuine Pauline. Cf. W. Munro, "Patriarchy and Charismatic Community in 'Paul,' " in Plaskow and Romero, *Women and Religion*, 2nd ed. (Missoula: Scholars Press, 1974), pp. 189–98; W. O. Walker, "1 Cor. 11:2–16 and Paul's View of Women," *Journal of Biblical Literature*, vol. XCIV (1975), pp. 94–110, and the rejection of his attempt to declare 1 Cor. 11:2–16 as non-Pauline by J. Murphy-O'Connor, "The Non-Pauline Character of 1 Corinthians 11:2–16?," *Journal of Biblical Literature*, vol. XCV (1976), pp. 615–21.

25. Almost all contributions that discuss the role of women in the New Testament grapple with this text. Cf. S. Lösch, "Christliche Frauen in Korinth," *Theologische Quartalschrift*, vol. CXXVII (1974), pp. 216–61; G. H. Gilbert, "Women in the Churches of Paul," *Biblical World*, vol. II (1893), pp. 38–47; E. Kähler, *Die Frau in den Paulinischen Briefen* (Zurich: Gotthelf, 1960); M. D. Hooker, "Authority on Her Head: An Examination of 1 Cor. 11:10," *New Testament Studies*, vol. X (1963–64), pp. 410–16; G. B. Caird, "Paul and Women's Liberty," *Bulletin of the John Rylands Library*, vol. LIV (1972), pp. 268–81; W. J. Martin, "I Corinthians 11:2–16: An Interpretation," in Gasque and Martin (eds.), *Apostolic History and the Gospel* (Grand Rapids: Eerdmans, 1970), pp. 231–41; R. Scroggs, "Paul and the Eschatological Woman," *Journal of the American Academy of Religion*, vol. XL (1972), pp. 283–303; J. B. Hurley, "Did Paul Require Veils or the Silence of Women? A Consideration of 1 Cor. 11:2–16 and 1 Cor.

14:33b–36," *Westminster Theological Journal*, vol. XXXV (1972–73), pp. 190–220; A. Feuillet, "La Dignité et le rôle de la femme d'après quelques textes Pauliniens," *New Testament Studies*, vol. XXI (1975), pp. 157–91 (for an English abstract of this article, cf. "Is Paul anti-feminist?," *Theology Digest*, vol. XXIV [1975], pp. 29–35); A. Joubert, "Le Voile des femmes," *New Testament Studies*, vol. XVIII (1972), pp. 422–24; J. Galot, *Mission et ministère de la femme* (Paris: 1973), pp. 123ff.; V. Ramsay Mollenkott, *Women, Men and the Bible* (Nashville: Abingdon, 1977).

26. Cf. G. Fitzer, *Das Weib schweige in der Gemeinde: Über den unpaulinischen Charakter der mulier taceat Verse in 1 Kor. 14* (Munich: Kaiser, 1963). Cf. also H. Conzelmann, *1 Corinthians* (Philadelphia: Fortress, 1975), pp. 246f.; S. Aalen, "A Rabbinic Formula in 1 Cor. 14:34," in F. L. Cross (ed.), *Studia Theologica, II, 1* (Berlin: Akademie Verlag, 1964), pp. 513–25; G. Dautzenberg, *Urchristliche Prophetie* (Stuttgart: Kohlhammer, 1975), pp. 257–73.

27. For the literature on the topic, cf. E. Lohse, *Colossians and Philemon* (Philadelphia: Fortress, 1971), pp. 154–63, and the notes above.

28. Cf. Dibelius and Conzelmann, *The Pastoral Epistles* (Philadelphia: Fortress, 1972), pp. 44–49 (literature); R. Falconer, "1 Timothy 2:14–15: Interpretative Notes," *Journal of Biblical Literature*, vol. LX (1949), pp. 375–79.

29. Cf. Dibelius and Conzelmann, pp. 65ff. and 116, on the "false Teachers" of the Pastoral Epistles; R. J. Karris, "The Background and Significance of the Polemic of the Pastoral Epistles," *Journal of Biblical Literature*, vol. XCII (1973), pp. 549–64.

30. C. Schlau, *Die Akten des Paulus und der Thekla* (Leipzig: Hinrichs, 1877); Hennecke and Schneemelcher, *New Testament Apocrypha*, vol. II (Philadelphia: Westminster, 1965), pp. 322–90, especially 353–64; E. Hazelton Haight, *More Essays on Greek Romances* (New York: Longdon, 1945), pp. 48–65.

31. Cf. Hennecke and Schneemelcher, pp. 331ff.

32. Tertullian, *De Baptismo*, 17: "But if certain Acts of Paul, which are falsely so named, claim the example of Thecla for allowing women to teach and to baptize, let men know that in Asia the presbyter who compiled that document, thinking to add of his own to Paul's reputation, was found out and though he professed he had done it for love of Paul was deposed from his position. How

could we believe that Paul should give a female power to teach and to baptize when he did not allow a woman even to learn in her own right? 'Let them keep silence,' he says, 'and ask their husbands at home.' "

33. Cf. M. Braun, *History and Romance in Greco-Roman Literature* (Oxford: Blackwell, 1938); P. J. Achtemeier, "Jesus and the Disciples as Miracle Workers in the Apocryphal New Testament," in E. Schüssler Fiorenza (ed.), *Aspects of Religious Propaganda in Judaism and Early Christianity* (Notre Dame University Press, 1976), pp. 149–86, especially 162ff.

34. R. Söder, *Die apokryphen Apostelgeschichten und die romanhafte Literatur der Antike* (1932; repr. Stuttgart: Kohlhammer, 1969), pp. 119–47; Sr. M. R. Nugent, *Portrait of the Consecrated Woman in Greek Christian Literature of the First Four Centuries* (Washington: Catholic University of America, 1941), pp. 77–78, 81ff.

35. Cf. E. Cothenet, "Prophétisme et ministère d'après le Nouveau Testament," *La Maison Dieu*, vol. CVII (1971), pp. 29–50; cf. also the literature and research review in G. Dautzenberg, *Urchristliche Prophetie*, pp. 15–42.

36. For Luke's redaction of the Joel material in Acts 2:17–21, cf. R. F. Zehnle, *Peter's Pentecost Discourse* (Nashville: Abingdon, 1971), pp. 28–34, 125ff.

37. This motif was further developed in the patristic period. Cf. A. Grillmeier, "Maria Prophetin," *Revue des Études Augustiniennes*, vol. XI (1956), pp. 295–312.

38. Eusebius, *Ecclesiastical History*, III, 31.

39. *Ibid.*, 39.

40. Cf. L. Zscharnack, *Der Dienst der Frau in den ersten Jahrhunderten der christlichen Kirche* (Göttingen: Vandenhoeck & Ruprecht, 1902), pp. 179–90.

41. Eusebius, *Eccl. Hist.*, V, 17.

42. Justin, *Dialogus*, c, Tryph. 88.

43. Irenaeus, *Adversus Haereses*, III, 11.

44. Hennecke and Schneemelcher, *New Testament Apocrypha*, vol. II, pp. 379f.

45. *Didache*, 10:7; 13:3; 15:1f.

46. M. E. Boring, "The Apocalypse as Christian Prophecy: A Discussion of the Issues Raised by the Book of Revelation for the

Study of Early Christian Prophecy," *SBL Seminar Papers*, vol. II (Cambridge: Society of Biblical Literature, 1974), pp. 43–62.

47. It is generally assumed that the followers of "Jezebel" are identical with the Nicolaitans (Apoc. 2:2–7) and with "those who hold the teaching of Balaam" (2:14). Yet it is not clear what their relationship to the later Gnostic group of the Nicolaitans was. Cf. my article "Apocalyptic and Gnosis in the Book of Revelation and Paul," *Journal of Biblical Literature*, vol. 92 (1973), pp. 565–81.

48. Cf. my article "The Quest for the Johannine School: The Apocalypse and the Fourth Gospel," *New Testament Studies*, vol. XXIV (1977), pp. 402–27, for the literature on the "school" question.

49. Most exegetes understand the address "elect lady" as a circumlocution for "church." However, the similarity in wording in Apoc. 2:20 and 2 John 1 suggests that the "elect lady" is the head of the community as "Jezebel" is the prophet-leader in the Apocalypse.

50. Cf. the excellent article by K. Thraede, "Frau," in *Reallexikon für Antike und Christentum*, vol. VIII (Stuttgart, 1973), pp. 197–269, especially 254–66.

51. Epiphanius, *Haereses*, LI, 3.

52. Cf. H. Kraft, "Die altchristliche Prophetie und die Entstehung des Montanismus," *Theologische Zeitschrift*, vol. XI (1955), pp. 249–71; P. de Labriolle, *La Crise montaniste: Les Sources de l'histoire du montanisme* (Paris, 1913); *idem*, " 'Mulieres in Ecclesia taceant': Un Aspect de la lutte anti-montaniste," *Bulletin d'ancienne littérature et d'archéologie chrétiennes*, vol. I (1911), pp. 1–24, 103–22.

53. Epiphanius, *Haer.*; XLVIII, 1:3; XLVIII, 14:1.

54. Cf. H. Lietzmann, *History of the Early Church*, vol. I, pp. 200f.

55. Eusebius, *Eccl. Hist.*, 16, 17. Cf. J. Pelikan, *The Christian Tradition: A History of the Development of Doctrine*, vol. I (Chicago: University of Chicago, 1971), pp. 105ff. But compare the severe judgment of Montanism by R. A. Knox, *Enthusiasm: A Chapter in the History of Religions* (New York and Oxford: Oxford University Press, 1950), p. 49: "The history of Montanism is not to be read as that of a great spiritual revival, maligned by its enemies.

It is that of a naked fanaticism, which tried to stampede the Church into greater severity . . ."

56. Cf. L. Zscharnack, *Der Dienst der Frau*, pp. 184ff.

57. Didymus the Blind, *On the Trinity*, III, 41:3.

58. Cyprian, *Epistolae* 75:10.

59. Epiphanius, *Haer.*, XLIX, 2.

60. Origen, *Fragment on 1 Cor. 74*.

61. Didymus, *On the Trinity*, III, 41:3.

62. *Apostolic Constitutions*, III, 6:1–23.

63. *Ibid.*, II, 58:4–6.

64. For an excellent review of church development in the question of women's ministry, cf. R. Gryson, *The Ministry of Women in the Early Church* (Collegeville, Minn.: Liturgical Press, 1976).

65. In the following section the English quotations of the texts are from W. Förster, *Gnosis: A Selection of Gnostic Texts*, vol. I, Engl. transl. ed. by R. McL. Wilson (Oxford: Clarendon, 1972).

66. K. Thraede ("Frau," *loc. cit.*, p. 237) maintains that Gnostic movements were known for the great participation of women in them. He suggests that the Gnostic dualism of "male and female" developed in reaction to the actual leadership of women in Gnosticism.

67. The standard work on Marcion is still A. v. Harnack, *Marcion: Das Evangelium vom fremden Gott* (1924; repr. Darmstadt: Wissenschaftliche Buchgesellschaft, 1960).

68. Epiphanius, *Panarion*, XLV, 2:1.

69. Cf. H. Jonas, *The Gnostic Religion: The Message of the Alien God and the Beginnings of Christianity*, 2nd enl. ed. (Boston: Beacon Press, 1963), pp. 236f.; R. A. Baer, *Philo's Use of the Categories Male and Female* (Leiden: Brill, 1970), pp. 65–80.

70. Hennecke and Schneemelcher, *New Testament Apocrypha*, vol. I, pp. 166f.

71. Pseudo-Clementines, *Homilies*, II, 15:3.

72. Cf. G. Strecker, *Das Judenchristentum in den Pseudoklementinen* (Göttingen, 1958), pp. 35–96; J. Jervell, *Imago Dei: Gn 1, 26f. im Spätjudentum, in der Gnosis und in den Paulinischen Briefen* (Göttingen: Vandenhoeck & Ruprecht, 1960), pp. 163f.

73. *Acts of Thomas*, 27.

74. Cf. L. Zscharnack, *Der Dienst der Frau*, pp. 156–79, especially 174f.

75. *Gospel of Thomas*, Log. 114. Cf. B. Gärtner, *The Theology*

of the Gospel of Thomas (London: Collins, 1961), p.253: "In the Gnostic systems the man–woman relationship is motivated basically by the structure of the heavenly world, the male and female powers which are striving after unity."

76. Tertullian, De Praescriptione Haereticorum, 6:6; 30:6; Eusebius, Eccl. Hist., IV, 13:2.

77. Tertullian, Adversus Marcionem, III, 11.

78. Tertullian, De Praescr. Haer., 30:6.

79. Cf. W. Förster, Gnosis, pp. 34–37; H. Kraft, "Gab es einen Gnostiker Karpokrates?," Theologische Zeitschrift, vol. VIII (1952), pp. 434–43.

80. Irenaeus, Adv. Haer., I, 25:1–6.

81. Clement of Alexandria, Stromateis, II, 2, no.6.

82. Ibid., no.6:1.

83. Ibid., no.8:1.

84. Ibid., no.10:1.

85. These accusations were made by pagans and Jews against the Christians in general, by mainstream Christianity against Montanist and Gnostic groups and vice versa, but also by various Gnostic groups against each other. Cf. R. Haardt, Gnosis: Character and Testimony (Leiden: Brill, 1971), p. 69 fn.1.

86. Simonianism also belongs to this type. For the Helene/Ennoia figure, cf. the analyses of K. Beyschlag, Simon Magus und die christliche Gnosis (Tübingen: Mohr, 1974), pp. 134–64; G. Lüdemann, Untersuchungen zur simonianischen Gnosis (Göttingen: Vandenhoeck & Ruprecht, 1975), pp. 55–81.

87. H. Jonas, The Gnostic Religion, p. 237.

88. R. A. Baer, Philo's Use of . . . Male and Female, p. 71.

89. Irenaeus, Adv. Haer., I, 23:3.

90. For the affinity of the Jungian system to the male-female principles of this second type of Gnostic dualism, cf. R. M. Stein, "Liberating the Feminine," in R. Tiffany Barnhouse and U. T. Holmes (eds.), Male and Female (New York: Seabury Press, 1976), pp. 76–86, and A. Belford Ulanov, "Jung on Male and Female," ibid., pp. 197–210. Cf. also the feminist theological evaluation of this dualism by R. Radford Ruether, New Woman, New Earth: Sexist Ideologies and Human Liberation (New York: Seabury, 1975), pp. 151–59.

91. Irenaeus, Adv. Haer., I, 14:1.

92. Gn. 1:27; Irenaeus, Adv. Haer., I, 18:2.

93. Irenaeus, *Adv. Haer.*, I, 23:3.

94. R. M. Grant, "The Mystery of Marriage in the Gospel of Philip," *Vigiliae Christianae*, vol. XV (1961), pp. 129–40.

95. Irenaeus, *Adv. Haer.*, I, 21:3.

96. R. McL. Wilson, *The Gospel of Philip* (London: Mowbray, 1962); cf. also W. A. Meeks, "The Image of the Androgyne," *loc. cit.*, pp. 191–95.

97. Wilson, *Gospel of Philip*, 71.

98. *Ibid.*, 78.

99. Even L. Zscharnack, *Der Dienst der Frau*, pp. 171ff., repeats the judgment of Irenaeus that Marcus was a "sorcerer."

100. Irenaeus, *Adv. Haer.*, I, 13:2.

101. *Ibid.*, 14:1.

102. *Ibid.*, 13:3.

103. *Ibid.*, 13:4.

104. Wilson, *Gospel of Philip*, 31.

105. *Ibid.*, 32, 35.

106. This is in my opinion overlooked by E. H. Pagels, "What Became of God the Mother? Conflicting Images of God in Early Christianity," *Signs*, vol. II (1976), pp. 293–303.

107. For the definition of woman as "other," cf. the classic work of S. de Beauvior, *The Second Sex* (New York: Knopf, 1953).

108. Tertullian, *De Praescr. Haer.*, XLI.

109. Tertullian, *De Virginibus Velandis*, IX. Cf. Ch. Stücklin, *Tertullian, De virginibus velandis* (Bern: H. Lang, 1974), pp. 189–203.

110. Cf. J. Pelikan, *The Christian Tradition*, vol. I, p. 109.

111. For the history of the formation of the canon, cf. the *Introductions to the New Testament*.

112. Cf. P. Perkins, "Peter in Gnostic Revelation," in *Proceedings of SBL: 1974 Seminar Papers*, vol. II (Washington: SBL, 1974), pp. 1–13, especially 1f.

113. Cf. M. Hengel, "Maria Magdalena und die Frauen als Zeugen," in Betz, Hengel and Schmid (eds.), *Abraham unser Vater* (Leiden: Brill, 1963), pp. 243–56, and my article "Mary Magdalene: Apostle to the Apostles," *UTS Journal*, April 1975, pp. 22ff.; U. Holzmeister, "Die Magdalenenfrage in der kirchlichen Überlieferung," *Zeitschrift für katholische Theologie*, vol. XLVI (1922), pp. 402–22, 556–84.

114. C. F. Parvey, "The Theology and Leadership of Women in the New Testament," in R. R. Ruether (ed.), *Religion and Sexism* (New York: Simon and Schuster, 1974), pp. 117–49, attempts a short description of the passages on women in Luke and Acts but does not give a critical evaluation of Luke's theological tendencies.

115. Hennecke and Schneemelcher, *New Testament Apocrypha*, vol. I, pp. 195ff.

116. *Ibid.*, pp. 243–48.

117. *Papyrus Berolinensis*, 124:9f.

118. *Coptic Gnostic Library*, Codex I, 106:16–23. Cf. Hennecke and Schneemelcher, vol. I, p. 251.

119. *Papyrus Ber.*, 127:16.

120. Hennecke and Schneemelcher, vol. I, pp. 248ff.

121. *Ibid.*, p. 339; Epiphanius, *Panarion*, XXVI, 8:2–3.

122. *Gospel of Thomas*, Log. 114.

123. C. Schmidt, *Koptisch-Gnostische Schriften*, vol. I, *bearb.* W. Till (Berlin: Akademie Verlag, 1954); Hennecke and Schneemelcher, vol. I, pp. 250–59.

124. For the special role of Mary Magdalene and "John"(?) in the Fourth Gospel, cf. R. E. Brown, "Roles of Women in the Fourth Gospel," *Theological Studies*, vol. XXXVI (1975), pp. 688–99, and the popular account of S. M. Schneiders, "Apostleship of Women in John's Gospel," *Catholic Charismatic*, vol. I (1977), pp. 16–20. In the Fourth Gospel we also find a certain tension between Mary Magdalene and Peter or the Beloved Disciple and Peter.

125. For the theological understanding of "becoming a virgin" in Philo and in Gnosticism, cf. R. A. Baer, *Philo's Use of . . . Male and Female*, p. 75.

126. Chap. 96; cf. Schmidt and Till, *Koptisch-Gnostische Schriften*, vol. I, pp. 148.25ff.

127. Chap. 36; also chap. 72; see Schmidt and Till, 36.3–25 and 104.17–39.

128. Published in W. C. Till, *Die gnostischen Schriften des koptischen Papyrus Berolinensis* (Berlin: Akademie Verlag, 1955), pp. 68–72; Hennecke and Schneemelcher, vol. I, pp. 340–44.

129. *Papyrus Ber.*, 18:1–21.

130. *Didascalia*, III, 6:2. Cf. R. H. Connolly, *Didascalia Apostolorum: The Syriac Version* (Oxford: Oxford University, 1929), p. 133. Also III, 6:1–2. Cf. F. X. Funk, *Didascalia et constitutiones*

Apostolorum (1905; repr. Turin, 1964), pp. 191, 8–18; transl. *The Ante-Nicene Fathers* (Buffalo: Christian Literature Publishing Co., 1885–96), vol. VII, p. 427.

131. *The Ecclesiastical Canons of the Apostles*, 24:1–28; English transl., J. P. Arendzen, "An Entire Syriac Text of the Apostolic Church Order," *Journal of Theological Studies*, vol. III (1902), p. 71.

132. Hennecke and Schneemelcher, vol. I, pp. 492f.

133. Cf. A. v. Harnack, *Mission and Expansion of Christianity in the First Three Centuries*, vol. II (New York: Putnam, 1908), p. 64. He argues, however, that the opposition to Gnosticism and Montanism led in the church to the exclusion of women. In a similar fashion argues F. Heiler, *Die Frau in den Religionen der Menschheit* (Berlin: De Gruyter, 1977), pp. 115f. Cf. also my article "Feminist Theology as a Critical Theology of Liberation," *Theological Studies*, vol. XXXVI (1975), pp. 605–26.

134. *Commentary on Romans*, 10:17 (PG 14, 1278A-C).

135. E. A. Clark, "Sexual Politics in the Writings of John Chrysostom," *Anglican Theological Review*, vol. LIX (1977), pp. 3–20, especially 15f.; D. F. Winslow, "Priesthood and Sexuality in the Post-Nicene Fathers," *The Saint Luke's Journal of Theology*, vol. XVIII (1975), pp. 214–27, argues that the Fathers took the incarnation seriously insofar as they were concerned with the whole person of Christ. However, they did not perceive that "sexuality was an integral part of the whole person. It follows that to deny the full participation in the life of the church to some persons (women) is to deny the reality of their full baptism into the one fully human articulation of God in Jesus Christ, as well as to deny the full 'assumption' of humanity of the incarnate Word" (p. 226).

TWO

Mothers of the Church: Ascetic Women in the Late Patristic Age

ROSEMARY RUETHER

The ascetic movement that came to dominate Christianity in the fourth century has not usually been seen as a liberating influence for women. The body-soul dualism of ascetic anthropology too readily identified the female with the sexual and bodily enemy to be suppressed. Asceticism placed women in double jeopardy: regarded as inferior as wives and mothers, and feared, even as ascetics, as the symbol of the carnal.[1]

I do not wish to deny this negative side of asceticism, but I wish to point to another side of its message for women. In its rejection of marriage and motherhood as the Christian norm, asceticism paradoxically suggested that women might now be liberated from their definition by these roles. As ascetics they were freed from the "curse of Eve" which defined their fate as that of bearing children in sorrow and being subject to their husbands (Genesis 3:16). Christ, founder of the new virginal humanity, had made them equals to men in the eschatological humanity that transcended this historical condition.[2] Women dedicated to asceticism could count on the support of the Church in making decisions against their family's demands that they marry and bear children for the patriarchal clan.

In antiquity women's lives followed a very different pattern from those of their brothers. At twelve, upper-class males were finishing the preparatory stages of their education and embarking on the higher studies of rhetoric that prepared them for a public career. Devotees of the public arts might pursue their education into their twenties. The education of females was cut off abruptly at puberty. Girls were married at twelve or thirteen or even earlier to husbands who might be forty years their senior and who had been chosen to cement the political and business ties of the family. Shifting family alliances governed marriages and remarriages, and women had little say in the matter. Unhappy marriages, early pregnancies, being shut out of the larger world of experience and education: these must have helped dispose many women to embrace the new alternative offered by the Church.

What individuals find "liberating" is relative, but perhaps the most important common denominator of the liberating choice is the sense of taking charge of one's own life; of rejecting a state of being governed and defined by others. One experiences the sense of moving from being an object to becoming a subject. I would argue that asceticism could and was experienced as that kind of liberating choice for women in the fourth century, for not only did it allow women to throw off the traditional female roles, but it offered female-directed communities where they could pursue the highest self-development as autonomous persons. It also offered security, for wealthy women endowed these communities for themselves and others. As a result, throngs of women were attracted to asceticism at this time, especially as the old Roman way of life was disintegrating.

The ascetic women best known to us by name come from the upper classes closely associated with the creative leadership of the Church. There is, for example, Macrina, sister of the Cappadocians Basil the Great and Gregory of Nyssa. She was the originator of the ascetic life for the family circle and perhaps should be credited with being the immediate source of the plan of life that came to be called the "Basilian rule." Macrina chose the ascetic life in her teens, refusing to accept further efforts of her family to arrange a marriage for her. She is described as having been the true "father, teacher, paedagogue and counselor" of her brother Peter, born after their father's death. She brought her mother into the ascetic life and turned the family estates into a monastic community of prayer and charitable service. When her brother Basil returned from his many years of study abroad, it was she who led him to abandon his wordly ambitions, some twenty years after she herself had embraced asceticism. Gregory of Nyssa gives us a vivid description of this event:

Her brother, the distinguished Basil, came home where he had had the practice of rhetoric for a long time. He was excessively puffed up by his rhetorical abilities and disdainful of all great reputations and considered himself better than the leading men of the district. But Macrina took him over and lured him so quickly to the goal of philosophy that he withdrew from worldly show and began to look down upon acclaim through oratory and went over to this life full of labors for one's own hand to perform, providing for himself through his complete poverty a mode of living that would without impediment lead to virtue.[3]

The apostolic model for ascetic women in this period was Thecla, the legendary disciple of Saint Paul. Great ascetic women were regularly dubbed "new Theclas." According to Gregory, Christ appeared at Macrina's birth and gave her the secret name of Thecla, thus predicting that she would follow the path of this famous prototype. Thecla, in the apocryphal *Acts*, is one who sacrifices all, her home and her fiancé, in order to follow Paul. She cuts her hair, travels as a man and stops at no threat from family or state to pursue her vocation. She even claims the right to baptize herself and escapes miraculously from various encounters with wild beasts in the arena. Ultimately she is commissioned by Paul to be an apostle of the Gospel. She ends her colorful career as a contemplative in a mountain cave, where she teaches and heals those who come to her.[4] Thecla was indeed an audacious role model for the Christian women. Her life clearly demonstrates that obedience to Christ can sanction sweeping disobedience to the established order of family and state.

The Roman Monastic Circle

The Roman aristocracy produced one particular circle of ascetic women of whom the central figures are two remarkable women, Paula and Melania, together with their namesake granddaughters, the younger Paula and the younger Melania. Other figures, especially Marcella, foundress of the Roman circle, have also a place in our narrative. Unfortunately, we are entirely dependent on their renowned male associates for an account of their lives. Although these women were highly literate and studious, not a line has survived from their pens. They wrote many scholarly epistles, but, unlike those of their male counterparts Jerome, Augustine and others, their letters were not collected and preserved. The reason for this seems to derive from the official Church's view that women, no matter how holy, cannot qualify as teachers of the Church. Their influence must be exercised only in private and behind a façade of male direction. This attitude toward the woman as teacher is evident in Jerome's remarks on Marcella:

Whatever in me was the fruit of long study and, as such, made by constant meditation a part of my nature, this she tasted, this she learned and made her own. Consequently, after my departure from Rome, in case of a dispute arising as to the testimony of Scripture on any subject, recourse was had to her to settle it. And so wise was she and so well did she understand what philosophers call *to prepon*; that is, what is becoming, in what she did, that when she answered questions she gave her own opinion not as her own, but as from me or someone else, thus admitting that what she taught, she had learned from others. For she knew that the apostle said, "I suffer not a woman to teach" and she would not seem to inflict a wrong upon the male sex, many of whom (including some priests) questioned her concerning doubtful and obscure points.[5]

This exclusion of even the holiest and most learned women from the public magisterium seems to have prevented work from their own hands from being included in the corpus of the Church's tradition. We are forced to reconstruct their lives and personalities through the uncertain mirror of their male admirers (or detractors).

Our primary information on the ascetic circle of women in Rome comes from Jerome. In A.D. 382 he arrived in the capital city from a sojourn in the East, already a seasoned rhetor, Biblical scholar, and dedicated monk. He quickly made his way into the network of highborn ascetic women. The foundress of the circle was Marcella, probably about fifty years old at this time, who some thirty years earlier had adopted the ascetic regime of prayer, fasting and study in her palace on the Aventine. Widowed after several months of marriage, she had resisted all attempts by her family to make a second advantageous match. Her mother, Albina, scion of the powerful Caionii Rufii clan,[6] had been drawn into her daughter's way of life. Marcella had been inspired by models of asceticism from Egypt, popularized during Athanasius' exile in Rome (A.D. 339–42) and again during the exile of Peter of Alexandria (A.D. 373–78).[7] She gathered around her a band of like-minded noblewomen who met for Scripture study at her home.

Included in this circle was the noblewoman Asella, perhaps Marcella's sister,[8] who had retired to monastic seclusion in her room at the age of twelve. She too was approaching fifty at this time. There was also the patrician widow Lea, who had made a break with the world at her husband's death. She is described by Jerome as "the head of a monas-

tery, she showed herself a true mother to the virgins in it." [9]
The prominent widow Paula was also a part of this network.
Her husband had died three years earlier, leaving her with
five children: Blesilla, Paulina, Estochium, Rufina and Toxotius. These matrons gathered around them younger relatives and daughters whom they led in the ascetic life.

Like most senatorial nobility, the members of this circle
were tied to each other by lines of marriage and kinship.
Eustochium, destined to be the lifelong companion of her
mother and of Jerome, was already an ardent disciple of the
discipline as a mere girl in her early teens. Paula's daughter
Paulina was to marry Pammachius, a cousin of Marcella and
a fellow student and friend of Jerome's. Paula's son Toxotius
would marry Laeta, daughter of Marcella's cousin Caeionius
Caecina Albinus. [10]

The ascetic regime adopted by these women was severe.
All trace of elegance and luxury normal to their class was
totally banished. They stayed secluded except for secret visits to martyrs' tombs or basilicas for worship. They fasted
stringently and continuously. Lavish clothing and cosmetics
were put aside for coarse, squalid dress, and they neglected
their personal appearance. Bathing was shunned. They slept
on hard mats on the floor and prayed and wept through the
night. The gossip of the dining table and the rounds of visiting were replaced by the Scripture study circle. The key to
their new life was chastity, as virgins and as widows. Sexual
appetite, along with all other desires of the flesh, was to be
suppressed by the ascetic discipline. [11]

Marcella was probably the first to draw Jerome into this
group, both as master of the monastic life and as tutor for
their Scriptural study. It was he who introduced them to the
controversial idea of studying Hebrew in order to read the
Old Testament texts in the original. [12] Marcella was the most
demanding philologist. Letter after letter from her between
tutorial sessions consulted him about difficult points of translation. What is the meaning of words such as *Selah*, *Ephod*
and *teraphim* in the texts? Jerome even complained that he

had been kept up until the morning hours dictating replies to her exacting questions.[13]

Jerome also was drawn into the household of Paula to become counselor and spiritual father. Her daughter Blesilla was beautiful and worldly, rejoicing in her coming marriage. Then, left a widow after seven months, she was converted to asceticism after a grave illness. Jerome and Paula had prayed for this turn of events and were delighted to see her turn to rigorous mortifications. Alas, these proved too much for her, and in four months the girl of twenty was dead. Paula fainted at the funeral, and an outpouring of rage against the monks, especially Jerome, went up among her relatives. "How long must we refrain from driving these detestable monks out of Rome? Why do we not stone them or hurl them into the Tiber?" went up the murmur from the crowd.[14]

The gentle Eustochium underwent no such violent turns of affection. According to Jerome, she had been trained in Marcella's cell since childhood.[15] Her commitment did not forbid her to offer girlish tokens of affection, however. On Saint Peter's Day she sent Jerome a present of doves, bracelets and a basket of cherries. For these Jerome thanked her in a letter of nicely turned rhetorical conceits that was the standard expression of educated *politesse*.[16] It was to Eustochium that Jerome dedicated his most remarkable treatise on virginity, as a proclamation of the new ideals to Roman society as much as personal counsel for her. The letter is notable for the vivid erotic imagination that revealed his suppressed sexual appetite. The girl of sixteen is advised to put aside all thought of marriage and sexual feeling, confining herself to her chamber in continuous mortification, to await the arrival of her bridegroom, Christ:

Ever let the privacy of your chamber guard you. Ever let the Bridegroom sport with you within. Do you pray? You speak to the Bridegroom. Do you read? He speaks to you. When sleep overtakes you He will come behind and put his hand through the hole of the door and your heart shall be moved for Him, and you will awake and rise up and say, "I am sick with love. . . . A bundle of myrrh is my well beloved unto me. He shall lie all night betwixt my breasts."[17]

This epistle is famous also for the acid bite of Jerome's best social satire, directed not only against the gaudy display of aristocratic life but also against the hypocrisy of the new groups of priests, nuns and monks who now swarmed through Roman society. There are the nuns whose chaste robes are only a mask for the new freedom to roam abroad for wanton adventures; the clergy who crowd around wealthy women with simpering gait, extorting food and gifts and performing the most disgusting tasks to win her last testament on her deathbed. Even monks make a display of their unkempt hair, black cloaks and bare feet to enter the homes of the wealthy, making up for their fasts by day in nocturnal feasting.[18]

This letter created a scandal. Antagonistic pagan society was more than happy to see the sins of the Church displayed before it, sins which many had wished to suspect. But Jerome's portrait of the insinuating monk in the homes of wealthy women was all too easily turned against himself.[19] The Roman clergy were not soon to forgive him this exposé, and it was one of the incidents that led to a worsening atmosphere around him in the capital. In the summer of A.D. 385 there was a formal synod of the Roman presbyterate to investigate the charges brought against Jerome. Their adverse judgment seems to have included a direct order to him to remove himself from the city.[20] Jerome rightly protested his innocence of all wrongdoing with these women, but it is obvious that the bonds of affection that united him with them, especially with Paula, were strong. Even as he wrote to Asella to make his farewells, he and Paula were laying plans to meet in the East and there construct a permanent monastic community.

The Bethlehem Community: Paula and Jerome

Paula left Rome a few weeks after Jerome, placing her remaining children in the hands of guardians, except for Eustochium, who was to share her mother's adventures. Paula's party arrived first in Cyprus, where they stayed with Bishop Epiphanius, previously their house guest in Rome. There Paula visited monasteries and left substantial relief for their maintenance.[21] Jerome's party met Paula's, probably in Antioch, and they undertook an extensive tour of the holy places of Palestine.

Bible in hand, Paula and Jerome searched out as many Biblical sites as possible. For them, this was holy ground filled with reminiscences of sacred history. The Palestine of the fourth century vanished from their mind's eye, to be replaced by the shimmering sight of an earlier era. Here was Elijah's town, there the house of Cornelius at Caesarea. Here was where Philip lived with his four prophetess-daughters. Here was where Jonah departed for his fateful journey, and there was where the Lord rested with his friends Mary and Martha. Old and New Testament sites alike attracted their avid attention, especially in Jerusalem and Bethlehem, the high points of their tour. Many of the sites had already been conjured back into existence by the eager tourism of the newly Christian world, but the Biblical erudition of the pair allowed them to add many lesser excursions.[22]

After the Palestine trip they journeyed down into Egypt, staying perhaps a month in Alexandria, where Jerome heard the famous teacher Didymus. But then they went on to their primary destination, which was to view the monks of the Nitrian desert. Jerome describes thousands of monks pouring out to greet the celebrated lady, including the illustrious Serapion. Paula was so moved by the experience that, "forgetful of her sex," she wished to establish her convent there among the monks. But she was also drawn back to the holy places of Palestine, doubtless with a little urging from Je-

rome, whose idea of a congenial monastery was something
other than a bare cave. By this time the heat of summer was
upon them, and so the party headed back to Palestine by
sea. They had already visited the monastic settlement there
that would be the model for their own.

Melania, an early member of the noble circle of Rome,
had departed for the East many years earlier. She had settled
in Jerusalem on the Mount of Olives, where she was joined
by Rufinus, an old colleague of Jerome's. The two had built
a double monastery for men and women where they could
pursue the disciplined life, engage in hospitality and also
teach and study. This was the model of a monastery suited
to Paula's and Jerome's needs.

Paula and Jerome decided to plant their establishment in
Bethlehem, a spot which had moved Paula deeply. There
was a basilica there at the site of the Nativity, as well as a
hospice and a monastery for men. Paula stayed in the hospice for three years while additional monastic buildings were
constructed. She had made appropriate financial arrangements for herself in her settlement of her vast family property, for it was her personal wealth that was used to build
and maintain first a men's monastery for Jerome to run, and
then a triple monastery for women which she was to head.
A group of women had accompanied her from Rome to form
the core of this female community. Finally, there was to be
a guest house for passing travelers. This was the "spiritual
kingdom" she was to rule until her death in A.D. 404. The
women's monastery had grown to some fifty virgins by the
time Eustochium inherited its leadership.

The women's communities lived an austere life of work
and prayer. They observed six hours of prayer: at dawn, at
the third, sixth and ninth hours, at evening and at midnight.
They were also assigned the study and memorization of por-
tions of Scripture and filled the rest of the day with the
menial tasks of monastic housekeeping. The three communities seem to have been divided according to class and social background, and the wealthier women retained a per-

sonal slave![23] The three companies worked and ate in their own houses, but met as one for prayer in a common chapel and trooped together to the basilica for the Eucharist on Sunday. They could own only the simplest change of clothing. Paula was the all-seeing mother of this community, reproving faults and encouraging backsliders, nursing those who fell ill. She herself always observed a stricter regimen than she imposed on the others.

Retirement allowed Paula and Eustochium to continue their textual studies with Jerome. Paula seems to have been attracted more by the allegorical method of searching out the moral and mystical meanings of the text. Jerome credits her with having learned Hebrew far better than he, being able to chant the psalms in that tongue without a trace of a Latin accent. Her daughter shared this accomplishment. Paula's probing mind would not let Jerome rest with easy answers: "Whenever I stuck fast and honestly confessed myself at fault she would by no means rest content, but would force me by fresh questions to point out to her which of many different solutions seemed to me most probable."[24]

Meanwhile, in Rome, Paula's family was undergoing changes. Paulina had married Pammachius. Rufina, the youngest daughter, died in A.D. 388. Toxotius, only a child when Paula departed, had grown and married Laeta. The young couple prayed for a child they could dedicate to virginity, and in A.D. 400 the younger Paula was born. Jerome immediately set himself to be the adviser of the babe in the paths of virtue. He wrote a long letter to the mother warning against the dangers of the luxurious city and spelling out the regimen for raising a Christian virgin.[25] Finally, despairing of her protection in Rome, he advised Laeta to send the child to be raised in the convent at Bethlehem. Old as he was (he was then near seventy), he promised to carry the little girl on his shoulders and be her tutor to train her stammering lips in Christian wisdom. This request was subsequently granted, though too late for Paula to see her granddaughter. Little Paula was to grow up under the care of her aunt and to inherit the leadership of the monastery at Eustochium's death in A.D. 419.

The Jerusalem Community: Melania and Rufinus

From Paula's community in Bethlehem, we turn now to the second Roman woman, Melania the Elder, who had preceded her to the Holy Land. Melania was probably born in A.D. 341 [26] and so was some years Paula's senior. She was well connected, and she married at about fourteen into the powerful Valerii clan.[27] Her husband, probably many years her senior, died in 364, leaving her a widow with three children at twenty-two. Soon after, two of her children died. Following these tragedies Melania was drawn into the ascetic circle in Rome, where she devoted herself to mortification and good works. In 372, her son now being of an age for her to give his education over to a guardian, she decided to tour the monastic settlements in the East.[28] Her noble relatives were bitterly opposed to this unusual decision, but she persisted and eventually had her way.[29] Within a decade, Melania's reputation as an ascetic was sufficiently great that Jerome hailed her the "new Thecla" and urged Paula to follow her example. Rufinus would remind Jerome of these praises when the two communities fell into acrimony some years later.[30]

Melania went first to the Nitrian desert to visit the solitaries in their caves. There she met such famous hermits as Pambo, Arsisius, Serapion, Paphnutius, Isidore the Confessor and Dioscorus. Palladius tells us that she remained with them in the desert for six months, traveling about to visit well-known monastic settlements.[31] The monk Macarius presented her a miraculous lamb's pelt given him by a hyena whose pup he had cured of blindness. This relic Melania was to treasure for over twenty years and then give to Paulinus

of Nola when she returned to Italy.[32] Melania had probably
joined Rufinus in Alexandria, but she was quite independent
of him in these journeys.[33]

After Athanasius' death (May 3, A.D. 373) a persecution
broke out against the Nicenes of Egypt. Many of these
monks, as well as priests and bishops, were banished to Dio-
caesarea in Palestine. Melania accompanied them and used
her wealth to minister to them, traveling to their place of
confinement by night disguised in a slave's hood. She was
thrown into prison by the consul for this offense, but she
immediately demonstrated the hauteur to which both her
rank and her dedication entitled her. She informed the consul, "For my part, I am So-and-So's daughter and So-and-
So's wife, but I am a slave of Christ. Do not despise the
cheapness of my clothing. For I am able to exalt myself if I
like and you cannot terrify me in this way or take any part of
my goods."[34] She was immediately released with apologies
and given leave to minister to the saints unmolested.

When the ban against the Nicenes was lifted, about five
years later, Melania settled in Jerusalem and there founded
a monastery on the Mount of Olives. Rufinus probably
joined her about 379–80, and together they developed a
monastery for men under his care and another for women
under hers for fifty virgins. It was primarily Melania's funds
that constructed both edifices.[35] The rule of Saint Basil,
which Rufinus was later to translate and spread to the West,
was probably the guide for their community. The day was
spent in a mixture of prayer, charitable work for the poor
and pilgrims, and the study of Scripture. Rufinus seems to
have developed a school where he taught.[36] There was also
a scriptorum, and the monastery partially supported itself by
copying manuscripts, developments that anticipate the cultural role characteristic of the later Latin monasteries. Rufinus was to chide Jerome afterward for ordering many manuscripts to be copied in this way and paying more for the
production of the pagan classical authors![37] Melania herself
was able to pursue her own studies in this learned setting.

Being very learned and loving literature, she turned night into day perusing every writing of the ancient commentators, including the three million [lines] of Origen and the two hundred and fifty thousand of Gregory, Stephen, Pierius, Basil and other standard writers. Nor did she read them once only and casually, but she laboriously went through each book seven or eight times.[38]

Jerome and Paula stayed at this monastery in A.D. 385 and made it the model of their own. Another notable visitor to the Mount of Olives was Evagrius of Pontus. He had fallen from grace in his native land and was in a state of physical and moral crisis. Melania nursed him back to health on both levels and restored his determination to live the ascetic life.[39] Melania is also credited with helping to win over four hundred monks of the region who had fallen into the heresy of the Pneumatomachoi (denial of the divinity of the Holy Spirit).[40]

In the 390s a dispute broke out over Origenism that was to rage through the whole Church, from Egypt and Palestine to Rome, embittering former friends and, thanks to the authority of Jerome, blackening the reputations of Melania and Rufinus until modern times. In retrospect, the differences between Jerome and Rufinus appear minor. Both agreed that Origen was a great scholar and theologian whose valuable work needed to be used, but who had strayed into errors that must be corrected. Jerome himself had praised Origen and followed a course of using his work not too different from that of Rufinus. Rufinus wished to deal with Origen's errors by making Latin translations that omitted them. Jerome, drawn into the anti-Origen camp, became the crusader against this suppression of Origen's errors.[41] Much of the heat surrounding this controversy was the result of enlarged personality conflict rather than substance. But, once inflamed, it embittered old friendships beyond repair.

Melania was marginal to the quarrel and became the object of Jerome's venom primarily because she was perceived as Rufinus' friend and supporter. The acrimony led John,

Bishop of Jerusalem and supporter of Rufinus, to put the
monastery in Bethlehem temporarily under an interdict. In
A.D. 397 the breach between John, Jerome and Rufinus was
healed with a ceremony of reconciliation in the Church of
the Resurrection. Rufinus returned to Italy and eventually
installed himself in what he hoped would be a more peaceful
setting in his old home in Aquileia. However, he also wrote
an apology for his method of translating Origen in which
Jerome was roundly criticized. Among other things, Rufinus
scored Jerome for his treatment of Melania. Having once
praised her as the new Thecla, he had wiped her name from
copies of his work to conceal the disparity with his later
denunciations.[42] Jerome rose to new heights of vehemence,
slashing Rufinus for his bad Latin![43] Old friends were drawn
into the fray. Marcella and Pammachius in Rome became
defenders of Jerome's side, even taking the liberty of sending
Jerome a stolen copy of Rufinus' unrevised manuscript of
Origen for refutation. They also suppressed a conciliatory
letter from Jerome to Rufinus[44] and in other ways heated up
the dispute.

This atmosphere of acrimony was one reason for Melania's decision to return home about A.D. 399, but her own
family affairs were the chief factor. Melania's son Publicola
was now about forty. He had married the noble Albina,
daughter of Caeionius Rufinus Albinus (and hence a cousin
of both Marcella and Paula's daughter-in-law Laeta). The
child of this marriage, Melania Junior, was married at the
tender age of thirteen to her cousin Pinianus, himself only
seventeen. Melania's purpose in returning home seems to
have been to urge the young couple to follow her in the way
of perfection by taking a vow of continence. In this matter
she had to contend against the worldly ambitions of her son
for his children.

We gain a vivid picture of the spirit of the elderly Melania
in an incident told by Palladius. On the return journey to
Italy the party paused to rest from the intense heat. Jovinus,
a deacon traveling with her, washed himself in cold water

and threw himself down to rest. Melania proceeded to scold him roundly for this indulgence, saying:

"How can a warm-blooded young man like you dare to pamper your flesh that way? Do you not know that this is the source of much harm? Look, I am sixty years old and neither my feet nor my face nor any of my members, except for the tips of my fingers, has touched water, although I am afflicted with many ailments and my doctors urge me. I have not yet made concessions to my bodily desires, nor have I used a couch for resting, nor have I ever made a journey on a litter."[45]

When Melania arrived in Italy a great entourage of her relatives came down to meet her at Naples. The party traveled to visit their relative Paulinus at Nola. Paulinus describes the arrival of the saint in the manner of a triumphal entry:

In that journey of mother and children I beheld the glory of the Lord. She sat on a tiny thin horse, worth less than an ass, and they attended her on the journey, their trappings emphasizing the extraordinary contrast. For they had all the pomp of this world with which honored and wealthy senators could be invested. The Appian Way groaned and gleamed with swaying coaches, decorated horses, ladies' carriages all gilded and numerous smaller vehicles. . . . I was astounded at the spirit of poverty shown by those rich people toward their mother's welfare, for they took pride more in her holy poverty than in all their own conspicuous wealth. . . . Those silk-clad children of hers, though accustomed to the splendor of a toga or a dress according to their sex, took joy in touching that thick tunic of hers, with its hard threads like broom and her cheap cloak.[46]

After this country sojourn, Melania went to the family palace in Rome. Here she was instrumental in bringing her niece Avita's pagan husband Apronianus into the Christian faith and persuading the couple to take the vow of continence.[47] But she was not immediately successful in her designs for Melania Junior. About A.D. 404 she made a visit to North Africa and was visiting Augustine there at the time of her son's death. Paulinus describes her deep sorrow at this event, not so much at death itself (which a good Christian should not fear), but at the fact that he had died still unconverted and having not yet renounced his ambitions for senatorial distinction.[48] Melania Junior and Pinianus also lost their two babies shortly after birth. These tragedies and Melania's near-death after childbed disposed the couple toward the way of asceticism.

The Ascetic Career of Melania Junior

The exact point at which Melania Junior decided to follow her grandmother's footsteps is unclear. Her hagiographer Gerontius dates this desire to before her marriage, but much of this account is pious romance. His story that the young couple in their twenties were already devoting themselves enthusiastically to the works of charity for the poor, the sick and the imprisoned, visiting the abused slaves in the mines, is probably true,[49] for Melania the Elder clearly saw her young niece as an appropriate successor. But the decision to follow the way of continence did not take place until later, not only after Publicola's death but after the sack of Rome forced the family to flee to Africa.

In August of 410 a terrifying advance of Germanic armies culminated in a three-day pillage of Rome. The family of Melania fled first to their estates in Sicily. There Melania the Elder spent some time giving Christian instructions to her grandson, Publicola's second child. She disposed of her property in that region and then returned to Jerusalem, where she died soon after her arrival.[50] Many of the others in the ascetic circle in Rome were also swept away by these events. Jerome, in Jerusalem, learned the tale of Marcella's heroic defense of the chastity of her young companion Prin-

cipia. The pillaging soldiers broke into the palace on the
Aventine and beat the elderly ascetic when she insisted that
the house held no gold. Her pleas that they spare her virgins
aroused their pity, however, and the women were conveyed
to the safety of the Basilica of Paul, where Marcella died
soon after.[51]

Melania Junior and Pinian settled for a time in Africa,
where the family had extensive estates. Their contacts with
Augustine encouraged them to look to him for guidance.
They took up residence first at Tegaste, where they had
property, and there they endowed two monasteries with suf-
ficient income to support eighty monks and 130 nuns. Melania was desirous of liquidating her vast estates in Italy,
Africa, Numidia and Mauretania in order to give the proceeds to the poor. But Pinian's brother Severus opposed
these pious designs. The couple also encountered a restrain-
ing force in the bishops of Africa. Augustine, Alypius and
Aurelius visited the couple and advised them to use their vast
incomes to endow churches and monasteries rather than
giving it away directly to the poor. "If you give money to the
poor, it is gone again tomorrow. If you give revenue to a
monastery, you will endow it permanently," was their pru-
dential admonition![52] Perceiving the fortune of the couple,
the people of Hippo attempted to force Pinian to remain
with them as priest and patron.[53] It was during this period
that Melania Junior and Pinian definitely adopted the ascetic
regimen. Melania took on a severe discipline of fasting,
prayer and intense study of the Scriptures and the lives of
the desert fathers.[54]

About A.D. 418 (Melania Junior then being about thirty-
five), the couple, together with Albina, decided to move on
to the East. They went first to Alexandria, where they visited
Bishop Cyril and were greeted by the holy Abbot Nesteros.
Then they continued on to Jerusalem, where they settled for
a time in the hostel of the Anastasis.[55] Time seems to have
cured the enmity between the Bethlehem and Jerusalem
communities. In 419 Jerome (then in his last year of life)

sent a note to Augustine in which he conveyed the friendly
greetings of their mutual friends Melania, Pinian and Albina, as well as the younger Paula, and mourned the recent
death of Eustochium.[56]

Melania's attraction to the heroics of Egyptian sanctity
soon led her on to new travels. Some funds from her estates
in Spain arrived. She took them and went off independently
to tour the cells of the monks in Nitria. She is said to have
traveled from cell to cell, seeking knowledge and blessings
from these holy ones and distributing largesse. But not all
the monks were pleased by her aristocratic patronage. One
aged Abbot Hephestion curtly told her that he had no need
of gold. Nevertheless she secreted some money in his basket
and hastily left, only to be surprised to see the monk hurry-
ing after her. "Give the money to those in need," she
pleaded, but he insisted, "No one is in need here." Faced
with his determination to return the gold, Melania finally
threw it into the river. But the habits of Roman largesse died
hard, and she repeated this secret deposit of wealth in the
cells of many other monks and nuns who had refused to
accept it. Melania Junior seems to have spent some months
of this tour meeting the monks of Alexandria as well as those
of the desert. Gerontius proudly recounts that she was received by them "as if she were a man."[57]

When she returned to Jerusalem, she found that Albina
had completed the monastery for the new community on
the Mount of Olives. Gradually a whole complex was built
up, with Pinian as head of the male compound and Melania
Junior in charge of a female community of ninety women.
Melania developed the rule for the governance of her convent, detailing the daily round of prayer and the rules of
spiritual growth. True humility is declared to be the most
important rule for the ascetic; rigorous mortifications can
still hide a prideful spirit. We are told that Melania was visited about this time by her cousin Paula Junior, who had
grown up with Jerome and Eustochium in Bethlehem and
was now a girl of about twenty. Paula is described as still

prideful, comporting herself with much of the hauteur of her family and class. Melania took the further guidance of the girl in hand and led her to turn from Roman pomp to true humility.[58]

In addition to the construction of the double monasteries, Melania Junior used her resources to build several churches; one was dedicated to the apostles, another to the Ascension. Another monastery for men was built, dedicated to the chanting of continuous psalmody.[59] Albina's and Pinian's deaths in 431–32 left her in exclusive charge of these church and monastic compounds.

Although she was now approaching fifty, her travels were not yet over. In A.D. 436 her uncle Volusian (her mother's brother) invited her to the imperial court in Constantinople for the wedding of the Western Emperor Valentinian III to Eudoxia, daughter of the Eastern Emperor Theodosius II. Melania Junior accepted, in the hope of bringing her still pagan uncle into the faith before his death. The great capital of the Eastern Empire was no easy place for a sheltered woman to make her way. Theodosius had grown up under the thumb of this powerful sister Pulcheria, who had taken a vow of virginity in her teens to assure her political independence. Pulcheria had governed until Theodosius' wife, Eudocia, had managed to oust her from influence.[60] The factions supporting the two women were linked with many other controversies that seethed in the capital. In A.D. 436 Theodosius and his wife were cementing the alliance of East and West by marrying their only child to Valentinian.

Melania threw herself into the religious strife of the city. She gathered about her a circle of women from the court whom she instructed in orthodox theology against the heresy of Nestorius, and she seems to have earned the friendship of the Empress Eudocia during her stay. The story of her success in converting her uncle Volusian is told in the romantic genre of the period, with many miraculous coincidences and combats with the Devil. She fell ill and recovered just in time to be carried to her uncle's deathbed after his baptism.[61] Having accomplished her purpose there, she returned to Jerusalem. The monk Gerontius, who accompanied her on this trip, describes her rigorous refusal to bend the rules of ascetic discipline even amid the snowstorms and other hardships of the journey.

Once back in Jerusalem, she again took up the work of her spiritual empire. New funds allowed her to build yet another edifice, a martyrium where a community of monks could chant perpetual praises. The Empress Eudocia had made a vow to go on pilgrimage to Jerusalem after her daughter's wedding, and Melania became her guide in this visit. She journeyed to Sidon to meet the Empress and escorted her to the holy city. There she showed her through the communities of monks and nuns and even miraculously cured her of a sprained ankle when she slipped and fell in a church! [62] Melania stayed with the Empress long enough to accompany her back to Caesarea. In A.D. 441 the Empress would fall from favor, having been accused of infidelity, and go into permanent exile in Jerusalem, but Melania was no longer alive by that time.

Melania is described as charismatic and a miracle worker. Among those healed by her powers was a young woman afflicted with a dead fetus which she could not deliver. Melania visited her in the company of her nuns and cured her, but not before making the case an object lesson for her virgins on the curses of childbearing from which chastity had delivered them! [63] Perhaps Melania recalled her own difficult childbearing many years earlier.

Melania died at Christmas of A.D. 448. Her passing is described as one filled with the odor of sanctity, surrounded by her virgins, including her cousin Paula. Troops of clergy and monks from the churches gathered about her. She completed the observance of the festival at Bethlehem and returned to Jerusalem to die in the bosom of her community. Gerontius makes clear his own prominent role at her side in these events and her specific commendation of the leadership of her communities to him at her death! [64]

Conclusion

We leave the story of Melania Junior at the moment when she passes from this earthly scene in a cloud of sanctity, her soul doubtless ascending directly to heaven to take its place in close proximity to the cherubim throne. These tales of ascetic women may not strike modern women as particularly attractive forms of feminism, but the ascetic way was one of the most interesting options open to women in the fourth and fifth centuries. It offered women possibilities which departed dramatically from their traditional role definitions under patriarchy. As ascetics, they could successfully combat demands for unwelcome marriage alliances. They could turn instead to intense study, self-development and an independent life in female-run communities. They were assured of absolute equality with men on the plane of their spiritual kingdom.

Women paid for this exodus with the sacrifice of worldly pleasures, sex and childbearing, but men were paying these same prices. They won no official office in the Church, although there is no doubt that, as saints and miracle workers, they belonged to the new class of heroes of the time. In a Christianized Roman Empire that believed that the ascetics were at least as important to its defense and favor as were armies and statesmen, they exercised a public and even political role.[65]

But in the ascetic view, this temporal world was doomed and fast disappearing. Another, more glorious kingdom was taking its place. Within this other world the ascetic woman was scaling the highest rungs of the angelic hierarchy to win eternal glory. For well-born Roman women accustomed to power but for the most part denied the right to exercise it themselves, here was more than enough challenge to attract their energies.

The tragedy of these women is not that they chose a path of accomplishment that was antisexual. In this they were no more than enthusiastic participants in the *Zeitgeist* of their age. Their tragedy, rather, is that in so choosing this path, accepting in good faith the ideals held out to them by the Church, they were nevertheless denied their rightful place in the Church's tradition. They were writers, thinkers, Scripture scholars, and innovators in the formation of monastic life, but because they were women they could have no public voice in the teaching Church here on earth.

NOTES

1. See R. Ruether, "Misogynism and Virginal Feminism in the Fathers of the Church," in *Religion and Sexism: Images of Woman in the Jewish and Christian Traditions*, ed. R. Ruether (New York: Simon and Schuster, 1974), pp. 150–83.

2. The idea that virginity frees women from the curse of Eve and represents her new equality with men in Christ is found in various patristic authors; for example, Leander of Seville, *De Instit. Virg.*, preface, and Cyprian, *De Habitu Virg.*, 22.

3. Gregory of Nyssa, *The Life of St. Macrina*, in *Ascetical Works: Fathers of the Church*, vol. LVIII (Washington: Catholic University of America, 1967), p. 167. Greek text: *Sources Chrétiennes*, no. 178, ed. Pierre Maraval (Paris: Éditions du Cerf, 1971). Macrina is also credited with being Gregory's mentor in his dialogue with her *On the Soul and the Resurrection*, in *Ascetical Works*, pp. 198ff.

4. *Acts of Paul and Thecla*, in *Ante-Nicene Fathers*, ed. Roberts and Donaldson, vol. VIII (1885–97), pp. 487ff. See also the note on "St. Thecla's Martyrium," in John Wilkinson (ed.), *Egeria's Travels* (London: SPCK, 1971).

5. Jerome, *Lettres*, Epistle 127:7, text and transl. by Jérome Labourt (Paris: Les Belles Lettres, 1949), vol. VII, pp. 143–44; Engl. transl.: *Nicene and Post-Nicene Fathers*, ed. Schaff and Wace, vol. VI (1890–1900), p. 255.

6. See Stemma 13, "Caionii Rufii," in A. H. M. Jones, J. R. Martin Dale and J. Morris, *The Prosopography of the Later Roman Empire*, vol. I, A.D. 260–395 (Cambridge: Cambridge University, 1971), p. 1138.

7. Jerome, Epistle 127:5.

8. *Idem*, Epistle 24.

9. *Idem*, Epistle 23:2.

10. Stemma 23, "The Family of Saint Paula," in Jones *et al.*, *Prosopography*, p. 1143.

11. Jerome, Epistle 24, to Marcellus on Asella.

12. *Idem*, Epistle 32. Because the Septuagint was regarded as verbally inspired, to go back to the Hebrew original was suspect as Judaiizing! Rufinus reflects this view in his *Apology against Jerome*, Bk. II, 32–33: *Nicene and Post-Nicene Fathers*, vol. III, p. 475 (*Patrologica Latina*, Latin text of Latin Church Fathers, ed. J.-P. Migne, 1844–82, vol. XXI, cols., 611–12).

13. Jerome, Epistles 28 and 29; also Epistles 25 and 26.

14. *Idem*, Epistle 39:6.

15. *Idem*, Epistle 127:5.

16. *Idem*, Epistle 31.

17. *Idem*, Epistle 22:25.

18. *Idem*, Epistle 22:13–14, 16 and 27.

19. For Jerome's protests against this criticism, see Epistle 27:2.

20. Jerome seems to have been accused of illicit relations with Paula, although the charge was later withdrawn by the informant; see Epistle 45:2 and his *Apology against Rufinus*, Bk. III, 21. The whole incident is discussed in J. N. D. Kelly, *Jerome: His Life, Writings and Controversies* (New York: Harper & Row, 1975), p. 113.

21. Jerome, Epistle 108:7.

22. *Idem*, Epistle 108:8–14.

23. *Idem*, Epistle 108:20. It is indicative of the deeply engrained character of slavery in antiquity that even in the community dedicated to evangelical poverty it was not seen as contradictory for a woman of noble birth to continue to have a slave. Jerome remarks only that she could not have the attendant of her former household, because this might perpetuate their worldly ways. But he finds nothing incongruous, as such, in the fact of having a slave in the convent.

24. Jerome, Epistle 108:27.

25. *Idem*, Epistle 107.

26. This dating has been established by F. X. Murphy, "Melania the Elder: A Biographical Note," *Traditio*, vol. V (1947), pp. 62–65, correcting the earlier estimates of her birth in 349 or 350.

27. See Stemma 20, "The Family of Melania I," in Jones *et al.*, *Prosopography*, p. 1142.

28. Palladius, *The Lausiac History (H.L.)*, 46:1: text and notes, Dom Cuthbert Butler (Cambridge: Cambridge University, 1898– 1904); Engl. transl., *Ancient Christian Writers*, vol. XXXIV, transl. Robert Meyer (Westminster, Md.: Newman Press, 1965), p. 123.

29. Paulinus of Nola attributes this resistance to the promptings of the Devil, but otherwise gives no further information on the causes of the opposition: Epistle 29:10, in *Ancient Christian Writers*, vol. II, *Letters of St. Paulinus of Nola*, transl. P. G. Walsh (Westminster, Md.: Newman Press, 1967), p. 112 (*Patrologica Latina*, vol. LXI, cols. 318– 19).

30. Rufinus, *Apology*, Bk. II, 26; Jerome originally praised her in his *Chronicle*, A.D. 377, but later erased her name from copies of the work. Cf. Jerome, Epistle 39:5, where the example of Melania is held up to Paula at the time of Blesilla's death.

31. Palladius, *H.L.*, 46:2: Butler, p. 135.

32. Palladius, *H.L.*, 18:27– 28: cf. Paulinus of Nola, Epistle 29:5.

33. See F. X. Murphy, "Melania the Elder," *loc. cit.*, p. 67.

34. Palladius, *H.L.*, 46:4.

35. Palladius, *H.L.*, 46:5– 6. Palladius errs in linking Melania and Rufinus in Jerusalem for 27 years. This figure represents the whole time spent by Melania in the East, A.D. 372– 399: see F. X. Murphy, "Melania the Elder," *loc. cit.*, p. 70.

36. Jerome ridicules Rufinus' poor Latin and draws a vicious picture of his pusillanimous teaching style: Epistle 125. See Francis X. Murphy, *Rufinus of Aquileia (345–411): His Life and Works* (Washington: Catholic University of America, 1945), p. 54.

37. Rufinus, *Apology*, Bk. II, 8 (2) (*Patrologica Latina*, vol. XXI, cols. 591– 92).

38. Palladius, *H.L.*, 55.

39. *Ibid.*, 38.

40. *Ibid.*, 46:6. See F. X. Murphy, "Melania the Elder," *loc. cit.*, p. 72.

41. Rufinus' two apologies against Jerome and Jerome's three apologies against Rufinus, as well as Rufinus' prefaces on the translation of Origen's *Peri Archon* and his treatise on the adulteration of the works of Origen, are translated in *Nicene and Post-Nicene Fathers*, vol. III. For the history of the controversy see J. N. D.

Kelly, *Jerome*, pp. 195–256, and F. X. Murphy, *Rufinus of Aquileia*, pp. 59–155. Also Monica Wagner, *Rufinus, the Translator* (Washington: Catholic University of America, 1945).

42. Rufinus, *Apology*, Bk. II, 26. Rufinus also scores Jerome for calling Paula the "mother-in-law of God"! This was Jerome's rhetorical conceit on Paula's maternity of virgins who were "brides of Christ," but Rufinus takes the infelicity seriously (*Apology*, Bk. II, 10 [2]). Jerome's acrimony toward Melania is evident in Epistle 133:4, where he puns on her name as one which "bears witness to the blackness of her perfidy."

43. Jerome, *Apology*, Bk. II, 9–11, and Bk. III, 6. Jerome was particularly annoyed by Rufinus' revelation of his continued attachment to secular learning: Rufinus, *Apology*, Bk. II, 6–9 and 8–9 (2).

44. Jerome, Epistle 81.

45. Palladius, *H.L.*, 55:2.

46. Paulinus of Nola, Epistle 29:12.

47. Palladius, *H.L.*, 54:4.

48. Paulinus of Nola in a letter to Augustine, Epistle 45:2.

49. Gerontius, *Vie de Sainte Mélanie*, transl. and ed. Denys Gorce, *Sources Chrétiennes*, No. 90 (Paris: Éditions du Cerf, 1962), secs. 8–9, pp. 140–43.

50. Palladius, *H.L.*, 54:6. The exact sequence of events from 404 to 410 is unclear. Palladius links Melania's sojourn in Sicily with her grandson with the flight from Rome in 410, and so probably the whole family went there first and then parted company, but Pinian, Melania Junior and Albina may have gone from Rome directly to Africa. See F. X. Murphy, "Melania the Elder," *loc. cit.*, pp. 76–77.

51. Jerome, Epistle 127:13.

52. Gerontius, sec. 20.

53. Augustine, Epistle 125:6.

54. Gerontius, secs. 21–33.

55. *Ibid.*, secs. 34–35.

56. See Jerome's Epistle 143 (Augustine, Epistle 202).

57. Gerontius, secs. 37–39.

58. *Ibid.*, secs. 40–48.

59. *Ibid.*, sec. 49.

60. Sozomen, *Church History*, Bk. IX, 1–3 (Engl. transl.: *Nicene and Post-Nicene Fathers*, 2nd ser., vol. II, pp. 419–21). See

Donald Attwater, "Pulcheria," in *Saints of the East* (New York: P. J. Kennedy, 1963), pp. 67f.

61. Gerontius, secs. 50–55.

62. *Ibid.*, sec. 58: cf. Socrates, *Church History*, XLVIII.

63. Gerontius, sec. 61.

64. *Ibid.*, sec. 63.

65. Peter Brown, "The Rise and Function of the Holy Man in Late Antiquity," *Journal of Roman Studies*, 1972, pp. 80ff.

THREE

Women, Power and the
Pursuit of Holiness
in Medieval Christianity

ELEANOR McLAUGHLIN

Recent shifts in the feminist movement and in American religious sensibilities have made attractive a search for models of wholeness and empowerment for women in the vast storehouse of traditional spirituality. We read that some of the many American women who are "turning East" do so in hope of recovering the woman in themselves and finding theories and disciplines for society.[1] Many are attracted to the mystical as well as the exotic corners of Eastern or heterodox spiritualities, ranging from Zen to witchcraft. One may search for religious meaning in the inner recesses of wild nature, as in Margaret Atwood's *Surfacing*, or choose the cooler quest of God the verb, but it seems intolerably remote to look for meaning and viable models in the lives of the medieval saints with their sturdy piety of obedience and order lived out as virgin brides of Christ. It would appear difficult for contemporary Christian women to find vital models in a culture so alien to our own, "The Age We Have Lost," as Peter Laslett, the demographer, terms that world before modernity.

An abbess may well have exercised the juridical powers of a bishop, but what woman today usefully aspires to the authority of the feudal *domina* over manors and serfs?[2] If anything, this is the kind of power that the women's movement has gracefully and prophetically criticized. So often medieval women exercised power out of the blood rights of family, clan or queenship which in their premodern familial and hierarchial contexts are interesting and admirable but hardly relevant to a postindustrial democracy.[3]

Perhaps even more difficult, because more subtle and fundamental for Christian women, are the ambiguities raised by the apparent characteristics of Christian spirituality implied in the lives of the saints. What does one do today with obedience, passivity, contemplative enclosure as a flight from the world, and the apparent loss of self in the pilgrimage toward dependence on God? There seems little in this traditional Christian view of human nature and God to attract contemporary women or men in search of meaning and personal authenticity.

Then, finally, even if the equivalence of women and men in the vocation to saintliness as pursued especially within the monastic life is granted, there is a suspicion among twentieth-century Christians that the female holy ones were not quite as equal as their brothers.[4] Was not the Queen of Sciences, theology, dominated by the lives and works of Saint Augustine, Saint Gregory I, Saint Anselm, Saint Bernard, Saint Dominic, Saint Bonaventura, Saint Thomas? It would seem that just as medieval businesswomen in the textile trade specialized in embroidery and small cloths,[5] so the female saints exemplified a piety extravagant or sentimental, marred by erotic, amorous imagery,[6] removed from the normative rigor and clarity of the Scholastic luminaries. If women today need to recover a history that is instructive beyond the legitimate delight of discovering "how it was then," must one not look to the corners, the fringes of medieval society, to meet with witches, heretics and the wise old women of the fairy tales? Is this so?

I would like to suggest that the foregoing is at best misleading; that historiography has often badly served the Christian woman who is also a feminist. Hints of an alternative interpretation are already abroad, and Francine du Plessix Gray, in her provocative review of Atwood's *Surfacing*, points in our direction with her title, "Nature as the Nunnery." She comments on the "demise of that monastic ideal that had prevailed in Europe until the Reformation, and had suggested that women's first allegiance is to a divine order, rather than to any patriarchal rule."[7] I wish to explore here how that empowering prior obedience to God needs to be seen in a context broader and deeper than the historical institution of monasticism with its real, although sometimes ambiguous, space for women. The focus here will be the pursuit of holiness, which was the reason for the existence of those monastic institutions, of anchorholds and Beguinages. I hope to show how the spirituality of the women who were called holy by their friends, their neighbors and the Church was a source of wholeness, meaning, power and authority. The effectiveness of these women was rooted in their holiness. Power out of holiness.

A second theme suggested by the lives and work of some medieval saints, both men and women, is the possibility that the ideal of human nature they exemplified—or their biographers set forth—represents a range of human possibility, a richness of human expression, that has been particularly hospitable to women and to whatever is meant today by the "feminine." Dangerous though this suggestion be in its implication of stereotypes, I want to explore the notion that these holy women exemplified a human nature and a vision of divine nature that gave more weight to affectivity, love and the integration of love and intellect, than has been the usual, acceptable or mainstream idea of "human nature," as we perceive it, since the seventeenth century. This more "feminized" human nature was *not* seen as "feminine" by men and women of the pre-Reformation Church but rather as Christian, typical and in the image of God, who was Mother as well as Father, Love more than Intellect. Holiness called forth a Christian theology and an anthropology radically *less* androcentric than that which dominates Christian piety today.

Such far-reaching assertions can at this stage be only a tentative beginning in the exploration of human meaning and possibility as recorded in the history of our own culture. The living context, local and political, economic and legal, must eventually be fully explored. Here we will approach these questions through lives and stories, limiting our attention to holiness—what it meant, and how the pursuit of holiness seemed to empower. Is this approach elitist historiography, even hopelessly romantic? Christians must say no to the first, for all are called to the wholeness of sainthood. One thinks of Mary Magdalene, who was a favorite medieval saint, a model for all Christians: repentant sinner, faithful disciple, joyful lover of God. A more serious objection is the instinctive sense that medieval religion, however attractive, speaks a mythic language and carries a dualist, hierarchical, magical world view that simply cannot work for twentieth-century people in any dialogue with contemporary reality.[8] All of this carries some weight. Yet, students of language, and of epistemology and religion, are suggesting today that our cultural, psychic and perhaps even physical salvation requires that we move to that "second naïveté" which can be nourished by the wisdom of mythic language and insight in a world near burned out by the historical/critical method and its scientific/technological counterparts.[9] In a culture starved by the language of the machine, image and vision, symbol and sacrament may once again enlighten and feed. Let us suspend our disbelief, and listen to the *Lives* of the saints.

Saint Lioba was an Anglo-Saxon nun of good Wessex family, a scholar, an abbess, a missionary in the wilds of Germany. She became the spiritual friend and confidante of Saint Boniface, bishop and Anglo-Saxon missionary to the Germans, who called her and a number of other women from the abbey at Wimborne to minister among the heathen of Saxony.[10] Lioba's *Life*, written half a century after her death in 779, was intended to edify, like all hagiography, but we can glean from its pages a sense of the strength and influence available to a woman within the eighth-century ideal of holiness.

In addition, unintended evidence of the grounds of her effectiveness can be read between the lines of the story itself. Both the ideal and the story, then, are sources for our understanding of how and why a holy woman functioned with power in the forests of eighth-century Germany. The basis of her esteem and power in that primitive, still virtually tribal society was twofold: learning and holiness. The importance of learning for holiness should be noted. The practical, almost administrative character of the sense of obedience and order which permeated the holiness may also be surprising to us, but both characteristics, learning and order, were central to the Benedictine monastic piety she represented.

Rudolf's *Life of Saint Leoba* begins with childhood. We see her mother sending the child, a miraculous birth of her old age, to be trained as a religious at Wimborne, where under Mother Tetta she was taught the sacred sciences. The translator records, ". . . she [Lioba's mother] gave her her freedom" [11]—that is, to live for God alone as a nun was to be freed of family under whom all women of that day lived as in bondage, to father, brother or uncle. The way in which the religious life transcended biological bonds is also symbolized by the observation that it was Lioba's wide reputation for learning and holiness which caused Boniface to summon her to work with him in Germany, not his blood relationship to her mother.[12] There is a self-conscious opposition between the bonds of sanctity and family which we will see repeated in later Christian literature. Also explicit is the wholly female context of Lioba's education. Mother Tetta was her intellectual and spiritual mentor, and Tetta herself, we are told, possessed the gift of prophecy as well as scholarship. Lioba also learned from her community of sisters:

She learned from all and obeyed them all, and by imitating the good qualities of each one she modeled herself on the continence of one, the cheerfulness of another, copying here a sister's mild-ness, there a sister's patience. One she tried to equal in attention to prayer, another in devotion to reading.[13]

Spiritual direction emerged out of community life as well as from the gifts of the abbess—and all was at the hands of women.

Boniface placed Lioba as abbess over the women, giving another English religious, Sturm, direction of the men. What Lioba did amid the wilderness, violence and moral chaos of eighth-century Europe is inextricably entangled with who she was—her doing cannot be separated from her being. The reasons for her call to Germany, learning and holiness, were elaborated in that new context, and these virtues were the source and the fruit of her effectiveness. Lioba, we are told, was a skilled classicist.[14] She sent Latin verses to Boniface.[15] She was never without a book to read, excepting only during times of sleep and prayer. She was learned not only in Holy Scripture, but in the works of the Church Fathers, in canon law and in the decisions of all the councils.[16] In the world of the eighth century, such erudition gave her an almost magical authority, and in addition afforded practical power in the vast administrative task of bringing order to the raw new church of Germany. Learning was no mere decoration, it was what made Lioba an abbess-founder, whose disciples and daughter houses spread like good seed over new-plowed fields. Her learning, then, was an aspect of her holiness, for it was the very stuff of that good order, that rootedness in faith and tradition, which the biographer finds so worthy in her monastic foundations. This good order was a "space" for Christian living and prayer which was at once revolutionary in its resistance to cultural (including male) pressures and in its effectiveness as a missionary strategy in the spreading and deepening of the Christian life among the newly converted Germans. We might say, from our twentieth-century perspective, the calm and order of the cloister was a space for women. We read that Mother Tetta (the sister of a king) was so powerful in her ability to lead her community that no man dared enter her monastery; even bishops were forbidden.[17] Cloister in the eighth-century context meant freedom, not constraint. From a historical perspective, Lioba's ability to create ordered, disciplined communities was perceived as the very core of her sanctity and as guarantee of the powerfulness of her prayers. In the midst of a terrible, destructive storm, the still half-pagan mob rushed to Lioba, an obvious Christ figure, to arouse her from prayer and seek her protection:

". . . arise, then, and pray to the Mother of God, your mistress, for us . . ." At these words Lioba rose up from prayer and, as if challenged to a contest, flung off the cloak which she was wearing and boldly opened the doors of the church . . . she made a sign of the cross, opposing to the fury of the storm the name of the High God . . . Suddenly God came to their aid. The sound of thunder died away, the winds changed direction and dispersed the heavy clouds, the darkness rolled back and the sun shone, bringing calm and peace. Thus did the divine power make manifest the merits of His handmaid. Unexpected peace came to His people and fear was banished.[18]

The miracles attributed to Lioba were often like this one— evidences of her power, her control, her calm equanimity. The holiness to which the miracles gave witness encompassed her learning, her constancy in prayer, her utter confidence in the power of prayer, the discipline and order of her life, her convents, her disciples. This holiness bore fruit in healing, as well as in calming storms, and in producing many vocations to the religious life. She visited the numerous convents, the abbesses whom she had trained, and stimulated the novices to vie with each other in pursuit of that life of perfection she so exemplified. She was venerated by all: "The princes loved her, the nobles received her, the bishops welcomed her with joy."[19] She was especially honored, we are told, by the great Emperor Charlemagne—an honor symbolic for the hagiographer of her leadership and competence as well as her piety. Her advice was sought by the powerful and, "because of her wide knowledge of Scriptures and her prudence in counsel they often discussed spiritual matters and ecclesiastical discipline with her." Lioba embodied an ideal of sainthood that included the tools of worldly authority.

Finally, we see in Boniface's esteem witness to Lioba's power and authority. Boniface gave her permission to pray at his monastery at Fulda, "a privilege never granted to any woman either before or since" [20]—a reminder that holiness and power were as charisms granted to individual women which relieved them, as it were, of the disabilities of their sex. More impressive is the fact that Boniface so respected his co-worker that he wished after his death that she be buried beside him, "so that they who had served God during this lifetime with equal sincerity and zeal should await together the day of resurrection." [21] This is nicely symbolic of the equality between men and women that existed among the saints—i.e., those moving toward freedom from worldly categories of the socially acceptable, because they belonged to God. The simple monks of Fulda, more bound by social convention than their master, failed to carry out Boniface's instructions, and Lioba was buried at Fulda apart from her colleague. Despite this resistance to Lioba and Boniface's experience of each other as sister and brother, one in Christ, it is significant that the hagiographer left to posterity an image of a woman whose holiness, whose claim to Christian perfection, was set forth in terms quite beyond sexual distinction. We hear of Lioba that "her deepest concern was the *work* she had set on foot." [22] Her work was grounded in an amalgam of prayer, rocklike faith, learning, instinct for order and discipline, and energetic dissemination of the monastic vision of radical Christian detachment which was purely and simply the Benedictine ideal. It was a sanctity neither male nor female. It was a sanctity powerful, public, practical, even administrative, and it was a power and holiness to which women were called coequally with men. The society was vaguely aware of the anomaly between the authority accorded Lioba and the usual "place" for women, but the ideal and expected living embodiment of holiness in their midst provided a place for women beside men (in life as in the tomb) beyond the conventions of social custom. There are, of course, complex sociological reasons why Anglo-Saxon family, political and ecclesiastical structures afforded a place for powerful women,[23] but we are choosing to focus here on the ways in which ideals of sanctity contributed to that space. We turn now to another time and a later date in English history to explore this issue—holiness and power—in the life of another Christian woman.

The *Life of Christina of Markyate* is again a work of edification, written in the latter part of the twelfth century by an anonymous monk of St. Albans who must have known Christina well.[24] The *Life* reads with the directness and immediacy of autobiography and is singularly free of the numerous miracles which twentieth-century individuals sometimes find difficult to accept. Christina's story is so powerful, the miraculous seems unnecessary. Her life gives evidence of three ways in which sanctity was empowering for a twelfth-century woman: it enabled her to defy family and social expectations, to challenge the church and enjoy churchmen's warm support, and to follow with success and esteem a life she chose for herself through which she shaped and affected the lives of the small and the great. As with Lioba, we will be interested to explore the character of that sanctity which seemed so empowering for Christina.

Her story can be briefly told, although losing in condensation the delight and emotional impact of rich detail and sometimes hilarious dialogue. Christina, baptized Theodora about 1096–98, was the daughter of an influential Anglo-Saxon noble family in Huntingdonshire. At age thirteen or so, while visiting St. Albans Abbey with her family, she made a vow to be the spouse of Christ and of no other. Firm in her resolution to remain a virgin and live for God only, Christina resisted the intention of her family to see her married, fending off all suitors, especially the young and persistent Burthred. She successfully defied the bishop who was bribed by her father to reverse his initial support and was pressuring Christina to relent. Finally, after some adventurous confrontations with Burthred and his friends, Christina escaped the family to take up hiding first with an anchoress, then more permanently with Roger, a hermit. Though Roger served initially as her spiritual director, the two of them grew into a maturity of spiritual friendship where each furthered the other in that pilgrimage toward God which was their common calling. Christina's fame as a holy woman and director of souls spread beyond England to the Continent. She became the particular spiritual friend and director of Geoffrey, abbot of St. Albans. The final years of her life were peaceful, combining a personal intimacy with God with a public ministry as director of souls and shaper of Christian life and practice far beyond the confines of the still point of her anchorhold.

Three aspects of this story throw special light on the relationship between holiness and power: Christina's resistance to family, society and church out of her sense of commitment to Christ; Christina's relationship with men in the context of her chosen vocation; and the character of that holiness which afforded her strength.

First, we need to appreciate the obvious and conscious rebellion against family and society supported by Christina's decision to belong to Jesus Christ alone. How symbolic is the fact that one of Christina's first acts after her decision was to discard her baptismal/family-bestowed name, to call herself Christina, belonging to Christ.[25] She named herself and chose her own vocation in the teeth of fierce resistance. Her family put her under virtual house arrest when she refused to consummate the marriage she had been forced into through unrelenting pressures. She was isolated from any "religious God-fearing man" and forbidden access to the chapel.[26] Her parents let Burthred into her bedroom to take her while asleep, but by "providential intervention" she was found dressed and awake, and she engaged the young man in a long theological discussion of the chaste marriage of Cecilia and Valerian.[27] When again her room was invaded, by Burthred and his drunken friends, she was emboldened in prayer to escape ingeniously by hanging from her fingertips between the wall and the bed curtains. At stake was the boy Burthred's virility: ". . . they joined together in calling him a spineless and useless fellow, . . . warned him not . . . to lose his manliness . . . all he had to mind was to act the man."[28] She resisted also the argument of her family's honor and her father's and mother's power and fury. At the onset of the campaign, in a conversation between the family and the prior of St. Mary's Huntingdon, these issues were made clear as her father complained,

". . . let her marry in the Lord and take away our reproach. Why must she depart from tradition? Why should she bring this dishonor on her father? Her life of poverty will bring the whole of the nobility into disrepute. Let her do now what we wish and she can have all that we possess."[29]

The prior Fredebert supported her father with traditional defenses of Christian marriage and assurances that mothers as well as virgins are saved, quoting heavily from Scripture in favor of the family and society's will for Christina. Encouraged, the father, Autti, and his noble friends went to the Bishop of Lincoln, expecting that he "would immediately order the betrothed woman to submit to the authority of her husband."[30] Autti was furious when the Bishop recognized both the priority of her vow to Christ and the unacceptability of the forced nature of the betrothal. The Church insisted in canon law that a marriage was invalid unless the free consent of both parties was obtained. Again the father angrily announced the real issues in his outburst:

"Well, we have peace today, you are even made mistress over me: the bishop has praised you to the skies and declared that you are freer than ever. So come and go as I do, and have your own life as you please. But don't expect any comfort or help from me."[31]

The Bishop, bribed by Autti's money and threatened by his family's wide influence in the country, then turned against Christina and tried with abundant Scripture quotes to force her submission. Christina, certain of her vocation and her vow, defeated the Bishop in the ensuing contest of prooftexting. Nor did the Church abandon her entirely; it was with the help of the priest Sueno, who was persuaded by her visions, that Christina made a dramatic escape from her family's house. The angry determination of her family to treat their daughter as nothing more than marriageable property is brutally apparent in the mother's reported sentiments: "In the end she swore that she would not care who deflowered her daughter provided that some way of deflowering her could be found."[32]

Supported by prayer and her total obedience to Christ, whom she loved as a spouse through all this, Christina finally fled, disguised as a boy. She is reported to have told herself to "put on manly courage and mount the horse like a man."[33] She found refuge in a safe though miserably uncomfortable hermitage, first with the anchoress Alfwen and then with the hermit Roger, with whom she remained until his death. She then took his place in the hermitage, having been absolved from her marriage, and made her vows as a religious to the abbot of St. Albans and before the Bishop of Lincoln.

If the first part of Christina's life is a story of ultimately successful resistance against great odds to familial and male authority of father, betrothed and bishop, what of this new stage in her vocation as a spouse of Christ? Did she merely exchange father and husband for submission to Roger and to the abbot of St. Albans? I think it possible to say such was not the case. To an extraordinary degree, Christina's relationship with Roger, her spiritual director and mentor, became one of mutuality in a common pilgrimage.

Furthermore, through their dwelling together and encouraging each other to strive after higher things their holy affections grew day by day like a large flame springing from two brands joined together. The more fervently they yearned to contemplate the beauty of the creator the more happily they reign with Him in supreme glory. And so their great progress induced them to dwell together.[34]

Their common "Holy Desire" for Christ bound them together in a mutuality of spiritual friendship which witnessed to an equality, a oneness in Christ, in which there was neither male nor female. Such a spiritual friendship was described by another twelfth-century English religious, the Cistercian Aelred of Rievaulx, as that bond which exists between two equals in the presence of and commitment to a third, Jesus.[35] I believe it possible to say that Christina and Roger could have been the personae of Aelred's Christian Ciceronian dialogue on friendship as well as the two male religious of whom he wrote so gracefully.

Even more persuasive of this interpretation is the record of Christina's friendship with Abbot Geoffrey of St. Albans, an intimacy which the hagiographer reports occasioned some malicious gossip during their lifetime. Christina here was the dominant figure, for the abbot, a worldly, powerful feudal ecclesiastic, was converted under her influence. Geoffrey grew under her tutelage into a serious Christian. We read he "became so changed a man from what he once was."[36] The account of his gradually deepened piety is so free of the supernatural, so human and straightforward in the telling, the reader is hard pressed to throw it out as hagiographical exaggeration. Geoffrey came to admire and love Christina. "He had deep respect for the maiden and saw in her something divine and extraordinary."[37] In fact, the mutuality of this spiritual friendship sometimes moved the newly converted abbot to an open dependence on Christina, whom he consulted in every act or political decision of importance. She was under obedience to his office as abbot, he was under obedience to her grace as a spiritual friend, powerful in prayer, clairvoyant in insight. "And he had to admit that the virgin's pure heart had more power with God than the factious and shrewd cunning of the great ones of this world." [38]

The mutuality of their love was sealed in the prayer by which Christina expressed her care for Geoffrey, whom she called her "beloved," confident that Jesus held them both.

> . . . she was rapt in ecstasy and saw herself in the presence of her savior; and she saw him whom she loved above all others, encircled with her arms and held closely to her breast. And whilst she feared that since a man is stronger than a woman, he would free himself from her grasp, she saw Jesus, the helper of the saved, closing her hands with his own loving hand, not by intertwining her fingers with His, but by joining them one over the other; so that by joining her hands no less than by the power of her arms she should feel greater strength in holding her friend back. She gave effusive thanks with joy both because she knew that her friend was relieved of trouble and also because she was aware of the presence of her spouse and Lord. [39]

This vision sets forth in great clarity the basis of Christina's power. Her spirituality was rooted in an affective experience of belonging to Christ, a radical belonging and desiring symbolized by the nuptial imagery—she was the spouse of Christ. Against this bond the gates of hell, her father, Autti, and Burthred and the bishop could not prevail.

Christina's holiness was grounded first in this unsparing obedience to the vision of her life in Christ. Her vocation, her vow to Christ, prevailed over every man, obstacle, misery or doubt. "My one desire, as thou knowest, is to please thee alone and to be united to thee for all time without End." [40] The erotic imagery, spouse of Christ, perfectly expressed the "Holy Desire," the love which lay at the center of her piety and kept her safe. God speaks: ". . . the key of your heart is in my safekeeping and I keep guard over your mind and the rest of your body. No one can enter except by my permission." [41] The freedom Christina enjoyed to name herself, to resist father, husband, bishop, flowed out of an obedience to God which was a *love affair*. She abandoned the world for this love affair with God and was in return girded against anything the world could inflict. Intimately involved in her life with Christ was a ready acceptance of the Way of the Cross; suffering was expected, and it was not simply transcended but was used to enable her to become the more loving person that being a spouse of Christ implied. "All who wish to travel to Jerusalem must carry this cross." [42] The external difficulties were met by Christina with constant prayer, a placing of herself in the loving presence of God. In that mode of prayerfulness, Christina was visited and encouraged and directed constantly by a "Presence of Love" in visions or dreams, some of which have been cited here.[43] It is interesting to note that the most frequent mediator of God to Christina was the Virgin Mother. Christina was comforted and instructed by the divine in female form far more often than by a direct encounter with her spouse, Jesus. And at a crucial time of sexual temptation Jesus came to her and was held by her, not as a male lover, but as a child taken to the breast of its mother—in this case Christina.[44] I would like to suggest that the spousal imagery, the prominence of the Virgin Mary in Christina's visions, and the virginity which freed her from male control make a unity with the great importance given to human spiritual friendship in Christina's troubled but ultimately triumphant realization of her vocation. The unity was love—and her strength was love. To be a virgin and spouse of Christ symbolized the enhancing, freeing, empowering love and touch of God in her life which gave her strength to stand victoriously against all who opposed her. It was a love, a friendship with God, full of affective, even erotic power in which she moved beyond all self-doubt or fear or internalized sense of female incapacity to name herself, to be herself, and to be recognized as a person of authority and power in the world beyond her cell.

The life of Saint Catherine of Siena (1347–80) presents to us a story very different from those of Lioba and Christina, but the three share important similarities in their consciousness of a common source of strength. Catherine also exemplified a particular kind of vocation to holiness that is especially attractive today. In her self-conscious combination of the active and contemplative life, she found God's will in action. Though the stillness of prayer, ascetical discipline, and contemplation were ever the starting point, a vigorous reform politics was the way in which the life of prayer shaped her will. I will outline in the briefest way her life and work and then ask again how the special character of her holiness issued forth in power and effectiveness for herself and her world.

Born Catherine Benincasa, the youngest of twenty-five children of a Sienese dyer, she was reported to have experienced visions of Christ at an early age, vowed herself to a life of virginity at seven, and thereafter resisted the pressure of her family to marry.[45] Catherine finally prevailed, and for the first three years of her formal religious vocation she lived as a Dominican Tertiary, a recluse or anchoress, in her own room, within that home with its numerous brothers and sisters. External peace was never Catherine's lot. After this period of seclusion and contemplation, she experienced a mystical marriage with Christ and was called back to a life of service and ministration within her own household and to the needy and sick of the city. Her gradual emergence into a life of intense reform activity was associated with a growing reputation for mystical gifts, ecstasies and visions. Catherine was surrounded by a group of disciples, her *famiglia*, as her reputation for sanctity and ecstatic prayer spread. In the mid 1370s she embarked on a public effort to return Pope Gregory XI from the Avignonese exile to Rome, seeing this effort as a necessity for the larger task of the reform of the

Church. At the same time she became heavily involved in diplomatic negotiations between the city of Florence and its implacable enemy the Pope, believing that the universal Christian brotherhood of all people could be effected only through obedience to the Church and its head. We cannot follow here the details of Catherine's work as ambassador, negotiator, reformer, gadfly, all of which she carried on with great personal presence and through a voluminous correspondence which is fortunately preserved. The letters are wondrously revealing of her wit and sarcasm, the depth and practical wisdom of her life with God, and her great ability to discern and speak to the particular strengths and weaknesses of her correspondents. The letters are a welcome addition to her confessor's *Life*, which was written primarily as an instrument for her beatification.[46]

Catherine's influence was a crucial factor in Gregory's return to Rome, but the victory was short-lived. Following Gregory's death and the confusing, disputed election of Urban VI, the Church was confronted with the chaotic claims of two popes, as the French cardinals, offended by Urban's immoderate or impolitic efforts toward reform, elected as pope a Frenchman, Clement VII, and declared Urban's election invalid. The last years of Catherine's life were spent in hapless attempts to rally support for the weak and often unworthy Urban. Through letters and personal persuasion, she attempted to realize her vision of a united humanity bound together by Christian love and justice under the leadership of the Church. Externally these efforts failed as the schism deepened its political ties. Catherine understood the source of this chaos to be sin, and, taking this sin upon herself, she died following a paralytic stroke. In that last turbulent year, she wrote her *Dialogue* on the spiritual life and successfully quelled a Roman revolt against Urban. During her final days she experienced a vision of the ship of the Church, its burden descending on her shoulders. She died, surrounded by her disciples, on April 30, 1380, giving herself in expiation for the sins of the Church.[47]

Catherine was a powerful and effective woman by anyone's standards. She dominated Pope Gregory and, to a lesser extent, Urban VI. She was held in highest regard in Florence and was widely recognized as a saint during her lifetime. The people of Rome witnessed her hours of ecstatic prayer in St. Peter's. She shared their poverty; they knew of her role in bringing the head of the Church back to Rome. We read that as her body lay in state at Santa Maria Sopra Minerva, there were those among the vast crowds who found themselves cured of their ills.[48]

What was the foundation of this energy and power in Catherine's life? The historian must say something other than the hagiographer who points to God met in prayer. Catherine seems first of all to have been a personality of charismatic force; her presence was irresistible. The Florentine businessmen who did not share her enthusiastic trust of Gregory could not say no to her peace proposals in her presence. They had to avoid her and treat by letter. This personal power can be explored from the perspective of her spirituality. Catherine was truly selfless in her capacity to identify in genuine humility with the sinner. She persuaded the Pope to share in her sense of sin by walking to the Vatican through the streets of Rome barefoot, an act of papal penitence never done before or repeated since. She was at the same time inflamed by a passionate vision of goodness, of the Church reformed, of the righteousness of God's will, an irresistible passion for the salvation of those persons she addressed. Her hatred for sin was combined with a love for the sinner which apparently moved many to seek their better selves and act accordingly. "If you are what you ought to be, you will set all Italy on fire," she wrote to a religious confraternity to move them to the support of Urban VI.[49]

Suffering and awareness of sin were part of this persuasiveness. She gave great importance to an identification with the suffering of Christ and was drawn to a Christlike vocation to take the sins of the world or those of the person before her onto her own shoulders. This embracing of the cross of suffering is a clue to the power of her persuasion. She shared all with those whom she urged on.

Fear and serve God, with no regard to thyself; and then do not care for what people may say, except to have compassion on them . . . if it shall be for His honor and thy salvation, He will send thee means and the way when thou art thinking nothing about it, in a way that thou wouldst never have imagined. Let Him alone, and lose thyself; and beware that thou lose thee nowhere but on the Cross, and there thou shalt find thyself most perfectly.[50]

Her ideal, her vision of holiness, her Holy Desire for God was a gift of contemplation which forced her and all who heard her into action for love of neighbor and reform of the Church. To a group of hermits whom she sought to bring to Rome to encourage Urban toward reform, she wrote:

Cursed are ye, the lukewarm! Would you had at least been ice-cold! This lukewarmness proceeds from ingratitude, which comes from a faint light that does not let us see the agonizing and utter love of Christ crucified, and the infinite benefits received from Him. For in truth, did we see them, our heart would burn with the flame of love, and we should be *famished for time*, using it with great zeal for the honor of God and the salvation of souls. To this zeal I summon thee, dear son, that now we begin to work anew.[51]

This movement from the love of God, stirred up by contemplation of God's love for humanity in the crucified Christ, into that zeal of being "famished for time" to honor God and save souls is a key to Catherine's activism, as it is also to the Puritan's zeal of three centuries later!

Inseparable from the love which issued in action, the love which embraced the cross, was obedience. Catherine's obedience was like that of Lioba and Christina—a radical, world-ignoring attachment to Jesus and God's will for her. Out of that obedience was forged a reformer of unshakable purpose. She spoke of obedience to vocation to one of her young followers: "Resist no longer the Holy Spirit that is calling thee—for it will be hard for thee to kick against Him. Do not let thyself be withheld by thine own lukewarm heart, or by a womanish tenderness for thyself, but be a man, and enter the battlefield manfully." [52]

Obedience was often associated with this militant sense of doing God's battle which she knew herself called to take up. She was a general, urging forth armies. Catherine's obedience was also very concrete. The very visible and sinful Church and its priests and popes were the symbols for her of God's presence in the world. She was obedient to the Church. But she insisted that pope and church be worthy of obedience and by the very stubborn loyalty of her attachment called churchmen from the inside, as it were, to be the pastors their office signified.

Alas, alas, sweetest "Babbo" mine, pardon my presumption in what I have said to you and am saying; I am constrained by the Sweet Primal Truth to say it. His will, father, is this, and thus demands of you. It demands that you execute justice on the abundance of many iniquities committed by those who are fed and pastured in the garden of Holy Church; declaring that brutes should not be fed with the food of men. Since He has given you authority and you have assumed it, you should use your virtue and power; and if you are not willing to use it, it would be better for you to resign what you have assumed; more honor to God and health to your soul would it be. [53]

Her obedience to Urban VI enabled her to insist that he exercise his authority as one who feeds, and who sees to it that the Church becomes the Mother she is called to be rather than a rapacious robber. Catherine's obedience to the Church seemed to be bound up with her image of the Church as mother and nurturer. The Fathers of the Church are to be mothers whose principal role is to feed the faithful. [54] Hers was no servile obedience to hierarchy but rather an obedience to the presence of God in the world in the sacramentality of the Church. And if Gregory XI was unwilling to fill out that office of good shepherd, resign or be damned, wrote Catherine. Such an obedience was a powerful instrument for change.

Another source of Catherine's strength was that peculiarly medieval marriage of passion and reason, mysticism and Scholasticism that she so preeminently lived out: ". . . love follows the intellect, and the more it knows, the more can it love. Thus the one feeds the other, and, with this light, they both arrive at the Eternal vision of Me, when they see and taste Me . . ." [55] The effectiveness of her political fervor was greatly enhanced by the strength and relentlessness of her mind. She brooked no nonsense.

The second and last way is, that we ought to recognize the truth about our neighbor, whether he be great or humble, subject or lord. That is, when we see that men are doing some deed in which we might invite our neighbor to join, we ought to perceive whether it is grounded in truth or not, and what foundation he has who is impelled to do this deed. He who does not do this acts as one mad and blind, who follows a blind guide, grounded in falsehood, and shows that he has no truth in himself, and therefore seeks not the truth. [56]

The love and the anger and the often violent urging were never disconnected from analysis.

Finally, as between love and reason, medieval spirituality chose the way of Holy Desire, and in this passion lies the bond between holiness and power. Constantly on her lips was the wonder at God's love shown to humankind in the Passion of Christ, which image in turn aroused in those who beheld it a love of God and neighbor which could move the world. "I beg you by that love of that precious Blood shed with such fiery love for you, that you give refreshment to my soul, which seeks your salvation," Catherine wrote to a recalcitrant queen, and she expected a positive action in response to her letter. [57] Catherine loved in a Godlike way, with a powerful desire which bound and carried sin and pain:

"But I wish to bind myself to bear you before God with tears and continual prayer, and to bear with you your penitence."[58] Her love therefore continually created relationships—it fed, nourished, forgave, and in this was maternal. It was also violent, militant, relentless. One of her favorite words of action was "manfully," *virilemente*. Catherine's love which moved cities and popes was expressed in metaphors both male and female. It was nurturing and judging: "I tenderly love your salvation . . . wait not for this rod; for it will be hard for you to kick against divine justice."[59]

Desire was her power, for God, for God's will on earth, for the salvation of individual souls, for the purifying of the Church. Everywhere the relationships that were formed out of this Holy Desire cemented the human basis for political authority. The love caught in mystical ecstasy was transformed into springs for action in every arena of life. And so she understood her power to lie in that meeting with God in prayer when, says Christ, in the *Dialogue* of souls, ". . . they are another myself, inasmuch as they have lost and denied their own will, and are clothed with Mine and are united to Mine, are conformed to Mine."[60]

Catherine of Siena is a singular example of the mystic reformer theologian who moved with power through medieval society by virtue of her sainthood. She referred to feminine weakness and identified virility with goodly and godly action, yet did not seem to perceive herself as suffering from the disability of "feminine vacillation" or softness. It appears that Catherine could use the theological and social stereotypes of female weakness without being personally touched, for she was among those whom "the Highest God Eternal . . . has placed in the battlefield as knights, to fight for His Bride (the Church) with the shield of holiest faith."[61] Yet this is the same woman who writes of humility as "the foster mother and nurse of charity, and with the same milk she feeds the virtue of obedience."[62] She wrote also of Christ as "man's foster mother enduring, with the greatness and strength of the Deity united with your nature, the bitter medicine of the painful death of the Cross to give life to you little ones debilitated by guilt." [63] The very mixture of the images for God and human nature points to a consciousness which embraced a fullness of possibility beyond the limitations of social or linguistic stereotype. Catherine's relationship to her womanhood was transformed by that loss of ego-self which was the prerequisite of the wholeness that was holiness. It is difficult, if not impossible, for us to judge that wholeness, especially in view of the violent ascetical assaults on her body that were part of her early religious practice—although never advised for others! Yet we can see in the vigorous activity of her life, as in that of Lioba and Christina, evidence of the personal integration and effectiveness that made all these women powerful and public figures.

The stories stand for themselves, their message is in the telling. Yet we can make some generalizations about the stories and their context which may permit that power and that holiness to be more readily appropriated today.

A first observation is that God's lovers, the saints, of the premodern Church exhibited a high degree of personal integration or wholeness in areas of human experience which in every age all too easily fall into conflict. Not every model of medieval sainthood illustrates this integrity, but many do, and our three women reveal that wholeness. They demonstrated an ideal of Christian perfection which united contemplation and action, learning and piety, preserved individual gifts in the context of obedience to community, embraced common sinfulness in the joy of experienced forgiveness, and held together the realities of a God transcendent and immanent, All-Might and All-Love, Father and Mother. This mystery of contained paradox resisted even the deeply held opposites of body and soul, for that metaphysical dualism was tempered in a sacramental understanding of self and cosmos, microcosm and macrocosm. The material universe of the world before modern science was never merely body stuff but rather mysteriously a vehicle for participation in the holy. Sainthood or holiness was a pilgrimage toward God which supported a human nature of paradoxical and mysterious wholeness, paradoxical for us especially because it was an integration sought within the confines of celibacy. Christian women like Lioba, Christina and Catherine through this ideal of sanctity moved beyond the limitations of biology and social convention, especially as these touched their womanhood, to an uncommon integration of act and vision, reason and love, obedience and self-affirmation. Their wholeness as human beings burns through every page of the record in the power and effectiveness of their personal and public lives.

If love was the driving force of holiness for these women, discipline and obedience were the forms in which that love was trained. In each of these lives we see a conjunction of highly personal experiences of God and the saints in dream, vision, in vow and contemplative prayer, with *obedience*, a disciplined following after that experience or vision. The obedience to God and the mediators of God's will, often female—Mary or other female saints—was the firm rock on which they stood for personal vocation against every familial and social, even ecclesiastical pressure to conform. Obedience was the form of holiness and power for these women. It was an obedience and a listening, self-imposed, which gave an inner sureness of direction and supplied an intellectual and moral clarity so characteristic of the Benedictine spirit that shaped much of medieval piety.

This obedience was also very concrete and incarnational, for their listening was to God whose Body was the Church. Christina's or Catherine's obedience to God through the Church was a powerful and personal support which when necessary could be turned against churchmen as well as family. Bishop Grossetest of Canterbury witnessed to this paradox of the revolutionary power of obedience when he wrote in the thirteenth century to Pope Innocent IV condemning a shameful appointment: "Because of the obedience by which I am bound to the Holy See, as to my parents, and out of my love of my union with the Holy See in the body of Christ . . . as an obedient son, I disobey, I contradict, I rebel." [64] This obedience carried a powerful potential for reform and was the opposite of passive submission. Catherine set before churchmen an ideal of Christ's Body, pure and holy, a vision which judged the historical reality. Her obedience to that vision of what office ought to be was a powerful fulcrum for change and a bulwark of personal integrity and autonomy over against church and world.

It is important for Christian women today to observe the power of obedience to which churchwomen witnessed in contrast to the fate of women who found their place within the medieval heresies. The historical evidence is overwhelming that Waldensian and Albigensian women played some leadership roles in those groups, teaching and preaching in the early years. After a century or so of the groups' existence, women disappeared almost wholly from the leadership as these "sectarian" groups developed a clerical hierarchy which mirrored the male clerical order of the Church and of feudalism. Unlike the Church, the "sects" retained no special vocation of holiness, sainthood or monastic community within their groupings to which women and men could be called equally. The *perfectae* disappeared as the *perfecti* became more like bishops than religious. [65] Before the sixteenth century, it was in the Church, not in sects, that women found the most enduring and powerful roles. Rebellion in the context of obedience, the vocation of the saint, provided more space for women than did sectarian protest.

Finally, I must hazard to suggest that the powerfulness of sanctity in women's lives had something to do with the peculiarly medieval apprehension of the holy. Medieval people wrote of their encounter with the holy in varieties of symbols reflecting a broader range of human experience than is the case within the mainstream of Christian expression today. Their language of prayer was less androcentric, more balanced between "male" and "female" metaphor and symbol for God and the holy, than is the case in the West since the seventeenth century. The realm of the holy in medieval spirituality was populated with female figures: the saints; the Queen of Saints, Mary; and even God himself was "as really our Mother as He is our Father." [66] There is not space here to document the great importance of female saints in the pre-Reformation Church beyond the mention of the obvious and not yet fully understood role of the Virgin Mother, [67] or, for example, the popularity among all Christians of devotion to that model of Christian penitence, love and ecstatic vision, Mary Magdalene. [68] My purpose in alluding here to this aspect of medieval piety (not forgetting the contrasting androcentrism, even misogyny, of the theological tradition) is to suggest strongly that the historical phenomenon of powerful and effective women is related to this context of worship and popular devotion. Jesus was experienced and sometimes addressed as a nurturing, caring Mother and mediated his will most frequently through his Mother; Christians were saved in the womb of God's Body, the Church, nourished at her breasts, fed and led by bishops and abbots whom Saint John Chrysostom and Saint Bernard bade to be mothers as well as fathers. [69] The scholars can with legitimacy point out that the mother-namings of Jesus or the bishops were not "mainstream," yet the existence of this current of female metaphor and naming was part of a total realm of the sacral which was heavily colored by an affective spirituality which twentieth-century Christians often apprehend as female or feminine. Obedience was balanced by nurturance, imagery of battle was accompanied by imagery of birth, labor and growth, and God's transcendence was contained within the immanence of sacramentality and the mystical union.

This affective spirituality was not, at least until the later Middle Ages, perceived as especially a woman's piety. [70] The sense of the Motherhood of God and the Church seems to have patristic roots, and it became more prominent in the emergence of devotion to the human, suffering Jesus at the hands of the medieval "Fathers," Saint Anselm, Saint Bernard and other Cisterican authors of the twelfth century. The flowering of Marian devotion and the widely popular cults of Saint Mary Magdalene, Saint Margaret, and Saint Brigid of Sweden served and were cultivated by men and women with like fervor. It is too early to be able to demonstrate with the rigor of modern historical method and canons of causality the relationship between the empowerment of medieval holy women and this affective piety and its associated peopling of heaven, including the Godhead, with female figures and metaphors. This is a thesis which requires our most serious attention, especially in view of the general loss of the affective and female God-language in Christian spirituality since the seventeenth century and the Enlightenment.

The dominance of love over reason, love rather than *sola fides*, in medieval piety was accompanied by a world view which was deeply sacramental, incarnational and even materialistic in character. This religious world view hallowed rather than overcame nature, was associated with a strongly immanent or mystical experience of God which expressed itself in images of growth, nurture and feeding, and love, erotic and filial. Such a piety seems to have fostered the existence of powerful and stubbornly obedient women who served as models of human excellence and divine will. Theirs was, to use Catherine's words, a religion of Holy Desire. The integration of mind and affect implied in this piety was opposed by theological and ascetical dualism, but never so defeated as has been the case since faith overshadowed love, and reason broke away from desire, in the centuries since the seventeenth. Of course family histories and economic, ecclesiastical and social structures play significant, even determining roles in the privatization of women and the loss of female sacral power. Yet it may still be possible for us today, seeking to discover meaning at the center of the self and the cosmos, to quicken the imagination and enrich our symbolic vocabulary by listening once more to the stories and the vision which lie readily at hand within the Western Christian tradition shaped by powerful, holy women such as Dame Julian of Norwich, who wrote:

. . . and the Second Person of the Trinity is Mother of this basic nature, providing the substance in which we are rooted and grounded. But he is our Mother also in mercy, since he has taken our sensual nature upon himself. Thus "our Mother" describes the different ways in which he works, ways which are separate to us, but held together in him. In our Mother, Christ, we grow; and develop; in his mercy he reforms and restores us; through his passion, death, and resurrection, he has united us to his being. So does our Mother work in mercy for all his children who respond to him and obey him.[71]

NOTES

1. Harvey Cox, *Turning East: The Promise and Peril of the New Orientalism* (New York, 1977), pp. 99–100.

2. See Joan Morris, *The Lady Was a Bishop* (New York, 1973).

3. See M. C. Facinger, "A Study of Medieval Queenship: Capetian France, 987–1237," *Studies in Medieval and Renaissance History*, vol. V (1968), pp. 3–48.

4. M. de Fantette, *Les Religieuses à l'âge classique du droit canon, recherches sur les structures juridiques de branches féminines des ordres* (Paris, 1967).

5. Marian K. Dale, "The London Silkwomen of the 15th Century," *Economic History Review*, vol. IV (1933), p. 329.

6. P. F. Chambers, *Juliana of Norwich* (London, 1955), p. 53.

7. Francine du Plessix Gray, "Nature as the Nunnery," quoting Margaret Atwood, *Surfacing*, in *New York Times Book Review*, July 10, 1977, p. 3.

8. See Keith Thomas, *Religion and the Decline of Magic* (New York, 1971).

9. Especially useful on this topic are Owen Barfield, *Saving the Appearances: A Study in Idolatry* (New York, n.d.); John S. Dunne, *A Search for God in Time and Memory* (New York, 1967); Paul Ricoeur, *The Symbolism of Evil* (Boston, 1967).

10. *Life of Saint Leoba*, by Rudolf, monk of Fulda, transl. and ed. C. H. Talbot, *The Anglo-Saxon Missionaries in Germany* (New York, 1954), pp. 205–26.

11. *Life of Saint Leoba*, p. 211.

12. *Ibid.*, p. 214: ". . . holding her in great affection not so much because she was related to him on his mother's side as because he knew that by her holiness and wisdom she would confer many benefits by her word and example."

13. *Ibid.*, p. 211.

14. *Ibid.*, p. 215.

15. *Letters of Saint Boniface*, transl. and ed. C. H. Talbot, *The Anglo-Saxon Missionaries in Germany* (New York, 1954), no. 17 (Tangl. 29), p. 88.

16. *Life of Saint Leoba*, *loc. cit.*, p. 215.

17. *Ibid.*, pp. 207–8.

18. *Ibid.*, pp. 219–20.

19. *Ibid.*, p. 223.

20. *Ibid.*

21. *Ibid.*, p. 222.

22. *Ibid.*, p. 223.

23. For the impact of evolving English political institutions on the role of noblewomen, see Betty Bandel, "English Chronicles Attitude Towards Women," *Journal of the History of Ideas*, vol. XVI (1955), pp. 113–18; see also Jo Ann McNamara and Suzanne Wemple, "The Power of Women Through the Family in Medieval Europe, 500–1100," in Mary Hartman and Lois W. Banner (eds.), *Clio's Consciousness Raised* (New York, 1974), pp. 103–18.

24. C. H. Talbot (ed. and transl.), *The Life of Christina of Markyate, a Twelfth Century Recluse* (Oxford, 1959), p. 6.

25. *Ibid.*, p. 35.

26. *Ibid.*, p. 47.

27. *Ibid.*, p. 51.

28. *Ibid.*, pp. 51–53.

29. *Ibid.*, p. 59.

30. *Ibid.*, p. 65.

31. *Ibid.*, pp. 65–67.

32. *Ibid.*, pp. 73–75.

33. *Ibid.*, p. 93. Once again we see this aspect of the anthropology of sainthood for women, in which the specifically female was left behind; to be holy is to regain the image of God, to become

more fully human and therefore, in this inheritance of patristic anthropology, to become male. See R. R. Ruether, "Misogynism and Virginal Feminism in the Fathers of the Church," *Religion and Sexism* (New York, 1974), p. 160.

34. *Ibid.*, p. 103.

35. Aelred of Rievaulx, *Spiritual Friendship*, transl. M. E. Laker, Cistercian Fathers Series, no. 5 (Washington, D.C., 1974).

36. Talbot, *Life of Christina*, p. 151.

37. *Ibid.*, p. 143.

38. *Ibid.*, pp. 165–67.

39. *Ibid.*, p. 169.

40. *Ibid.*, p. 91.

41. *Ibid.*, p. 133.

42. *Ibid.*, p. 107.

43. She is referred to as a "lover of Christ," *ibid.*, p. 173.

44. *Ibid.*, p. 119.

45. See Alice Curtayne, *Saint Catherine of Siena* (London, 1929); Sigrid Undset, *Catherine of Siena*, transl. Kate Austin-Lund (London/New York, 1954).

46. Saint Raymond of Capua, *The Life of St. Catherine of Siena*, transl. George Lands (London, 1965). Citations of her letters here are from Vida D. Scudder (ed. and transl.), *Saint Catherine of Siena as Seen in Her Letters* (New York, 1911).

47. Curtayne, *Saint Catherine*, pp. 196–98.

48. *Ibid.*, p. 202.

49. *Ibid.*, p. 184.

50. Scudder, *Letters*, p. 297.

51. *Ibid.*, p. 305.

52. *Ibid.*, p. 298.

53. *Ibid.*, p. 234.

54. *The Dialogue of Saint Catherine of Siena*, transl. Algar Thorold (Rockford, Ill., 1974), pp. 65–66.

55. *Ibid.*, p. 185.

56. Scudder, *Letters*, pp. 285–86.

57. *Ibid.*, p. 283.

58. *Ibid.*

59. Scudder, *Letters*, p. 289.

60. *Dialogue*, transl. Thorold, p. 27.

61. Scudder, *Letters*, p. 345.

62. *Dialogue*, transl. Thorold, p. 284.

63. *Ibid.*, p. 69.

64. Robert Grossetest to the Papal Notary (1253), in Marshall Baldwin, *Christianity Through the Thirteenth Century* (New York, 1970), p. 383.

65. Eleanor McLaughlin, "Women and Medieval Heresy," *Concilium*, vol. CXI (1976), pp. 73–90.

66. Julian of Norwich, *Revelations of Divine Love*, ed. Clifton Wolters (Baltimore, 1973), chap. 59, p. 167.

67. New books on the significance for Christian anthropology of the cult of the Virgin are numerous. Andrew Greeley, *The Mary Myth: On the Femininity of God* (New York, 1977), or John de Satgé, *Down to Earth: The New Protestant Vision of the Virgin Mary* (Wilmington, N.C., 1976), need to be read with reference to basic research, as, for example, K. E. Børresen, *Anthropologie médiévale et théologie mariale* (Oslo, 1971).

68. V. Saxer, *Le Culte de Marie Magdelène en occident des origines à la fin du moyen âge* (Paris, 1959).

69. "André Cabassut, une dévotion médiévale peu connue: La dévotion à Jesus notre mère," *Revue d'ascétique et de mystique*, vol. XXV (1949), pp. 234–45; Elaine Pagels, "What Became of God the Mother? Conflicting Images of God in Early Christianity," *Signs*, vol. II (1976), pp. 293–303; Eleanor McLaughlin, "Christ My Mother: Feminine Naming and Metaphor in Medieval Spirituality," *Nashotah Review*, vol. XV (1975), pp. 228–48; Caroline Walker Bynum, "Maternal Imagery in Twelfth Century Cistercian Writing," 7th Cistercian Conference, Kalamazoo, Mich., May 5–8, 1977.

70. For what I believe to be a controversial discussion of the issue of "female piety," see John Bugge, *Virginitas: An Essay in the History of a Medieval Ideal* (The Hague, 1975).

71. Julian of Norwich, *Revelations*, ed. Wolters, chap. 58, p. 166. See also Kari Elisabeth Børresen, "Christ notre mère, la théologie de Julienne de Norwich," *Mitteilungen und Forschungsbeiträge der Cusanus-Gesellschaft*, 13 (Mainz, 1978).

FOUR

Virgins in the Service of Christ: The Dispute over an Active Apostolate for Women During the Counter-Reformation

RUTH P. LIEBOWITZ

During the Counter-Reformation, women engaged in a remarkable effort of religious creativity, striving to establish new kinds of communities in which they could effectively pursue an active apostolate. Foremost in this movement were Angela Merici, Mary Ward and Louise de Marillac, the founders respectively of the Ursulines, the Institute of the Blessed Virgin Mary (in America, the Ladies of Loretto) and the Daughters of Charity. Their efforts aroused great controversy and intense opposition both from the clerical hierarchy and from the larger society of Roman Catholic Europe. By the middle of the seventeenth century, the issues had begun to resolve themselves in a way which represented a partial—and, it should be stressed, a *very* partial—success for these women's goals.

This dispute is revealing in two ways: it throws light on Counter-Reformation attitudes toward women in religion, both those of the women themselves and of the Church and society at large; and it suggests that, in the formation of these attitudes, Christian theology, economic and social forces, and the conflicts of the Reformation all played a part. An awareness of these attitudes and their institutional consequences in turn can add something to our far from complete picture of the religious opportunities open to women in the Reformation era.[1]

Here I wish to take up the women reformers' self-image and goals, along with the sources and the nature of the opposition they aroused. I want to explore some possible reasons for the outcome of the dispute and its larger significance. Finally, I will make some very brief comparisons between the experiences of these Roman Catholic reformers and developments affecting women in early Protestantism.

Whereas in Protestantism the rejection of the ideals of virginity, celibacy and religious vows made for a situation in which women's religious life was restructured from the ground up, in Roman Catholicism women continued to pursue religious experience, though often in new ways, within the inherited framework of medieval ideals and forms. Women who sought an active apostolate were highly innovative in terms of defining new spiritual vocations and institutional structures appropriate to express them. Yet it is striking how none of them questioned basic medieval assumptions about the religious life.

The early Church Fathers had posited that to achieve the fullest life of prayer and service of God several things were essential. It was necessary to make a permanent self-dedication to this end, to practice sexual abstinence and to adopt an appropriately organized form of daily living (sometimes on an individual basis but more usually in a community). The emphasis on abstinence, with its underlying eschatology and body-soul dualism, led these writers to rank virginity as the highest state, with widowhood rededicated to celibacy as the second best.[2]

The founders of active women's orders in the Counter-Reformation all continued to adhere to these notions of celibacy, self-dedication and organized discipline. The ideal of virginity in particular remained strongly emphasized. For example, Angela Merici's rule for her new Company of Saint Ursula reminded her daughters and sisters "how many great persons there are, empresses, queens, duchesses, and the

like, that would wish to be considere⬚ ⬚ f the least of
your handmaids, esteeming *your* ⬚ much more
worthy, so much better than ⬚

Underlying this ideal ⬚ of womanhood which was ⬚ ⬚semary
Ruether has sh⬚ ⬚mula-
tion in the ⬚ cre-
ated i⬚ ⬚or-
rupted ⬚ ⬚st
spiritual ⬚
her body ⬚
usually had ⬚
man whose fu⬚
suitable to serv⬚

While not disp⬚
ists nevertheless ⬚ ⬚
dence. They revele⬚ ⬚r virginity in a highly cha⬚ ⬚erici lauds
the heroism of militar⬚ ⬚ in the world,
staunchly reject its tem⬚ ⬚ding that, "like Ju-
dith, spiritedly cutting of⬚ ⬚ of Holofernes, we, de-
capitating the devil, may g⬚ ⬚ously go on to the heavenly
country, in such wise that to all, in heaven and earth, great
glory and triumph shall arise." [5] The Ursuline rule and the
writings of Vincent de Paul and Louise de Marillac for the
Daughters of Charity imply that their vocation in the world
is more meritorious than the cloistered virtue of their contemplative sisters. This sense of élan extended to their view
of themselves in relation to male religious. The Daughters of
Charity were reminded that women could exert themselves
as heroically as men in works of charity. Although their sufferings and sacrifice of life in this cause often went unno-
ticed, their vocation was greater for this very reason. [6]

In the area of vocations and especially of institutional arrangements, Angela Merici and other women activists proposed some striking innovations. The apostolate of service
in Christian society that they envisioned included a number

of activities—catechizing, moral instruction, female education, nursing and works of charity—to be carried on either singly or in combination. Toward this end, these women endeavored to create appropriate new forms of religious community, ones that permitted their members to be out in society, mobile and engaged efficiently in their spiritual and charitable pursuits. They called these new communities congregations or societies rather than orders to distinguish themselves from the established pattern of female monasticism.

They were, in effect, proposing an alternative to female monasticism with its orientation toward contemplative spirituality and its conventual organization. The latter in its fully elaborated form called for the nuns to take solemn, public vows (poverty, chastity and obedience), to devote much of their time to reciting the Divine Office, and to participate in a highly regulated and scheduled communal life, always in some degree of cloister. By contrast, the female activists of the Counter-Reformation generally wanted to simplify and deformalize all these arrangements. They made their vows privately, or at most took simple ones in public.[7] Instead of a habit, they chose to wear a sober form of everyday dress, sometimes including a specifically religious article of clothing.[8] So as to allow for an open, flexible schedule, they greatly reduced the time spent in reciting the Office, and they substituted living at home or in a noncloistered, informal community for the traditional convent structure.

Each of these groups also struck out individually in new directions. Angela Merici, for instance, sought to avoid the social stratification which had crept into the old orders, where upper-class nuns were served by lower-class lay sisters. In the first Ursuline congregation, which was formed in Brescia in the early 1530s, the ideal of a spiritual democracy prevailed. There were no lay sisters, and its members were drawn from all ranks of society.[9] Although the original scheme for Mary Ward's Institute, begun about 1610, retained lay sisters, it proposed a radical departure in the area

of governance. It was customary for houses of female religious to be placed under the jurisdiction of a local male
ecclesiastic—either the bishop, the provincial of a male
order or the prior of a nearby monastery. Mary Ward wanted
the organization of her Institute, which planned to educate
English Catholic girls, to parallel that of the Jesuits—that is,
to be headed by a mother general who was directly subject
to the Pope.[10]

These activist women were moving in a direction different
from that of their contemporaries like Teresa of Ávila, whose
Reformed Carmelites sought to revive and purify contemplative life. Nevertheless, the ideals of the two groups were not
necessarily mutually exclusive, and in at least one instance
they were jointly envisioned. Jeanne de Chantal and Francis
de Sales in their original plan for the Visitation Order, which
they worked out in the first decade of the seventeenth century, wanted to combine a conventual form of life with simple vows, recitation of a shorter Office, and provision for the
nuns to go out and tend the sick on a regular basis. This plan
was partly inspired by the open Ursuline congregations in
Milan.[11]

It cannot be said that these women's conceptions were
entirely new. In the Middle Ages there had been the Beguinages, informal communities of women dedicated to prayer
and religious activities. Important in northern Europe during the thirteenth and fourteenth centuries, by the time of
the Reformation they were in a state of decline.[12] There was
also, especially in Italy, the female branch of the Third
Order of Mendicants (Tertiaries). The friars' ideal of a mixed
active and contemplative life had been transformed into a
purely contemplative form among their sister Dominicans
and Franciscans (Clarisses), but it was still accessible to female Tertiaries, particularly those Franciscans who had retained their original loose form of organization.[13]

On the whole, there were few medieval precedents for
active female religious orders. It is possible that the "open"

state of many traditional convents in the Renaissance, especially in Italy and Spain, may have encouraged thoughts of fully open communities.[14] However, in the sixteenth-century revival of the mendicant ideal among the Franciscans, the Capuchins, its female branch (Capuchinesses) was once again strictly cloistered from the start.[15] The medieval lay confraternities dedicated to works of charity seem to have been largely male [16] and therefore probably suggested counterpart all-female organizations for this same purpose. These confraternities and the Tertiary movement did serve as starting points for the Ursulines' founder, but what is significant is the way she moved beyond them. After a life of living singly as a Franciscan Tertiary, and participating in charitable work in Brescia, Angela Merici, in her late fifties, began to organize a group of young women for charitable work, especially for the religious instruction of young girls. Unlike the male confraternities, the girls of her company were not to remain in a lay state but would consecrate themselves to a life of virginity. Her rule also provided not simply for an association but for a structured organization in which the efforts of its members were to be carefully supervised and coordinated.[17]

This new theme of rational organization for more effective action appears again in Mary Ward's Institute and in the Daughters of Charity, founded in 1633. Louise de Marillac's plan for a mobile congregation devoted primarily to nursing worked out a varied form of life for its members, alternating between a structured community at their home base in Paris and flexible arrangements when they were on the road at work.[18]

These programs for an active apostolate were, of course, by no means unique to women during the Counter-Reformation. They run parallel to the better-known creations on the male side, above all the Jesuits. They all reflect the Roman championing of the value of good works in answer to Luther's doctrines, and possibly also the Renaissance humanists' praise of the *vita activa*, as well as their ideas for a more organized and moralistic approach to social problems.[19]

Once their unity of impulse is recognized, however, it has to be stated immediately that there were significant differences both in the character and in the outcome of male and female efforts in this period. Most of the active male congregations, such as the Theatines, the Barnabites, the Mission Fathers of Vincent de Paul (Lazarists) and the Jesuits, were conceived of in terms of specifically *priestly* pastoral work— above all preaching and administering the sacraments. Their associations (clerks regular, in church terminology) thus inevitably were all male, because of the traditional exclusion of women from the priesthood.[20] Whereas the ideal of the contemplative monastic life could be jointly aspired to by brother and sister orders, the priesthood admitted of no female counterpart. The activist women's movement focused itself around a set of activities that were considered spiritually appropriate for women. Thus the pastoral emphasis of the Counter-Reformation tended to accentuate differences in sex roles within Roman Catholicism.

This emphasis also tended to accentuate the inequality between these sex roles. The activist women, as has been mentioned, accepted the principle that they owed obedience to male ecclesiastics, whether individually to their confessor or as a community to whoever had jurisdiction over them. The institutional vow of obedience had always been central to Western monasticism. During the Counter-Reformation, the confessor role was expanded into that of a spiritual director and became more significant. The church hierarchy, in response to the Reformation challenge to priest and sacraments, emphasized the authority of the spiritual director and the corresponding obligation of obedience to him. Also the increasing interest in the psychological aspects of spirituality tended to make this relationship personal.[21] For Jeanne de Chantal and Louise de Marillac, their long collaboration with and submission to their spiritual directors, Francis de

Sales and Vincent de Paul respectively, was central to their whole religious experience.[22]

At first glance Mary Ward would seem to be an exception to this principle. Her proposal to have her Institute headed by a mother general subject only to the Pope did reject the necessity for local male superiors. However, the grounds on which she based her plan seem to have been pragmatic rather than ideological. They related to the organizational logic of a mobile international group working in a missionary area, and also to Mary Ward's aristocratic assurance that she could deal directly with people at the top. She early on displayed great obedience to her confessor and later to directives from papal officials.[23] Her writings and career do not indicate any rejection of the notion that spiritual women still needed male guidance, or any alternative theology of women.[24] This frame of mind has to be taken into consideration when looking at the women's responses to the opposition their new congregations aroused.

The congregations became controversial almost as soon as their formation began. As Evennett says, "neither social nor ecclesiastical opinion . . . was prepared" for them.[25] Just why they were not "prepared" or, to put it more accurately, why they were strongly opposed relates to some basic concerns shared by the Church and the higher ranks of society. The opposition generally focused around two main points: the congregations' lack of cloister and the question of their members' dowries.

Most of these concerns were stated explicitly when the constitution of the new Visitation sisters came up for approval in 1615. Their ecclesiastical superior, the Archbishop of Lyons, expressed his dissatisfaction with their lack of cloister as follows:

In the first place he did not approve of the sisters visiting the poor; in France, nuns were not allowed by their rule to walk in the streets. He admitted that the saintliness of Madame de Chantal and of her sisters justified this experiment and even made it praise-

worthy. If, however, as he had seen happen in other Orders, the
first fervor should wane, he feared that these daily visits might
become a source of distraction, dissipation and perhaps of scandal.[26]

The Archbishop's sensitivity to potential scandal reflects the
Counter-Reformation's determination to eliminate laxity,
worldly living and periodic sexual scandals among nuns,
abuses which were frequent in Renaissance convents and
which had provided the early Protestant reformers with a
great source of ammunition in their anti-papal polemics.
The remedy for this problem arrived at by the Counter-
Reformation Church was the legally questionable but simple
and presumably effective one of reducing to the absolute
minimum the nuns' contact with everyone. Through a decree passed at the last session of Trent and a subsequent
papal edict, the Church renewed and extended the obligation of strict cloister to all female religious. It declared that
female religious who up to then had taken only simple, public vows or private ones were now obligated to take solemn
vows, and that these in turn automatically entailed the obligation of strict enclosure.[27] Cloister thus became a tool in
combating Protestant influence, and in shoring up the reputation of the clergy in the states of Europe remaining loyal
to Rome.
In its pressure for cloister, the Church generally received
support from the civil authorities, who saw the moral example of the religious and the priests as conducive to social
order and political stability.[28] Similarly, the families of
upper-class nuns had an interest in preventing their daughters in convents from disgracing their family name. This
concern reflects a broad set of social mores focused around
the idea of honor, both of the house and of the individual.
For unmarried women, honor was synonymous with virginity, and to protect it families favored a form of seclusion for
young, unmarried girls at home as well as in the convent. Of
course, the families had contributed greatly to convent sex-

ual scandals in the first place by using these religious institutions as respectable, subsidized residences for daughters they either chose not to or were unable to marry off.[29] Nevertheless, they continued to have expectations for their daughters' conduct in this state.

It is indicative of the fear of scandal shared by the Church and society that in the 1540s, even before the Counter-Reformation was under way, the Ursulines were already ordered to wear a distinctive habit.[30] In this way the society could recognize the maidens whose religious commitment they were supposed to respect. Similarly, the Barnabites, who began as an unusual company of both men and women dedicated to charity in Milan in the 1530s, were soon forced by these fears to separate into single-sex groups, and the female Barnabites (also called the Angelicas) assumed a conventual form.[31] In at least one instance, this concern prevented a new congregation from emerging at all. When, in the 1580s, the Archbishop of Siena heard of a young girl who had started an Ursuline-type group in the city, his immediate reaction was fear for her honor, and he persuaded her to transform the group into a more acceptable house of enclosed Capuchinesses.[32]

The second and related point of issue, the question of dowries, also aroused much controversy. The Archbishop of Lyons pointed out with displeasure that because the Visitation sisters had taken only simple vows, which according to canon law were reversible, they could obtain permission to retrieve their convent dowry and return to the world, where they might marry and then make claims on their families for a much larger marriage portion. This could obviously happen even more easily when women had merely pledged their vows privately. Solemn vows created more security for both convents and families, because according to canon law they were irreversible and excluded a girl from inheriting or bequeathing property, and from ever validly marrying.[33] Like the highly controversial Tridentine edict against clandestine marriage, the insistence on solemn vows and cloister represented a way for social institutions to better control the young.[34]

The informal and mobile nature of the new congregations also raised questions about their abilities to manage financially. Angela Merici had sought to counter this by obtaining a papal bull that guaranteed the members of her company the right to have their dowry from their family as securely as if they were marrying or entering a convent.[35] Mary Ward's rapidly growing and still unapproved Institute aroused concern in the 1620s about the management of its members' dowries. Church officials feared that if the womens' dowries were consumed, being so distant from their families the women might be led into prostitution for survival. Besides being beset by these general kinds of opposition to the new congregations, Mary Ward's Institute aroused a particularly bitter furor because of her proposal that it be subject only to the Pope. In one way or another, this antagonized vested jurisdictional interests throughout the entire hierarchy.[36]

In addition to arousing opposition from contemporaries, the departure of these new groups from the set marks and forms of the established orders sometimes simply left people in doubt about their religious vocation.[37] All these problems made the position of the women's congregations extremely difficult. The stress of sustaining controversial new practices led to internal divisions in the early Ursulines and the Institute of the B.V.M.[38] It was essential for the groups to stay outside cloister if they were going to carry on the activities they envisaged. However, after the 1550s there was strong pressure from ecclesiastical officials for them to conform to the cloistered, conventual model. Jeanne de Chantal's director, Francis de Sales, submitted to the negative judgment of his superior, the Archbishop of Lyons, regarding their plan for the Visitation sisters. The latter gave up visiting the sick, took solemn vows and became a traditional cloistered order, developing only the contemplative side of Jeanne de Chantal's inspiration.[39]

The outcome for other groups varied. Mary Ward's Institute was suppressed by papal order in 1629, after a series of skirmishes and intrigues in Rome which remind one of the Galileo affair, and she herself was briefly imprisoned as a heretic.[40] Some groups were pressured into solemn vows and cloister, and they moved into the one active function compatible with these, namely the kind of female education where students boarded and observed the same cloister as the nuns. This was the destiny of many Ursulines in France and in some areas of Italy by the middle of the seventeenth century. It was also the form taken by the second, modified Institute of the B.V.M., which gradually regrouped out of the ruins of the suppressed original and which received papal approval in 1703.[41]

The Ursulines in and around Milan, however, retained something of their early form because the Church needed their services in the society. Charles Borromeo, the leading figure of the Counter-Reformation, who was archbishop of Milan from 1560 to 1584, followed most of the Tridentine prescriptions in dealing with the new congregations. He put the Ursulines in Brescia and Milan more closely under episcopal jurisdiction and established modified rules for them which brought their structure closer to that of the majority of congregations. He also encouraged them to take a formal vow of virginity and to form communities.[42] However, the special rule drawn up under his authority for the Ursulines living in community (a minority through the seventeenth century) did not prescribe complete cloister as directed by Trent. It called for contemplative practices and an internal school, but permitted the sisters to continue to go out for such work as teaching in the schools of Christian doctrine which Borromeo had set up all over the diocese. Without their assistance, he could not have run this catechism program, which was his response to Protestant charges of religious ignorance in Papist lands.[43]

In the course of all these changes, the response of the women founders and the members of the congregations had generally been, after some initial protest, to comply in the

spirit of obedience. It was Mary Ward and some of her colleagues who showed the greatest degree of persistence in
their goals possible within the limits of obedience. After the
suppression of her Institute, Mary Ward got papal permission to gather some former members together in Rome,
now, however, as a group of individuals with no rule, wearing secular dress. From this base they reemerged to form the
second Institute.[44] Thus she ensured the survival of her
group and the memory (and eventual vindication) of her
goals. There was one woman who refused to accept the
changes in her original plan: the founder of the female Barnabites, Lodovica Torelli de Guastalla. When her already
conventualized group in Milan was enclosed in 1557, she left
and founded a school for girls under the aegis of the civil
authorities.[45]

The first active women's congregation to succeed in get-
ting complete church approval for its original rule was the
Daughters of Charity, founded by Louise de Marillac in
1633, just four years after the suppression of the Institute.
Because the creators of its rule managed to overcome the
previously discussed objections of contemporaries, they were
able to proceed with their admittedly much-needed hospital
work. Louise de Marillac gave careful thought to the possibility of scandal. Her Daughters soon came to wear simple
but recognizable habits, and their schedules were supervised
by a sister-servant in charge. When they went out to visit the
sick, they always traveled in pairs, and each was supposed to
help the other keep "well-recollected."[46] Rather than be
subject to the Archbishop of Paris, Louise managed to have
the Daughters put under Vincent de Paul's Mission Fathers,
with whose work she felt close ties. Also she apparently was
a very competent administrator.[47]

Most important of all were the arrangements made regarding vows. Louise de Marillac herself had taken solemn vows
to mark and dignify her personal commitment, but Vincent
de Paul realized that this practice could not be institutionalized for her Daughters, because then they would be obli-

gated to cloister and unable to carry on their nursing. Instead, the Daughters took simple, temporary vows which were renewed annually. The cost of this workable solution, however, was that despite their heroic spiritual vocation, their rule and their willingness to make a lifetime commitment, the Daughters and other groups who followed them in France had to accept a status as something other than and less than real religious.[48] As Vincent de Paul reminded them, this title was reserved for nuns who observed solemn vows and cloister.[49]

In addition to their founders' careful provisions, the social composition of the Daughters of Charity may have enabled them to retain their original form more successfully than the other groups. It is fairly clear that the members of the Institute and the Visitation Order came from the upper classes.[50] The social origins of the Ursulines are less clear, and they probably varied considerably, depending on the time and the region. However, the kind of broad education they provided in France, like that of the Institute, presupposed teachers from a fairly well-off background. By contrast, at least the initial membership of the Daughters of Charity was drawn from the poorer, rural classes, and they served those in special need.[51] It seems likely that concerns about dowries, family reputation and the social niceties would not matter in the case of the Daughters, who otherwise would be leading a hardy, mobile life in domestic service or farm labor.[52]

After this initial breakthrough, acceptance of other features of the congregations came very slowly. At the beginning of the eighteenth century, the Papacy recognized the right of self-government in women's congregations.[53] The idea of active religious orders of women gained acceptance slowly, although they were still considered second-class religious. In the middle of the nineteenth century, the Papacy granted these active congregations with their simple, public vows full legal recognition as religious under canon law, and thus placed the sisters on an equal plane with the nuns.[54] Angela Merici's original rule for the Ursulines was revived

by a group of women in Brescia and received papal approval
in 1901. Mary Ward's rehabilitation as founder of the Institute of the Blessed Virgin Mary took place only in 1907.[55]

The story of women's efforts to establish an active apostolate during the Counter-Reformation thus turns out to be
a very mixed epic. These new congregations arduously endeavored to make the point that women could and should
work in Christian society. Yet their story, unlike that of the
Jesuits and the Capuchins, was not one of speedy and brilliant success. For the most part, the groups failed to achieve
their original goals. Although they made a significant contribution spiritually, and socially also, to female education, it
was not the one they had initially envisioned. The single
success of the Daughters of Charity suggests that, in the
Counter-Reformation, congregations could achieve their
aims only under certain conditions.

An awareness of these realities contributes something to
our understanding of the broader picture of women's roles in
the Reformation era. Natalie Davis has compared what Catholicism and Protestantism had to offer city women. She
feels that Roman Catholicism gave women somewhat more
because the religious orders offered them the possibility of a
separate identity and the opportunity to exercise organizational creativity. As an example of the latter, she cites the
work of Angela Merici, Mary Ward and Louise de
Marillac.[56] In light of the history of their groups, one would
have to add that when churchmen feared the release of
women's creativity, they did not allow it to survive without
modification.

In the short term, as Natalie Davis has noted, the position
of women on both sides of the Reformation division was
characterized by subordination. She describes the relation
of women to men in Protestantism as "together but unequal"; the Catholic version for religious could be termed
"separate but unequal." [57] Both in the mainstream of Protestantism and in Roman Catholicism, women were excluded
from the ministry. During the Counter-Reformation, more-

over, female religious saw a lessening of the independence they had enjoyed in an earlier period.

In the long term, the struggles of the women activists of the Counter-Reformation had significance not only for the evolution of female orders in Roman Catholicism but for the larger history of women. Working within a religious context, they pioneered a departure from the limited options of marriage or the convent, with their private, fixed and generally stationary character. By advancing the idea of public, mobile and diversified roles for women in religion, they helped to lay the groundwork for a more modern view of women as a whole.

NOTES

An earlier version of this chapter was presented as a paper at a Reformation Colloquy, Wellesley College, June 7, 1977. The author wishes to thank George Williams, David Steinmetz, Ian Siggins, Mark Edwards, Carl Estabrook, Sharon Elkins and Timothy George for their provocative questions and comments, from which the final version has greatly benefited.

1. For the literature on this subject, see Natalie Davis, "City Women and Religious Change," in her volume of essays, *Society and Culture in Early Modern France* (Stanford, Calif., 1975), pp. 65–95; also Jane Douglass, "Women in the Continental Reformation," in Rosemary Ruether (ed.), *Religion and Sexism: Images of Woman in the Jewish and Christian Traditions* (New York, 1974), pp. 292–319.

2. These theological notions are discussed in connection with their impact on women in Rosemary Ruether, "Misogynism and Virginal Feminism in the Fathers of the Church," in her *Religion and Sexism*, pp. 150–79.

3. Angela Merici, "Rule of the Company of St. Ursula (1536)," reprinted in Sister M. Monica, *Angela Merici and Her Teaching Idea, 1474–1540* (New York, 1927), pp. 246, 254–55, 257–58. (My emphasis.)

4. Ruether, "Virginal Feminism," especially pp. 156–59. See also her *Liberation Theology: Human Hope Confronts Christian*

History and American Power (New York, 1972), pp. 99–108.
Thomas Aquinas' reformulation of Augustine's views is discussed
by Eleanor McLaughlin, "Equality of Souls, Inequality of Sexes:
Woman in Medieval Theology," in Ruether, *Religion and Sexism*,
pp. 213–67.

5. Merici, "Rule," *loc. cit.*, p. 247.

6. M. V. Woodgate, *St. Louise de Marillac, Foundress of the
Sisters of Charity* (St. Louis, 1942), pp. 81–86, 132–37.

7. Simple vows are less canonically binding than solemn ones.
For some of the ramifications of this difference, see p. 141, and
also the *New Catholic Encyclopedia*, vol. XIV, p. 758.

8. The members of Mary Ward's Institute, for instance, wore a
linen band over the forehead, one of the marks of a nun, with
their widow's dress (Sister Monica, *Angela Merici*, pp. 327–28).
The matter of dress in these congregations is rather tricky because
often what started out as ordinary clothing became gradually with
the change of fashion a distinctive dress; for examples see Woodgate, *St. Louise de Marillac*, pp. 66, 130–31, and Mary Oliver,
Mary Ward (New York, 1959), pp. 74, 155.

9. H. O. Evennett, "The New Orders," *New Cambridge Modern
History*, vol. II, p. 289. For social stratification in Florentine convents, see Richard Trexler, "Le Célibat à la fin du moyen age: Les
Religieuses de Florence," *Annales*, vol. XXVII (1972), pp.
1334–37.

10. Peter Guilday, *The English Catholic Refugees on the Continent* (London, 1914), vol. I, pp. 172–75.

11. For these congregations, see pp. 142–45. For the Visitation
sisters, see Maurice Henry-Couännier, *Saint Francis de Sales and
His Friends* (Chicago, 1964), pp. 203–4, 253–54, 274; also Sister
Monica, *Angela Merici*, p. 331, and Thérèse Ledochowska, *Angèle
Mérici et la compagnie de Ste. Ursule à la lumière des documents*
(Rome, 1967), vol. II, p. 179.

12. For a discussion of the Beguines of Cologne, see R. W.
Southern, *Western Society and the Church in the Middle Ages*
(London, 1970), pp. 319–31.

13. The career of Catherine of Genoa in hospital work furnishes
a good example. Whereas Dominican Tertiaries, whose members
included Catherine of Siena, developed early on a contemplative,
conventual (but noncloistered) form, some Franciscans continued
to live at home or in informal communities. For the variety of

vows taken by Tertiaries, see Raimondo Creytens, "La riforma dei monasteri femminili dopo i Decreti Tridentini," in *Il Concilio di Trento*, vol. I (Rome, 1965), pp. 46–49.

14. This meant that the nuns could receive visitors without intervening grilles and themselves go out to visit. In France, the monastic reforms of the early sixteenth century had strengthened enclosure. (Davis, "City Women," *loc. cit.*, pp. 75–76.)

15. Evennett, "New Orders," *loc. cit.*, p. 290.

16. For French data, see Natalie Davis, "City Women," *loc. cit.*, p. 75. The new Company of Divine Love, though in close relations with individual female religious, seems to have had an all-male membership, as also did the confraternities of Venice (the *scuole*); see respectively Ledochowska, *Angèle Mérici*, vol. I, pp. 46–55, and Brian Pullan, *Rich and Poor in Renaissance Venice: The Social Institutions of a Catholic State to 1620* (Cambridge, Mass., 1971), Part I.

17. It envisioned a two-layer structure with young virgins directed by older widows, who were to meet in citywide and neighborhood assemblies. The major part of Angela Merici's rule was taken up by the description of this structure; see Angela Merici, "Rule," *loc. cit.*, pp. 257–77.

18. Woodgate, *St. Louise de Marillac*, pp. 124–34; see also Louise de Marillac, *Textes choisis*, ed. Jean-Pierre Foucher (Namur, 1959), pp. 79–81.

19. H. O. Evennett, *The Spirit of the Counter Reformation* (London, 1968), chap. 2, especially pp. 41–42. For humanist attitudes toward poverty, see Pullan, *Renaissance Venice*, pp. 223–31.

20. Evennett, "New Orders," *loc. cit.*, pp. 276, 285–89.

21. Evennett, *Counter Reformation*, pp. 36–37. The period saw the emergence of some famous spiritual circles revolving around charismatic figures, ranging from the unorthodox Juan de Valdés and Miguel de Molinos to Loyola, Francis de Sales and Fénelon.

22. These spiritual relationships, discussed lengthily but sentimentally in popular religious biographies like Woodgate and Henry-Couännier, could well be studied further.

23. Guilday, *English Catholic Refugees*, pp. 170–72, and Oliver, *Mary Ward*, p. 63.

24. Ruether, *Liberation Theology*, pp. 109–11.

25. Evennett, "New Orders," *loc. cit.*, p. 290, and *Counter Reformation*, pp. 84–85.

26. Henry-Couännier, *Saint Francis de Sales*, p. 311.

27. The 1298 bull of Boniface VIII, *Periculoso*, which the Tridentine decree on cloister (Session XXV, Decree on Regulars, v) renewed, applied only to certain convents. In his subsequent edict of 1566, *Circa Pastoralis*, Pius V applied it to all nuns and Tertiaries. This meant setting aside parts of established rules, disregarding the nuns' customary rights, and obligating them to regulations stricter than those they had accepted at their entrance. For a thorough discussion of the legislation, see Creytens, "La riforma," *loc. cit.*, and also his "La giurisprudenza della Sacra Congregazione del Concilio nella questione della clausura delle monache (1565–1576)," *Apollinaris*, vol. XXXVII (1964), pp. 251–85.

28. For this attitude in the grand dukes of Tuscany, see Ruth Liebowitz, "The Medici and the Sienese Church, 1557–1577," unpublished Ph.D. thesis, Harvard University, 1972, pp. 8–9, 11–12.

29. Family placing of daughters in convents, stimulated by the great inflation of marriage dowries, is discussed in Trexler, "Le Célibat," *loc. cit.*, pp. 1338–45. For an example of this policy in France, see Robert Forster, *The House of Saulx-Tavanes* (Baltimore, 1971), pp. 4 and 7. Sometimes the Counter-Reformation Church's pressure for these less than inspired nuns to conform to strict cloister caused them to rebel openly and even leave the convent. In this situation, sometimes both their families and the civil authorities felt threatened and they in turn exerted pressure on the Church to ease its demands somewhat; for instances in Tuscany and Venice, see Liebowitz, "The Medici," pp. 292–95, 307–8, 384–93.

30. Ledochowska, *Angèle Mérici*, vol. II, pp. 29, 42.

31. Mario Bendiscioli, "Politica, amministrazione e religione nell' età dei Borromei," *Storia di Milano*, vol. X (Milan, 1957), pp. 166–72.

32. *Bulletino senese di storia patria*, Terza Serie, Anno II (1943), pp. 88–109.

33. Sister Monica, *Angela Merici*, pp. 330–31. According to Richard Trexler in conversation, however, even solemn vows did not prevent many lawsuits for return of convent dowries in Florence. It would be interesting to see if there was a higher rate of defections in the new congregations than in the old orders.

34. For the edict on clandestine marriage and its history in

France, see David Hunt, *Parents and Children in History* (New York, 1970), pp. 61–64.

35. Sister Monica, *Angela Merici*, pp. 237–38.

36. On one hand, the similarity of her plan to the Jesuit structure aroused anti-Jesuit sentiment from all the older orders and the secular clergy. On the other hand, it elicited hostility from the Jesuits themselves because of their refusal to connect themselves in any way with women's houses. For the various kinds of opposition, see Guilday, *English Catholic Refugees*, pp. 174–96, and a much fuller account in J. Grisar, *Die ersten Anklagen in Rom gegen das Institut Maria Wards* (Rome, 1959).

37. See the account of Mary Ward's group cited by Guilday, *English Catholic Refugees*, p. 184, note 1.

38. See, respectively, Sister Monica, *Angela Merici*, pp. 306–8 (with a fuller account in Ledochowska, *Angèle Mérici*, vol. II, pp. 10–36) and Guilday, *English Catholic Refugees*, pp. 180–81, 185, 199.

39. Henry-Couännier, *Saint Francis de Sales*, pp. 311–14.

40. Oliver, *Mary Ward*, pp. 128–54; Guilday, *English Catholic Refugees*, pp. 188–209.

41. For the Ursulines, see Evennett, "New Orders," *loc. cit.*, pp. 289–90, and the longer account in Sister Monica, *Angela Merici*, pp. 300–327, 336–51. For the second Institute, see Guilday, *English Catholic Refugees*, pp. 209–14.

42. In addition to providing protection for young virgins without a suitable home, they also supported those without adequate means of self-support, or the sick and aging in need of care (Ledochowska, *Angèle Mérici*, vol. II, pp. 69–85, 111–31).

43. *Ibid.*, pp. 85–98, 131–51.

44. Oliver, *Mary Ward*, pp. 154–64.

45. Bendiscioli, "Politica," *loc. cit.*, pp. 166–72.

46. Louise de Marillac, *Textes*, p. 71.

47. Woodgate, *St. Louise de Marillac*, pp. 105–10, 131.

48. The attitudes of obedience and submissiveness noted for the Daughters apparently have continued to permeate these French foundations down to the present day, and are reflected in a lack of awareness of the value of their records. See Dora B. Weiner, "A Guide to Research in Archives of Active French Women's Orders," *French Historical Studies*, vol. IX, no. 2 (Fall 1975), pp. 362–64.

49. Woodgate, *St. Louise de Marillac*, pp. 64–65, 127–32. The post-Tridentine restriction of the title of religious to those with solemn, and more recently to those with at least simple, public vows has created difficulties in terminology for modern Catholic writers dealing with the private vows of the early Ursulines and members of the first Institute. They move back and forth from calling them "lay groups" and forerunners of the modern lay apostolate to discussing them as religious and members of new kinds of orders. For example, see Oliver, *Mary Ward*, pp. xi, xii; and Evennett, "New Orders," *loc. cit.*, pp. 289–90, and *Counter Reformation*, p. 85. While the appellation "lay" is technically correct in canonical terms, it is misleading to overmodernize these groups, when their general orientation follows the traditional conception of the religious life.

50. For the Institute, see Oliver, *Mary Ward*, *passim*. The first lay sisters of the order were the servants whom Mary Ward and her companions had brought with them from England (Guilday, *English Catholic Refugees*, p. 169). For the Visitation sisters, see Henry-Couännier, *Saint Francis de Sales*, pp. 159–62, 234–37, 244–58.

51. Woodgate, *St. Louise de Marillac*, pp. 51–56, 126–27.

52. It would be interesting to see if, in the orders founded after 1650, there continued to be a correlation between their social composition and their observance of cloister.

53. In connection with the approval of the second Institute in 1703, Clement XI uttered the memorable phrase "*Lasciate governare le donne dalle donne*" (Sister Monica, *Angela Merici*, p. 328). But episcopal jurisdiction seems to have continued to be an issue (Guilday, *English Catholic Refugees*, p. 213).

54. *New Catholic Encyclopedia*, vol. XIII, p. 261.

55. For the Ursuline revival, see Sister Monica, *Angela Merici*, p. 335; for Mary Ward, see Guilday, *English Catholic Refugees*, pp. 163–64, 191.

56. Davis, "City Women," *loc. cit.*, pp. 85, 93–94.

57. *Ibid.*, pp. 82–93.

FIVE

"A Woman Must Not Speak": Quaker Women in the English Left Wing

ELAINE C. HUBER

Arrested at the home of a friend in 1657, an Englishwoman named Dewens Morrey was taken before the justice to face her accuser, the parish priest of Hawkchurch. When she inquired what evil she had done the priest said, "A woman must not speak in the church." Her punishment is recorded in a volume called *First Publishers of Truth:* "So in conclusion they ordered her to go back to Hawkchurch that Night, and there she was to be whipt untill the Blood did come, which was done the next Morning Early, she receiving many Cruell, bloody stripes." [1] For a woman to speak aloud in church was indeed a punishable crime, and the verdict for Dewens Morrey was "guilty," yet she and hundreds of other Quaker women continued to defy ecclesiastical authority by their public preaching and thus helped to shape the current of seventeenth-century religious history.

The Society of Friends experienced a phenomenal period of growth in the latter half of the seventeenth century. George Fox had begun to spread the message of the Inner Light shortly before midcentury, and by 1690 there were sixty thousand Friends, or one out of every 130 persons then living in England. [2] Many of those first preachers were women. Although there is no way to determine how many

of the early converts were won over through the efforts of
the intrepid women preachers, it is possible to examine what
may have attracted women preachers to the Quaker ranks.
Those Spirit-filled meetings of the early Quakers spoke to
women as well as men, for they called on all to recognize
the limitless possibilities within themselves; but perhaps the
effect of this challenge on women was greater because they
had heard it so seldom.

Early Quakers exhibited a fervor that in many ways resem-
bled that of the first-century Christians. At least four characteristics that set this group apart from the more "established" churches would have appealed to women of that (or
any) age: (1) simplicity, (2) empowerment in the present moment, (3) a sense of adventure and (4) opportunity for full
participation. Religion for Quakers was not an hour set aside
for Sunday services but a transformed way of being in the
world. And the world found it difficult to ignore their presence. Neither civil nor ecclesiastical authority was able to
force conformity on those belonging to the Society of
Friends. Because they believed that all persons were equally
beloved by God they refused to use deferential titles,
whether for monarchs, magistrates or bishops. Their rejection of all forms of warfare prevented them from serving in
the army and from paying taxes that would support a military
budget. Finally, their insistence on freedom of conscience
meant that they could not support a state church by paying
tithes. Punishment followed swiftly. When it became clear
that this rapidly growing group of religious rebels was threat-
ening the social order, the powers of church and state combined to coerce them into submission, using methods that
became increasingly more outrageous. Yet the same practices that aroused the wrath of the authorities attracted many
courageous souls, and their numbers grew in proportion to
the severity of their persecution. In this setting where
women were encouraged to share full responsibility, many
of them rose quickly to positions of leadership.

Quaker Simplicity

The early half of the seventeenth century was a turbulent era in English history. The struggle between Parliament and the Crown resulted in the beheading of Charles I and the establishment of the Commonwealth under Oliver Cromwell. The churches were in a state of turmoil following the Reformation. Maria Webb describes it this way: "During these boisterous times the British Protestant people formed three great sections . . . Neither the Episcopalians, the Independents, nor the Presbyterians, were men of peace. Each of their Churches, where it had power, persecuted the other for not conforming to its religious rites." [3] At this point the Society of Friends came forth insisting that true gospel principles were being obscured by the violence of the church-and-state quarrels. Boldly they declared that liberty of conscience was a God-given right belonging to every man, woman and child. This simple challenge was perceived as such a threat by those in authority that the Quakers were persecuted by whatever group held power. Ironically, these advocates of gospel principles met their fiercest opposition at the hands of the clergy. For the Quakers denied the need for a "hireling priesthood" and for "steeple-houses" in which to gather for prayer. Theirs was a direct and immediate experience of the presence of God. Geoffrey Hubbard, a twentieth-century Quaker, describes it in this way:

The Quaker discovery in worship was . . . extremely simple when once recognized. The whole idea was that Christians, or anybody else for that matter, can come together with the double freedom to engage in words or to be released from the necessity of uttering words . . . ; they were not bound to any form of words; they were not bound to silence. They simply *gathered*, *listened*, *waited*, and sought to be *obedient*. [4]

The simplicity of the Quaker approach stands out in stark contrast both to the elaborate formal rituals and to the lengthy sermons which prevailed in the other worship services of that age.

The early Quakers also managed to avoid most of the wordy theological controversies which marked the post-Reformation period. While they were eager to share their own perception of "Truth," they believed that this sharing would be primarily accomplished through the work of the Spirit. They were confident that the spark of divine life within each person was capable of responding to their witness. Thus they saw no need for lengthy theological treatises or closely reasoned arguments. Theirs was a dynamic, experiential theology that led directly to a practical ethic. George Fox says in his *Journal*: "Now, when the Lord God . . . sent me forth into the world, to preach His everlasting gospel and kingdom, I was glad that I was commanded to turn people to that inward light, spirit, and grace by which all might know their salvation, and their way to God; . . . That they might know the pure religion, might visit the fatherless, the widows, and the strangers . . ."[5] Not surprisingly, professional ministers took a dim view of this direct contact which eliminated the need for their intervention. Such stark simplicity must have baffled those who had spent years undergoing a rigorous theological training. The Quakers did not deny the validity of intellectual understanding, but insisted that the *essential* ingredient was inward experience. Hubbard offers this view of the controversy:

Intellectuals, and particularly academic and theological intellectuals, often attribute lack of rigorous thought to others, where the truth of the matter is that simple thought appears inept to those given to complexity. Real rigour is more dependent on a grasp of fundamentals; the creator of complex intellectual structures cannot forgive those who disregard the edifice and cast penetrating glances at the foundations.[6]

The Quaker message could never have spread so rapidly had not many of the English people been ready for this return to

simplicity. The Reformation had made vernacular translations of the Bible available, so that Scripture was not only
widely read but freely discussed by "nonprofessionals." No
longer revered as the sole interpreters of God's Word, the
clergy were now being criticized for having usurped too
much power. Two excerpts from Samuel Pepys' *Diary* illus-
trate the discontent which had become so widespread:

Aug. 31, 1661—At Court things are in very ill condition, there
being much emulacion, poverty, and the vices of drinking, swear-
ing, and Loose amours that I know not what will be the end of it
but confusion. And the Clergy so high, that all the people I meet
with do protest against their practice. In short I see no content or
satisfaction anywhere, in any one sort of people.

Nov. 9, 1663—[Mr. Blackburne] told me how highly the present
clergy carry themselves everywhere, so as that they are hated and
laughed at by every body: among other things, for their excom-
munications, which they send upon the least occasions that can
be.[7]

In the midst of quarrels, recriminations and conflicts, the
Quakers somehow managed (divine inspiration was their explanation) to get hold of a vision of human society where
resources were shared, initiative was encouraged, and relationships between people of high or low estate were marked
by mutual respect. Little wonder that great crowds gathered
under their banner. And women, who had had no share in
formulating any policy, whether civil or religious, must have
been delighted to be offered a part in shaping this new order.

Empowerment in the Present Moment

An immediate effect of the experience of the Inner Light
was that the recipient recognized the God-within and began
immediately to operate out of the assumption that she/he

now possessed a spark of divine life. This conviction had immediate ramifications in every aspect of their lives, both public and private. For instance, if *each* person possessed God-within, then it made no sense for a woman to promise to "love, honor and obey" in marriage. New forms then evolved within Quaker worship meetings which incorporated this insight into mutuality. Here are the words spoken by the bridegroom in an early Quaker wedding ceremony: "I take this my friend Alice Perry to be my wife, promising through divine assistance to be unto her a faithful and affectionate husband until Death shall separate us." The damsel Alice, we are told, repeated words "of like import." [8] Thus the recognition of women as full sharers of the Inner Light quickly began to reshape the powerful institution of marriage.

At another level the women themselves, quickly sensing their potential power, began to form groups in order to share their strength. During these years of formation many Quaker women suffered imprisonment under inhuman conditions. Medieval dungeons were still in use as places of confinement, and besides being filthy and ill-lighted they were frequently either so hot and smoky or so cold and wet as to be fatal. So many Quakers suffered in prisons, sometimes dying at the hands of sadistic jailers, that in 1659 one hundred forty-four Friends petitioned the House of Commons begging to take the place of those then in prison so that prisoners who were weak and ill could be released. [9] Women were not spared the cruelty of these punishments. One set of statistics from Norwich lists sixty-nine Quaker prisoners of whom twenty were women, ranging from seventeen to above sixty years of age. [10] There is no evidence, however, that these women saw themselves as submissive sacrificial victims. One letter, jointly written and signed by five women prisoners at Guildhall, embodies so well the growing sense of solidarity and protest among Quaker women that it deserves to be quoted in full:

Sher: Stubbing. We, thy prisonrs, being 5 women here in ye hole over Jno Blanchert, undr thy great severity, ye room being so little & so hot, And being it is thy strick ordr that we should not haue ye door open into ye little room next us for a little Air, there being no use made of it, wch is far from yt Christian Comand to do as thou wouldst be done unto, we being thy fellow Creatures. Jf we haue broken any Just Law, Let us be tried thereby, and not first smother us, for then 'twill be too late to trie us. We haue done nothing agt thee or any other, but only suffer for our Tendr Conscience towards God. Men ought not to usurp Authority over ye Consciences, for ye apostle saith, "Let every man be perswaded in his own mind, and if any be otherwise minded, God will reveal it to them," 'Tis not man's work. And thou wouldst think it hard to be put into such a stinking Hole, for thy Conscience. We would desire thee to Consider it, & let us haue a little Air, and not smother us privatly. We rest in ye will of the Lord, who is ye searcher of all hearts, & will reward every one according their doings,

> PRISCIL WEBB,
> LID. WEEDS,
> JANE ENGLAND,
> THEADO KENDAL,
> MARY MONK.[11]

This forthright letter bears no hint of humble supplication. These are five staunch citizens conscious of their rights under the laws of God and the English Crown. The fact that Sheriff Stubbing has temporary custody over their persons does not deter them from issuing him a stern warning about his behavior.

George Fox, founder of the Society of Friends, deserves generous credit for insisting on leadership roles for women within the group. Separate meetings for Quaker women, who were to be answerable to no one and were to handle their own finances, were defended by him. From the earliest days of the Society he had freely accepted advice from women, and Elizabeth Hooton, credited by historians with being the first Quaker convert, was immediately accepted as a public preacher. Fox's marriage with Margaret Fell was in many ways a model for the mutual relationships that characterized Quaker couples. At the time of their marriage she was the mistress of Swarthmore Hall, possessing not only wealth and social status but the responsibility of being head of the "manor house" for the market town of Ulverston. George Fox refused to claim what, by English law, would have been their joint estate. Although their correspondence testifies to their deep affection and concern for each other, they were frequently apart and both continued to make their own plans, consulting each other when it was convenient, but in no way depending on each other's approval.

Near the beginning of his *Journal* Fox describes the revelation that came to him in Leicestershire, where a great meeting of Presbyterians, Independents, Baptists and Common Prayer men were involved in dispute. At the time of Fox's revelation a priest had just refused a woman the right to speak publicly in the assembly. Here is the incident in Fox's words:

At last one woman asked a question out of Peter, what that birth was, viz., a being "born again of incorruptible seed, by the Word of God, that liveth and abideth for ever." And the priest said to her, "I permit not a woman to speak in the church"; though he had before given liberty for any to speak. Whereupon I was wrapped up, as in a rapture, in the Lord's power; and I stepped up in a place and asked the priest, "Dost thou call this place a church? Or dost thou call this mixed multitude a church?" For the woman asking a question, he ought to have answered it, having given liberty for any to speak. But, instead of answering me, he asked me what a church was: I told him the Church was the pillar and ground of Truth, made up of living stone, living members . . .[12]

On this as on other occasions Fox met with violent opposition for his courageous defense of the right of women to receive the fullness of the Spirit. At the "steeple-house" in Leicestershire the dispute ended with the priest coming out of the pulpit and the people coming out of the pews while

George Fox retreated to a nearby inn. But he refused to waver on the essential of full participation for women, even when later he met opposition from men within the Society to the formation of separate women's meetings. Quaker women of the seventeenth century responded so fully to the movement of the Spirit that it was impossible for onlookers to deny their power. Jailers were astonished at their capacity to withstand suffering, congregations at the eloquence of their preaching. Experiencing their own empowerment, these women moved into new arenas as quickly as the doors were opened to them.

A Sense of Adventure

There is a marked quality of adventure in the lives of early Quaker women, as well as a great diversity in the kinds of adventures upon which they embarked. Frequently they had no need to leave home, because their challenges came to meet them. Loveday Hambly, one of the earliest and most renowned Quaker women, served the cause by generously opening her home at Tregangeeves. There she allowed meetings to be held and extended hospitality to traveling preachers. As a convinced Quaker she resolutely refused to pay tithes, despite repeated pressures from the magistrates. In 1662 she was imprisoned at Bodmyn. Conditions in the jail were so oppressive that she became ill, but still she refused to comply. Next the magistrates allowed her livestock to be taken, and five cows, four heifers and one steer were removed from her farm. The following year the constables returned, this time carrying a "warrant of rebellion" for her arrest. Although then in her sixtieth year, she was forced to ride on a "poore bad horse which did throw & in the going to Austle town did often stumble to the endangering of her life." [13] Undaunted by this persecution, she continued to befriend her fellow Quakers until her death, refusing always to pay the unjust tithes.

A schoolteacher named Barbara Blaugdone also exercised much of her ministry in her home town, resisting the somewhat extreme measures of the Bristol authorities to rid themselves of her presence. Soon after she joined the Quakers her pupils were taken from her. Then she was imprisoned for three months for having spoken in the church. After that she was beaten, and finally she was sent out of town with a company of gypsies! A woman of great determination, she left the gypsies as soon as the sheriff's back was turned and returned to Bristol, where she continued the work of the Lord.[14]

For Dorothy Waugh it was necessary only to travel from Westmorland to Carlisle, where she testified on market day, to find herself in trouble. There she was confronted by Mayor Peter Norman, who asked whence she came. She answered, "Out of Egypt, where thou art." At this, we are told, "his wrath was so kindled against Truth and her, that he caused a bridle to be put upon her, which is said to be a stone weight, and another on her companion, & put them into ye Mute-hall, until his heat was abated."[15]

But for other Quaker women the call of the Spirit meant starting out for untried territory, frequently under hazardous conditions and with little equipment or provisions.

The academic bastions of Oxford and Cambridge provided the "untried territory" for resolute Quaker women. Recognizing that an overly academic and "professional" approach to the ministry had resulted in an alienation of believers, the early Quakers did not hesitate to challenge the "hireling priesthood." There were constant confrontations with local ministers at the time of the Sunday services. Even so it must have required considerable bravery for women to approach the powerful universities and issue a challenge to the very professors and students who considered religion their private bailiwick. In 1653 Mary Fisher and Elizabeth Williams went to Cambridge, where they "discoursed about the things of God" with the young theologians and preached publicly at the gate of Sidney College.[16] Their behavior so affronted the mayor of Cambridge that he ordered them to be taken to Market Cross, where they became the first of the Friends to be publicly scourged. Elizabeth Fletcher, a comely maid of seventeen, and her friend Elizabeth Leavens received no gentler treatment within the confines of Oxford. Their visit took place in 1654, and the scholars must have been angry beyond measure at being publicly rebuked by women. The confrontation there is described in *The First Publishers of Truth*:

. . . they suffered by the black tribe of scholars—for they dragged them first through a dirty pool, afterwards had them to a pump, and holding their mouths to the pump, endeavoured to pump water thereinto with other shameful abuses; after threw the said Elizabeth Fletcher down upon a grave stone . . . and bruised her so sore that she never recovered it.[17]

Many women left England as part of the remarkable early Quaker missionary effort. A letter produced at the Skipton general meeting in 1660 depicts the scope of these travels. Included are such farflung places as Tuscany, Turkey, Norway, Barbados, Bermuda and Newfoundland.[18] Although courage, vitality and a willingness to endure privation marked all of the traveling preachers, it could be fairly stated that the women showed a certain propensity for arriving first. Women led the way to Malta, Corinth, Smyrna and the new American settlements in Massachusetts and Virginia.[19]

The account of Mary Fisher's travels provides an astonishing example of constancy in the face of overwhelming obstacles. After her cruel treatment at the hands of the Cambridge magistrates she sailed to the West Indies. While she was witnessing there she felt a clear call to communicate the new message to the Turkish Sultan, Mohammed IV. Setting out alone for his headquarters at Adrianople, she got only as far as Smyrna, where she was detained by an overly conscientious English consul who feared for her safety. Unable to dissuade her, he arranged for her to be taken on board a vessel that was sailing back to Venice. Undaunted, Mary persuaded the ship's captain to put her ashore on the coast of Greece. From there she traveled on foot through Macedonia and the mountains of Thrace. After finally reaching the Sultan's encampment, she had trouble finding anyone bold enough to speak to the Grand Vizier on her behalf. When this had been accomplished, however, the young Sultan agreed to grant her an audience. He and his assembled court listened attentively as an interpreter translated what she had to say. The content of her message has not been recorded, yet the Sultan must have been impressed, because he invited her to remain for a time in his domains. But Mary Fisher had other work to do. Declining the Sultan's offer of a protective escort, she returned to England "without the least hurt or scoff." [20]

Elizabeth Hooton was also a woman of boundless stamina and perseverance. Her journeys, undertaken at the promptings of the Spirit, continued throughout her long life. Born in 1600, this first convert to the Quaker cause met George Fox in 1646, near the beginning of his public ministry. Fox notes their meeting in his *Journal*: "Traveling on through some parts of Leicestershire and into Nottinghamshire, I met with a tender people, and a very tender woman, whose name was Elizabeth Hooton; and with these I had some meetings and discourses. But my troubles continued . . . for I was a man of sorrows in the times of the first workings of the Lord in me." [21] At the time, Elizabeth Hooton, twenty-four years Fox's senior, was a comfortably established married woman, already a successful preacher of the Gospel. The deep faith of this woman undoubtedly had a profound effect on the troubled young man of twenty-two, and their discussions must have affected the subsequent development of the Society of Friends. They remained close friends and co-workers throughout Elizabeth's lifetime. Elizabeth Hooton's first missionary work was among the Quaker groups in the north of England. In the records of Henley-on-Thames is written: "Also Eliz Hutton . . . came, and vised us early." [22] During this period she suffered repeated imprisonments but continued to carry on her successful ministry, preaching to fellow prisoners while she was in jail. Besse records that in 1651 she was imprisoned at Derby for "speaking to one of the Priests there, who so resented her Reproof that he applied to the Magistrate to punish her. For it is common with Men who most deserve Reprehension, to be most offended with those who administer it." [23] Later Elizabeth was imprisoned at York Castle for sixteen months for having spoken in the church at Rotherham. While in jail she also carried on a lively correspondence with those in high places. A letter written to Oliver Cromwell in 1653 shows that while an inmate she was critically observant of the corruption of the prison system:

Your Judges Judge for reward, And at this Yorke many wch Comitted murder escaped throughe frends & money, & pore people for Lesser facts are put to death; . . . many was but delivred from the psence of the Judges in to the hands of two greate Tirantes viz. the Gaoler & the Clearke of the Assize & these two keepes many pore Creatures still in prison for fees . . . They [the prisoners] Lighe worse then doggs for want of strawe . . . [24]

The letter typifies Elizabeth Hooton's concern for the poor and her outspoken approach to correcting the evils of her day.

The reception of Mary Fisher and Ann Austin, the first two Quakers to visit Boston, had been unreasonably hostile. Word of their ill-treatment and of the subsequent harassment of Quakers in the American colonies reached England and was the cause of grave concern. Elizabeth Hooton and her friend Joan Broksopp felt called to visit this new territory in the year 1661. At this time the political climate in the Massachusetts Bay Colony was particularly repressive. The close ties between the magistrates and the ministers resulted in religious liberty being considered by the authorities as dangerously close to treason. The Reverend Mr. Ward of Ipswich, Massachusetts, stated this viewpoint succinctly: "It is said that men ought to have liberty of conscience and that it is *persecution* to debar them of it. I can rather stand amazed than reply to this. It is an astonishment that the brains of a man should be parboiled in such impious ignorance." [25] Elizabeth Hooton certainly understood the physical dangers that awaited her in New England; she also recognized the inconsistency in the behavior of Puritan leaders who had earlier fled England to ensure their own religious liberty. The following comment shows her assessment of their policies:

This is to lay before friends or all where it may come of the sufferings & persecutions which we suffered in newe England I Elizabeth Hooton have tasted on by the prefessours of Boston & Cambridge, who call themselves Independents who fled from the bishops formerly, which have behaved themselves, worse then the bishops did to them by many degries, making the people of God to suffer much more then ever they did by the bishops which causeth their name to stink all over the world becaus of cruelty. [26]

So greatly did the Massachusetts authorities fear a Quaker incursion that they passed a law forbidding ship captains (under penalty of £100) to deliver such undesirables to the port of Boston. Thus the ship bearing Elizabeth Hooton and Joan Broksopp was forced to land in Virginia. From there the two resolute women, advanced in years and unaccustomed to the perils of the wilderness, proceeded to walk toward New England. Fortunately, they obtained passage on a small ketch, which helped them cover part of the distance. Upon their arrival in Boston they were immediately imprisoned, but Governor Endicott decided that they presented too great a danger to be allowed to remain, even under confinement, and they were banished a two days' journey into the wilderness escorted by armed men on horseback. After this episode the practical Elizabeth decided that

it was necessary to have a Quaker homeowner in Boston.
This homeowner would then be able to provide immediate
aid to fellow Quakers when they suffered persecution there.
Returning to England, she petitioned the King for permission to purchase land in Boston so that she could build a
house. The following excerpt concerning her negotiations
with Charles II shows how little she was concerned with
courtly protocol:

I waited upon the King which way souer he went, I mett him in
the Parke, and gave him two letters . . . but the people murmered
because I did not Kneele, but I went along by the King and spoke
as I went . . . I waited for an answer many dayes, and watch for
his goeing up into the Coach in the Court, and some souldiers
began to be favorable to me, and soe let me speake to the King,
and soe the power of the Lord was raised in me, and I spoke freely
to the King and Counsell, that I waited for Justice . . .[27]

Finally the King granted permission, and she sailed off once
more for Boston. There, however, the royal authorization
was ignored and Elizabeth Hooton was sentenced to the
savage punishment of being tied to the tail of a cart and
forced to walk to the whipping posts in the towns of Cambridge, Watertown and Dedham. At each post she was
stripped to the waist and beaten with a three-corded whip.
Finally she was taken deep into the wilderness on horseback.
In matter-of-fact fashion she describes this ordeal: "So they
put me on a horse and carried me into ye wildernesse many
miles, where was many wild beasts both bears and wolves &
many deep waters where I waded through . . . but ye Lord
delivered me."[28] She not only survived intact but later embarked with George Fox on a missionary journey to Jamaica.
There she died a peaceful death, far from her native village
in Nottinghamshire.

Mary Dyer was well known to the Boston magistrates.
Unlike the other Quaker women, she was a member of the

Massachusetts Bay Colony, having been one of the earlier and more prominent settlers. As early as 1635 she and her husband, William, had arrived from England and been immediately accepted as members of the Boston church. During the time of the Antinomian Controversy, Mary Dyer was one of Anne Hutchinson's most faithful supporters. On the day that Anne Hutchinson was publicly banished from the church in Boston, Mary Dyer left her place in the congregation to walk out at the side of her friend. At that time there were no Quakers in the Bay Colony, but the principles espoused by the "Antinomians" (ongoing revelation and immediate experience of the divine) were similar to those later developed in the Society of Friends. Mary and William Dyer left Massachusetts in protest over Anne Hutchinson's banishment and, in 1638, were among the eighteen founders of Portsmouth, Rhode Island.[29] Shortly after their arrival there William Dyer was made secretary of Portsmouth and Newport, and by 1649 he was the attorney general of the colony.[30] Mary was also well respected. An account written at the time of her death calls her "a comely grave Woman, and of a goodly Personage, and one of good Report, having a Husband of an Estate, fearing the Lord, and a Mother of Children."[31] When in 1651 William Dyer left the colony it was to join Mary, then visiting in England, where she remained for another five years. It was during this interval that she joined the Quakers. Thus she had been out of the country when Ann Austin and Mary Fisher first brought the Quaker message to Massachusetts in 1656.

Apparently she was not arrested upon her return by way of Boston (although the law forbidding Quakers free entry was then in effect), because she was coming to rejoin her family in Portsmouth. But she was not satisfied to remain in Rhode Island, which had become a haven for religious freedom. Following that first law requiring ship captains to pay a fine for transportation of Quakers, the treatment of Quakers by the General Court of Massachusetts became increasingly harsh. Every Quaker coming into the jurisdiction was to be taken immediately to prison and "soundly whipped at the entrance."[32] A later law fined those who harbored Quakers, at the rate of forty shillings per hour, and threatened Quakers who returned after a first offense with having an ear cut off.[33] Incredible pressures were placed on local residents who refused to join in the persecution. In Salem an elderly couple, Lawrence and Cassandra Southwick, were fined and later whipped for lodging Quakers. They refused to attend church under these conditions and were repeatedly fined until their property was completely gone. The General Court then authorized the county treasurer to sell their children into slavery. This law, enacted May 11, 1659, states:

Whereas Daniell and Provided Southwicke sonne and daughter to Lawrence Southwicke, have been fyned by the County Courts at Salem & Ipswich, ptending they haue no estates, resolving not to worke, and others likewise haue binn fyned, & more like to be fyned, for siding with the Quakers & absenting themselves from the publicke ordinances—in ansr to a question, what course shall be taken for the satisfaction of the fines, the Court, on pervsall of the lawe, Title Arrests, resolve, that the Treasurers of the seuerall countjes are and shall hereby be impowered to sell the sajd persons to any of the English Nation at Virginia or Barbadoes.[34]

It must have appeared to Mary Dyer and her fellow martyrs, William Robinson and Marmaduke Stephenson, that only drastic measures could prevail against such barbarism. Perhaps their deaths would so horrify the people that the magistrates would be forced to repeal their unjust laws. Mary Dyer expresses her intention clearly in a letter to the General Court in Boston written just after she had received the first sentence of death: "Whereas I am by many charged with the Guiltiness of my own Blood; if you mean, in my coming to Boston, I am therein clear, and justified by the Lord, in whose Will I came, who will require my Blood of you, be sure, who have made a Law to take away the Lives of the Innocent Servants of God . . ."[35] Only a firm conviction that she acted in a just cause could have strengthened her to refuse her own reprieve from the gallows unless the law were annulled. An early account, printed in London the following year, describes the event:

She stept up the Ladder and had her Coats tied about her feet, and the Rope put about her neck, with her face covered, and as the Hangman was ready to turn her off, they cryed out to stop, for she was reprieved, and loosing her feet and bid her to come down, but she was not forward to come down, but stood still saying she was there willing to suffer as her Brethren did; unlesse they would null their wicked Law, she had no freedom to accept their reprieve . . .[36]

After the reprieve, which had been secured by her family, she spent the winter on Shelter Island. Recognizing that her task was unfinished, she returned to Boston in May. Once more she was sentenced by the General Court to be hanged. This time there was no reprieve, and Mary Dyer died on May 31, 1660. As she had hoped, there was strong public opposition to her death. Word reached England, and shortly thereafter the King commanded Massachusetts authorities to rescind the death penalty for Quakers.

These pioneer Quaker women differed greatly from one another in their response to the call of the Spirit, yet there are certain similarities in their stories. They moved with apparent ease from positions of dependency or supportive roles within their families. Elizabeth Hooton's husband objected to her ministry, and William Dyer tried repeatedly to prevent his wife from reaching the gallows, yet these women made autonomous decisions and carried them out. Traveling alone, frequently under dangerous conditions, presented no problem for them. In some cases, their well-meaning "protectors" (as in the case of the English consul who feared for Mary Fisher's safety) simply presented an additional obstacle to be overcome. Finally, it should be noted how frequently they received their support from other women. Elizabeth

Fletcher and Elizabeth Leavens, Mary Fisher and Ann Austin, Elizabeth Hooton and Joan Broksopp were just a few among the many teams of Quaker women who traveled together. And Mary Dyer's long friendship with Anne Hutchinson certainly must have prepared her for her final courageous sacrifice. From reading their stories, singly or collectively, it would be difficult to conclude that there is any inherent weakness in women's nature.

Opportunity for Full Participation

The sense of joy and enthusiasm that pervades the lives of these early Quakers cannot be explained in any of the ordinary ways in which we define human happiness. They had little material security, they suffered ridicule from their fellow citizens, and they lived under the constant threat of imprisonment. What they did possess, though, was a sense that they were participating in the creation of a new order. The Quakers of the seventeenth century believed in the possibility of changing the social order. In a simple, straightforward manner they began to implement such changes in their daily lives. High officials might be angered at not being addressed by their deferential titles, but on this seemingly insignificant matter the Quakers could not be swayed, because it provided them with an opportunity to demonstrate mutual respect between human persons. In the same manner they refused to take oaths, because speaking under oath implied a lesser standard of honesty for ordinary discourse. Somehow the very newness of what they attempted provided different ways of sharing both private and public responsibilities. In the public sphere particularly, this meant increasing openness to participation by women.

Throughout English history all major religious groups had reserved public preaching for men. But Quaker women were encouraged to listen for the voice of the Spirit and follow its lead, even into the pulpit. Women addressed small groups gathered for worship as well as vast public gatherings. As we have seen, these women preachers encountered a great deal of opposition, especially from the professional male ministry. But there was no way for the Quakers to give in on this point without rejecting the principle of direction by the Inner Light. A spirited defense of this practice, written by Margaret Fell in 1666, is entitled *Women's Speaking, Justified, Proved, and Allowed of by the Scriptures*. It contains not only a well-wrought argument (based on Scripture) for the right to preach, but also a strong plea for the recognition of spiritual equality between women and men. In an expanded version published the following year Margaret Fell challenged the priests for putting the songs of Elizabeth and Mary into the Book of Common Prayer if they did not believe in the capacity of women to receive the Spirit of God. She also refers to the powerful prophecy of Huldah found in 2 Kings 22, saying, "Now let us see if any of you, blind Priests, can speak after this manner, and see if it be not a better Sermon than any of you can make, who are against Women's Speaking." [37]

Women were quick to seize the opportunity to speak in public. Besides the well-known traveling preachers already considered, there were many lesser-known women who began by speaking out in their family circles and developed confidence to move into the public realm. Alice Hayes, author of an autobiography called *A Legacy: or Widow's Mite*, followed such a pattern. In her book she describes her progress from a shy witness of the Quaker faith to the effective preacher she eventually became. She tells of an incident when her father-in-law voiced his opposition to her Quaker conversion:

My Father-in-Law used many bitter Expressions . . . He began to Curse and Swear, for which I could not forbear reproving of him, and that in the *Plain Language*, and that enrag'd him, that he was like a mad Man, Cursing and saying, "Do not Thee and Thou me"; and in a despising Manner said, "A Quaker! Away with it: If you had been any Thing else; had you been a Baptist, and gone to hear them every Day in the Week, it had not been so bad as this." [38]

Having survived this family confrontation, she progressed to a public discussion with the Anglican parish priest which resulted in many of the parishioners coming to Quaker meetings. Finally, as a public preacher, she led a group of Friends in a protest against paying tithes. The opportunity to speak in public was welcomed by many Quaker women as a way to participate more fully in the Christian community.

Equally important contributions were made by means of the printed word. In a book entitled *The Literary Life of the Early Friends*, Luella M. Wright explains why the writings of the Friends are important in the history of English literature: "They represent the ideals of a nonconformist group, impregnated with concepts of the spirituality of life and of religious liberty which they were willing to write for, die for, and live for." [39] Quaker writings fulfilled an immediate need for the members of the Society during the 1660s. Many of the leaders had been imprisoned, and so many of the others had departed on missionary journeys that the group needed a way to keep an ever-expanding membership in touch with each other. Lloyd talks about the way that books and pamphlets helped to consolidate the group at this time:

The method of buying Monthly Meeting subscription, used as early as 1656, gave individual members access to a great variety of more expensive books than they could have afforded themselves and the joint-ownership of the library was itself a unifying influence. . . . It is quite impossible to estimate the influence of books in moulding the character, in setting the standards and, it may be said, in enhancing the self-esteem of the Quakers during the formative period of the growth of their society. [40]

From the earliest days of the Society women were part of the writing and the publishing of such influential works. Margaret Fell wrote tracts explaining the position of the

Quakers on important issues of the day. Her collected works also contain powerful letters addressed to the King, and to the magistrates and people of England. She is also credited with writing the first Quaker poem.[41] The beginning of her letter written to King Charles in 1666 gives the flavor of her direct style:

KING CHARLES, I desire thee to Read this over, which may be for thy Satisfaction and Profit.

In the Fear of the Lord God stand still, and consider what thou and you have been doing these six years . . . What Laws have you made or changed, save such as have laid Oppression on the Consciences of God's People . . .[42]

Such a letter, circulated through the monthly meetings, would surely have strengthened and encouraged those present. Besides numerous pamphlets and letters there are travel accounts, such as that written by Elizabeth Hooton, and autobiographies. Two of the autobiographies written at this time have been cited in a recent study for their narrative skill and ability to convey psychological complexity.[43]

Still other women were involved in the business operations of the Quaker press. The scope of this enterprise is illustrated by the fact that more than 2,500 books and pamphlets had been published by the turn of the century. Lloyd emphasizes that this is one new title for every week from the beginning of the Society.[44] Little is known of the lives of the women printers, but we do know some of the works for which they were responsible. The widow Inman printed a tract written by a Quaker named William Smith. A woman printer, Mary Westwood, printed Quaker pamphlets which, Lloyd notes, were done throughout "in italics." Elizabeth and Giles Calvert printed and published so many "seditious" works that in 1663 Elizabeth was forced to sign a bond for the amount of £600. Finally there is Tace, daughter of master printer Andrew Sowle, who took over her father's business in 1691.[45]

Women were also adept at handling finances in the early years of Quaker history. In this area also we see the strength of Margaret Fell's leadership. During the period of the Commonwealth most of the Quaker finances were handled through the Kendall fund, originated by Margaret Fell, to which funds were contributed by groups in Cumberland, Lancashire and Westmorland.[46] Her daughter, Sarah, was a competent bookkeeper and kept accurate accounts in the Swarthmore Account Book, still preserved in London. Because women were charged with handling the finances of their own meetings, many of them gained valuable experience in accounting procedures. Ross describes the "box meeting" which is another of their enterprises:

The Box Meeting (which still exists in London, and has an unbroken record of minutes from 1671) was composed entirely of women, and got its peculiar name from the fact that it gathered money into a box, and disbursed it for the relief of the poor and needy. . . . It met once a week, and was not accountable to any other body.[47]

The nonhierarchical structure of Quaker meetings ensured that decision-making would be shared, and many women welcomed the opportunity to try these new experiences. How seriously they took their responsibilities can be seen in the following instructions for quarterly women's meetings, written by Sarah Fell in 1681:

The first business to be done is to call over the Meetings, and see that there be some women from every particular meeting in the county . . . At the meeting which is in the 7th month of every year, inquiry must be made how it is with the women in every particular meeting in the county as to the clearness of their testimonies against tithes, unrighteous demands, touching the priest's wages and steeple-house repairs . . .[48]

An important factor for encouraging the full participation of Quaker women is that they had Margaret Fell as a model of a resourceful woman. She wrote powerful letters to those in authority condemning the unjust laws and challenging them to live up to the promises they had made. A great part of her correspondence was with the women and men from the north of England who are known as the "First Publishers of Truth." Isabel Ross explains the key role played by Margaret Fell's strategic planning in this venture:

The seed-sowing time . . . was not an unrelated wandering of inspired individuals; it had Swarthmoor Hall as its base, and Margaret Fell as its guiding mother, providing also spiritual and material help. The travellers reported to her in what towns and counties they were working, and where they believed God was leading them to go next, and they frequently reported the movements of their fellow-preachers. It was Margaret at Swarthmoor who seemed to keep a plan of their movements, so that there was no overlapping, and so that all places could be covered.[49]

It would be difficult to overestimate the contribution of Margaret Fell to the formation of the Society of Friends.

The open and accepting attitude of most of the men in the Society also encouraged the women to join in the collective activity. An incident that well illustrates this openness is that concerning William Penn's decision at Pennsylvania's one and only witchcraft trial.

After a Quaker jury had found the woman innocent, Penn asked her "Art thou a witch? Hast thou ridden through the air on a broomstick?" To her affirmative reply, Penn answered that she had a perfect right to ride on a broomstick, that he knew of no law whatever against it, and ordered her discharge.[50]

An interesting footnote to that story is that William Penn had borrowed a sum of £300 from the London women's meeting to help establish the colony of Pennsylvania.[51]

Quaker history for the first fifty years is so filled with confidence and hope that it is discouraging to note the signs of conformity that begin to appear at the end of the first half century. Margaret Fell, in her final letter to the Friends, warns them of the dangers of quenching the Spirit. She insists that legal ceremonies are far from gospel freedom and begs them not to lead young Friends to an observation of "outward things":

Away with these whimsical narrow imaginations, and let the Spirit of God which He hath given us, lead us and guide us . . . Jesus saith that we must take no thought what we shall eat, or what we shall drink, or what we shall put on, but bids us consider the lilies . . . But contrary to this we the Quakers must look at no colours, nor make anything that is changeable colours as the hills are . . . This is a silly poor gospel. It is more fit for us to be covered with God's eternal spirit.[52]

Margaret Fell was disturbed at the tendency toward conformity in dress which was just beginning to appear among the Quakers. But somehow her wholeness of vision is dimmed in the move toward external conformity. The vital young society which had successfully challenged the abuse of power in both ecclesiastical and civil courts began to turn inward on itself and insist on "Quaker grey." At the same time women were slowly pushed back into subordinate roles.

Here are two examples of this disheartening trend. Elizabeth Redford, in her ministry at the Wandsworth meeting in June of 1695, encouraged Friends to withhold taxes that would support the current war; she was then threatened with disownment because her witness contradicted the judgment of the Meeting of Ministers.[53] In London, where the women ministers had begun to hold Saturday meetings in order to plan their schedules for the following day's services, the men decided in 1701 to suppress the women's planning meetings because the women ministers were taking up too much time and thereby preventing men from serving. It was decided that in the future women who wished to minister at any particular meeting should "leave their names at the central office."[54]

In a reversal of the spontaneous surge of spiritual power that had occurred fifty years earlier, women's leadership roles were now being discouraged, and at the same time official policy concerning methods of civil disobedience was becoming more conservative. Nevertheless, the history of Quaker women during the latter half of the seventeenth century deserves to be studied more closely. The vital women of this period exemplify an astonishing range of possibilities. We need to understand more about the social conditions and the sense of personal empowerment that enables such women to break through old boundaries.

NOTES

1. Norman Penney (ed.), *First Publishers of Truth* (London: Headley Brothers, 1907), p. 87.

2. John P. Fry, *The Advent of Quakerism* (London: Forsaith, 1908), p. 15.

3. Maria Webb, *The Fells of Swarthmore Hall* (Philadelphia: Longstreth, 1884), pp. 29, 30.

4. D. Elton Trueblood, *The People Called Quakers* (New York: Harper & Row, 1966), pp. 87, 88.

5. George Fox, *Journal*, revised by Norman Penney (New York: Dutton, 1924), p. 21.

6. Geoffrey Hubbard, *Quaker by Convincement* (Middlesex: Penguin Books, 1974), p. 53.

7. Samuel Pepys, *The Diary of Samuel Pepys* (New York: Croscup & Sterling, 1893).

8. Caroline Hazard, *Narragansett Friends' Meeting* (Boston/New York: Houghton Mifflin, 1900), p. 129.

9. Hubbard, *Quaker by Convincement*, pp. 37, 38.

10. Penney, *First Publishers*, p. 184.

11. *Ibid.*, pp. 190, 191.

12. Fox, *Journal*, pp. 14, 15.

13. L. V. Hodgkin, *A Quaker Saint of Cornwall: Loveday Hambly and Her Guests* (London: Longmans, Green, 1927), p. 153, quoting *Record of Suffering of Friends in Cornwall, 1655–1792*.

14. Charles Evans, *Friends in the Seventeenth Century* (Philadelphia: For Sale at Friends Bookstore, 1876), pp. 73, 74.

15. Penney, *First Publishers*, p. 69.

16. Frances Anne Budge, *Annals of the Early Friends* (London: Samuel Harris, 1877), p. 188.

17. Penney, *First Publishers*, pp. 258, 259.

18. Trueblood, *People Called Quakers*, p. 250.

19. Evans, *Friends*, p. 155, and Budge, *Annals*, p. 190, for Mary Fisher's travels; Douglass S. Brown, *A History of Lynchburg's Pioneer Quakers and Their Meetinghouse* (Lynchburg: J. P. Bell Co., 1936), pp. 19 and 29, for arrival of Elizabeth Harris, Mary Fisher and Ann Austin; Penney, *First Publishers*, p. 228, for Malta trip of Katherine Evans and Sarah Cheevers.

20. Budge, *Annals*, pp. 190–192.

21. Fox, *Journal*, pp. 7, 8.

22. Penney, *First Publishers*, p. 219. Spelling for her surname appears as Hooton, Houton and Hutton.

23. Besse, *Sufferings of the Quakers* (1753), vol. I, p. 137, quoted in Emily Manners, *Elizabeth Hooton: First Quaker Woman Preacher* (London: Headley Brothers, 1914), p. 6.

24. Manners, *Elizabeth Hooton*, p. 10.

25. *Ibid.*, p. 18, quoting Callender, *Historical Discourses* (Boston, 1739).

26. *Ibid.*, p. 30.

27. *Ibid.*, pp. 36, 37.

28. *Ibid.*, p. 41.

29. George Hodges, *The Hanging of Mary Dyer, The Apprenticeship of Washington and Other Sketches of Significant Colonial Personages* (New York: Moffat, Yard and Co., 1909), p. 53.

30. *Ibid.*, p. 54.

31. *Ibid.*, p. 52.

32. Richard P. Hallowell, *The Quakers in New England* (Philadelphia: Merrihew & Son, 1870), appendix, p. 30.

33. Hodges, *Hanging of Mary Dyer*, p. 68.

34. Hallowell, *Quakers in New England*, appendix, p. 32.

35. Horatio Rogers, *Mary Dyer of Rhode Island: The Quaker Martyr That Was Hanged on Boston Common* (Providence, R.I.: Preston & Rounds, 1896), Appendix II, p. 84.

36. G. T. Paine (ed.), *A Call from Death to Life, being an account of the sufferings of Marmaduke Stephenson, William Robinson and Mary Dyer in New England, in the year 1659* (Printed by Friends in London, 1660), p. 46.

37. Margaret Fell, A *Brief Collection of Remarkable Passages and Occurrences Relating to the Birth, Life, Conversion, Travels, Services and Deep Sufferings of that Ancient, Eminent, and Faithful Servant of the Lord, Margaret Fell* (London: J. Sowle, 1710), p. 345.

38. Catherine La Courreye Blecki, "Alice Hayes and Mary Penington: Personal Identity Within the Traditions of Quaker Spiritual Autobiography," *Quaker History*, vol. LXV (Spring 1976), p. 24.

39. Luella M. Wright, *The Literary Life of the Early Friends, 1650–1725* (New York: Columbia University, 1932), p. 238.

40. Arnold Lloyd, *Quaker Social History 1669–1738* (New York: Longmans, Green, 1950), p. 154.

41. Mary H. Jones, *Quaker Poets Past and Present*, Pendle Hill Pamphlet 102 (Wallingford, Pa., 1975), p. 11.

42. Fell, *Brief Collection*, p. 325.

43. Blecki, "Alice Hayes and Mary Penington," *loc. cit.*, p. 31.

44. Lloyd, *Quaker Social History*, p. 147.

45. *Ibid.*, pp. 147–50.

46. *Ibid.*, p. 157.

47. Isabel Ross, *Margaret Fell: Mother of Quakerism* (London/New York/Toronto: Longmans, Green, 1949), p. 284.

48. Webb, *The Fells*, pp. 355, 356.

49. Ross, *Margaret Fell*, pp. 45–47.

50. A. Ruth Fry, *Quaker Ways* (London/Toronto/Melbourne/Sydney: Cassell, 1933), p. 69.

51. Lloyd, *Quaker Social History*, p. 113.

52. Letter from MS. at Devonshire House, Post 25–66, dated "2nd mo. 1700," quoted in W. K. Baker, *George and Margaret Fox* (London: Routledge, 1927), pp. 113–14.

53. Lloyd, *Quaker Social History*, p. 92.

54. *Ibid.*, p. 118.

SIX

Jane Lead: The Feminist Mind and Art of a Seventeenth-Century Protestant Mystic

CATHERINE F. SMITH

The idea that mysticism and feminism share common elements is generally unfamiliar, even unacceptable. Mysticism is idealist in its philosophy, apolitical in its ends, and often patriarchal in its concepts. Feminism is materialist, activist, and is usually traced to rational thought rather than nonrational, to logical theories of equality rather than visions of unity. Until now, mainly the unsympathetic, with an eye toward the lunatic fringe, have connected feminism with irrationality. A recent historian of the occult, for example, has observed that the sort of people who joined the nineteenth-century Theosophists were

> hosts of women, those on whose hands time hung heavy, and to whom every tick of their drawing-room clock spelled boredom and imprisonment. It is significant that the Movement for Woman's Suffrage and the Theosophical Movement ran in England simultaneous courses.[1]

I cite this hostile example only to agree that the coincidence is indeed significant and to propose that the reasons for it deserve serious attention. To study mysticism and feminism together is to learn more about the links between envisioning power and pursuing it. Idealist analogues of transcendence may shape political notions of sexual equality as much as materialist or rationalist arguments do. In the revolutionary body of thought called Romanticism, this mixture is well documented. The double inheritance of idealist and materialist philosophy in Romantic thought leads clearly to an "as above so below" mirroring of the imaginative world of ideal forms and the actual one of politics.[2]

In contrast, study of the intellectual history of feminism lacks a developed consideration of its debts to nonrational, nonmaterialist traditions. As a result, we know too little about the structure of vision in feminist politics. Major studies of both mysticism and feminism have ignored or distorted these questions. In her pioneering *Essentials of Mysticism*, Evelyn Underhill treats a majority of female mystics but does not comment on their gender. Their erotic imagery to express spiritual conditions and their craving for protective love are described as regrettable lapses in the quality of their mysticism.[3] Simone de Beauvoir's *The Second Sex* explains women mystics as pathological personalities, as masochists and narcissists. De Beauvoir adds that some women mystics present a vision of redeemed life that is essentially feminine, but rather than considering the possible backgrounds of their vision she faults them for wanting to redeem femininity. Better to transcend it, she suggests.[4] Alice Rossi's social history *The Feminist Papers* is a tantalizingly incomplete study of related religious and feminist thought. Rossi convincingly shows that orthodox theology carried over into moral reformism and influenced feminist activism in Elizabeth Cady Stanton and others. But Margaret Fuller's early interest in Transcendentalism, a blend of esoteric theology and occult philosophy, is treated as an intellectual cocoon, an idealist limbo from which she surprisingly emerged to active, radical humanism.[5] Mary Wollstonecraft's continuing associations with political radicals who were also theological radicals are not discussed.[6]

Critical views seem thus to hold that while orthodox religion may lead indirectly to advocacy of women's rights, unorthodox or mystical beliefs relate to feminism very little, if at all. But, as Katharine Hepburn says in *The African Queen*, coming out of that swamp thought to be impenetrable, "Nevertheless . . ." Feminist poetry and theory reveal the integral link that critical opinion has neglected. Robin Morgan, in a poem called "The City of God," observes:

> *Politics is not enough.*
> *Poetry is not enough.*
> *Nothing is not enough.*
>
> *If I could smash the carapace.*
>
> *Only God would be enough, and She*
> *is constricted inside my torture-chamber ribs,*
> *this whole planet one bubble that floats briefly*
> *from her drowning mouth*
> *up toward breaking.*
>
> *Oh my God, if I could wholly love Thee,*
> *Wholly be mine Own, then I would not be snared*
> *in loving all these fragments of Thee.*[7]

Sylvia Plath, in imagery of honey bees in "Stings," says:

> *. . . but I*
> *Have a self to recover, a queen.*
> *Is she dead, is she sleeping?*
> *Where has she been,*
> *With her lion-red body, her wings of glass?* [8]

Jill Johnston, in her utopian work *Lesbian Nation: The Feminist Solution*, resolves: ". . . except a woman be born again she cannot see the Kingdom of Goddess a woman must be born again to be herself her own eminence. . . ." [9]

The idea of woman's god-self or queen-self in these three statements comes from no orthodox theology. Rather, the idea is traditional within esoteric thought, notably certain types of mysticism. Occult philosophy and religion have always formed a countertradition offering an alternative epistemology and a protest against prevailing orthodoxies. That countertradition may have been more congenial to women as thinkers, and to the development of feminist thought, than mainstream theology in any age. Each age has had its women mystics, even when its otherwise outspoken women were few. The numbers of those mystics and the spiritualists, transcendentalists, artists and activists drawn to occult thought may be a misunderstood signal from several related areas of women's history. By widening the intellectual history of modern feminism to include its share of mysticism, we recognize a grafting onto ancient roots of thought, and we discern a joined root of patriarchy and feminism. By critically examining women's mystical writing, we rediscover a special and neglected category of literary history. Women mystics in many ages, like feminists in ours, have found a language for visions of female power in the literary type called revelations. The work of those mystics may have long been a significant form of women's protest and self-affirmation within patriarchal culture.

Jane Lead, who lived from 1624 until 1704, demonstrated these dimensions of thought and art in her life and work. Her life spanned three quarters of the turbulent seventeenth century—the age of the Reformation in Europe and of Puritanism, the execution of a king, and civil war in her native England. During that time, Copernican theories redesigned the universe, and large-scale emigration from the Old World to the New remapped world politics. Ancient world views faded, carrying with them particular systems such as magic, astrology, alchemy, established mystic theology, and much else that had respectably fed imaginative life for centuries. But while commitment to Enlightenment rationalism grew, resistance to the philosophical shift was continuous. Active disagreement came from the proliferating religious sects such as the Ranters, the Diggers, and the Quakers, who drew on the receding authority of nonrational thought to support their belief in a transcendent spirit and their hopes for immediate apocalypse in those politically unstable times. Such groups varied in their expectations of a universal millennium, but all stressed individual, personal transformation. As Norman Cohn describes this period in *The Pursuit of the Millennium*, prophecies were uttered all around and ecstasies were everyday occurrences.[10]

Within this context, Jane Lead, an ordinary Englishwoman in her forty-sixth year, was left a widow in 1670. Her emotional and intellectual life profoundly deepened after her husband's death. Like many others, she had frequently experienced ecstatic trances, which now became her guides for living. Through Enthusiast friends, she discovered the mystic thought of the German philosopher Jacob Boehme (1575–1624) and interpreted her experience by its perspectives. A new life began for her as a prophet and prolific writer of visionary revelations. A practical mystic more interested in spiritual guidance than in metaphysics, she was a principal organizer of the Philadelphian Society, a sect of Boehme's advocates and a forerunner of the Theosophists, who coincided with nineteenth-century feminism and who are still active in the twentieth century.[11]

Boehme was a major conduit of traditional occult and mystical thought for Lead, as he was for a number of other, better-known European and English thinkers. His syncretistic work combined Gnosticism, hermeticism, astrology, alchemy, and Jewish and Christian mysticism. Those bodies of thought had reemerged along with Neoplatonism earlier in the Renaissance and had served as a corrective to the rationalist basis of humanism. Boehme's work gave them new energy to oppose the new rationalism of the Enlightenment. He developed the idealist hybrid known as Theosophy and contributed to the theology of Protestant "Inner Light" mysticism. His thought had entered the brew of English sectarian controversy around 1644, several decades before Lead encountered it.[12]

A striking component of Boehme's writing is his systematic sexual metaphor. From the Wisdom literature of Scripture, the Jewish Kabala, and alchemical philosophy, Boehme structured a cosmology in sexual imagery to express the processes of existence and the unity underlying them that he had ecstatically perceived. From Gnostic heresies, he drew on the concept of a primary female ground of unconditioned being called Sophia, or Wisdom. In Boehme's system, this female ground of being is prior to and then coexistent with the creating, masculine deity. Existence begins when the creative male will of God disturbs the prior, female possibility. Along with existence inevitably comes opposition and loss of potentiality. No thing comes into being without reductiveness and without simultaneously projecting its opposite, not-self. Originally patterned by attraction and repulsion, then, existence is a continual dialectical relationship of potentiality and actuality that Boehme images as female–male struggle. Ideal unity is a product of this dialectic that Boehme images as the androgyne, or male enclosing the female, most often symbolized by Christ's reunion with his mother/bride, Sophia. United erotically or through an alchemical marriage of subject and object, they form a virginal, apocalyptic self.

The significance of Boehme's symbolic sexual cosmos cannot be overlooked. It has expressively accompanied his wide influence in science, philosophy, religion, literature and the visual arts. Its parts had been familiar but scattered throughout his own sources in tradition. Boehme schematized them and passed them on to makers of modern thought such as Isaac Newton, Schelling, Hegel, Nietzsche, Schopenhauer, Marx and Bergson. His ideas spread principally, at first, by sectarian advocates such as Lead, a point that has been obscured where women are concerned. For example, Chambers' *Cyclopaedia* in 1781 described the "English female fanatic, named Jane Leadley, who seduced by her visions, predictions and doctrines, several disciples, among whom were some persons of learning." Her Philadelphian Society is described as "an obscure and inconsiderable society of mystics." [13] But, partly due to groups and people such as Lead's Society, Behmenist thought was part of the intellectual environment in which poet John Milton framed his metaphor of woman and man in *Paradise Lost*. Major poets of the next three centuries—William Blake, Samuel Taylor Coleridge and William Butler Yeats—acknowledge Boehme's importance in their own early thought. When Blake's poetry characterizes the creative mind as male and the mind's creations as female, it echoes the patriarchal aspects of Boehme's sexual metaphor that have marked the mystic's contribution to symbolic thought. Yet, when Blake exults in his apocalyptic poem *Jerusalem* that sexes must vanish and cease to be in the fully realized imagination, he again echoes Boehme, and we find him quoted with approval in the twentieth-century feminist debate over androgyny. Boehme's thought, with its synthesis of the long occult tradition, is a main current in the hidden river of androgyny traced by Carolyn Heilbrun and Mary Daly.[14] Hence the tangled history of patriarchal and feminist thought in one strand of radical, mystical thought.

But what effects has that thought had on the imaginations of little-known women such as Jane Lead? Most immediately, its Inner Light theology offered utterance to her spiritual crisis. Lead probably viewed her writing largely as passionate religious witness. She was, after all, an ecstatic who thought of herself as a prophet. Yet, modern readers observant of her imaginative processes and her expression as well as her religious statement can recognize the outlines of an implicit visionary feminism. Hers is a gynocentric vision that perceives universal spiritual transformation, modeled on her own, in predominantly female, not male, terms. Inherited ideas of the primacy of one's own "inner light" and the femaleness of the soul fused with Lead's fantasies and her social experiences as a woman to produce an intriguing form of apocalyptic literature. "Now give me leave," she writes in *A Fountain of Gardens*,

to tell you the Beginning of my Way that the Spirit first led me into. In the first place, then, after some Years that I had lived in some good Degree of an Illuminated Knowledge, Setting under the Visible Teachings of Men, that could give no further light than that they had arrived from others, through all of which I traced as a wandering Spirit that could find no Rest: but something still I found within myself that did open to draw in from a more pure Air, than I could meet without me: whereupon I introverted more into my own Inward Deep, where I did meet with that which I could not find elsewhere. . . .[15]

When Lead traces the progression from acquired knowledge, or the "Visible Teachings of Men," to personally revealed knowledge, she appropriately draws from her own experience to adapt the symbolism she encountered in Boehme's thought. For example, elsewhere in A *Fountain of Gardens* she asks how to free her spirit from the husk of material concerns and ordinary life.

After a little while of suspending my outward Senses, this Answer I obtained, that this could not be, till there were a Total Death of the Body of Sin; referring to that in the Seventh of the Romans, ver. 6. That being Dead wherein we were held fast, we should serve in the Newness of Spirit; as being discharged from the Law of the first Husband, to which we were married, after the Law of a Carnal Command: Whence we are now free to be Married unto him that is raised from the Dead, and so shall become the Lamb's Wife, jointured into all the Lands and Possessions that he hath. The Eternal Revenues are belonging to her, whether Invisible or Visible: all Power in Heaven and Earth is committed to her . . . whether it be Gifts of Prophecy, or of Revelation, or of Manifestation, or of Discerning of Spirits: or that high Tongue of the Learned, which only speaks from Wisdom's Breath.
At which Opening, my Spirit even failed within me, as desponding ever to get rid of my First Husband . . . that First Husband who so long hindered my Marriage with the Lamb.[16]

This answer is given through her offspring Christ by Sophia, the Gnostic figure of Wisdom who centers Lead's meditations. Boehme's female ground of being is muse, mother and mate for female writer Jane Lead. Sophia guides her daughters, the souls of humanity, back to herself, their origin. They find her only by the Inner Light of their reflections, in the double meaning of that term. By intuitive or reflective thought, they discover that individual existence mirrors or reflects original, undifferentiated potentiality. In her *Revelation of Revelations*, Lead describes this territory as "one's own Native Country and original Virginity."[17] It is, she says in *A Fountain of Gardens*,

the deep Magical ground where [Wisdom] is an absolute Princess to create and generate spirits in her own express likeness, knowing well what her Offspring have right unto; and therefore their Education is to be answerable to their high Birth.[18]

Lead sees Sophia's submerged presence throughout Christian history, just as she finds her within herself. It is a Behmenist alchemical merger of subject and object, or the personal and the universal, that Lead makes work for her here. First of all, Lead "raises" Eve, as she puts it. After recounting a dream vision of sighting an eagle's nest in a lofty tree and receiving in her apron the fledglings who had fallen out of the nest, Lead explains:

In plainness of Speech, then, it is Eve her self, that hath lain long as dead under the Tree of Good and Evil, whose time of raising is very nigh . . . Eve lost her Virgin Eagle Body, and so hath long been sown into a slumbering Death, in Folly, Weakness, and Dishonour. . . . But now . . . raise Eves dead body. . . . Wisdom hath made choice of Eve, for to be her mate . . . Thus choice Eagle Spirits, will be raised up, out of old Eves dust. . . .[19]

Lead also reinterprets Ruth, Rebecca and Mary as types or vestiges of the goddess, Sophia. Their disobedience and dependency, like Eve's "Folly," are recognized as the strategies of the victim who must disguise their original power to keep it alive in displaced circumstances.

[Wisdom] would now be to me as Rebecca was to Jacob, to contrive and put me in a way how I should obtain the Birth-right-Blessing. Know thee (said the same Voice) thou shalt supplant thy Brother Essau, who according to the Figure, is a cunning hunter in the out-birth and field of Nature, while he with his subtilty [is] seeking it abroad, in the wild Properties of the External Region; I will now help thee to it near at Hand, even in thy own enclosed Ground.[20]

In this vein of reinterpretation to show the workings of a feminine principle, Lead sounds much like a seventeenth-century Elizabeth Gould Davis, rediscovering the female first state of the spirit as Davis traces the female first sex hidden in history.[21]

Continuing her revisions, Lead draws on the woman in the Biblical Revelation who "had a Place prepared for her in the Wilderness" to characterize the necessity for lonely isolation to rediscover the soul's original country. The antagonists in that quest are female, too. Revelation's Whore of Babylon and her accompanying Beast represent the carnal command of sensual and conventional life that binds the soul. If she defeats that command, the soul's separatism is rewarded. "Her Wilderness shall become a Sharon-Pasture, a Land of Unknown Plenty, where Gold, Silver, and precious Stones shall be as the Dust under the Feet of these separate Virgins."[22]

Rejoining Sophia involves the female imagination in a dizzying series of transformations. Using the symbolism she has inherited, Lead sometimes limits herself to the patriarchal model of soul as remnant, the female aspect seeking to marry with the male will. But she also adapts that symbolism to mythologize her own actuality as a sentient human being. In her myth, as in her life, a female soul integrates a female will. The stylistic effect is that Lead's narrator, the I who reveals, sometimes plays both roles as bride and bridegroom. When that speaker identifies with Christ, it is not as victim but as the offspring and apocalyptic mate of Mother Wisdom. The image for the newly unified personage, as with

Eve mated with her mother, is a double female or female androgyne as symbol for ideally integrated humanity. "The whirling Wheel of my spirit finding no stay for itself," she writes,

I resolve to make my Application, as not to be put off with any-thing less than the Kingdom and Reigning-Power of the Holy Ghost . . . and . . . to grasp in with Love-violence, this my fair, wise, rich and noble Bride, well knowing her Dowry was so great [that] it would . . . set me free.[23]

This marriage accomplished, the soul becomes the Woman Clothed with the Sun, as the Biblical Book of Rev-elation names her. Jane Lead often calls her "the Wonder Woman."[24] She is

the Wonder of all Wonders, which hath been since Time's Crea-tion. The Birth of Jesus was great and marvellous, but this shall far excell it . . . for the Virgin that brought forth Jesus is a Fleshly Figure . . . remained still the same, no transformation came upon her . . . but this is a Birth of meer Spirit without any commixture of Humanity . . . so that here the Mother of the Virgin-Birth will be more dignified and honoured then the foregoing Ministration in the Birth of Jesus was. Therefore an oriental bright flaming Garment is allotted her, with a Crown beset with Stars, plainly declaring that to her is given . . . Command and Power . . . that operates in every creature and after a Magical manner.[25]

A poem introducing Lead's *Fountain of Gardens* celebrates the redeemed souls who attend this Wonder Woman as an "Illustrious Troop of Heroins Divine/ Celestial Amazons; un-taught to yield. . . ."[26] This troop and their "Mother and Bride in One" create the Heavenly Metro-polis, or Mother-City, imaged in visionary architecture but actualized only in renewed souls, the "Jerusalem within."

That Lead's Wonder Woman is somewhat revolutionary, even within mystical tradition, is suggested by a note inserted in the *Fountain* by Francis Lee, the Oxford Orientalist who became Lead's son-in-law, editor, and secretary of the Philadelphian Society. The author does not derogate Christ or Mary, Lee cautions, but tries to shift thought from mortal, temporal forms to transcendent ones "before all time."[27] Apart from the editorial acknowledgment of possible conflict, it is apparent from the text that the Wonder Woman competes in Lead's own imagination with the inherited male androgyne and its related female imagery of vicarious transformation through giving birth to another. Those received versions of apotheosis, by comparison with the exultant Wonder Woman, seem mechanical and tame.

I had in the Night a Vision: it was the Sight of an Infant, new born, that was brought to me; and it was said to be Mine. But I wondered at it: for I knew not When, or How, I brought it forth. Then I Questioned, whether it was Male, or Female? And it being examined, there was no mark for Distinction upon it. Which was Marvellous . . . And when I call'd it over in the Divine Sense, it was said, *This Figures Out the Mysterious high Birth, that will be Mighty in Power, and Wonderful in Wisdom and Majesty.*

And it is open'd to me thence that this Child, being a Masculine Virgin figured out, doth represent the Eternal Spiritual Offspring, that Adam should have brought forth from God's Eternal Virgin in Himself. And so it is to be renewed again, and to have its Succession, As Christ the Second Adam becomes the new Birth in us, Being Male and Female, and so multiplying himself: tho' under the Covert of a Mortal Figure.[28]

This male androgyne has led feminist critics to reject the art of women writing within mystical tradition.[29] But the patriarchal limitations of mystical thought are not the main point when women writers are concerned. Rather, mysticism has given women a voice, a literary form capable of describing both their reduced condition and their native powers. It has also provided them with an indirect language for protesting sexual politics.

Jane Lead was a woman, a new writer, and an outsider to

educated and artistic circles. Mystical writing gave her a tradition, an audience, and a set of conventions that were particularly useful in her circumstances. The tradition was Protestant mysticism, growing out of nonrationalist philosophy.
Her recognitions gained legitimacy from association with respected ways of knowing, and from contemporary shared
belief. To publish an account of her life was an impropriety
for a woman in the seventeenth century, *except* within the
sectarian audience hungering for spiritual models. Inner
Light theology stirred the impulse and provided a vocabulary
for autobiography.[30] Because of the ascribed femaleness of
the soul in that theology, women were considered especially
appropriate witnesses. Jane Lead and others responded to
the sectarian audience with numerous journals of dreams,
fast-paced narratives of lives in crisis, and volumes of polemic commentary on the Bible. Lead herself published fifteen books or tracts in the twenty-three years between 1681
and 1704.

Lead's style exhibits conventions that some feminist critics
suggest may be characteristic of women writing under patriarchy.[31] Their felt powers of energy and competence conflicting with their societal powerlessness, women may rely
extensively on techniques of indirection—ambiguity, equiv-
ocation and elaborate symbolic structure—to express their
understanding. Highly contrived, the resultant style reflects
the tensions and convolutions in the author's mind and
obliquely challenges the external controls hampering that
mind. Jane Lead gained from traditional mysticism a symbolic language that objectified her own consciousness. The
sexual metaphor within that language indirectly protested
rigid societal dichotomies of gender as well as spiritual ones.
It also quietly attacked conventional female social experience, such as a woman's material necessity for marriage, a
"first husband." Most important, Lead gained a self-affirm-
ing female image for fully actualized humanity, the wonder-
woman capacity "to act from a creating Power, the Virgin's

Omnipotency [that] will enable them to give a new Form, Virtue, and Purity to all things . . ."[32]

Lead also inherited a traditional literary type, the revelation in the form of a confessional journal, letter or essay. These are the conversational art forms, intended to suggest proximity to the direct workings of mind or spirit. But, as Virginia Woolf has noted, they are also the most accessible forms of expression for a woman influenced by the belief that writing was an act unbefitting her sex.[33]

The literary form brought with it a traditional narrator who is ambivalent about self-expression. Such an authorial voice in mystical writing usually speaks under compelling force of inner conviction or divine command, but speaks only to serve as a guide for others. Jane Lead is clearly drawing on that mystical stance, but perhaps also from her feminine experience of displaced power and equivocal authority, when she declares:

It was in my purpose to have suspended . . . any further manifestation of the Revelation that still followed me . . . but Christ, the bright Banner of Glory stood before me, and said, *Keep in Record the Journal of the new raised Life*, according to the Progression thou art going on in. . . . Forbear not writing . . . Seeing it hath pleased the Lord to over-rule my Resolution . . . I shall no longer be backward to reveal what is of great weight and importance. . . .[34]

The authority of this artless narrator comes from the inner world of insight and not from knowledge of the external world. A journal of travels in that interior world is at once both an expansion of the author's socially limited experience and a critique of rational authority and acquired explanations.[35] That mind-set, at once subjective and critical, is the inner light that Lead hopes to kindle in each reader. She relies on dreams, a familiar entrance to mental reality, as her own cognitive guides and as her rhetorical devices. By the literary dream convention, she can present the benefits of redeemed life, including heightened sensation and direct awareness of mental or spiritual phenomena. One such episode, dated February 9, 1678, is titled "A Transport." The punning title is typical of Lead's varied play with language to achieve compressed, double statement.

In the morning after I was awaked from Sleep, upon a sudden I was insensible of any sensibility as relating to a corporeal Being, and found my self as without the clog of an Earthly Body, being very sprightly and airy in a silent place, where some were beside my self, but I did not know them by their Figures, except one, who went out and came in again: and there was no speaking one to another, but all did set in great silence, and I my self with my Eye fixed forward. And I did suddainly see at a pritty distance, where I was, a rich splendrous thing come down all engraven, with Colours, the Ground whereof being all of Gold. It was in the form of a large Ship with Wings, I cannot say, whether more than four, which spread themselves out, being like varnished Gold, it came down with the greatest swiftness as is imaginable. Upon which amazing sight, I asked some by me, do you see this wonderful sight? And they said no. But I saw my self, or something like my self, leaping and dancing and greatly rejoicing to meet it. But when I came up to it, then it did as suddainly go up again, withdrawing out of all sight, unto the high Orb from whence it came. After which I found my self in my Body of Sence, as knowing I had been ranging in my Spirit from it a while, that I might behold this great thing.[36]

In her own day, Lead was producing popular literature. The flying ships, gardens of living statues, bloody hands dropping onto her breast, strange births, monsters who creep from holes in the ground, and the narrator who continually argues against reductive rationality that would negate her flights of fantasy—all suggest the Gothic stories that were beginning to entertain popular imagination in Lead's age and the centuries to follow.[37] Apart from the common reader, the polemicist in contemporary sectarian controversies was equally well served by Lead's frequent question-

and-answer formats, her full indices, and her brief entries of sometimes only a paragraph, with provoking titles ("Queries Concerning the Wonder Woman") and interpretation immediately following.

To the twentieth-century reader, however, Lead's text suggests the fiction of the unconscious. With the apparatus of polemic removed, her narrative resembles a stream of consciousness or interior monologue. She writes in epiphanies, as novelist James Joyce called them—moments of sharp apprehension placed in the framework of a mind and spirit's ongoing development.[38] These sudden, intense recognitions are separated by flats of depressed loss of vision or the obligatory interpretation. Their peaking relies on the imagery of flying figures, traveling, "transport" and rushing sensation similarly employed by Joyce, Virginia Woolf and other modern psychological fiction writers. Jane Lead and the other women who wrote like her are little-recognized sharers in the religio-literary heritage that shaped, first, Romantic thought and, later, modern theory and art of the unconscious.

Lead makes of that heritage, in part, a myth of evolving feminist consciousness. The narrative of peaks, depressions and hopes for apocalypse traces a pattern as familiar to feminists as it is to mystics. It is the feeling of living on the edge, in the feminist and the mystic spatial sense, with the center at the circumference.

With these converging literary, political and religious qualities, the writing of Jane Lead and others like her cannot be categorized simply as mysticism. It needs a new name. It is a special, integrative language built from occult thought by creative discontent in certain women. It speaks from the fusion of fear and wish, of powerlessness and power. Sally Gearhart comes close to naming it in her theory of a new epistemology, "womanknowing":

Astrology, the Tarot, numerology, the I Ching, the Kabala—all these and others . . . redeemed from their masculist emphasis and

filtered anew through the channels of womanknowing, woman-
sight, . . . dreams, visions, dream-and-vision sharing [create] an
affirmation of the intuitive, a song of praise to the non-logical . . .
a reconstruction of reality that will be unequalled in history.[39]

I would add to that definition only that it is not a new
epistemology, just an unfamiliar one. It has been a women's
tradition, carried on importantly by sectarian Protestant
mystics whose resources were occult philosophy, radical theology and their own dreams. All of those resources had been
sadly damaged by patriarchy. In spite of that, those women
mystics reforged an ancient language to create a new universe, one that we are still trying to realize.

NOTES

*Special thanks for their contributions to this study go to Cynthia
Secor, Joan Critchlow, Désirée Hirst, Mary Porter, John Smith,
Helen Caldwell, Annelies Gray, Sally Gearhart and Robin Morgan.
Funds granted by Bucknell University and the kind consideration
of the Dr. Williams's Library, London, made the research possible.*

1. James Webb, *The Occult Underground* (La Salle, Ill.: Open
Court Publishing Co., 1974), p. 105.
2. M. H. Abrams, *Natural Supernaturalism: Tradition and Revolution in Romantic Literature* (New York: Norton, 1971), offers
a recent discussion of this connection.
3. Evelyn Underhill, *The Essentials of Mysticism and Other
Essays* (1920; reprint ed., New York: Dutton, 1960), p. 20.
4. Simone de Beauvoir, *The Second Sex*, transl. H. M. Parshley
(New York: Knopf, 1953), p. 674.
5. Alice Rossi, *The Feminist Papers: From Adams to de Beauvoir*
(New York: Columbia University, 1973), pp. 145, 150.
6. Joseph Priestley, scientist and English sympathizer with the
American and French revolutions (along with Wollstonecraft and
her husband, William Godwin), was also a scholar of religion. His
four-volume *History of Early Opinions Concerning Jesus Christ*
(Birmingham, 1786) collected documents from Gnosticism and

other controversies. Godwin himself, best known as a rationalist philosopher, showed continuing interest in occult practices. In 1834, two years before his death, he published *Lives of the Necromancers: or, an Account of the Most Eminent Persons in Successive Ages, who have claimed for themselves, or to whom has been imputed to them by others, the Exercise of Magical Power.*

7. Copyright 1974 by Robin Morgan. Published in *Lady of the Beasts* (New York: Random House, 1976), p. 38. Quoted with permission of the author.

8. *Ariel* (New York: Harper & Row, 1966), p. 62. Thanks to Sandra M. Gilbert, University of California, Davis, for bringing this poem to my attention in this context.

9. *Lesbian Nation* (1970; reprint ed., New York: Simon and Schuster, 1973), p. 267.

10. Norman Cohn, *The Pursuit of the Millennium* (Fairlawn, N.J.: Essential Books, 1957), p. 316.

11. Désirée Hirst, *Hidden Riches: Traditional Symbolism from the Renaissance to Blake* (New York: Barnes and Noble, 1964), p. 103. This study, along with Margaret Lewis Bailey, *Milton and Jakob Boehme: A Study of German Mysticism in Seventeenth-Century England* (London: Oxford, 1914), contains the fullest generally available information on Jane Lead. D. P. Walker, *The Decline of Hell: Seventeenth-Century Discussions of Eternal Torment* (Chicago: University of Chicago, 1964), is informative, though hostile to Jane Lead as prophet.

12. Biography and social context are discussed in Bailey and in John Joseph Stoudt, *Sunrise to Eternity: A Study in Jacob Boehme's Life and Thought* (Philadelphia: University of Pennsylvania, 1957). For this study, I have used the "William Law" edition, by George Ward and Thomas Langcake, *The Works of Jacob Behmen, The Teutonic Theosopher* (1764–81).

13. Chambers' *Cyclopaedia*, vol. III (1781), quoted by Désirée Hirst, letter, 1975.

14. Carolyn G. Heilbrun, *Toward a Recognition of Androgyny* (New York: Knopf, 1973), and Mary Daly, *Beyond God the Father: Toward a Philosophy of Women's Liberation* (Boston: Beacon Press, 1973).

15. *A Fountain of Gardens Watered by the Rivers of Divine Pleasure and Springing Up in All the Variety of Spiritual Plants . . .* (London, 1697–1701), vol. I, p. 6.

16. *Ibid.*, pp. 68–71.

17. Lead, *The Revelation of Revelations Particularly as an Essay Toward the Unsealing, Opening and Discovering the Seven Seals, the Seven Thunders, and the New Jerusalem State* . . . (London: A. Sowle, 1683), p. 47.

18. *Fountain*, vol. I, pp. 77–78.

19. *Ibid.*, vol. II, pp. 105–7.

20. *Ibid.*, vol. I, pp. 25–26.

21. Elizabeth Gould Davis, *The First Sex* (New York: Putnam, 1971).

22. Lead, *Revelation*, p. 41.

23. *Fountain*, vol. I, p. 118.

24. *Ibid.*, vol. II, table of contents and *passim*.

25. *Ibid.*, vol. I, pp. 468–70.

26. *Ibid.*, "Solomon's Porch . . ." (unpaginated). The authorship of this poem is uncertain. Francis Lee, Jane Lead's editor, attributes it to Richard Roach in "Three Epistles, addressed by Francis Lee to the learned and pious Peter Poiret in Holland . . . ," MS. Walton 186.18 c. 5.30, Dr. Williams's Library, London.

27. *Fountain*, vol. II, p. 527.

28. *Ibid.*, vol. IV, pp. 311–12.

29. Barbara Charlesworth Gelpi, "The Politics of Androgyny," *Women's Studies: An Interdisciplinary Journal*, vol. II (1974), no. 2, pp. 151–60.

30. Abrams, *Natural Supernaturalism*, pp. 48ff.

31. The following discussion of style owes much to Barbara Bellow Watson, "On Power and the Literary Text," *Signs: Journal of Women in Culture and Society*, vol. I, no. 1, pp. 111–18, and to Patricia Meyer Spacks, *The Female Imagination* (New York: Knopf, 1975).

32. *Revelation*, p. 53.

33. Virginia Woolf, *The Second Common Reader* (1932; reprint ed., New York: Harcourt, Brace and World, 1960), p. 51.

34. *Revelation*, p. 1.

35. Ellen Moers discusses the indoor travels of heroines in Gothic novels by women in *Literary Women: The Great Writers* (Garden City, N.Y.: Doubleday, 1976), pp. 122–40. Her remarks illuminate accounts of spiritual travels by women as well.

36. *Fountain*, vol. III, pp. 66–67.

37. Moers, *Literary Women*, pp. 90–110, 122–40.

38. Robert Scholes and Richard M. Kain (eds.), *The Workshop of Daedalus: James Joyce and the Raw Materials for A Portrait of the Artist as a Young Man* (Evanston, Ill.: Northwestern University, 1965), pp. 3–5.

39. Sally M. Gearhart, "Womanpower: Energy Re-sourcement," unpublished essay, 1975, p. 4. Quoted with permission of the author. Published (revised) in *Womanspirit*, vol. II, no. 7 (Spring Equinox Issue, 1976), pp. 19–23.

SEVEN

The Feminist Thrust
of Sectarian Christianity

BARBARA BROWN ZIKMUND

Scholars may debate the nature and character of "sectarian Christianity," but popular understanding points to a rather simple definition: those groups which consciously set themselves apart from the culturally dominant beliefs and practices of a particular time and place. In America, sectarians have defined themselves over against the consensus Anglo-Protestant religious ethos and have remained aggressively uncomfortable with, and critical of, the values, goals and practices of all mainline religious groups. Although many radical religious sects are eventually absorbed into, or transformed into, a mainstream denomination, some sectarian movements continue to flourish on the fringes of American religious life. It is appropriate, therefore, to label the Shakers, the Christian Scientists, the Mormons, the Perfectionists and the Pentecostals as "sectarian."

Contemporary religious studies have noted the masculine bias and limited attitudes toward women in most Western religion. Within sectarian Christianity, however, particularly in the United States, this masculine bias has been modified repeatedly. American women have claimed and gained personal and political rights years before their sisters in other parts of the world. The development of feminism and the growth of sectarian Christianity in America are not unrelated. It is almost as if women who were ignored by mainline religious groups sought out, or developed, sectarian places and positions to fully express their faith. Long before female leadership, female imagery, or community life sympathetic to women emerged in dominant American Christianity, sectarian Christians honored and followed women.

The correlation between feminism and sectarianism is most obvious when we look at the first half of the nineteenth century—a period when women began to move out of the home into the broader society to occupy themselves in ways other than keeping house and raising children. Barbara Welter argues that from 1800 to 1860 American religion underwent a feminization process. As religion declined in force and strength from a position of colonial importance, "it entered a process of change whereby it became more domesticated, more emotional, more soft and accommodating—in a word, more 'feminine.'"[1] These changes are reflected, according to Welter, first in the increased visibility of women in the life of the churches, second in a theological shift toward interest in the suffering Christ, and finally in a preoccupation with religious humility evident in the most popular hymns of the period.

It would appear, argues Barbara Welter, that the woman who wanted a more active role in religion than enduring or teaching Sunday school had two options: she could become a missionary and thereby be able to practice her old religion in a new setting, or she could join a new religion which gave women a more active role.[2] When we look at the development of sectarian options on the American scene, we find a high correlation between this "feminization" process and the increase in sectarian movements and organizations. Indeed, Sydney Ahlstrom calls this very period examined by Welter the "sectarian heyday."[3]

It is my thesis, therefore, that this sectarian growth took at least part of its impetus from women who felt more at home in religious matters than their colonial ancestors, but considered themselves severely limited by dominant tradi-

tional religious practices. There is a distinct feminist thrust
to sectarian Christianity in the nineteenth century.

But first a distinction needs to be made between those
women who responded to new possibilities by becoming sectarian Christians and the majority of women who continued
to worship and increase their commitment within the existing churches.

Beverly Wildung Harrison has called the latter group "soft
feminists." [4] These were women who perceived subtle
changes in the church and society, but accepted the "social
dictates of woman's place." Following the logic of Catherine
Beecher and other moderates, these "soft feminists" sought
to preserve feminine values in a social order that was predominantly male. These women took serious responsibility
for the sphere that had been granted them—the care of
children, the sick, the disabled and other women. The record of female concern on the domestic scene and female
leadership in the foreign mission field stands as witness to
the contributions of "soft feminism."

It is obvious, however, that women in this tradition con-
sented to a view of woman as "different" or of a "special
nature." At first, acceptance of this special nature was eman-
cipating—pushing many women out of the home into social
action. Eventually, however, the basic premise of inequality
and female second-class status, even in the churches, deprived women in the mainline churches of their full intellectual self-respect. Harrison points out how this "soft feminism," by focusing upon woman's place, kept most women
from fighting for more room. [5]

Sectarian women did not accept the logic of "soft feminism." Although some women withdrew from the churches
totally and denied the claims of all religion, "feminized" or
not, large numbers of women turned to new forms of religious expression to meet their rising awareness of themselves
and the world. It is possible to document this feminist presence in sectarian movements in three ways: first, in the ideological or theological emphasis of some sectarian groups;

second, in the social or institutional order which produced new life styles for many sectarian Christians, particularly women; and, third, in the leadership roles held by many strong women in nineteenth-century sectarian groups.

Sectarian Concepts of God

The United Society of Believers in Christ's Second Appearing, commonly called Shakers, is a good place to begin. Founded as a variation of English Quakerism in the mideighteenth century, by the early nineteenth century this sect had developed a new theology which stressed striking feminine principles. The key person in Shaker development was Ann Lee.[6] Not only was this woman the founder and leader of the sect in colonial America, but eventually her teachings and person were interpreted to identify her as the female Messiah. In 1806 Elder Benjamin S. Youngs wrote *The Testimony of Christ's Second Appearing* in an effort to clarify Shaker doctrine. This little volume argued that true spiritual life, based upon the practice of celibacy and abstinence from all sins of the flesh, was revealed by Jesus and Mother Ann. The book proclaims the idea of a dual deity and dual messiahship (through Jesus and Ann Lee). The Godhead is defined in four persons—Father, Son, Holy Mother Wisdom and Daughter. Twenty years after the death of Ann Lee the Shaker leadership codified these principles and laid a foundation for the most phenomenal growth of the sect.[7]

The Shakers upheld an egalitarian and bisexual view of God and human life. In a popular religious broadside published in the early nineteenth century this androgynous theology was clearly stated:

All life and activity animated by Christian Love is Worship. Shakers adore God as the Almighty creator, Fountain of all Good, Life, Light, Truth and Love,—the One Eternal Father-Mother. They recognize the Christ Spirit, the expression of Deity, man-

ifested in fulness in Jesus of Nazareth, also in feminine manifestation through the personality of Ann Lee. Both, they regard as
Divine Saviors, anointed Leaders in the New Creation. All in
whom the Christ consciousness awakens are Sons and Daughters
of God.[8]

In the 1830s, when most of the original followers of Ann
Lee had died, the Shakers experienced a rebirth of spiritual
vitality based upon a series of strange manifestations and
messages that reemphasized the importance of Mother Ann
and Holy Mother Wisdom. In this manner the female principle and the mother-father understanding of God remained
a central tenet of Shaker doctrine. A popular hymn published in an 1813 Shaker hymnal, *Millennial Praises*, witnesses to the dual nature of God.

> *Long ere this fleeting world began*
> *Or dust was fashioned into man*
> *There Power and Wisdom we can view*
> *Names of the Everlasting Two.*
>
> *The Father's high eternal throne*
> *Was never fill'd by one alone:*
> *There Wisdom holds the Mother's seat*
> *And is the Father's helper-meet.*[9]

Another sectarian movement that brought female images
into its theology was Christian Science. Founded almost a
century after the Shakers, Christian Science also emphasized the idea of an androgynous God. Mary Baker Eddy, a
woman plagued by ill-health, found physical relief in the
concept of infinite Spirit.[10] In 1875 she published *Science
and Health: With Key to the Scriptures*. Reality was spiritual
mind, she argued, and God was Mother and Father of us all.
Indeed, Mrs. Eddy believed that the discovery of Christian
Science carried with it the revelation of the Motherhood of
God. She writes, "In divine science we have not as much
authority for considering God masculine, as we have for

considering Him feminine, for Love imparts the clearest idea of Deity."[11]

One of the most prominent windows in the original mother church of the Church of Christ, Scientist, in Boston, Massachusetts, portrays God as woman. It builds upon the vision in the Book of Revelation (Chapter 12) of a woman "clothed with the sun, and the moon under her feet, and upon her head a crown of twelve stars." In the tradition of Christian Science there is no question but that this window was designed to portray God.

Christian Science aggressively supported women's rights. In fact, Mrs. Eddy spoke out on behalf of women more explicitly than on any other issue. She was not an active feminist during the late-nineteenth-century suffrage campaign, but she did believe in the equality of the sexes before the law and supported the campaign for the vote.[12]

A third sectarian group, the Mormons, did not reject patriarchal theology as directly as the Shakers or the Christian Scientists, but they expanded their view of deity to include a divine family. God the Father had a wife, the eternal Mother.

Mormons believed that a certain kind of human marriage extended into eternity. It was only logical, therefore, that Mormon theology developed the belief in a married God. When the prophet Joseph Smith consoled one of his daughters at her mother's death, he promised that she would meet the "eternal Mother, the wife of your Father in Heaven," when she herself went to heaven.[13] Again, it is revealing to quote a verse from another hymn. This one was printed in the Deseret Sunday-school songbook

> *In the heav'ns are parents single?*
> *No! The tho't makes reason stare!*
> *Truth is reason; truth eternal*
> *Tells me I've a mother there.*[14]

In 1915 a Mormon authority reinforced this theological belief by calling humanity "literally the sons and daughters of

Divine Parents, the spiritual progeny of God, our Eternal Father and of our God Mother." [15]

Sectarian Life Style

Sectarian religious commitment in the nineteenth century was far more than a set of beliefs or concepts, it was a new way of life. Those women who left traditional Christianity to join radical groups changed their way of living. Sectarian groups challenged social practices and experimented with new alternatives, and the ways in which various groups attacked social institutions in the name of the faith affected the situation of women. Some groups challenged the narrow vision of family life, others focused particularly upon marriage or motherhood, while others transformed the vision of the institutional church. In working out these emphases, it was action rather than belief that witnessed to a feminist theme. In fact, in some instances no feminist message was articulated, but in practice women lived radically transformed lives.

The family is a good example. Women of that period spent most of their adult lives caring for the physical and emotional needs of large families. There was a great deal of loneliness, pain and hard work in women's lot. It is no accident that many sectarian groups condemned classical family structures and struggled to develop alternatives for women. The Shakers considered carnal lust and sexual intercourse (which almost invariably led to childbirth) to be at the root of all human problems. If the faithful wanted to enter into the higher order, a celibate life was the answer. This way of life was not for everyone, but those who accepted it participated in the Resurrection Order. Jesus had said, "For in the resurrection, they neither marry, nor are given in marriage, but are as the angels of God in heaven." It soon became apparent that the most expedient way for the Shakers to preserve purity and be strengthened in a celibate life was to form communes. Eventually communal living itself offered new opportunities for female leadership and personal growth.[16]

Some sectarian groups began with the communal ideal as a basic tenet. Taking seriously the Gospel promise that all were one in Christ, they sought to work out a life style that allowed all persons equality. These communities were particularly appealing to women, promising, as they did, economic security and social equality. Some scholars argue that few women were attracted to these options independently.[17] But the evidence shows that women did participate in utopian and sectarian communes with enthusiasm. If a communal group could relieve women from the burdensome chores of housekeeping and caring for children, provide companionship among peers, and even save a marriage that was cracking under the strains of individualism and economic pressure, women were willing to give it a chance. Inequities did persist in most communities, but sectarian women believed that they were on their way to a better life. Unlike their counterparts who stayed within the churches and developed an ideology supporting a special status for women, the sectarians usually espoused a relatively egalitarian ideology within a less than perfect world.

The most notorious example of a sectarian group that upheld a feminist position was the Oneida Perfectionists. John Humphrey Noyes, the founder and leader of this group, believed that monogamy and unchecked childbearing had limited women unduly. He argued for "complex marriage" grounded in "Bible Communism." Unlike the Shakers, Noyes did not reject sex as evil; rather, he argued that monogamy had placed undue limitations on human relationships. If we are charged to love one another, argued Noyes, then women and men should freely relate to each other at all levels. He carried to its logical conclusion the rejection of private property fundamental to the communitarian ideal.[18]

Noyes further supported the need for women to be freed from repeated pregnancies. In an era when abstinence seemed to be the only way to control fertility, Noyes argued for "male continence." By intellectual discipline and practice Oneida men learned to participate in intercourse without ejaculation. Noyes claimed that the technique was simple and satisfying. It certainly allowed women to explore their own sexuality in new ways.

Coming at the problems of women from a totally different direction, it is even possible to argue that the Mormons' practice of polygamy fulfilled certain feminist goals. Here the motivation to attack the straitjacket of traditional marriage is still present. Instead of rejecting marriage and turning to celibacy, or developing an egalitarian option such as complex marriage, the Mormons developed an expanded and idealized style of patriarchal marriage. Not only was it important for a nineteenth-century woman to find her social place as someone's wife, in Mormon doctrine it becomes essential for all the saints to participate in marriage as part of their salvation.

Joseph Smith believed that plural marriage was a "duty" that human creatures had to assume in order to provide fleshly tabernacles for those in the spiritual realm. Following Old Testament practice, it was appropriate for a man to take multiple wives.[19] (In Mormon theology there are different levels of marriage. Telestial marriage is the practical union between a natural man and woman. Terrestrial marriage is a good honorable marriage where a couple is committed to each other and their children. Celestial marriage, however, is marriage contracted under the law of God and validated by the Holy Spirit in the church. These marriages are sealed only between two believers in a Mormon temple. They are for eternity.[20])

The interesting thing about the Mormon understanding of marriage is its superiority to the single life. When persons "not married in the new covenant" die, they are appointed to be angels in heaven to "minister to those who are worthy of far more." These angels remain separate in their saved condition to all eternity, and they are not gods. Those who marry, however, shall inherit all things, shall be gods, and all things will be subject to them. Marriage, therefore, is an *essential* key to eternal life and the promise of divinity.[21]

With this view of marriage, women are a means to salvation. Combined with the stipulation that multiple marriages can be contracted only with the consent of each wife, it becomes possible to imagine how nineteenth-century women willingly participated in polygamy. Each Mormon household became a small commune of shared responsibilities and freedoms. Because multiple wives meant multiple obligations for the male, Mormon polygamy was claimed to be more popular with women than with men. According to some observers, "Thousands of women walked from St. Louis to Salt Lake to take part in it." [22]

Sectarian Church Reform

The sectarian impulse was not always separatist and radical. In some cases efforts were made to transform church life from within to make women more welcome, while in others the commitment to formal ecclesiastical structure was adapted to encourage more direct female leadership. The development of the evangelical Holiness movement and the founding of the Salvation Army were two instances of sectarian church reform.

In certain ways the evangelical movement and sectarianism overlapped at some points. When Phoebe Palmer, for example, started her Tuesday meetings for the promotion of holiness, these gatherings were very popular with women. They upheld the legitimacy of personal religious experience and provided channels for sharing. Women, often intimidated by and hesitant to speak out in more formal church sessions, thrived on the informality. Many women were able thus to define their faith in their own terms and declare theological independence from male systematic categories. Furthermore, armed with the strength of their convictions, many of these women assumed leadership roles in the new organizational structures that proliferated within and outside the traditional churches. Women were empowered by the informality of separate gatherings to claim a new vision of the church and themselves.

Secondly, at least one sectarian group, the Salvation Army, developed *formal* structures to encourage female gifts within organizational Christianity. When William and Catherine Booth founded the Salvation Army in England, they were forced to establish a separate organization because the regular Christian churches would not accept them. From the very beginning the Army was organized on a quasi-military model, with women having total equality in service and status. During its spread in the late nineteenth century, the role of women on all levels of its leadership stood in striking contrast to prevailing church practice. Evangeline Booth, one of the daughters of the founders, enjoyed thirty years of leadership, from 1904 to 1934, over the American Salvation Army.[23] Women were empowered in this structured sectarian group (patterned after the male military model) to claim a new vision of the church and themselves.

Sectarian Female Leadership

The feminist thrust of sectarian Christianity is expressed first through creative theological insights; second, in the alternative life styles offered by sectarian groups; and third, in those church reform movements that valued and encouraged female participation. In a world dominated by male standards and control, it is also significant that women actually founded or established several sects, and that many more exercised significant power in sectarian organizations. One is surprised to learn that female leadership was generally accepted in sectarian Christianity long before mainline American churches had so much as confronted the issue of women in ministry. These sectarian women provide the contemporary church with inspiring historical models.

The impact of Ann Lee on Shaker life and doctrine has been pointed out. But it was Eldress or Mother Lucy Wright who became the "first leading character in the female line." In 1796 she assumed leadership of the central Shaker ministry. She was extremely interested in forms of worship and brought greater variety and vitality to already unusual Shaker worship practices. Her extra songs, lively dances and union marches became hallmarks of Shaker life. Lucy Wright encouraged Shaker expansion into Kentucky, Ohio and Indiana in 1804. Under her guidance, until her death in 1821, the Shakers enjoyed their period of greatest expansion.[24]

The Quakers are often overlooked in research and writings on women in sectarian groups. Yet this group, more than many, offered able women opportunities for leadership. The concept of the Inner Light meant that Quakers would not tolerate human social distinctions (free–slave, priest–worshiper or male–female). All persons were equal before God's spirit.

Mary Dyer, who, as we have seen in an earlier chapter, was hanged in Massachusetts in 1660 for defying the ban against her sect, was the first in a long line of strong Quaker women. In the eighteenth century, the names of Hannah Jenkins Barnard, Rebecca Jones and Sophia Wigington Hume witness to the contribution of Quaker women. Although the Quaker life style was quiet and unassuming, it offered articulate women an arena for self-expression and social impact during an era when women were generally seen and not heard.

In the nineteenth century Quaker women became more visible, and some of them played key roles in the rise of nineteenth-century feminism. Elizabeth Leslie Rous Comstock, of rural Michigan, became an outspoken itinerant Quaker minister and reformer. She worked with the Underground Railway before the Civil War and then after the war concentrated her energy on prison reform and political solutions to the social problems developing in America's urban ghettos. Eliza Paul Kirkbridge Gurney and Sybil Jones were enthusiastic Quaker evangelists. They were committed to the fervent spread of Quaker Christianity and worked in several ways to promote the Society of Friends. Eliza Gurney was one of the founders of Earlham College. Sybil Jones served as a missionary to Canada and Liberia and founded a Friends school for girls in Syria.[25]

Finally, no list of nineteenth-century Quaker women can be complete without some word about Lucretia Coffin Mott, who remains the most striking example of a Quaker woman as wife, mother, preacher, reformer and feminist. She grew up a Quaker, but her theological inclinations caused her to forsake the rigidity of Quaker discipline and join the liberalizing wing of "Hicksite" Friends. She was also influenced by the Unitarian movement. Furthermore, she became a radical abolitionist when many Friends were committed to gradual emancipation. Out of her antislavery activity Lucretia Mott developed a commitment to women's rights—and, with Elizabeth Cady Stanton, she called for the historic Seneca Falls convention of 1848 that started the drive for women's suffrage. In the years that followed, Lucretia Mott tried to be a moderating influence in the feminist struggle, for, although she was committed to women, she did not always agree on tactics. Her sectarian roots and experiences, however, continued to influence and inform her feminist leadership.[26]

Female leadership is a logical consequence of Quaker doctrine. It is a bit more surprising to discover female leadership in traditional Biblical movements spawned by Adventist revivalism. Nevertheless, the role of Ellen Gould Harmon White in the development of the Seventh-Day Adventists cannot be overlooked.

Ellen Harmon was raised a Methodist, but converted to the Adventist message of William Miller that Christ would return to earth in 1843. When the Second Coming did not take place as predicted, many Millerites went back to their old churches or abandoned religion altogether. Ellen Harmon was only eighteen years old, but shortly after the "Great Disappointment" she began having visions reinterpreting the nature of the Advent hope by declaring that Christ's return was still imminent though of indeterminate date. She further became convinced that the Ten Commandments required the faithful to observe the seventh-day Sabbath. She moved about the frontier sharing her visions.

Ellen Harmon married James White, a man committed to the Adventist cause and an elder in the movement. In the 1850s she wrote down some of her visions and published a number of pamphlets, the beginning of a long stream of publications. In 1855 the family settled in Battle Creek, Michigan, which eventually became the base of Adventist operations.

Adventism limped along as a disjointed movement until 1860, when the Battle Creek group chose the name Seventh-Day Adventists and organized as a denomination. In this period, Ellen White, relying upon the authority of her numerous visions, guided the sect. The unquestioned acceptance of her visions and their divine origins became basic to Seventh-Day Adventist orthodoxy. As the group grew in size she continued to influence its direction. Her concern for health, education and temperance caused the sect to endorse a healthful diet dominated by whole-grain foods. The cereal empire of W. K. Kellogg and the numerous educational institutions founded by Seventh-Day Adventists are a direct result of her influence.

In an era when the religious leadership of women was limited, Ellen White exercised almost unquestioned power over the Seventh-Day Adventists for over fifty years. She wrote and preached and traveled and governed the church with considerable skill until her death in 1915 at the age of eighty-seven.[27]

Although we have already mentioned the theological insights of Christian Science, it is important to recognize the leadership of Mary Baker Eddy. As a strong woman, she was convinced that her ideas and opinions could and should govern her church. Out of her self-confidence she insisted that Christian Science offer no barriers to women as readers or practitioners. So it was that Augusta Emma Simmons Stetson became the leader of a rival New York City faction of Christian Science which eventually challenged the authority of Mrs. Eddy.[28] For many years, female leadership in Christian Science has remained visible and important.

Another, more general area of female leadership may be found within the Holiness movement, which later spawned a number of Holiness sectarian "denominations." Even within mainline churches, when Holiness factions developed, women enjoyed important leadership roles.

Phoebe Worrall Palmer was not exactly a sectarian, and yet her impact upon the sectarian Christianity of late-nineteenth-century America must not be overlooked. Mrs. Palmer was a Methodist who took Wesley's interest in "entire sanctification" seriously. In the 1830s she began holding meetings in her home dedicated to the search for holiness. These meetings continued for thirty-seven years, and Phoebe Palmer became a key figure in a widespread Holiness Revival. She wrote a number of books and contributed regularly to the principal journal of the Perfectionist movement, the *Guide to Holiness*.

Phoebe Palmer never left the Methodist Church to join or found a new sect. She was, however, the key leader of a sectarian movement which did produce many new groups and denominations committed and recommitted to holiness. She is the spiritual mother of sectarian bodies such as the Pilgrim Holiness Church and the Church of the Nazarene.[29]

A final name to be lifted up in this consideration of female leaders in sectarian groups is that of Aimee Semple McPherson. She stands in the tradition of strong female leadership in nineteenth-century sectarian movements, although she is a twentieth-century figure.

Aimee began her life in the Salvation Army, where her mother was a committed worker. As she grew older she was converted at a Pentecostal revival and felt the call to preach. Soon she was traveling the country preaching a gospel that emphasized crisis conversion, speaking in tongues, healing, and a fundamentalist interpretation of the Bible. She was a great success, becoming known throughout the world, and was supported handsomely by Pentecostal churches.

In 1921 she began the construction of the Angelus Temple near Los Angeles, which she dedicated as "the Church of the Foursquare Gospel." Aimee Semple McPherson emphasized the fourfold ministry of Jesus as Savior of the World, giver of the Holy Spirit, healer of our bodies, and King of kings to come. Although she did not intentionally set out to found a new sect, by 1927 the International Church of the Foursquare Gospel existed as a new Pentecostal denomination. "Sister Aimee," as her followers called her, was an able administrator, a flamboyant public figure and a sensitive leader. She used her talents to minister to the many spiritual needs that respectable churches failed to fill. She was not a feminist, but her strong and visible leadership carried a message of female leadership that became an inspiration to many women.[30]

It has only been quite recently that many major denominations in American religious life have recognized and encouraged female leadership in the churches. Yet, beginning with the Shakers, and moving through Quaker, Adventist, Christian Scientist, Holiness and Pentecostal sectarian groups, there has been a steady pattern of female opportunity, experience and success. These women provide concrete models of able leadership for all of contemporary Christendom.

The proliferation of sectarian Christianity during the nineteenth century was diverse and unsystematic. Large numbers of women moved into many sectarian groups, at least partly motivated by latent or open feminist ideas, practices and leadership. Women were won over through the theological appeal of an androgynous or married deity expressed by the Shakers, the Christian Scientists or the Mormons. Women were intrigued by the vision of an easier way of life, be it celibate, polygamous or one of complex marriage. Within the church itself women were emancipated through informal structures or given power in militaristic equality. Finally, women were exposed to the able leadership of capable and articulate women among Shakers, Quakers, Seventh-Day Adventists and Christian Scientists, and in the Holiness and Pentecostal revivals. Nineteenth-century sectarian Christianity empowered many women in leadership roles, despite its ambiguity about the symbolic relations of the "masculine" and the "feminine."

NOTES

1. Barbara Welter, "The Feminization of American Religion: 1800–1860," in Mary Hartman and Lois W. Banner (eds.), *Clio's Consciousness Raised: New Perspectives on the History of Women* (New York: Harper & Row, 1974), pp. 137–57.

2. *Ibid.*, p. 143.

3. Sydney E. Ahlstrom, *A Religious History of the American People* (New Haven: Yale, 1972), p. 472.

4. Beverly Wildung Harrison, "Sexism and the Contemporary Church: When Evasion Becomes Complicity," in Alice L. Hageman (ed.), *Sexist Religion and Women in the Church* (New York: Association Press, 1974), pp. 195–216.

5. *Ibid.*, pp. 204–5.

6. Edward Deming Andrews, *The People Called Shakers* (New York: Dover, 1963), p. 11.

7. *Ibid.*, pp. 97–99.

8. Reproduced in Nardi Reed Campion, *Ann the Word: The Life of Mother Ann Lee, Founder of the Shakers* (Boston/Toronto: Little, Brown, 1976), p. 87.

9. Quoted in Andrews, p. 158.

10. Stephen Gottschalk, *The Emergence of Christian Science in American Religious Life* (Berkeley: University of California, 1973), p. 47.

11. Mary Baker Eddy, *Science and Health* (Boston: A. V. Stewart, 1910), p. 517.

12. Gottschalk, p. 269.

13. Welter, p. 140, quoted from Susa Young Gates, *History of the Young Ladies' Mutual Improvement Association of the Church of Jesus Christ of Latter Day Saints* (Salt Lake City: Deseret News, 1911), p. 16.

14. Eliza R. Snow Smith, *Poems, Religious, Historical and Political* (Salt Lake City: Latter Day Saints Printing, 1877), p. 173.

15. Thomas F. O'Dea, *The Mormons* (Chicago: University of Chicago, 1957), p. 127.

16. Raymond Lee Muncy, *Sex and Marriage in Utopian Communities: Nineteenth-Century America* (Bloomington: Indiana University, 1973), pp. 19–21.

17. This position is argued by Muncy, pp. 215–25.

18. Muncy, pp. 160–84.

19. O'Dea, pp. 60–61.

20. Rodney Turner, *Woman and the Priesthood* (Salt Lake City: Deseret, 1972), pp. 66–75.

21. O'Dea, pp. 62–63.

22. Kenneth Rexforth, *Communalism: From Its Origins to the Twentieth Century* (New York: Seabury, 1974), p. 297.

23. John A. Hardon, *The Protestant Churches in America* (Garden City, N.Y.: Doubleday, 1969), pp. 215–27.

24. "Lucy Wright," in *Notable American Women* (Cambridge, Mass.: Belknap Press, 1971).

25. See articles in *Notable American Women* on the Quaker women mentioned in these paragraphs.

26. Otelia Cromwell, *Lucretia Mott* (Cambridge, Mass.: Harvard University, 1958).

27. "Ellen G. White," in *Notable American Women*.

28. "Augusta Emma Simmons Stetson," in *Notable American Women*.

29. Timothy L. Smith, *Revivalism and Social Reform: In Mid-Nineteenth-Century America* (Nashville, Tenn.: Abingdon, 1957), p. 117, and John L. Peters, *Christian Perfection and American*

Methodism (Nashville, Tenn.: Abingdon, 1956), pp. 109–12. Also the biography in *Notable American Women*.

30. Aimee Semple McPherson, *The Story of My Life* (Waco, Texas: Word, 1973), and the biography in *Notable American Women*.

EIGHT

Women in the Holiness Movement: Feminism in the Evangelical Tradition

NANCY HARDESTY,
LUCILLE SIDER DAYTON AND
DONALD W. DAYTON

On May 21, 1835, at 2:30 P.M., Sarah Worrall Lankford experienced assurance of entire sanctification. In August she consolidated the prayer groups she attended at both the Allen Street and Mulberry Street Methodist churches in New York City into one meeting held at 54 Rivington Street, the home she and her merchant husband, Thomas, shared with her sister Phoebe and her sister's husband, Walter Palmer, a physician. That prayer meeting, known around the world as the "Tuesday Meeting for the Promotion of Holiness," continued for more than sixty years.

Although Phoebe was a member of the prayer circle, she herself did not experience sanctification until after an experience "on the evening of July 26th, 1837, between the hours of eight and nine o'clock," when "the Lord gave me such a view of my utter pollution and helplessness, apart from the cleansing, energizing influences of the purifying blood of Jesus, and the quickening aids of the Holy Spirit, that I have ever since retained a vivid realization of the fact."

Thereafter, Phoebe became the more famous of the sisters. Through the publication of *The Way of Holiness*, *Faith and Its Effects* and *Present to My Christian Friend on Entire Devotion to God*, she substantially changed the concept of holiness. The influence of the Tuesday Meeting, combined with the Palmers' evangelistic activities along the East Coast and into Canada, culminated in the Holiness Revival of 1857–58, which was telegraphed across the country.

The Lankfords and the Palmers were of English stock and were Methodists, the offspring of John Wesley. In fact, Sarah and Phoebe's father, Henry Worrall, had heard Wesley preach early one morning in a field in England. A priest of the Church of England, John Wesley lacked assurance of his own salvation. A life of strict discipline and sacramental devotion had not satisfied his soul. Moravian Pietists told him that all he needed was faith. On May 24, 1738, about nine in the evening during a reading of Luther's commentary on Romans in a small prayer meeting on Aldersgate Street in London, his heart was "strangely warmed." He felt sure at last that Christ had indeed died for his, Wesley's, sins.

Yet he continued to strive for perfection, for complete victory over all intentional sin. In *A Plain Account of Christian Perfection* Wesley declared that sanctification was a lengthy process likely to be completed only near or at the point of death. As he taught this idea, however, he began to meet those who affirmed they had attained it. All their actions, they said, were guided by perfect love.

Women were prominent in the Evangelical Revival generated by Wesley's preaching. Perhaps his receptivity to women's participation was due to his respect for his mother, Susanna. Even before his birth, in her husband's absence from his parish in Epworth, Susanna had turned her Sunday-evening family worship into a public service attended by as many as two hundred persons. When her husband objected she explained, "It came into my mind that though I am not a man nor a minister of the Gospel, and so cannot be employed in such a worthy employment as they were, yet if my heart were sincerely devoted to God, and if I were inspired with a true zeal for his glory and did really desire the salvation of souls, I might do something more than I do."[1] She remained John's confidante and counselor until her death, encouraging him to use lay people, and particularly women, wherever possible.

In 1739 Wesley began to appoint women as leaders of "classes" in Bristol. Their roles enlarged as opportunities presented themselves. Sarah Crosby found two hundred people at her class meeting. The presence of such a crowd obviously precluded the usual practice of "leading" each person individually. Instead, Mrs. Crosby decided to share her own testimony. Wesley applauded her actions and simply asked her to avoid, if possible, the appearance and scandal of a woman "preaching" by restricting her Scriptural expositions to four or five minutes. Two years later Mrs. Crosby's successful ministry forced Wesley to give her, and other women as well, permission to preach.

Influential in Wesley's formulation of Christian perfection was John Fletcher. When Fletcher died, Wesley encouraged his wife, Mary Bosanquet Fletcher, to take over many of his parish duties. She preached to crowds as large as three thousand, and he described her manner as "fire, conveying both light and heat to all that heard her," and as "speaking smooth, easy and natural, even when the sense is deep and strong."[2] She defended her work by appealing to Scriptural precedent:

No, I do not apprehend Mary could in the least be accused of immodesty when she carried the joyful news of her Lord's resurrection, and in that sense taught the teachers of mankind. Neither was the woman of Samaria to be accused of immodesty when she invited the whole city to come to Christ. . . . Neither do I suppose Deborah did wrong in publicly declaring the message of the Lord . . .[3]

Mrs. Fletcher's life story became must reading in nineteenth-century American Holiness circles.

Wesley countenanced Mary Fletcher's preaching in the 1770s on the basis of her "extraordinary" character and "call." By 1787 he was willing to give more formal recognition to the general ministry of women. He wrote to the Manchester conference: "We give the right hand of fellowship to Sarah Mallet, and have no objection to her being a preacher in our connexion, so long as she preaches the Methodist doctrines and attends to our discipline."[4] Although Wesley never approved of the formal ordination of women, he did allow them to serve as local preachers and itinerant evangelists as well as local class leaders.

The exemplary lives of women such as Hester Ann Rogers, who visited the sick and the poor, instructed penitents and counseled believers in several classes, became compelling role models for both women and men in the Holiness movement. One could cite many other eighteenth-century examples: the Countess of Huntingdon, leader of the Calvinistic Methodists; lay preachers Hannah Ball, Frances Pawson, Mary Taft and Sarah Bentley. The first organized Methodist Church in the United States and the first in Canada were both begun at the instigation of Barbara Heck. By the early nineteenth century these women were being self-consciously appropriated as models by American women beginning to find new places of Christian service in benevolent, missionary, temperance, reform and Sunday-school societies.

Further impetus to such expansion of women's roles in religious life came from the revival sparked first in upstate New York by the preaching of Charles Grandison Finney. Settling the question of his own soul's salvation on October 10, 1821, the promising young lawyer began reading for the ministry. Ordained by the Presbyterian Church in 1824, he began to preach, and revival resulted. Abolitionist Theodore Dwight Weld was converted during the revival in Utica in the winter of 1825–26. Weld later told Angelina and Sarah Grimké:

. . . the very week that I was converted . . . and the first time I ever spoke in a religious meeting—I urged females both to pray and speak if they felt deeply enough to do it, and not to be restrained from it by the fact that they were females. . . . The result was that seven females, a number of them the most influential female Christians in the city, confessed their sin in being restrained by their sex, and prayed publickly in succession at that very meeting. It made a great deal of talk and discussion, and the subject of female praying and female speaking in public was discussed throughout western New York.[5]

Finney accepted the practice without question and allowed women to participate freely in public prayer during social meetings, and to give their testimonies.

East Coast revivalists called it a great "evil to be apprehended" and accused Finney of allowing the practice to split churches. "Whoever introduces the practice of females praying in promiscuous assemblies, . . . will ere long find to his sorrow, that he has made an inlet to other denominations, and entailed an everlasting quarrel in those churches generally," charged Asahel Nettleton.[6] When they met with Finney and his men at New Lebanon, New York, in July 1827 to discuss Finney's "New Measures" in promoting revivals, the group was able to draft compromise agreements on all issues except one: whether or not women should be allowed to pray in mixed assemblies. Noted Boston pastor Lyman Beecher argued that the practice was "unscriptural and inadmissible." Finney's friend Nathaniel Beman argued its propriety from Scripture in a manner "manifestly too conclusive to admit any refutation," according to Finney.[7] After several days' discussion the matter was simply dropped.

Many women later prominent in women's-rights activities were involved in or influenced by Finney's revivals. Elizabeth Cady Stanton was converted in Troy, her husband-to-be in Rochester. Antoinette Brown's father was a convert in Rochester, too. Caroline Severance remembered the revival in Auburn. After Finney's revival near LeRoy, Paulina Kellogg Wright Davis wanted to be a missionary. After reviving the state of New York and much of the northeast seaboard, Finney settled down in 1835 to commute between the pastorate of the Second Free Presbyterian Church in New York City and a professorship in theology at Oberlin College in Ohio. Oberlin was the first coeducational college in the country. Early graduates included Lucy Stone, noted suffragist and abolitionist; Antoinette Brown, first woman to be ordained; Betsey Mix Cowles, one of the founders of the Ohio Women's Rights Association; Sallie Holley, abolitionist lecturer and educator; and Hannah Conant Tracy, journalist and educator of the handicapped.

During a revival meeting for "prayer, praise, and inquiry" in October 1836 an Oberlin student asked President Asa Mahan and Professor Finney, "When we look to Christ for sanctification, what degree of sanctification may we expect from him? May we look to him to be sanctified wholly, or not?" Mahan promised to give the question "prayerful and careful attention" and to offer a "full and specific answer" in "due time"[8] Finney and Mahan spent the winter of 1836–37 in New York City reading Wesley's works and other books concerning holiness. Mahan experienced a second blessing in which Christ "filled and occupied the entire compass of his being."[9] By the spring they had begun to formulate an answer which Finney expounded in *Letters to Professing Christians*.

In order to counteract rumors that they favored the Antinomian Perfectionism of John Humphrey Noyes, they published their views in the *Oberlin Evangelist*. The first issue contained a sermon by Mahan titled "Is Perfection in Holiness Attainable in This Life?" His answer was affirmative. The sermon became a chapter in *The Scripture Doctrine of Christian Perfection* (1839), about which a reviewer in the *Methodist Quarterly Review* declared: "Though it is not to be maintained that he expresses himself Methodistically upon all the points of this great doctrine, we are satisfied that the thing which we mean by Christian Perfection is truly set forth in that work."[10]

By 1840 Perfectionism in a variety of forms was becoming a central theme in American social, intellectual and religious life. In order to foster the Methodist concept, Timothy Merritt of Boston founded *The Guide to Christian Perfection*. The last page of the first issue carried a special notice:

> A WORD to the Female Members of the CHURCH.—Many of you have experienced the grace of sanctification. Should you not then, as a thank-offering to God, give an account of this gracious dealing with your souls, that others may be partakers of this grace also? *Sisters in Christ*, may we not expect that you will assist us both with your prayers and pens? [11]

Many women responded. In addition the paper carried excerpts from the stories of spiritual heroines of the past and contemporary leaders such as Phoebe Palmer. News of the Tuesday Meeting and reports from the Palmers on their preaching tours often appeared in its pages. Her book *Fragments from My Portfolio* and their book *Four Years in the Old World* both appeared serially in what was by then called *The Guide to Holiness*. In 1865 the Palmers purchased the magazine, and Phoebe became its editor.

From the beginning the doctrine of holiness caused division within the church. Sanctified Christians came to believe that slavery was a sin in society and especially within the Methodist Church. In 1843–44 the Wesleyan Methodist Church was formed in New York and New England, and in 1844 the Methodist Episcopal Church South was formed as a separate entity. It was in a Wesleyan Methodist Church in Seneca Falls, New York, in 1848, that Elizabeth Cady Stanton and Quaker Lucretia Mott convened the first women's-rights convention. It was a Wesleyan Methodist minister, Luther Lee, who in 1853 preached the ordination sermon for Antoinette Brown. The question of the ordination of women was raised in the church's General Conference of 1864 by the ordination of a woman elder in Illinois. A resolution against the licensing of women preachers failed, and so the issue was left to local conferences. Women preachers became common in the church by the early twentieth century.

The climax of holiness sentiment came in 1858, *annus mirabilis*, a year of phenomenal revival which spread like wildfire across the prairies. Nurtured entirely by laypeople, it has been called the "Prayer Meeting Revival." Across the nation business people and factory workers, housewives and farmers turned out to sing hymns, pray and give their testimonies. The Palmers were in eastern Canada for most of that year, leading fervent revival camp meetings there. Finney was in Boston. Meetings held by his second wife, Elizabeth Ford Atkinson, "became so crowded, that the ladies would fill the room, and then stand about the door on the outside, as far as they could hear on every side."[12] In December 1858 the Finneys sailed for England, where Elizabeth had begun her own speaking ministry a decade before. Again her meetings were crowded.

In June 1859 the Palmers arrived in England. Phoebe had just completed a 429-page defense of woman's right to preach titled *The Promise of the Father; or a Neglected Specialty of the Last Days*. She argued from the promise of Joel 2:28, reiterated by Peter at Pentecost in Acts 2:17–18, that God the Father has promised that in the latter days the Holy Spirit will be given to women as well as to men, and that both will be expected and compelled to pray, prophesy and preach. In the book's introduction she explained that she decided to write the book after hearing the anguished story of a woman who felt called by God to speak publicly but was reprimanded by the leaders of her church.

A woman in the pulpit did arouse some ire among British Methodists, and Phoebe's ministry in Newcastle was attacked in a pamphlet by a Reverend Arthur A. Rees. A young pastor's wife named Catherine Mumford Booth, an ardent feminist since childhood, read it and responded in a letter to her mother:

Mr. Rees was once a Church [of England] clergyman, and is now an Independent minister with a congregation of upwards of a thousand people. I hear he talks of publishing another pamphlet. I hope he will wait a bit till I am stronger! And if he does bring out any more in the same style, I rather think of going to Sunderland and delivering an address in answer to him. William says I should get a crowded house. I really think I shall try, if he does not let us ladies alone! . . . I am determined he shall not go unanswered.[13]

And so she wrote a reply titled *Female Ministry*. Soon afterward God called Catherine to an active pulpit ministry. The Booths eventually left the Methodist Church to found the Salvation Army in 1878, committed to a doctrine of holiness and a ministry to the poor. In organization it was committed to equality between men and women: "No laws can be good in effect that profess to care for and guard the interest of one sex at the expense of the other."[14] All of the Booth daughters retained their family name, hyphenating it with that of their husbands: Booth-Tucker, Booth-Clibborn, etc. In 1934 daughter Evangeline Booth became worldwide General of the Salvation Army.

Upon their return to the United States, the Palmers traveled westward. In the winter of 1866 they held meetings in Evanston, Illinois, where a younger teacher named Frances Willard was in faithful attendance. On behalf of the American Ladies Centenary Association of the Methodist Church she had just raised $30,000 to build Heck Hall, the first building of Garrett Biblical Institute, a project dear to Phoebe Palmer (who was also influential in the founding of Drew Theological Seminary). After "Mrs. Palmer had spoken with marvellous clearness and power," Willard responded to an altar call for those who wished to enter "the higher Christian Life." Although the ardor of her initial experience of holiness waned, she testified in 1887 that "since then I have sat at the feet of every teacher of holiness whom I could reach."[15]

Willard was a product of Finney revivalism. Her parents had studied at Oberlin when she was a child, and she remembered Lucy Stone. She claimed a lifelong commitment to woman suffrage. A decade after her experience of sanctification she received a "call" to become involved in the suffrage movement, even though "suffrage was too advanced and radical a thing, connected in those days with too much ridicule and scorn, a thing unwomanly and unscriptural, and to touch it was contamination." [16] She testified:

While alone on my knees one Sabbath, in the capital of the Crusade state [Columbus, Ohio], as I lifted my heart to God crying, "What wouldst thou have me to do?" there was borne in my mind, as I believe from loftier regions, this declaration, "You are to speak for woman's ballot as a weapon for protection for her home." Then for the first and only time in my life, there flashed through my brain a complete line of arguments and illustrations. [17]

Although she was first denied permission to speak on the subject and then ostracized from the Women's Christian Temperance Union, she persuaded the Illinois chapter to take up the cause and in 1879 had amassed enough support to become national president, an office she held until her death in 1898. In addition to the WCTU's own work for suffrage and Willard's work in forming political coalitions such as the Populist and Prohibition parties, she trained in the WCTU many of the women who later became officers in the National American Woman's Suffrage Association. One was Anna Howard Shaw, medical doctor and ordained Methodist Protestant minister, who served as superintendent of the WCTU's Franchise Department from 1888 to 1892 and as president and vice-president of the NAWSA from 1892 to 1915.

Another colleague was Hannah Whitall Smith, who in 1883 became the first superintendent of the WCTU's Evangelistic Department. She was already a prominent leader in the Holiness movement, noted for her 1875 book *The Christian's Secret of a Happy Life*, which can still be purchased from supermarket book racks. She and her husband, Robert Pearsall Smith, helped to found the English Keswick "deeper life" movement.

Following Phoebe Palmer's death in 1874, her sister Sarah
married Walter Palmer and they continued the Tuesday
Meeting and publication of *The Guide to Holiness*. The
movement, however, had begun to institutionalize. In 1867
the camp meetings which had been such a fruitful field of
ministry for the Palmers were "nationalized" into the National Camp Meeting Association for the Promotion of Holiness. Under the leadership of the Reverend John Inskip, the
group held national conventions in such places as Vineland,
New Jersey; Manheim, Pennsylvania; Round Lake, New
York; Urbana, Ohio; and Sacramento, California—a total of
fifty-two from 1867 to 1883. Walter Palmer died in 1883 while
ministering in Ocean Grove, New Jersey, established and
still operating as a "Christian seaside resort."

One woman whose ministry began at a national Holiness
camp meeting in Oakington, Maryland, was evangelist
Amanda Smith. Born a slave, she was working as a washerwoman in 1870 when she felt led by God to go to the meeting. Converted as a young woman, she found sanctification
in September 1868 under Inskip's preaching at his Greene
Street Church in New York. "I wanted to shout Glory to
Jesus! but Satan said, 'Now, if you make a noise they will put
you out,' " she said. "I was the only colored person there and
I had a very keen sense of propriety." But at the end of the
sermon, she said, "I seemed to feel a hand, the touch of
which I cannot describe. It seemed to press me gently on
the top of my head, and I felt something part and roll down
and cover me like a great cloak! I felt it distinctly; it was done
in a moment, and O what a mighty peace and power took
possession of me!" [18] That day, with a reminder of Galatians
3:28, God also delivered her from her fear of white people.

She began to attend camp meetings around the East, tes-
tifying and singing. In Kennebunk, Maine, "the Lord cured
a good old brother, Jacob C., of prejudice . . . When he saw
me about in the meetings he was much disturbed. But still
he felt that he needed the blessing, and had come to camp
meeting for that purpose. Whenever the invitation was given

for those who wanted a clean heart, he would go forward and kneel down." But then, reported Smith, "the black woman would . . . sing, or pray, or testify. He could not get on." He finally found victory over his prejudice while praying alone in the woods and was then able to "make a full surrender of himself" in the meetings. He even found strength to give up chewing tobacco.[19]

When Smith felt led by the Spirit to attend a national camp meeting in Knoxville, Tennessee, even Mrs. Inskip discouraged her, fearing she would be treated discourteously. When she arrived at the camp, the meetings had been in progress for three days without much success. However, when she gave her testimony, one of the leading opponents of holiness began to weep. Stepping onto the platform, he told how many years he had been a Methodist minister and how prejudiced he was against the subject of holiness. "When I heard this colored sister tell how God had led her and brought her into this blessed experience, the darkness swept away and God has saved me, and I see the truth as I never did before. Glory to God!"[20]

Amanda Smith took her message of holiness to the British Isles as well, where she spoke at Keswick and the Broadlands conferences. She traveled across the Continent to India, where Methodist Episcopal Bishop J. M. Thoburn observed: "She possessed a clearness of vision which I have found seldom equalled. . . . During the seventeen years that I have lived in Calcutta, I have known many famous strangers to visit the city, but I have never known anyone who could draw and hold so large an audience as Mrs. Smith."[21] She also spent a number of years in Africa, particularly in Liberia. When she finally felt too old to travel, she returned to the United States in 1890 and founded an orphanage near Chicago, which she served until her death in 1915.

The National Camp Meeting Association represented those who wished to keep the movement within the Methodist Episcopal Church. However, the camp meetings were ecumenical in scope, and soon local and regional Holiness

associations began to form. They held regular, sometimes
weekly, meetings, put out journals, published books and
pamphlets, sponsored charitable institutions—in short, they
took on the trappings of an institutional church. National
Camp Meeting leaders fought successfully to keep most of
their followers within the Methodist fold, but peripheral
groups began to form and break away. One of the earliest
splits was that of the Free Methodist Church in 1860 in
upstate New York. Founder B. T. Roberts was an ardent
feminist who fought, unsuccessfully, until his death, for the
ordination of women. In 1891 the denominational publishing house printed his *Ordaining Women*. Bishop W. A. Sel-
lew also defended the right in an 1894 book, *Why Not?* In
1907 women were allowed to be deacons, but they were not
given full ordination as elders until 1974.

Other Holiness denominations that emerged from the
controversy about such teaching in the late nineteenth century all allowed women full participation. Women played a
prominent role in the early days of the Church of God (Anderson, Indiana), founded in 1881 by Daniel S. Warner. Historian John Smith wrote that, from its beginning, women
were considered essential to its leadership and served equally
with men. In a 1902 publication, *Familiar Names and Faces*,
fifty of the church's two hundred leaders mentioned were
women. Says Smith: "Forty years before the time of
woman's suffrage on a national level, a great company of
women were preaching, singing, writing, and helping to determine the policies in this religious reform movement."[22]
Outstanding preachers and evangelists Mary Cole, Sarah
Smith, and Lena Shoffner all faced considerable criticism.
In her autobiography, *Trials and Triumphs of Faith*, Cole
noted that although she had to explain the Scriptural teaching on the subject of women preachers at almost every meeting, people found salvation under her ministry.

The right of women to preach was not even debated in
the early days of the Church of the Nazarene, for the matter

was settled at its founding near the turn of the century. Its original constitution specifically affirmed that right. The first woman to be ordained, Lucy P. Knott, had been associated with founder Phineas Bresee from the beginning of his ministry in Los Angeles. Women were primarily responsible for starting the church's missionary work, its youth work and the Pacific Bible School, its first educational institution, whose faculty, the second year, consisted of five women and three men headed by a female principal. For a time one entire conference of the church in west Tennessee consisted solely of women ministers. Severely criticized, twelve of the Nazarene women ministers defended their right to preach in a book, *Women Preachers*, edited by Fannie McDowell. Says historian Timothy Smith of these women, who included his own mother:

The women who carried on this independent gospel work seem to have combined piety and practicality to a remarkable degree. Between revivals they maintained a normal and apparently stable family life, if the few surviving letters may be taken at face value. Their husbands joined happily in their meetings when they were near home and accepted periods of separation without much protest. Only one of the women seems ever to have gone to extremes of religious emotionalism, and on that occasion the sound common sense of the others shook her out of it.[23]

The Pilgrim Holiness Church grew out of the International Holiness Union and Prayer League, founded in Cincinnati in 1897. Seth Cook Rees served as its president from 1897 to 1905. He declared that one of the fourteen marks of "the ideal Pentecostal church" was the fact that there was no distinction because of gender. In fact:

Nothing but jealousy, prejudice, bigotry, and a stingy love for bossing in men have prevented woman's public recognition by the church. No church that is acquainted with the Holy Ghost will object to the public ministry of women. We know scores of women who can preach the Gospel with a clearness, a power, and an efficiency seldom equalled by men. Sisters, let the Holy Ghost fill, call and anoint you to preach the glorious Gospel of our Lord.[24]

Manuals for this denomination show that through the 1930s as many as thirty percent of its ministers were women. Among them was Rees's wife, Hulda, known as the "Pentecostal Prophetess" after her Biblical namesake. She preached from the age of sixteen until her death, accompanying her husband as co-pastor and co-evangelist. Her stepson Paul S. Rees says of her: "Like Catherine Booth, she was a balanced soul in whom domestic virtues and platform gifts developed apace."[25]

Alma White, who claimed to be the first woman bishop in church history, founded the Pillar of Fire, a small sectarian Holiness body that originated around the turn of the century. She believed that while men filled the priestly office in the old dispensation, the fact that the veil of the Temple was rent asunder at Christ's crucifixion meant that now both men and women are invited into the Holy of Holies: "Let Christ reign in the heart, and woman will take her place beside man and help to fight the battles of life, and not only be a helpmeet, but socially and mentally his equal."[26] For years the Pillar of Fire published a paper titled *Woman's Chains*, advocating the enfranchisement of women and their full participation in all levels of government, including the Presidency, in all sectors of society, and throughout the whole church. Continued interest in the topic is revealed by the fact that the Pillar of Fire in 1955 reprinted Lee Anna Starr's *Bible Status of Women*, originally published in 1926 by Fleming H. Revell. White was a friend of Starr, pastor of the college church at Adrian (Michigan) College, a Methodist Protestant school.

Holiness denominations still, by and large, have a higher percentage of ordained women than does their mother church, the United Methodist Church, which is the leader among mainline Protestant groups.

What could account for the Holiness movement's consistent feminist thrust? At least six factors.

First, the Holiness movement had a theology centered in experience. Both the Wesleyan and Finneyite revivals stressed conversion and a subsequent, separate experience of sanctification. Arminian in theology, they saw salvation as available to all who would accept it. Elizabeth Cady Stanton summarized Finney's preaching: "The way to salvation was short and simple. We had naught to do but to repent and believe and give our hearts to Jesus, who was ever ready to receive them." [27] Antoinette Brown said her father "had accepted the Calvinistic idea that it was God who must convert him in his own time and had waited years for that time to come," but during a Finney revival he learned that "Prof. Finney laid the whole stress of his preaching on the duty of the sinner himself to work actively for his own conversion. Although a partial Calvinist, he had in that matter taken a new departure." [28]

Just as Wesley found at Aldersgate and Finney learned in the woods of New York, Holiness people believed that one could know *now* that one was sanctified. And, echoing the activism and immediacy of Finney, Phoebe Palmer told seekers of Christian perfection in *The Guide to Holiness*: "Resolve that you WILL HAVE IT NOW, and it may be yours at once." [29]

Palmer altered the Methodist understanding of sanctification to bring it more in line with Finneyite revivalism. For Wesley, assurance of perfection was given by the Holy Spirit as the culmination of a long process, the goal of a committed Christian life. Palmer taught a second crisis experience marking the beginning of full Christian commitment. Using controversial "altar" terminology, she outlined the process in three simple steps. First, one must "lay one's all on the altar," consecrate everything to God. Second, one must exercise faith that "if God has enabled you to bring it, will he not, now that you bring it and lay it on his altar, accept it at your hands?" "Apart from any excitement of feeling, other than the sacred awe inspired by the solemnity of the act," one must simply "lay hold upon the terms of the covenant, by which God has condescended to bind himself to his people."[30] Third, one must make immediate public confession that one has received the blessing. Usually a feeling of assurance will follow. Testimonies recorded in *The Guide to Holiness*, in books of testimonies, in accounts of the Tuesday Meeting, in reports of Palmer's own meetings, almost always bear this design—as does Finney's account of his own "baptism of the Holy Spirit."[31]

In the first phase people felt compelled to renounce their attachment to their possessions, their children, their spouses, in that ascending order, and sometimes to their own reputation or pride. Although Holiness people were eminently faithful to their marriage vows and were devoted parents, this act of consecration did reorder their priorities and give them a certain distance from and perspective on domestic responsibilities. For example, Lydia Sexton, first woman licensed as an "approved preacher" (in 1851) by the Ohio quarterly conference of the United Brethren Church, a German Methodist body, was criticized for being away on a preaching trip when her son Thomas died. She responded: "If you were working for God in a work that would tell to your advantage and the advantage of hundreds of others in the human family in time and eternity . . . if your motive-force was to promote the glory of God and the salvation of never-dying souls, you would then feel as I do. . . . My children belong to God."[32]

The third step compelled women as well as men to speak in public. Willard lamented the fact that she lost the assurance of sanctification because she failed to continue to speak of it. Historian Melvin Dieter has commented:

It was the theology of the [Holiness] movement and the essential nature of the place of public testimony in the holiness experience which gave many an otherwise timid woman the authority and the power to speak out "as the Holy Spirit led her." . . . To those who allowed the theology, the logic was irrefutable.[33]

Phoebe Upham, writing on "Woman's Freedom in Worship," declared: "To *impart* what one receives from God, is the out-going life of the new Christ-nature. . . . How opposed then to the new Christ-nature, and to God's Word, is the sealing of woman's lips in the public exercises of the Church."[34]

As part of their sanctification experience many women felt called to preach. Palmer told the story of Wesley's friend Sarah Mallet, who resisted that call for several years. She began having "fits" or seizures, during which she imagined herself in another town, preaching. As soon as she yielded to the Spirit and began to speak, the "fits" ceased.[35] Sadie J. Hart, a Presbyterian, admitted to readers of the *Guide* that her refusal to pray at prayer meetings was "the one step between me and the kingdom." She kept denying the right of women to preach and pray in public until a Methodist elder gave her a "talking to," and, thus convinced, she immediately experienced sanctification.[36] Osee Fitzgerald of Newark, New Jersey, mother of a Methodist bishop who also championed holiness, told of her quest for sanctification in 1856. She consecrated her children, her husband and all her property to God, but when the Spirit asked, "If I give you a clean heart and sanctify you wholly, will you speak before this people and tell them what I have done for you?" she explained that she was a Presbyterian and opposed to women speaking in church. When she finally acceded to this request, she experienced sanctification. Soon she felt led to speak in a meeting, but hesitated until it was too late. Chided the Spirit: "What but a man-fearing or a man-pleasing spirit prevented you?"[37]

"HOLINESS IS POWER," promised Phoebe Palmer.[38] "Dear

Darling, get the blessing of holiness, and it will be a gift of power," Sarah Lankford advised Martha Inskip.[39] The experience of this power "nerved for holy achievement." It encouraged, indeed compelled women to burst the cocoon of "woman's sphere." Palmer's biographer cited an example: "In Tully [N.Y.] Mrs. Palmer's loving instructions were blest, to the entire sanctification of a minister's wife, who was changed from a timid, shrinking, silent Christian, into one of tearful, modest, but pentecostal power, and who afterwards spoke in public, with remarkable effect."[40]

Second, the doctrine of holiness was rooted in Scripture. Experience was tested by its conformity to the Word of God, and Scriptural truth was illustrated by personal experience. In every work by or about Palmer there appears some variation of the following statement: "THE BIBLE, THE BLESSED BIBLE, IS THE TEXT BOOK. Not Wesley, not Fletcher, not Finney, not Mahan, not Upham, not Mrs. Phoebe Palmer, but the Bible—the holy BIBLE, is the first and last, and in the midst always. The BIBLE is the standard, the groundwork, the platform, the creed."[41] Subjectively interpreting Scripture in line with experience, Holiness people could criticize the status quo. They claimed Biblical authority, but they were not bound by literal interpretations. Actually one can find at least three types of hermeneutic operating in the course of the movement.

One type, which originated in abolitionist circles surrounding Finney, was based on Galatians 3:28's affirmation that "there is neither Jew nor Greek, there is neither bond nor free, there is neither male nor female: for ye are all one in Christ Jesus." Fighting those who appealed to a "Bible defense of slavery," Theodore Weld wrote *The Bible Against Slavery*. Appealing to an egalitarian "spirit" of Scripture over against the "letter," Weld, and the women who adapted his arguments to support women's rights, sought to implement kingdom norms which would usher in the millennium on earth. Sarah Grimké in her *Letters on the Equality of the Sexes and the Condition of Woman* argued that "Men and women were CREATED EQUAL; they are both moral and accountable beings, and whatever is *right* for man to do, is *right* for woman." [42] Grimké, and almost every other nineteenth-century feminist, quoted from British Methodist scholar Adam Clarke's commentary. Concerning Galatians 3:28 he wrote: "Under the blessed spirit of Christianity, [women] have equal *rights*, equal *privileges*, and equal *blessings*, and let me add, they are equally *useful*." [43] Luther Lee used this text and this approach in his ordination sermon for Antoinette Brown. This position accepted the fact that Scriptures and first-century culture could not be imported uncritically into the present. A more developmental and historically oriented view that permitted the new to emerge was needed. Many Holiness people argued that the women's-rights movement was, in fact, the culmination of New Testament teachings. Just as in the case of slavery, where, "while yielding for a time to the form of the institution," the apostles "laid down principles that would cut away the foundations of the system," so the "same method was adopted in the case of woman." "The apostles began the elevation and education of woman, and left the movement to flow on so far and in such channels as Providence and the current of events might open for it, thus preparing the way for a much broader and grander work than they themselves were permitted to perform." [44]

A second type of Biblical interpretation used Pentecost as the key. Peter's citation of Joel's prophecy in Acts 2:17–18 became the relevant text to argue that both sons and daughters should pray, preach and prophesy. In the 1890s the *Guide* ran a column describing the work of women in various organizations and headed it with the quotation "Upon the handmaidens . . . will I pour out my Spirit." Regular corresponding editor Jennie Fowler Willing was a colleague of Willard in the WCTU, a licensed Methodist local preacher and ardent suffragist. She called Pentecost "Woman's Emancipation Day" and declared that "Pentecost laid the axe at the root of the tree to social injustice. The text of Peter's sermon that marvelous day was the keynote of woman's enfranchisement." [45] She explained that Paul did not insist on freedom for women at every point because people were too prejudiced to accept it. Rather, he gave "axioms which believers would grow to apprehend, with now and then an illustrative side-light." [46] Pentecost was spoken of as inaugurating a "new age" or "dispensation." This way of interpreting Scripture coincided with a shift from a post-millennial position held by Finneyites to a premillennial position. Although she was not premillennial, Palmer subtitled *Promise of the Father* "A Neglected Specialty of the Last Days." Holiness people argued that wider ministries for women were a sign of the "latter rain," the special outpouring of the Spirit before Christ's Second Coming.

A third and later line of interpretation, showing the impact of the fundamentalist controversy, affirmed the inspiration and authority of Scripture. Using a more literal hermeneutic, Lee Anna Starr in her *Bible Status of Women* and Katharine Bushnell in *God's Word to Women: One Hundred Bible Studies on Woman's Place in the Divine Economy* [47] both managed feminist reinterpretations of the entire Bible, including the Levitical laws!

A third major characteristic of the Holiness movement was its growing emphasis on the work of the Holy Spirit. Wesley had spoken of the Holy Spirit as witnessing to the believer's sanctification, but his teaching was basically Christocentric. In antebellum America one can chart a shift of emphasis from the "Scripture Doctrine of Christian Perfection" which Asa Mahan described in 1839 to an understanding of sanctification as the "Baptism of the Holy Ghost," the title of Mahan's second book on the subject, published in 1870. The use of Pentecost and baptism of the Spirit as central metaphors for the experience of holiness reinforced the idea that believers could expect extraordinary gifts and manifestations of power. This led naturally to a charismatic concept of leadership and ministry. Preaching was not a product of human effort or training endorsed by the proper ecclesiastical authorities, but rather the result of direct influence of the Spirit.

These characteristics led to a fourth: a freedom to be experimental. Although a strong supporter of the ancient catholic traditions of the Church of England, Wesley was open to experimentation with new forms: field preaching, lay ministers, women preachers, class meetings. Finney took such Methodist innovations as the "anxious meeting" and "bench" and incorporated them into his own "New Measures." Building on the revival techniques of Wesley and Finney, the Palmers founded the Tuesday Meeting and did most of their revival work at camp meetings, which became a Holiness institution. From the movement emerged a new style of preaching called "Bible readings," in which a speaker simply read a passage, interspersing appropriate comments. Hannah Whitall Smith was famous for hers. It allowed women and laymen to preach without actually giving a formal "sermon." The criterion for acceptability was success. If the means was successful in winning souls and encouraging holiness, it was approved. Said Finney, "if [God] blesses the *measure itself*, it is rebuking God to pronounce it unwise. . . . The success of any measure . . . . demonstrates its wisdom." [48]

Fifth, the emphasis on perfection and holiness is always an implicit critique of the status quo and is thus intrinsically reformist, even revolutionary. The Finneyites and the Wesleyan Methodists were particularly concerned about the abolition of slavery. Wesley and many later Holiness denominations such as the Salvation Army, the Church of the Nazarene, and the Christian and Missionary Alliance felt that their mission was to the poor. Holiness churches grew out of mission agencies such as homes for unwed mothers, orphanages, rescue missions, schools to train missionaries, social agencies for the poor, etc. They saw needs that the established churches were not meeting, and they tried new ways to fight injustice.

This led to the formation of sects, a sixth characteristic of the movement. Initially the Holiness associations were strongly ecumenical. The Palmers boasted of the ecumenical nature of the Tuesday Meeting, how it attracted Congregationalists, Quakers, Presbyterians, Baptists and even Episcopalians. This diluted any emphasis on specifics. When the associations became small struggling sects, they were more fluid, flexible in terms of organization and rules. Women leaders were available and needed. Leaders emerged on the basis of spiritual gifts; organization was more congregational. As the Holiness sects have evolved into churches, the number of ordained women has decreased.

Why has this story remained unknown for the most part? Several reasons are apparent.

When one thinks of the nineteenth-century American feminists, one thinks immediately of Elizabeth Cady Stanton and Susan B. Anthony because they wrote *The History of Women Suffrage*. We think of them and the suffrage issue. They told their story. Suffragists like Lucy Stone and Alice Paul are ignored. Feminists like Frances Willard who worked for suffrage outside the official organizations are also ignored. Because of Stanton's and Anthony's and many subsequent historians' bias against religion, the movement for women's rights within the churches (both ordination and laity rights were contested issues in many churches during this period) are overlooked.

One could argue that the feminism of the Holiness churches was not as radical, as "hard," or that religious feminists were not as "militant." They did not, for the most part, criticize the family or advocate divorce reform. Many still believed in some final "headship" of the husband—though B. T. Roberts argued that "the greatest domestic happiness always exists where husband and wife live together on terms of equality." If business partners could operate without submission of one to the other, married couples surely could. When comparing religious feminists to others, one must remember, however, that Stanton, Paul and the labor union organizers were considerably more militant than the vast majority of their followers. Stanton's *Woman's Bible* was condemned by her own organization. As for rhetoric, in terms of "militancy" Frances Willard's castigation of the Methodist Church after it denied her a seat as an elected delegate to its 1888 General Conference or the editorials and cartoons in *Woman's Chains* compare favorably with anything that emanated from the more "secular" quarters of the movement. Churchwomen and their supporters fought for admission to the decision-making bodies and for control of their own social agencies within the churches. They won, and their victories endured.

But history moved on. After the Civil War, the Holiness movement, along with many of the other "Perfectionist" movements, lost its radically egalitarian thrust engendered by the drive for abolition. After the First World War, both secular and religious feminists settled down to consolidate their gains, assuming that suffrage would ensure equality. And following World War II, women in every sector of society suffered from the repression of women's rights and the elevation of "the feminine mystique."

Within the churches, several factors contributed to the waning of the nineteenth-century feminist vision. One was a change in leadership. When the first-generation charismatic leadership of any movement dies, the movement slows down. In moving from informal prayer meetings to formal associations, from sects to churches, the Holiness movement got caught up in a professionalization of leadership. When the movement was young, it founded Bible institutes and small colleges where many of the faculty members were women, in the Bible and theology departments as well as in English and rhetoric. But as these institutions became full-fledged colleges, higher academic degrees were required in a time when few women were attaining them. Women in the ministry faced the same problem when even the Holiness denominations began to move to the suburbs and to require seminary-trained pastors. In the 1930s to 1950s daughters did not follow in the footsteps of their preacher and professorial mothers and grandmothers; thus these role models were lost, for the present generation to rediscover.

Phoebe Palmer, in concluding *The Promise of the Father*, summed up the state of the church in her day—and in ours. She also issued a challenge to her Christian brothers and sisters:

The church in many ways is a sort of potter's field, where the gifts of woman, as so many strangers, are buried. How long, O Lord, how long before man shall roll away the stone that we may see a resurrection?

> *Daughters of Zion, from the dust*
> *Exalt thy fallen head;*
> *Again in thy Redeemer trust.—*
> *He calls thee from the dead.*[49]

NOTES

1. F. Townley Lord, *Great Women in Church History* (London: Cassell, 1940), p. 161.

2. Thomas M. Morrow, *Early Methodist Women* (London: Epworth Press, 1967), p. 98.

3. Quoted in Phoebe Palmer, *The Promise of the Father* (Boston: Henry V. Degen, 1859), p. 11.

4. *Ibid.*, p. 117, relying on Zechariah Taft, *Biographical Sketches of Holy Women*.

5. Theodore Weld to Angelina and Sarah Grimké, New York, Aug. 26, 1837, in Gilbert Barnes and Dwight Dumond (eds.), *Letters of Theodore Dwight Weld, Angelina Grimké Weld and Sarah Grimké, 1822–44* (New York: Appleton-Century-Crofts, 1934; reprint ed., Gloucester, Mass.: Peter Smith, 1965), vol. I, p. 432.

6. Bennet Tyler, *Memoir of the Life and Character of Rev. Asahel Nettleton, D.D.* (Hartford: Robins & Smith, 1844), p. 251.

7. Charles Grandison Finney, *Memoirs* (New York: A. S. Barnes & Co., 1870), p. 214.

8. Asa Mahan, *Scripture Doctrine of Christian Perfection* (Bos-

ton: D. S. King, 1839), p. 188. See also p. 232. For an understanding of Mahan, read Donald W. Dayton, "Asa Mahan and the Development of American Holiness Theology," *Wesleyan Theological Journal*, vol. IX, Spring 1974, pp. 60–69.

9. Asa Mahan, *Out of Darkness into Light* (New York/Boston: Willard Tract Repository, 1876), p. 135, quoted in Barbara Zikmund, "Asa Mahan and Oberlin Perfectionism," Ph.D. dissertation, Duke University, 1969, p. 122.

10. *Methodist Quarterly Review*, vol. XXIII, April 1841, pp. 307–8.

11. *Guide to Christian Perfection*, vol. I, July 1839, p. 24.

12. Finney, *Memoirs*, p. 443.

13. F. de L. Booth-Tucker, *The Life of Catherine Booth: The Mother of the Salvation Army* (London: Salvation Army Printing Works, 1892), vol. I, p. 243. This pamphlet was *Female Ministry; or, Woman's Right to Preach the Gospel* (London, 1859). An expurgated version was published in London by Morgan & Chase (n.d.) and in *Papers on Practical Religion* (London: International Headquarters, 1890); and in New York by the Salvation Army Supplies Printing and Publishing Dept. (1975).

14. *The Salvation Army: Its Origin and Development* (London: Salvationist Publishing and Supplies, 1951), p. 63.

15. Olin Garrison, *Forty Witnesses* (1888; reprint ed., Freeport, Pa.: Fountain Press, 1955), pp. 73, 75–76.

16. Ray Strachey, *Frances Willard: Her Life and Work* (New York: Fleming H. Revell Co., 1913), p. 209.

17. *Ibid.*, p. 208.

18. Amanda Smith, *An Autobiography: The Story of the Lord's Dealings with Amanda Smith* (Chicago: Meyer and Bros., 1893; reprint ed., Nobelsville, Ind.: Newby Book Room, 1972), pp. 77, 79.

19. *Ibid.*, p. 185.

20. *Ibid.*, p. 211.

21. *Ibid.*, p. vi.

22. John W. Smith, *Heralds of a Brighter Day* (Anderson, Ind.: Gospel Trumpet Co., Church of God, 1955), p. 125.

23. Timothy L. Smith, *Called unto Holiness* (Kansas City, Mo.: Nazarene Publishing House, 1962), p. 155.

24. Seth Cook Rees, *The Ideal Pentecostal Church* (Cincinnati: M. W. Knapp, 1897), p. 41.

25. Paul S. Rees, *Seth Cook Rees: The Warrior Saint* (Indianapolis: Pilgrim Book Room, 1934), p. 13. See also Byron Rees, *Hulda A. Rees: The Pente-Prophetess* (Philadelphia: Christian Standard Co., 1898).

26. Alma White, *The New Testament Church* (New Jersey: Pentecostal Union, 1912), p. 227.

27. Elizabeth Cady Stanton, *Eighty Years and More* (1898; reprint ed., New York: Schocken Books, 1971), p. 41.

28. Mrs. Claude Gilson, "Antoinette Brown Blackwell: The First Woman Minister," Blackwell Family Papers, Schlesinger Library, Radcliffe College, Cambridge, Mass., p. 49.

29. Phoebe Palmer, "The New Year," editorial in *Guide to Holiness*, vol. XLVII, January 1865, p. 14.

30. Phoebe Palmer, *The Way of Holiness* (New York: printed for the author, 1854), pp. 34, 30.

31. Finney, *Memoirs*, pp. 373–79.

32. Lydia Sexton, *Autobiography of Lydia Sexton* (Dayton: United Brethren Publishing House, 1882), pp. 342–43.

33. Melvin Easterday Dieter, "Revivalism and Holiness," Ph.D. dissertation, Temple University, 1972, p. 50.

34. Mrs. P.L.U. (Phoebe L. Upham), "Woman's Freedom in Worship," *Guide to Holiness*, vol. XLIII, April–May 1863, pp. 114–15.

35. Palmer, *Promise*, pp. 115, 117.

36. Sadie J. Hart, "My Experience," *Guide to Holiness*, n.s., vol. VI, April 1869, pp. 114–15.

37. Garrison, *Forty Witnesses*, pp. 141–42, 144.

38. Richard Wheatley, *The Life and Letters of Mrs. Phoebe Palmer* (New York: W. C. Palmer, Jr., 1876), p. 67.

39. *Ibid.*, p. 67.

40. *Ibid.*, p. 283.

41. *Guide to Holiness*, vol. XXXI, May 1857, p. 135. For similar quotations see Palmer, *Promise*, p. 227, and Wheatley, *Palmer*, p. 251.

42. Sarah Grimké, *Letters on the Equality of the Sexes and the Condition of Woman* (1838; reprint ed., New York: Burt Franklin, 1970), p. 16.

43. Adam Clarke, *The Holy Bible* . . . (various editions). Cf., for example, B. T. Roberts, *Ordaining Women* (Rochester, N.Y.: Earnest Christian Publishing House, 1891), p. 59.

44. David Sherman, "Woman's Place in the Gospel," in John O. Foster, *Life and Labors of Mrs. Maggie Newton Van Cott* (Cincinnati: Hitchcock and Walden, 1872), pp. xxxiv–xxxvi.

45. J. Fowler Willing, "Woman and the Pentecost," *Guide to Holiness*, vol. LXVIII, January 1898, p. 21. See also "Woman in Gospel Evangelism," *Guide*, vol. LXIV, January 1896, p. 22; "God's Great Woman," *Guide*, vol. LXVII, December 1897, p. 226; and "Women under the Pentecostal Baptism," *Guide*, vol. LXX, February 1899, p. 52.

46. Willing, "Women under the Pentecostal Baptism," *loc. cit.*, p. 53.

47. Katharine Bushnell, *God's Word to Women* (Piedmont, Oakland, Calif.: published by the author, n.d.; reprinted by Ray B. Munson, Box 52, North Collins, N.Y., 1976).

48. Charles G. Finney, *Lectures on Revivals of Religion*, ed. William G. McLoughlin (Cambridge, Mass.: Belknap Press, 1960), p. 189.

49. Palmer, *Promise*, pp. 341, 347.

BIBLIOGRAPHY

Additional works which might be helpful are:

Dayton, Donald W. *Discovering an Evangelical Heritage*. New York: Harper & Row, 1976.

———. "Evangelical Roots of Feminism," *The Covenant Quarterly*, vol. XXXIV, November 1976, pp. 41–56.

———, and Lucille Sider Dayton, "Evangelical Feminism: Some Aspects of Its Biblical Interpretation," *Explor*, vol. II, Fall 1976, pp. 17–22.

———, and Lucille Sider Dayton, "Women as Preachers: Evangelical Precedents," *Christianity Today*, May 23, 1975, pp. 4–8.

Dayton, Lucille Sider, and Donald W. Dayton, " 'Your Daughters Shall Prophesy': Feminism in the Holiness Movement," *Methodist History*, vol. XIV, January 1976, pp. 67–92.

Hardesty, Nancy Ann, " 'Your Daughters Shall Prophesy': Revivalism and Feminism in the Age of Finney," Ph.D. dissertation, The University of Chicago, 1976.

Harrison, Beverly, "The Early Feminists and the Clergy," *Review and Expositor*, vol. LXXII, Winter 1975, pp. 41–52.

Jones, Charles Edwin, A *Guide to the Study of the Holiness Movement*. Metuchen, N.J.: Scarecrow Press, 1974.

——, *Perfectionist Persuasion: The Holiness Movement and American Methodism, 1867–1936*. Metuchen, N.J.: Scarecrow Press, 1974.

Lee, Luther, *Five Sermons and a Tract by Luther Lee*, ed. Donald W. Dayton. Chicago: Holrad House, 1975.

Magnuson, Norris, *Salvation in the Slums: Evangelical Social Work, 1865–1920*. Metuchen, N.J.: Scarecrow Press, 1977.

Rosenberg, Carroll Smith, *Religion and the Rise of the American City*. Ithaca, N.Y.: Cornell University Press, 1971.

Rossi, Alice, ed., *The Feminist Papers from Adams to de Beauvoir*. New York: Columbia University Press, 1973.

Smith, Timothy, *Revivalism and Social Reform in Mid-Nineteenth Century America*. New York: Abingdon Press, 1957.

Synan, Vinson, *The Holiness-Pentecostal Movement in the United States*. Grand Rapids, Mich.: Eerdmans, 1971.

NINE

Removing the Veil:
The Liberated American Nun

MARY EWENS, OP

Catholic nuns, though they belonged to an extremely patriarchal church whose male hierarchy defined female roles
according to medieval notions that women were irresponsible, soft-brained and incapable of logical thought, were in
some ways the most liberated women in nineteenth-century
America. The first nuns to serve in North America arrived
in Canada in 1639; their work in the continental United
States began in New Orleans in 1727. Since that time nuns,
or "sisters" as they are popularly called, have conducted numerous philanthropic projects: built hospitals, churches,
schools and orphanages; raised money to support their charitable works; and made a tremendous contribution to the
liberation of other women, particularly through education.

In their personal lives and in their work they have enjoyed
many of the freedoms and opportunities that feminists are
pleading for today. They have supported themselves, owned
property, received an advanced education, and held executive positions. They have not feared success; have had men-
tors who gave them encouragement and advice; and have
been freed from the responsibilities of marriage and motherhood. They have transcended sex-role stereotypes and enjoyed friendships based not on sexuality but on common
interests and a sharing of the deepest aspirations of the

human soul. Their numbers reached more than 180,000 in the United States by 1966. Yet they are hardly mentioned in bibliographies of women's history or women's studies. It is time to remove the veil that has too long obscured the story of these women, and to add their chapter to the history of American women.

Liberating Experiences

Many historians have documented what Page Smith calls "the Great Repression," which forced American women back into their homes and into the roles of wife, mother and helpmate in the nineteenth century, when the Industrial Revolution had deprived them of meaningful occupations outside the home. A study of the lives of American nuns in the nineteenth century reveals that their experiences were strikingly different from those of their married sisters. Relieved of the responsibilities of marriage and motherhood, they enjoyed the personal fulfillment that comes from opportunities for meaningful and useful work, education and economic independence, and lived in groups that gave them warm sisterly support and encouragement. The hard-pressed bishops and priests for whom and with whom they worked usually supported them with gratitude for their help, advice, encouragement, contacts, and warm friendship and whatever financial resources they could muster. In those instances in which churchmen tried to interfere with their work or overstep the limits of their authority, the nuns were protected by their constitutions, which clearly defined responsibilities and obligations on all sides and could not usually be changed at the whim of a single individual.

There are a number of reasons, both theological and cultural, why nuns were able to transcend the usual sex-role stereotypes for women. Most women who joined the convent had been deeply imbued from childhood with an understanding of the importance of the spiritual life and a desire to imitate the life of Jesus, to grow in virtue, and to conquer weakness through penance and mortification. The Mass, the sacraments (except for holy orders), the virtues of faith, prudence, justice and fortitude, and the gifts of wisdom, understanding, knowledge, and piety were for all, and the young woman was encouraged to take advantage of them. At home, in the parish, and in the convent schools that they often attended, girls were surrounded by role models in the Christian virtues, both male and female, in living exemplars and in the lives of the saints whom they were taught to imitate, and whose intercession before the throne of God they were encouraged to seek.

The high calling of the nun was to a life of prayer, of imitation of the life of Christ, of service to Christ through service to others, of response to his command to spread the Gospel to all nations. One who answered this call felt that she had been specially chosen by God for a noble vocation, and thus her self-image was enhanced. Life was seen in terms of action rather than passivity, and submission to the will of Christ prepared one to undertake great works in order to spread his kingdom. The religious habit which concealed her body under layers of serge proclaimed to the world that the nun was not an object of sexual exploitation, but wished to relate to others on a deeper level than that of physiology. Even the practice of sometimes taking the name of a male saint, and choosing him as a model or patron, had its positive aspects. If the more heroic virtues were seen oftener among male saints, then women who chose them for their models might be encouraged to strive for "male" virtues and transcend the usual stereotypes for women. The nun who modeled her life on that of Christ was ready to carry difficult projects through to a successful conclusion.

In the novitiate new members deepened their spiritual life and learned to live and work in sisterly support of one another. Talents and abilities that would enable them to do useful work were carefully assessed and developed and defects of character or personality were rooted out. The most successful teachers or nurses supervised the apprenticeship of those just beginning the work, and those with administrative talents had internships to prepare them for positions of authority. In a world in which males administered the sacraments but females held all other posts of responsibility, one expected to find work that would fulfill her highest ambitions in due time. Florence Nightingale was poignantly aware of the contrast between the opportunities enjoyed by nuns and those that were open to other women, and she thought at one time of becoming a nun herself. She wrote to the man who would become Cardinal Manning:

You do know now . . . what a home the Catholic Church is. And yet what is she to you compared with what she would be to me? No one can tell, no man can tell, what she is to women, their training, their discipline, their hopes, their home. . . . For what training is there compared to that of the Catholic nun? . . . I have seen something of different kinds of nun, am no longer young, and do not speak from enthusiasm but from experience. There is nothing like the training (in these days) which the Sacred Heart or the Order of St. Vincent gives to women.[1]

Thus from the time they were very young, Catholic girls were made aware, at home, at school and in church, of a highly esteemed alternative to marriage. The fact that convents had been abolished in France and other countries during and after the French Revolution gave a greater impetus among European Catholics for the founding of new communities and the reestablishment of old ones, as soon as the religious persecutions abated.

Mother Caroline Friess

Mother Caroline Friess, superior of the American houses of the School Sisters of Notre Dame in the last half of the nineteenth century, was one who was formed in this tradition. Josephine Friess was born in Paris in 1824 to a Bavarian couple who returned to their native land and their highly successful family leather goods business four years after her birth.[2] Her strong-willed mother was an excellent manager of business and domestic affairs, and her father was known for his erudition and linguistic ability. He valued education so highly that he decided to leave the four-year-old Josephine with her uncle, Father Michael Friess, and her grandmother in the town of Donauwörth, where there was a well-known Benedictine school, until her education should be completed. Her mother's objections brought about a compromise whereby Josephine would spend her summers with her family.

Father Friess devised a comprehensive plan for the education of his precocious protégée, and he supplemented the school lessons she began at five with training in concentration and good study habits, a carefully guided reading program (including the doctors of the Church and accounts of foreign missionaries) and encouragement in the acquisition of virtue and the curbing of her impatience and pride. He himself chose her playmates and stressed good sportsmanship and self-control in the games he supervised. Her grandmother taught her the basics of housekeeping, neatness and good health habits. In the summers spent with her family, she enjoyed the games of her brothers more than those of her sisters, and proved herself a born leader.

As her uncle's abilities as a preacher came to be recognized, he was assigned to positions of greater importance, and Josephine and her grandmother accompanied him to his new posts. When she was ten, he became an assistant to Bishop Reisach of Eichstädt, and she began five years of education at the old Benedictine convent of St. Walburga, founded in 870. Here she would have imbibed the spirit of the great Benedictine women of the past, Saints Walburga, Lioba, Thecla, Hilda, Gertrude and Hroswitha, whose accomplishments as missionaries, as executives ruling both men and women, as scholars and as writers would make them powerful role models for her. Her special patrons throughout her life were the Virgin Mary, Saint Joseph, and Saint Catherine of Siena, whose names she had been given in baptism, and Saint Aloysius Gonzaga, the patron of youth. The sisters who taught her would have been living examples of virtuous and rewarding lives. In her uncle's home Josephine took part in the conversations when statesmen, clergymen and other friends came to call, and she was the special protégé of Bishop Reisach, who was her spiritual director and gave her conferences on prayer, moral uprightness and obedience. In her last years at St. Walburga's she spent a part of each day at the Bishop's residence learning domestic science so that no facet of womanly accomplishments would be unknown to her.

At the age of fifteen, Josephine finished her education at St. Walburga's with a brilliant academic record and a certificate as an elementary-school teacher. She had wanted to become a nun since the day of her First Communion in 1836, and she began to consider which community she would enter. Neither her uncle nor Bishop Reisach felt that her health could stand the rigors of a cloistered community, so she decided to join the new congregation of the Poor School Sisters of Notre Dame, which Mother Theresa had founded under the guidance and direction of Bishop Michael Wittmann of Ratisbon in 1833. Its rules were based on those of an earlier group of similar name which had been disbanded by government decree in 1809, but they were modified to allow the sisters to teach outside the cloister in small towns and rural areas. Their chief work was parochial education.

When her mother opposed her entrance into this community in 1840 at the age of sixteen, Josephine looked to her patron, Saint Aloysius Gonzaga, whose father had blocked his entrance into the Jesuits, for help in convincing her. She weathered the storm and soon entered the novitiate, in which the character development so assiduously pursued by her uncle was continued, and she was imbued with the idea that "every God-given endowment of mind and body entails a corresponding duty on the part of the receiver to cultivate it . . . for the Creator's honor and glory." [3] Mother Theresa and Father Matthias Siegert, who had become the community's chaplain in 1833, were her chief teachers, and in 1841 she passed with the rank of Number One the examination for certification as a secondary-school teacher. She received the habit and the name of Sister Mary Caroline in 1842, and took vows of poverty, chastity and obedience in 1845. During these years, in addition to her secular and religious studies, she taught for a part of each day in the boarding school attached to the convent, and thus became acquainted with the sisters' educational methods.

In 1847 the Redemptorist priests who had gone to America to work among the German immigrants there sought Mother Theresa's help in ministering to the needs of their countrymen, who were in danger of losing their Catholic faith because there was no one to instruct them in their own language. The Redemptorists had established a number of parishes and wanted Mother Theresa's sisters to teach in the parish schools. The King of Bavaria urged Mother Theresa to accede to their request and promised to help defray the cost of the expedition. She acquiesced, and decided to accompany the first band of four sisters herself, that she might become acquainted with the needs and conditions of the American Church.

Sister Caroline, at the age of twenty-three, was among this first group of volunteers who set out in 1847, eager to use the talents, which had been so carefully nurtured by her teachers, in the service of her countrymen, and to imitate the exploits of the foreign missionaries whom she admired. The experiences of these sisters and their reactions to the alien and in many ways hostile American culture are typical of those of thousands of other immigrant nuns who left comfortable, refined homes to spread the Gospel on the frontiers of America. Mother Theresa's long letters to Father Matthias Siegert, the motherhouse chaplain who was her adviser, helper, confidant and close friend, spoke candidly of the problems they faced in establishing their American foundations and included wise observations on all facets of American life.[4] She recounted their sufferings on shipboard, the seasickness, fever, thirst and storms they had endured, and described the poverty of the Pennsylvania backwoods log cabin that was their first American convent. This cultured and educated woman of fifty was aghast at what she saw of American schools, child-rearing practices and social equality, and she agonized over the plight of the German immigrants. Shortly after her arrival in America she wrote to King Ludwig I of Bavaria thanking him for his financial aid and noting,

How pitiful is the plight of the poor Germans. Entire families grow up and die without being baptized or instructed in their religion, especially those who live in the primeval forests. English institutions receive assistance in abundance so that the English way of living may prevail, although English morals are not the best. The poor Germans are left empty-handed; the German priests receive no support for their churches, schools, and parishes. Anything German is an object of contempt to the British, and is suppressed, even by the Bishops.[5]

The Redemptorist Father (later Bishop and Saint) John Neumann welcomed them with great kindness and took a personal interest in their affairs, but they encountered the ethnic antipathies so prominent in the nineteenth-century Church when they sought approval of their work from bishops. Mother Theresa lamented to Father Siegert,

Germans are not liked here. It is openly stated that German schools should close, so that the Germans can be assimilated into the English-speaking nation, and become one with her. The superior here . . . spoke emphatically against this when he discussed with the Most Reverend Bishop the establishment of a branch house of our order here at Pittsburgh. The latter did not even state whether he would permit us to be here. He is afraid of jealousy

and disharmony on the part of the sisters he requested from Ire-
land. Since he himself is Irish, these sisters are his favorites and
darlings. He has entrusted the hospital, the orphanage and the
English-speaking schools to them.[6]

Sister Caroline was given charge of the first school, at St.
Mary's, Pennsylvania, but was later called to open another
in Baltimore. "I am training her to become a superior,"
wrote Mother Theresa to Father Siegert, but she also expresses certain doubts about her abilities: "Sister Caroline
needs direction for five or six years; she must be instructed
and taught humility. She is young and inexperienced. Neither of the two sisters understands building, and the order
could be made financially liable."[7] She took Caroline with
her on visits to places where they had been asked to open
schools, and made sure she was aware of the circumstances
and conditions of each. "She will, without doubt, become a
good superior general if, in the course of time, she grows in
humility, holy seriousness, the love of God, and the spirit of
the order," she wrote.[8]

Mother Theresa wasted no time in turning to the opening
of schools. Leaving two sisters at St. Mary's, she proceeded
to Baltimore, where St. James' School was opened on October 8, St. Michael's on October 11, and St. Alphonsus' on
November 3. Fortunately some young women asked to join
the community, and she put them to work in the schools
immediately. In a little more than three months she had
opened four schools, which were staffed by a nucleus of five
sisters. (She was to establish 291 houses of her congregation
in all parts of the world before her death in 1879.) Now
Mother Theresa wrote to Munich for reinforcements, and
stipulated that the persons sent should be

healthy, strong, robust and courageous; each must be capable of
filling the post of superior, and must be a competent teacher in the
elementary school and in the Industrial Arts department. . . .
Great prudence is needed to manage the children and their par-

ents successfully, and only a keen insight and strong will can meet
and conquer the various difficulties that arise in the school room
and outside it. Without these qualities it is not apparently possible
to hold one's own in a German-American school. Neither are
mannish, rough sisters acceptable. . . .[9]

Her suggestion that the sisters who came should "reduce the
amount of luggage as much as possible" and "not take more
than they are able to carry and watch personally"[10] sounds
a familiar note to today's transatlantic traveler, but the more
homely instructions such as "Horsetail and zinc bloom do
not grow in America; please send some of each," connote
another world of folk wisdom and home remedies.

In March of 1848 Mother Theresa, Sister Caroline, and
Father Neumann undertook a 2,500-mile journey to inspect
places where the sisters had been asked to open schools, and
then Mother Theresa began to plan for her return to the
motherhouse in Munich. She was troubled at the thought
that the sisters she was leaving behind in America were
young and inexperienced, and she was very much aware of
the clashes between European and American religious values that they would have to face. She wrote to Father Siegert, "I feel less capable of being a superior here than in
Europe, and I must take steps to resign; otherwise, I shall
spoil everything. Sisters Caroline and Seraphina have a calling for America; their views are opposite mine, and I am
sure the Lord will assist them when they are in a position of
authority."[11] Hesitant to impose the burdens of being a superior on Sister Caroline, the youngest of the sisters, she
named the eldest among them, Sister Seraphina, to that post
and put Sister Caroline in charge of the schools. She left in
July 1849, happy that Father Neumann had promised to
guide and direct the sisters during the next five years.

In August 1849, Sister Caroline opened St. Peter's School
in Philadelphia. In this City of Brotherly Love where there
had been anti-Catholic riots in 1844, the sisters were insulted
on the streets and pelted with mud. (It was experiences like

these that impelled all American sisters to wear secular dress when walking the streets or traveling.) At night they slept in specially prepared robes, so that they might be decently attired should they suddenly have to leave their convents. The burning of the Charlestown, Massachusetts, convent in 1834 had not been forgotten.

As they gained experience of the American milieu, and the needs and demands of the people they served, it became clear to Sister Caroline, her companions and her advisers that certain changes had to be made in their rules if their work for the Church was to prosper. The Church's canon law regulations for religious congregations were formulated in medieval times, and revised in the sixteenth century, in order to correct abuses that had crept in when, consigned to convents by their fathers or others, women who did not really choose to live lives of poverty, chastity and obedience had been professed. Among the most onerous of these regulations were cloistral prescriptions which restricted contact with the world outside the convent walls. Based on a European attitude that the nun was a *jeune fille*, childlike, irresponsible, incapable of directing her own life and in need of constant surveillance, these rules were singularly inappropriate in America. One of the chief problems faced by American nuns, even into the 1970s, has been that of determining the extent to which cloistral practices that were carried over from another age and an alien culture could or should be adapted to an American setting.

According to the rule of enclosure, nuns could not venture beyond their convent walls, nor could others enter, except with the bishop's permission. A grating in the parlor called a grille separated a nun from her visitors, whom she never saw without a companion. The convent had to be built in such proximity to the church that the choir or chapel would open onto the sanctuary of the church, thus enabling the sisters to attend Mass without leaving their convent precincts. The school too had to be built adjacent to the convent, and sisters could confer with parents, pastors, etc., only in the convent parlor, where the nun sat behind the grille. They would have to leave their classrooms unattended in order to escort visitors to the parlor if some business matter came up during school hours. Arrangements such as these proved very difficult in America, where the convent might be several blocks from church or school.

Sister Caroline saw clearly that changes had to be made and remembered that adaptation to local conditions had been one of the chief characteristics of her congregation at the time of its founding. Father Neumann and other priests encouraged her to take a stand, but Mother Theresa ignored all of her letters to the Munich motherhouse. Wanting to settle the matter once and for all, the sisters decided that Sister Caroline should go to Munich as their representative and place the matter before Mother Theresa and Father Siegert in person. They neglected to inform the motherhouse of this decision, however.

Caroline set out alone on the third anniversary of her arrival in America and was received with suspicion at the motherhouse. There she was assigned a room in the guest quarters, where she could not contaminate the other sisters with her dangerous ideas. She pleaded the cause of the Church in America with great courage, however, and was rewarded when her uncle and her old friends Archbishop Reisach and Father Siegert took her part. So powerful were their arguments that Mother Theresa not only relented but gave Mother Caroline, as she then came to be called, complete authority over all of the American missions and instructed her to build a new motherhouse in Milwaukee. Though Mother Theresa gave grudging consent to changes in the rules, she continued to share with many European priests, bishops and superiors a hostile attitude toward American freedom and democracy, and to voice these sentiments in her letters. She wrote to the cardinal protector of the congregation in Rome in 1854:

If the superior in Milwaukee, Mary Caroline Friess permits herself so many irregularities now when she has the approved Rule in her hand, what will she do in the future if she becomes a provincial superior with the power and authority of a superior general? The Rule will be changed to her taste; she will put the sisters in classes with young boys, send them into open fields to work, and into stores to make purchases, put on shows, and take them to the theatre after the conclusion of examinations. . . . We wish only to regulate the unbridled freedom of the American people according to Christian maxims. How long can our order survive in America in this fashion? Besides, what will it profit us if we gain all of America and in so doing perish ourselves? [12]

Strengthened by the success of her difficult mission to the Munich motherhouse, and armed with the authority to adapt the constitutions to American needs, Mother Caroline set out for Milwaukee upon her return to America, and began the remarkable career for which her training had so carefully prepared her. She and the pioneer sisters arrived in Milwaukee on December 15, 1850, and from that day until her death on July 22, 1892, it was the center from which her activities and her influence radiated across the country. Her life was a constant round of religious exercises, building projects, provision for the instruction of new recruits, supervision of schools, correspondence with pastors and bishops, and interminable travel. By the time of her death she had opened 265 schools in seventeen states and Canada, and had given the habit of her order to over three thousand young women.

This remarkable growth was no doubt attributable to Mother Caroline's head-on confrontation with the problem of adapting European ways to the needs of the American Church. Many other communities experienced an uneasy tension because of conflicting expectations that strained the relations between, on the one hand, American nuns and their European superiors and, on the other, their local pastors and bishops. Even those communities which had been founded in America without any European ties usually had to contend with the European backgrounds of the priests who were their advisers, who wanted religious life to be lived as strictly on the American frontier as it was in Rome. Fortunately, most local superiors were willing to forget the niceties of aristocratic European customs and get on with the work of the Gospel.

Children of the leading families of a city often attended the sisters' schools, as in Milwaukee, because they were the best schools available. Through them the most advanced European pedagogical methods might be introduced in remote settlements. In many instances a majority of the students were Protestants, who became the sisters' staunchest defenders against the slurs of bigots and helped to change public attitudes toward nuns and the Church they represented.

Tuition money helped to defray the expenses of the sisters' institutions, and Sister Caroline and others instituted a system of "pay schools" and "free schools" in order to finance works of charity for the poor. Other adaptations to the American economic scene had to be made as well. European convents were traditionally supported by the income from endowments given by wealthy benefactors, often members of the nobility, and from the dowries that members brought with them when they entered a community. Income from the ownership of property, from the sale of surplus crops and perhaps from educational activities might supplement the interest on endowments. Thus active communities were able to serve the poor *gratis*. In America, where there were few wealthy Catholics, the financial security of religious communities was much more tenuous, and nuns had to find new sources of income in order to survive.

As we have seen, Mother Theresa's initial venture in America was supported by King Ludwig I of Bavaria. Her community continued to receive donations from the Louis Mission Society and the Leopoldine Association of Vienna for a number of years. The sisters sent careful annual reports and descriptions of the works they were able to carry on because of the generous gifts of their countrymen, and their letters show that they had a highly developed sense of public relations.

Mother Theresa studied the economic situation in America and concluded,

We cannot use sisters and young ladies who desire only to live a quiet, retired conventual life, those who can not be employed in school; unless they bring with them considerable funds which bear a yearly interest of at least 200 dollars. This is considered the lowest amount annually needed for the support and needs of an individual.[13]

She had various suggestions for increasing the sisters' income. "Small wax figures of the Infant Jesus might . . . find a market here," she noted,[14] and again, "The publishing of school books might well be a good source of income; however, you would have to have a good school man, an experienced educator to assist in this; otherwise, you might expose yourself to much criticism. Text books by women usually have no value, and receive little respect." [15]

The School Sisters of Notre Dame devoted themselves almost exclusively to schools in which children could learn religious doctrines while at the same time they prepared for their future positions in society. Other communities, however, carried on a variety of works for the public good—nursing the sick, visiting the imprisoned, caring for orphans, helping the poor—as the need arose. In times of local or national crises such as epidemics or wars, even the teaching sisters turned out to care for the suffering. During the cholera and yellow fever epidemics, which ravaged the country in 1838–39, 1849–50 and 1855, all but the most strictly cloistered gave devoted service.

It was in military nursing that American nuns really distinguished themselves, however. They nursed the wounded in every war fought on American soil, but gave exceptional service during the Civil War, in which one fifth of all female military nurses were nuns. They led the way in assisting the surgeons in the thick of battle and won for all women the right to nurse on the battlefield. Other nurses such as Mary Livermore and Kate Cumming paid high tribute to their work in the war and explained why surgeons preferred nuns to all other nurses. Cumming, matron of a Confederate hospital in Tennessee, confided to her diary how sick she was of people who said that nursing was not a proper occupation for ladies, and noticed how nuns were able to break through this barrier:

A very nice lady, a member of the Methodist Church, told me that she would go into the hospital if she had in it a brother, a surgeon. I wonder if the Sisters of Charity have brothers, surgeons, in the hospitals where they go? It seems strange that they can do with honor what is wrong for Christian women to do. Well, I cannot but pity those who have such false notions of propriety.[16]

Letters, diaries and journals kept by sisters during the war record the grisly scenes they had witnessed, the courage of the wounded, the ways in which the nursing services were organized, and the nuns' spiritual ministrations to the suffering: preparing soldiers for death, instructing them in Christian truths, preparing them to receive the sacraments.

The result of the sisters' nursing during the Civil War was a complete reversal of the popular image of the nun and in the attitudes of the American public toward nuns. The religious habit that had attracted ridicule in the 1850s was a badge of honor in the 1870s.

As schools, hospitals and orphanages multiplied, the influence of the sisters grew. Their institutions were patronized by people of all faiths, and their schools were a strong civilizing influence. They dispelled anti-Catholic sentiment among all with whom they came in contact. There was scope indeed for personal fulfillment—meaningful work, service to others and to the Church, and even high adventure—in the life of the nun, and thousands of women embraced it. In 1850 there were 1,375 nuns in America, and the number had grown to almost 40,000 by 1900.

Though the Catholic Church excluded women from its hierarchy and did not even allow them to hold official roles in its liturgy or ritual, it did give its approval to the religious communities through which women exerted a powerful influence on church members and society. Sisters worked closely with priests and bishops in providing for the needs of the people in a given area, and they probably had more to do with the Christian formation of children and young women than did the clergy. It was often the women who did the spadework in religious instruction, preparing people to receive the sacraments, visiting the sick, the needy, the orphan, the aged; the priests then did the actual baptizing, hearing of confessions, anointing of the sick, marrying and burying. If power is "the ability to act," "the capability of producing or undergoing an effect," "the possession of sway or controlling influence over others," as *Webster's New Collegiate Dictionary* holds, then who is to say that Catholic nuns held less power in their unofficial positions in the Church in the nineteenth century than did the churchmen who filled the official posts of authority? The evidence reveals that Catholic nuns in nineteenth-century America did indeed enjoy far more freedom than other women in most areas of their lives. They were soon to experience their own Great Repression, however, one which was similar to that which had forced many women back into their homes at the beginning of the nineteenth century.

The Great Repression of the Twentieth Century

While some of the shift in roles for American nuns at the beginning of the twentieth century may have been the consequence of the evolution from the hardships of early beginnings to a more stable and secure situation, much of it had to do with the tightening of their ties with Rome. I have discussed the evolution of canon-law regulations for nuns in detail elsewhere;[17] here I will condense and simplify this complex subject.

By the twentieth century, the Roman Catholic Church had developed a uniform system for granting official approval to the constitutions of religious communities. Its criteria were published and explained in the bull *Conditae a Christo* of 1900 and in the *Normae* of 1901. In 1917 the Church's canon law was codified for the first time in six hundred years, and the application of its prescriptions to the minute details of daily life became a science engaging a whole corps of priest experts. The very different approaches of English common law and Roman law to the application of regulations in specific instances led Americans to interpret general rules more stringently than was intended by Roman lawmakers, complicating the situation yet further.

Now specific cloistral regulations that must be followed by all sisters were spelled out in detail, and heads of religious congregations were required to answer and submit to Rome every five years a detailed questionnaire, which measured the degree to which they were following the prescriptions of canon law. Among the kinds of work considered unsuitable for religious women were the care of babies, the nursing of maternity cases and the staffing of coeducational schools.

Sisters were pushed back behind their cloister walls and were no longer so free to respond to contemporary needs. The most obvious change that one notes when one studies the lives of twentieth-century nuns is in the emphasis on the dangers of "particular friendships," and the absence of the warm, supportive relationships with men which were so much a part of the lives of earlier nuns and contributed so much to the success of their work. The essentials of religious life, the vows, an intense prayer life, the virtues, participation in the sacraments, etc., continued to be valued, but the emphasis on the letter of the law and on external details of behavior sometimes obscured the message of the Gospel. Fortunately, there are many examples that prove that some nuns were able to become truly liberated women under this regime, despite the petty restrictions of canon law.

In the 1960s, with the convoking of the Second Vatican Council, religious communities were told to reexamine their rules and their lives in the light of the Gospels, the spirit of their foundresses and the demands of contemporary culture. They were once again free to create a life style in which they could enjoy the opportunities that are the goals of the women's movement, and to be liberated and liberating. Whether or not they will take full advantage of their freedom remains to be seen. Surely the story of their struggles and of the accomplishments of the thousands of American nuns who have led the way in the past is an important chapter in the history of American women.

BIBLIOGRAPHICAL SOURCES

There is an abundance of material available to one who wishes to study the contribution of nuns to American society. Many American communities began as missionary projects emanating from European motherhouses. Business arrangements and contact with European superiors and with families and friends necessitated a tremendous volume of correspondence. Mother Theodore Guerin, foundress of the American Sisters of Providence, for example, records the sending of over five thousand letters in her journals, and there are 5,337 extant documents written by Mother Theresa Gerhardinger, foundress of the School Sisters of Notre Dame. Whether a community originated in Europe or America, the operation of its charitable works and the organization of its internal affairs entailed the keeping of records, letters, reports, etc., on file at the motherhouse or elsewhere. Some communities have preserved the custom of appointing an annalist for each house who records the significant events that occur there.

The extent to which primary materials such as these have been saved, collected and catalogued varies tremendously from one religious community to another. Many have not kept archives until very recently; others have had a keen historical sense and have a rich store of materials. Though many circumstances such as fire, flood, persecution, frequent changes of residence, and lack of space have caused the loss of primary materials, other factors have led to their preservation. The memory of the pioneer sisters of a community, particularly of its foundress, is usually held in great reverence by their spiritual daughters, who seek to emulate their virtues and therefore cherish anything connected with their lives. Should their sanctity seem to merit consideration for canonization as saints of the Church, transcripts of everything ever written by or about them must be sent to Rome. This results in the collection of all relevant materials at a central location, and careful study and preservation.

Often the biography of a foundress or an outstanding sister will be written and published so that the history and essential spirit of a community and its heroines may be transmitted to future generations of nuns, or the silver or golden jubilee of a group will be the occasion for the writing of its history. Dozens of histories of American communities and biographies of outstanding members have been published, many of them written by members of the order with some training in historical method. These accounts vary tremendously as to quality of scholarship, use of primary materials, and discussion of community problems and incidents that reflect the human failings of individual members or others with whom they have dealt. Even those that are not models of scholarship, however, often include enough facts, biographical sketches and quotations from primary sources to convey some idea of the achievements and contributions of the community.

An analysis of 130 histories, biographies, articles and autobiographical books dealing with nineteenth-century American nuns [18] reveals that eight percent are diaries, collections of letters, and journals, while another forty-five percent are of high quality, with generous use of primary sources and scholarly documentation. Twenty percent are more popular works that do not include documentation, and eighteen percent are primarily chronological listings of factual information such as the opening of new hospitals and schools, the names of the personnel assigned, and brief biographies. Only eleven of these 130 books could be said to belong to the realm of pious legend rather than history. Four fifths of them have been written by women, many of them trained sister-historians who deserve credit for their contributions to women's history. Sisters engaged in graduate study have often examined

certain aspects of their community's history or of Catholic education or history in their master's theses and doctoral dissertations.
Sister Elizabeth Kolmer includes a survey of the literature in her
article "Catholic Women Religious" in the Summer 1978 issue of
American Quarterly.

Since the Second Vatican Council, when sisters were told to
reexamine their roots and study the charisms of their foundresses,
there has been considerable interest among nuns themselves in
the history of their communities. In many instances a diligent
search has been made for relevant materials, and these have been
studied in the light of modern historiographical methods. Volumes
of letters have been collected and published, and earlier histories
have been reissued or rewritten. The School Sisters of Notre
Dame provide one example of this trend among many that could
be cited. Their Sister Mary Hester Valentine has translated and
edited the letters of the German foundress, Mother M. Theresa
Gerhardinger, and published selections in three volumes, one of
which is devoted solely to letters having to do with the community's North American foundations.[19] These letters contain invalu-
able insights into the attitudes, problems, and customs of nineteenth-century religious, particularly the immigrant groups, and
shed light on many aspects of their experiences in America. Some
communities like the Sisters of Charity of the Blessed Virgin Mary
and the Benedictine Federation have published volumes that reflect the thinking behind the many changes that these groups have
made since the Second Vatican Council.[20] The Sinsinawa (Wis-
consin) Dominican Sisters have begun, under the leadership of
Sister Elizabeth O'Hanlon, an oral-history collection of tape-re-
corded interviews which focus on the history of this congregation
and supplement its written records.

The Bicentennial year saw the sponsorship by the Leadership
Conference of Women Religious, with a grant from the National
Historical Publications and Records Commission, of a series of
workshops for community archivists as the first step toward a general survey of source materials in the archives of religious women's
communities. This survey, conducted by Sister Evangeline
Thomas, is scheduled to be completed and the results published
by 1981. The Women's History Resources Survey of the University
of Minnesota is also studying the availability of materials of this
kind.

Information of a more specialized kind can be found in such places as the archives and histories of individual dioceses, the offices of diocesan superintendents of Catholic schools, parish archives, the Catholic Hospital Association, the archives of the Bureau of Catholic Indian Missions at Marquette University, the Center for the Study of American Catholic Church History at Notre Dame, and the files of the Catholic newspapers of the various dioceses. Organizations of sisters such as the Leadership Conference of Women Religious, the Sister Formation Conference, the National Assembly of Women Religious, the National Black Sisters Conference, the National Coalition of American Nuns, Sisters Uniting, the Consortium Perfectae Caritatis, Las Hermanas, the Association of Contemplative Sisters, the Tekakwitha Conference and the National Sisters' Vocation Conference are also sources of information.[21] *The National Catholic Reporter* publishes items on newsworthy people, and *Sisters Today* and *Review for Religious* contain theoretical discussions. A perusal of this material reveals the great variety of activities carried on by thousands of American nuns, both in the present and in the past.

NOTES

1. Shane Leslie, "Forgotten Passages in the Life of Florence Nightingale," *The Dublin Review*, vol. CLXI, October 1917, p. 181.

2. All details about the life of Mother Caroline are based on information contained in Sister Dympna Flynn, *Mother Caroline and the School Sisters of Notre Dame in North America*, vol. I (St. Louis: Woodward & Tiernan, 1928).

3. *Ibid.*, p.22.

4. *The North American Foundations: Letters of Mother M. Theresa Gerhardinger, School Sister of Notre Dame* (Winona, Minn.: St. Mary's College, 1977), *passim*.

5. *Ibid.*, p. 43.

6. *Ibid.*, p. 63.

7. *Ibid.*, pp. 81, 88.

8. *Ibid.*, p. 92.

9. *Ibid.*, p. 68.

10. *Ibid.*, pp. 71–72.

11. *Ibid.*, p. 77.

12. *Ibid.*, p. 116.

13. *Ibid.*, p. 68.

14. *Ibid.*, p. 69.

15. *Ibid.*, p. 133.

16. Kate Cumming, A *Journal of Hospital Life in the Confederate Army* . . . (Louisville: Morton, 1866), p. 178.

17. Mary Ewens, *The Role of the Nun in Nineteenth-Century America* (New York: Arno, 1978), *passim*.

18. These are listed in the bibliography of *ibid*.

19. Gerhardinger, *North American Foundations*.

20. Joan Chittister, O.S.B., et al., *Climb Along the Cutting Edge* (New York: Paulist Press, 1977); Sister Rita Mary Benz and Sister Rosemary Sage (eds.), *Self-Study for Renewal* (Dubuque: Mount Carmel, 1968), and *Kinetics of Renewal* (Dubuque: Mount Carmel, 1969).

21. Further information about these organizations may be found in annual editions of *The Catholic Almanac* and *The Official Catholic Directory*.

TEN

"Their Prodigious Influence": Women, Religion and Reform in Antebellum America

DOROTHY C. BASS

"The sects called evangelical were the first agitators of the woman question," declared Lydia Maria Child, author and abolitionist. By convincing women of "their prodigious influence, and consequent responsibility, in the great work of regenerating a world lying in wickedness," churchmen who had sought women's aid in spreading the Gospel had incidentally—and inadvertently—contributed to the emancipation of women themselves. As missionaries and as members of benevolent societies spawned by a militant Protestantism in the first half of the nineteenth century, Child argued, women had found that their "sympathies and thoughts" became "active, and enlarged far beyond the bounds of the hearth and the nursery." Indeed, by 1837, as she spoke, some women had begun to apply "the zeal and strength of newly exercised freedom" to the cause of women's rights—much to the horror of their clerical patrons.

Child found an apt parallel in an old fable, one which relied on an appropriately domestic metaphor—the fable of the sorcerer's apprentice. After watching his master turn a broom into a man capable of carrying water from a nearby river, the apprentice decided to lighten his work by using the spell himself. At first he was delighted to see the bewitched object sprouting arms and legs to do his bidding—until he realized that he had forgotten how to turn it back into a broom. As tubs, floor and furniture overflowed with water, the terrified apprentice cried, "Stop! Stop! We shall all be drowned, if you don't stop!" Child drew the lesson with a smile: "Thus it is with those who urged women to become missionaries, and form tract societies. They have changed the household utensil to a living, energetic being; and they have no spell to turn it into a broom again."[1]

Since historical change proceeds neither by sorcery nor by transparent logic, the actual transformation of activist churchwoman to women's-rights crusader lacked the simplicity of Child's allegory. But during the course of the Second Great Awakening (1795–1835), many women turned the dynamic spirit of religious reform in a variety of new directions unforeseen by those who had first enlisted their aid in regenerating a world lying in wickedness. Beginning modestly as helpmeets to their brethren in the voluntary associations of a massive evangelical crusade, some went on to become organized agents of charity and morality on their own account. By the end of the period, female moral reformers and abolitionists had applied the methods and ideas of social regeneration in two causes of striking import for the status of their sex. As the reaction of many conservative evangelical clergymen to the movement of these women from the obscurity of the pew to new positions of visibility demonstrated, evangelical religion was not in itself necessarily subversive of the old pattern of women's secondary status. Rather, it was a profoundly social fact that made the evangelicals the first agitators of the woman question: religious reform was the largest and most important extrafamilial activity of middle-class women in this period, and it became the arena in which many of the tensions surrounding their role in a modernizing and expanding society surfaced.

Most eighteenth-century Americans had assumed that the role of woman in church and society was decisively settled, and, in comparison to their descendants, they seemed to find it unnecessary to say much about her.[2] In an essentially hierarchical society, a male clergy stood over a mostly female laity in matters religious just as husbands stood over wives in matters legal. Preindustrial patterns of production assured the typical woman of a central place in her family's economic life, however, and intense private devotion and, perhaps, membership in a female prayer circle likely helped her to find in religion some quiet satisfaction of her own needs for both introspection and sociality. But changes apparent in the Northeast by early in the nineteenth century created a large class of women whose lives differed substantially from those of their mothers. Residents of growing cities and towns, and increasingly relieved of household production by the forces of industry and their husbands' cash-earning jobs, the women of the rising middle class adopted the tasks of modern domesticity: child care, homemaking, consuming. Though hardly less subordinate than under the old order, they were both more leisured and more aware of the differences between their own lives and those of men. These were the women who would join the evangelical crusade.

The crusade itself was nurtured by the rapid social change which so affected the lives of women. In a new nation whose yet unformed moral character hung in the balance, growing cities seemed to churchmen to harbor vice, ignorance and poverty, while the sprawling frontier seemed the abode of atheism and anarchy. Millennial hopes that the young republic might become the new Zion clashed with the realities of a democracy which seemed unwilling to respect either Gospel morality or clerical leadership. With too great a capacity for confusing the two—but with a genuine, if parochial, concern for the sinners they sought to reclaim—the evangelical clergy seized the initiative with a massive campaign for the souls and minds of Americans.[3] Forced by democracy, disestablishment, pluralism and mobility to win by voluntary assent what they could not impose from above, large segments of several older denominations—Presbyterians, Congregationalists, Baptists and, to a lesser extent, Episcopalians—and a rapidly growing younger one, Methodism, relinquished Calvinism to offer salvation on increasingly democratic terms, to all who would have it, in widespread revivals. Institutional innovations accompanied theological ones. Voluntary associations formed to support a variety of religious and humanitarian ends. Missions to the heathen abroad and to the unchurched at home, Sunday schools, the distribution of Bibles and tracts, charitable relief of the poor consolidated the participation of laypeople in the crusade while reaching outward to regenerate a world lying in wickedness by regenerating all the individuals who inhabited it. New Englanders, heirs of a theocratic tradition and a myth of past moral order not unlike their hopes for America's future, led the way, with hearty support from evangelicals in the Middle Atlantic States and from the uprooted New Englanders who peopled the vast interior of the Empire State and the Western Reserve. A religious movement whose goals and activities extended far beyond the walls of any church, the militant Protestantism of the Second Great Awakening stood ready to claim the energies of all who were on its side in the struggle to turn the disorder of the present age from a harbinger of national dissolution into a final victory over Satan. Indeed, it stood ready to claim even the energies of women.

The simultaneous appearance of a militant Protestantism in need of workers and a large group of willing and able women encouraged the rapid development of female voluntary associations. Before 1815, the members of hundreds of female mite societies contributed a cent each week to the extension of the Gospel, while after that date newly organized national bodies such as the American Bible Society and the American Sunday School Union added fuel to the fire by sending out traveling agents ordained to the formation of yet more societies.[4] In 1811, Ann Judson and Harriet Newell carried female benevolence further by going out as missionaries with their husbands to the Far East. Although few churchwomen could follow their example, many would take part vicariously, with all the zealous imagination they possessed as evangelicals and as women, in the trials and triumphs of these and later women missionaries—yet another impetus to their own dedication to the tasks of organized benevolence.

Urban societies were more likely to blend humanitarian with religious goals than were societies located in towns and villages. While female Bible societies typically met weekly to sew, receive donations, pray and study, members of Bible and tract societies in New York, Boston and Philadelphia could hardly ignore the fact that the wonted subjects of their evangelization were right under their noses: the unchurched, possibly illiterate and probably licentious poor. Benevolent women who entered the slums to distribute sacred literature sometimes returned to alleviate the human distress they had discovered, distributing food, founding charity schools which taught the three R's as well as religion, or providing shelter for homeless women and children. Other related societies with explicitly charitable goals also abounded, beginning in 1796 with Isabella Graham's Society for the Relief of Poor Widows and Small Children in New York City. With similarly conservative social ends—but with a program which required a great deal more of their members—female charitable societies were complements, not competitors, to specifically religious organizations, and urban evangelical ladies were likely to belong to societies of both types. One Boston woman, for example, belonged at the time of her death in 1826 to the Female Orphan Asylum Society, the Graham Society (to further Isabella's work), the Female Society of Boston and Vicinity for Promoting Christianity among the Jews, the Female Bible Society of Boston, the Widows' Society, the Boston Female Education Society (for the schooling of ministers, not women), the Old South Charity School Society, the Boston Female Tract Society and the Boston Maternal Association.[5]

By virtue of their social status, middle-class evangelical women shared the desire of their brethren for a society immunized by religion against the excesses of a disorderly democracy. When the benevolent women of Boylston, Massachusetts, heard an address by Reverend Ward Cotton on "Causes and Effects of Female Regard to Christ" in 1816, they surely sympathized with the unveiled social conservatism with which he praised their support of missions to the rabble of the West as "the means not only of the salvation of their souls, but also of the political salvation of our country."[6] At the same time, however, organized women were not unaware of the unprecedented nature of their own extrafamilial efforts, and their self-consciousness lent another layer of meaning to their role in the evangelical crusade. "The men could not allow our sex the steadiness and perseverance necessary to establish such an undertaking," said Isabella Graham in an address to the "angelic band" who had proven the men wrong by offering "their own personal services to instruct the ignorant, and become the saviours of many of their sex."[7] Bereft of preindustrial usefulness, these women rejected passive isolation in nonproductive homes for exhilarating responsibilities as "co-workers with God in spreading that Gospel, which bringeth glad tidings of great joy to this miserable world."[8] Electing one another officers, handling funds, conducting business meetings, publishing appeals to the public, they mastered procedures of the commercial society in which they lived, but from which they were otherwise excluded. Furthermore, participation in female societies nurtured the gender-group identification which was developing among middle-class women as the social distance between home (feminine) and marketplace (masculine) increased, providing opportunities for mutual support and collective reflection on the burdens of womanhood. In fact, one group resolved that its members were never to make "an illiberal remark . . . respecting the performance of any of the [other] members, neither shall they report abroad any of the transactions of the society to the prejudice of any of its members."[9]

If organized female benevolence fulfilled some of the needs of women, it surely suited the clergymen who led the evangelical crusade at least as well. Glad for help in the work of redemption, but steadfastly committed to their own supremacy as men and as clergy, they led the way in the development of a new definition of womanhood capable of explaining and encouraging female benevolence while sharply limiting its potentially dangerous implications. "Women have a work to do in the House of God," Presbyterian Matthew Perrine told the first annual meeting of the Female Missionary Society for the Poor of the City of New York and Its Vicinity in 1817,[10] benignly noting that "the error among Christians has been to limit [women's] exertions and to confine their influence." Praising the Society as "a noble enterprise [which] indicates . . . the approaching splendors of the millennial day," the preacher assured the worthy women before him that the Gospel already (and "the Gospel alone") had elevated them to "receive the confidence of the other sex, and become their real companions, their associates, their counsellors, and their helpers in the discharge of duties social and religious." As he elaborated, however, it became clear that his emphasis fell on the word "helpers."

Domesticity dominated Perrine's discussion of how "pious females . . . may greatly assist the public ministers of the Gospel in promoting the general cause of truth and piety." Their primary duties, religious and social, lay in the homes to which both nature and divine wisdom ordained them. "No voice like that of a tender and affectionate wife can reach the heart of a rational man," said Perrine, assigning women a crucial salvific role even while contrasting the distinct and unequal natures of male and female. A sanctified motherhood had even greater evangelical potential, for to women were entrusted the developing characters of "children, the hope of the Church." Benevolent activities outside the actual home—in "the House of God"—were the mere externalization of these natural and primary functions. Through their charitable endeavors, even childless women could mother "the children of poor and careless parents";

through their support of missions, they could say to distant ministers, "We will give you water and bread." In Perrine's own telling summation, *"female hands* shall be employed in the finest *needle-work* to adorn [the Church] for her presentation to the King."

The linchpin in the argument of Perrine and his colleagues was the interpretation of all female exertion not as the work of human beings, nor even as the duty of Christians, but as the effusion of a distinctly defined femininity. In 1831, one association of clergy and laymen endorsed the charitable efforts of Philadelphia women by stating "that women by their constitution and habits are more suitable for the work . . . [and] that they possess superior intuitions, are more sympathetic, more self-denying, gentler, and that their time as a rule is more generally at their command." [11] Religious pronouncements on the separate natures, characters and appropriate activities of men and women fed and were fed by similar statements by other arbiters of value—including a new, commercialized mass media aimed at the middle class—to create a cult of domesticity which dominated American thought about womanhood by 1840. Tocqueville noticed it (with approval) in the 1830s: "in no country has such constant care been taken . . . to trace two clearly distinct lines of action for the two sexes." [12] Harriet Martineau, an English visitor with no sympathy for either evangelical religion or the subjection of her sex, agreed—and was particularly shocked by the ethical implications of the distinction: "the prevalent persuasion that there are virtues which are peculiarly masculine, and others which are peculiarly feminine" seemed almost to suppose that "a separate gospel" existed for each sex. [13]

There were many reasons for the acceptability of the cult of domesticity to this generation of Americans. Not the least of these was the hope that it could contribute to the pursuit of that much desired social order yet another institution whose newly idealized image suggested morality and stability: the Christian Home under the dominion of a Pure Womanhood. Unwilling or unable to enforce observance of the gentler virtues in the economic and political activities which occupied the middle-class men of a rapidly growing society, America's moral leaders entrusted them to women. More than agents of morality through the voluntary associations of the evangelical crusade, women were to embody morality in their very persons. And in the circuitous logic of the cult, women's acceptance of this character involved no relegation to secondary status but was the basis of what Lydia Maria Child had playfully called "their prodigious influence." "The appropriate duties and influence of women . . . are the sources of mighty power," declared a group of Massachusetts clergymen. "When the mild, dependent, softening influence of woman upon the sternness of man's opinions is fully exercised, society feels the effects of it in a thousand ways." [14]

But in the 1830s, just as the leaders of the evangelical crusade consolidated its institutions of regeneration and the terms of their alliance with women, a new phase of religious reform announced that the millenarian impulse had escaped conservative control. The new reformers—abolitionists, temperance advocates, or campaigners against a host of other social evils—built on the thought of earlier moral crusaders, but with significant differences. Turning the hope of regeneration into the bolder promise of human perfectibility, they thought less about containing the disorderly individualism of a democracy than about encouraging its attacks on stifling institutions. The belief that religious conversion and social salvation were closely linked was intensified and inverted as they argued that the sins of society were the main inpediments to individual sanctity and as they attacked those sins directly. Concurrently, lingering theological scruples about the efficacy of human agency in the work of redemption vanished before both secular celebrations of "the common man" and the spectacular successes of revivalist Charles Grandison Finney. [15] The projected millennium of the new reformers would look more like an egalitarian community of perfect individuals than like an eighteenth-century

New England town under clerical control. And its coming would require even more strenuous exertion on the part of the faithful.

The new reform spirit, which engaged the imaginations of many benevolent persons of both sexes, did not initially propose a distinctly new role for women. When in 1833 the founders of the American Anti-Slavery Society solicited women's aid in the cause by encouraging the formation of female auxiliaries, they simply endorsed the institutional arrangements of their predecessors. That women attended the first national antislavery convention but that they were neither listed as present in the minutes nor invited to sign its "Declaration of Sentiments" seemed generally unremarkable to these heirs of the evangelical crusade. One who did remark upon these and other restrictions, Lucretia Mott, a Philadelphia Quaker, was hardly surprised by them. "We could not expect that women should be fully recognized in such assemblages as that, while the monopoly of the pulpit existed," she commented, foreshadowing the anticlericalism of the women's-rights movement she would later help to found. And even this exceptional woman admitted that she spoke "with diffidence," for she and other women were present at the convention only "by sufferance."[16]

Still, Mott and her sisters brought to the new phase of religious reform a species of moral capital their mothers had not possessed at the turn of the century, for the advances of the preceding generation had become the commonplaces of 1833. Women's "right" to associate for extrafamilial purposes was established, and its duties assumed with skill and confidence. Furthermore, even the cult of domesticity recognized the superior moral endowments of women; and what might happen if "their prodigious influence" escaped clerical control, as the reform spirit itself was escaping? With eyes sharpened to social corruption and will strengthened to its uncompromising combat by the Perfectionism of the 1830s, the new generation of benevolent females invested their moral capital in two causes which would prove particularly important to the status of their sex: moral reform and the fight against slavery.

The New York Female Moral Reform Society was founded in 1834 by a group of evangelical ladies intent on ridding the world of a sin whose very mention demonstrated their pious defiance of public opinion: the sin of sexual licentiousness. Their claim that "it is the duty of the virtuous to use every consistent moral means to save our country from utter destruction" by violators of the Seventh Commandment apparently struck a responsive note in the hearts of other women, for by 1838 the New York Society had 445 auxiliaries, and the similar New England Female Moral Reform Society had another twenty-nine.[17] Turning the religious fervor they shared with evangelical men to a cause with distinctive import for women, moral reformers approached their task with an absolutism befitting the inauguration of a perfectionist millennium. They publicly castigated sinners: their newspaper published the names of respectable gentlemen suspected of seduction, of landlords suspected of renting space to brothels, and of employment agencies suspected of directing women to dangerous places. They coupled spiritual righteousness with bodily purity, religious conversion with reclamation from social evil: praying bands of women invaded the very haunts of sin to hold revival meetings among residents and customers, and wives and mothers evangelized their male relatives. Building on the intellectual and social legacy of the evangelical crusade, moral reformers recognized in the unity of a pure and benevolent womanhood the best guarantor of a social order untarnished by female degradation. They sought to reclaim prostitutes, educate girls to the wiles of seducers, and, most grandly, to create "A UNION OF SENTIMENT AND EFFORT AMONG . . . VIRTUOUS FEMALES FROM MAINE TO ALABAMA."[18]

Consistent as it was with both the new spirit of religious reform and the moral bifurcation of male and female posited by the cult of domesticity, moral reform provided respectable middle-class women with an opportunity to express some of their deepest anxieties about their own role in American society. Its annals are filled with anger at the prevailing double standard: "Why should a female be trodden under foot and spurned from society and driven from a parent's roof, if she but fall into sin—while common consent allows the male to habituate himself to this vice, and treats him as not guilty?" the New York Society's executive committee asked. "Has God made a distinction in regard to the two sexes in this respect?"[19] And the contrast between "open-hearted, sincere, and affectionate" woman, the victim of licentiousness, and "reckless . . . bold . . . mad . . . drenched-in-sin" man,[20] its perpetrator, expressed no less ire, as chords struck in the sexual arena sounded overtones of male aggression and female helplessness in other parts of life. Asserting that their own moral preeminence gave them the right to shape male behavior, the moral reformers seized the initiative in a cause to which, they believed, even the churches' leaders had been apathetic.

Moral reform was a women's crusade, and one of the innovations by which it expressed its independence was by hiring laywomen, not ministers, as agents and missionaries. One of the earliest of these, Margaret Prior of New York—a Methodist with previous experience in female prayer, Bible, tract, mission, temperance, charity-school and poor-relief societies—stretched the prerogatives of benevolence to their limits. Her visits to 350 poor families each month anticipated modern social work, while her more heroic deeds—posing as a washerwoman to gain entry to a brothel, or intervening in an alleyway brawl to distribute moral-reform tracts to a gang of teen-aged toughs—earned her a reputation as an avenging angel among both her supporters and the city's less pure elements. Benevolent limits could be stretched but not broken, however. Far from representing an abandonment of femininity, Prior's activism was comprehensible to herself and to her colleagues as proof of an abundance of true femininity itself. "Few know or practice better 'the art of making *home* happy,' or more highly appreciate duty in this respect, than did this humble, self-denying Christian," attested her biographer.[21] Accepting domesticity in its broad contours, but resisting with religious zeal the temptations of vanity and dependence which ran rife in a commercial society—"unnecessary visiting, idle gossiping, undue attention to dress, and needless expenditure"—Prior was the quintessential "mother in Israel."[22] Her goal was to press the moral image of her Christian home on the malleable features of the metropolis.

Like many other members of the New York Female Moral Reform Society, Margaret Prior was also an abolitionist. It was no accident that the campaign to convert the American public to the immediate and unconditional emancipation of the slaves emerged at roughly the same time and with many of the same adherents as the campaign against sexual licentiousness, for the two shared the uncompromising spirit and the direct attack on social evil as the root of human misery which characterized the new phase of religious reform. As scores of female antislavery societies sprang up in the old regional haunts of female benevolence between 1832 and 1837, abolitionism carried less an air of avenging the wrongs of woman than did moral reform. But by the end of the decade it was clear that women's participation in the antislavery movement would have much greater consequences for the cause of women's rights.

In the early years, the terms of women's participation in the cause were essentially the well-established ones which characterized their alliance with the clergy. One firm abolitionist vowed to do everything in her power to end slavery—everything, that is, "consistent with a necessary devotion to domestic duty."[23] Antislavery women promised to prick the consciences of the slaveholders with the points of their needles, applying old methods of fund-raising to the new reform. Shocked by slavery's denial of the sanctity of marriage, its separation of husband and wife, parent and child—evils similar to those combated by moral reformers—women stepped comfortably into abolitionist roles as guardians of domestic morality, but drew back at first from stronger action. Notably absent from early appeals were suggestions that women had any inherent civil right to meddle with so grave a political and economic issue as slavery. Female abolitionism was rather to be an extension of women's charitable concern for other women and children, a humanitarian rescue effort for "the one million of OUR OWN SEX" who lay in chains. It was to be one more effusion of woman's special virtue. "It is not in the nature of the female heart to look unmoved upon scenes of misery," the Ladies' Department of *The Liberator* proclaimed in 1832. Indeed, so consistent was abolitionism with femininity that it was "incredible" that so many women could "so far forego their own natures" as *not* to be abolitionists.[24]

Yet by 1840, one major segment of abolitionism had relinquished the inherited model of female participation in favor of a model which permitted women to speak in public, vote and hold office in societies composed of members of both sexes, and work for the once all-male American Anti-Slavery Society as editors and traveling agents. As one of the earliest female lecturers put the justification for the innovations, "show me the difference between a soul that may have taken up its abode, during its sojourn in this vale of tears, in a female tenement, and one that inhabits a male tenement, and then I will begin to discriminate between 'male and female virtues,' and the duties and responsibilities resting upon men, as differing from those on women, in reclaiming the world from sin."[25]

There were many reasons for the rapid institutional and intellectual change which marked women's participation in the antislavery movement in the 1830s. One was the unpopularity of a reform which poked relentlessly at such sore points in the body politic as racism, profit and the fragile Union between the states. The armor of benevolent domesticity simply could not shield female abolitionists from opponents set on the defeat of their cause. "In every other

department of philanthropy we are told in flattering terms of
female influence and woman is represented as a ministering
angel relieving the distressed, and comforting the afflicted;
but the Anti-Slavery cause in which it would seem every
feeling of humanity would impel us to be active—this we are
told does not come within our appropriate sphere of labor,"
the Fitchburg, Massachusetts, Female Anti-Slavery Society
wryly noted.[26] A second reason was the fortuitous advent of
two former slaveowners from a prominent South Carolina
family whose talents made them among the most effective
of abolitionist lecturers—and who happened to be women.
Charged with violating womanly propriety by their public
lecturing, Angelina and Sarah Grimké responded with a
forthright assertion that "men and women were CREATED
EQUAL: they are both moral and accountable beings, and
whatever is *right* for man to do is *right* for woman." [27] A
third was a fruitful mix of religious traditions: evangelicals
attuned to social sinfulness and the possibilities of regenera-
tive social conversion, Quakers accustomed to hearing
women's voices in church, and Unitarians steeped in the
legacy of the Enlightenment. The reason with the greatest
significance for women's role in religion and reform, however, was the new understanding of the nature of moral authority held by a radical faction of abolitionists.

Sanguine hopes that the churches would speedily recognize the identity of the emancipation message with the
Christian Gospel had inspired abolitionists of both sexes in
the early 1830s. The truth that the church and its clergy
soon proved themselves almost as unwilling to welcome a
threat to the economic and social order as were the public
and its politicians hit hard. Disillusion heightened the anti-
institutional spirit of these new religious reformers as they
seized the keys of moral authority and social order from the
hands of church and clergy to place them in the hands of
regenerate individuals. The result, for women, was a moral
freedom which relied on neither clerical allies nor the special virtues of femininity for its exercise. "Let us remember

dear sisters that our opposers cannot if they would answer for us in the great day of retribution," wrote an obscure member of the Dorchester, Massachusetts, Female Anti-Slavery Society, emboldened by the belief that the Judge would approve every Christian action by women, "however publicly done." [28]

It was little wonder that "the clergy, as a body, have been extremely sensitive on the subject . . . of woman's rights," as Lydia Maria Child mildly put it, [29] for the novel moral autonomy of female abolitionists broke the terms of the benevolent alliance which had served them so well. Confronted with Pauline injunctions against her public activities, Sarah Grimké countercharged that men had purposefully translated the Bible to the detriment of women and then withheld instruction in the sacred languages from their victims. [30] When her clerical critics attempted to lure the reformist energies of women back into safer channels by announcing that they appreciated "the unostentatious prayers and efforts of woman in advancing the cause of religion at home and abroad, in Sabbath-schools; [and] in leading religious inquirers to the pastors for instruction," Grimké replied that she utterly denied "that all pastors are better qualified to give instruction than woman." [31] In a humorous poem spoofing three particularly agitated ministers, abolitionist Maria Weston Chapman put the issue of women's autonomy bluntly: "But for spiritual guidance no longer they look/To Fulsom, or Winslow, or learned Parson Cook." [32] By the decade's end, some of the most radical, though still firmly religious, abolitionists had decided for this and other reasons to "come out" of religious institutions altogether.

Not all abolitionists were as radically anti-institutional as these; indeed most, female and male, were not. Discord between radicals ("woman's rights abolitionists" to their enemies) and moderates ("clerical abolitionists" to theirs), who chose to wage the antislavery campaign within the inherited institutional forms of church, political party, and separate and unequal male and female societies, led to a division in the American Anti-Slavery Society in 1840. The women who seceded with the clerical faction—including the New York Female Anti-Slavery Society, to which Margaret Prior belonged—faded rapidly from antislavery visibility, retreating from explicit avowals of women's rights to the rewards of leadership in the less volatile reforms justified by their special nature and the clergy's blessing. As rapidly, women in the radical faction acted on the promise of sexual equality in reform. Abby Kelley and, a few years later, Lucy Stone and Sallie Holley were among the most active of antislavery lecturers. Lydia Maria Child became editor of the official organ of the American Anti-Slavery Society. Several women served on the executive and business committees of the Society. In London for a World Anti-Slavery Convention from which they were excluded on the ground of sex, Lucretia Mott and Elizabeth Cady Stanton began to lay plans for a new movement to be devoted exclusively to the cause of woman. Their plans would finally bear fruit in 1848 at Seneca Falls, New York.

By midcentury, the lives and thoughts of middle-class American women differed fundamentally from those of their ancestors of 1800, and the variety of their activities in the overlapping areas of religion and reform were a sign, if not the cause, of the difference. Furthermore, ideas and institutions born in the ferment of antebellum religious reform would continue to frame the extrafamilial efforts of Protestant women for decades to come. Female voluntary associations in support of missions continued, enlivened after the Civil War by the growing tendency of churchwomen to administer the funds they had raised themselves, usually for the work of women missionaries.[33] Religiously motivated charitable endeavors carried on the work begun by Isabella Graham and others; but by the 1850s Holiness leader Phoebe Palmer, a founder of the Five Points Mission in New York City, could combine a career of theological and ecclesiastical innovation with her acts of feminine compassion.[34] Temperance advocates, such as Amelia Bloomer in the 1850s and

Frances Willard two decades later, echoed many of the themes of moral reform, depicting every act of male drunkenness as an assault on woman and the home—but going on to demand not only male conversion but also such positive assurances of female autonomy as the vote and the right to decent labor.[35] And suspicion of institutional religion persisted as a theme of the small but dauntless band who fought for woman suffrage through the second half of the century.[36]

Women's participation in antebellum religious reform left not one legacy but several. Even as the initial task of regenerating a world lying in wickedness ended in a proliferation of reform positions not always in harmony with one another, so different women responded in different ways to the variety of opportunities and interpretations for female activism which arose. The result was not a conclusion to the question of women's appropriate social and religious role, but rather a vigorous opening of the question itself. If the rapid social change of the period had made the question unavoidable, the ferment of militant Christianity had provided the intellectual and psychological resources which made religious reform a crucial setting for women's adaptation to and initiative within a changing society. Although middle-class Protestant women had hardly been mere "household utensils" at the beginning of the Second Great Awakening, there can be little doubt that many were "living, energetic beings" by the time of the Civil War. They had discovered the possibilities of their prodigious influence.

NOTES

1. *The Liberator*, vol. XI, (July 23, 1841), p. 118.

2. For example, late-eighteenth-century ministers who wrote about exemplary female Christians generally ignored the sex-specific qualities and duties of their subjects, a theme of great concern to later authors in this genre. See Dorothy C. Bass, "Memoirs of Eminently Pious Women: A Study in the Evangelical Religion of

New England, 1790–1840," paper delivered at the Third Berkshire Conference on the History of Women, 1976.

3. Historians argue heatedly over whether the efforts of evangelical crusaders resulted from their desire for social control or from their benevolent concern for their contemporaries. Many have entered the debate; important statements of conflicting interpretations may be found in Clifford S. Griffin, "Religious Benevolence as Social Control, 1815–1860," *Mississippi Valley Historical Review*, vol. XLIV, no. 3 (December 1957), pp. 423–44, and Lois W. Banner, "Religious Benevolence as Social Control: A Critique of an Interpretation," *Journal of American History*, vol. LX, no. 1 (June 1973), pp. 23–41.

4. For summaries of the proliferation of hundreds of local voluntary associations, see Keith Melder, "Ladies Bountiful: Organized Female Benevolence in Early Nineteenth-Century America," *New York History*, vol. XLVIII, no. 3 (July 1967), pp. 235–38, and Nancy F. Cott, *The Bonds of Womanhood: "Woman's Sphere" in New England, 1780–1835* (New Haven, 1977), pp. 134–35.

5. Benjamin B. Wisner, *Memoirs of the Late Mrs. Susan Huntington* (Boston, 1826), pp. 123–24.

6. Cited in Cott, *Bonds of Womanhood*, pp. 148–49.

7. *The Power of Faith: Exemplified in the Life and Writings of Mrs. Isabella Graham* (New York, 1819), pp. 299–300.

8. Wisner, *Mrs. Susan Huntington*, p. 113.

9. From the records of the Jericho Center, Vermont, Female Religious and Cent Society, cited in Cott, *Bonds of Womanhood*, p. 143.

10. Quotations in this paragraph and the next are from Matthew LaRue Perrine, *Women Have a Work to Do in the House of God* (New York, 1817).

11. Cited in Melder, "Ladies Bountiful," p. 239.

12. Alexis de Tocqueville, *Democracy in America* (New York, 1945), vol. II, p. 223.

13. Harriet Martineau, *Society in America* (New York, 1837), vol. II, p. 233.

14. From a pastoral letter of the General Association of Massachusetts (Orthodox) to the churches under their care, 1837, in Elizabeth Cady Stanton, Susan B. Anthony and Matilda Joslyn Gage (eds.), *History of Woman Suffrage* (New York, 1881), vol. I, p. 81.

15. On the new phase of religious reform, see John L. Thomas, "Romantic Reform in America, 1815–1865," *American Quarterly*, vol. XVII, no. 4 (Winter 1965), pp. 656–81. On Finney's democratization of evangelicalism, see William G. McLoughlin's introduction in Charles Grandison Finney, *Lectures on Revivals of Religion*, ed. William G. McLoughlin (Cambridge, Mass., 1960).

16. *Proceedings of the American Anti-Slavery Society at Its Third Decade* (New York, 1864), p. 42.

17. Carroll Smith Rosenberg, "Beauty, the Beast and the Militant Woman: A Case Study in Sex Roles and Social Stress in Jacksonian America," *American Quarterly*, vol. XXIII, no. 4 (October 1971), p. 576; and Cott, *Bonds of Womanhood*, p. 152. The quotation on "the duty of the virtuous" is cited in Smith Rosenberg, p. 566.

18. Cited in Smith Rosenberg, "Beauty, the Beast and the Militant Woman," p. 577. In this paragraph and the next, I have relied heavily on Smith Rosenberg's excellent study of the New York Female Moral Reform Society.

19. Cited in *ibid.*, p. 572.

20. Cited in *ibid.*, p. 571.

21. Sarah R. Ingraham, *Walks of Usefulness, or Reminiscences of Mrs. Margaret Prior* (New York, 1851), p. 18.

22. *Ibid.*, pp. 73 and 5.

23. *Liberator*, vol. II (Oct. 27, 1832), p. 174.

24. *Ibid.* (Jan. 7, 1832), p. 1 and (Dec. 1, 1832), p. 189. Even Angelina Grimké, who would become the voice and symbol of a much different interpretation of women's role in 1837, could write in 1836 that women should "frankly acknowledge [man] as 'the head' " and make her own contribution to reform a distinctly feminine one: "Her gentle influence is *felt* like falling dew—her soft & tender voice is *heard* in the heart, tho' never in the forum." (Angelina Grimké to L. L. Dodge, July 14, 1836, in the Theodore Dwight Weld Papers, Library of Congress.)

25. Abby Kelley in *The Liberator*, vol. IX (Sept. 6, 1839), p. 142.

26. *Proceedings of the Anti-Slavery Convention of American Women* (Philadelphia, 1838), p. 18.

27. Sarah M. Grimké, *Letters on the Equality of the Sexes and the Condition of Woman* (Boston, 1838), p. 16.

28. Sarah Baker to Abby Kelley, May 31, 1838, in the Abby Kelley Foster Papers, American Antiquarian Society.

29. *Liberator*, vol. IX (Sept. 6, 1839), p. 142.

30. Grimké, *Letters on Equality*, p. 16.

31. Pastoral letter, in Stanton *et al.*, *History*, vol. I, p. 81; Grimké, *Letters on Equality*, p. 19.

32. "The Times That Try Men's Souls," in Stanton *et al.*, *History*, vol. I, p. 83.

33. On women's missionary activities, see R. Pierce Beaver, *All Loves Excelling: American Protestant Women in World Mission* (Grand Rapids, Mich., 1968).

34. The life and work of Phoebe Palmer are discussed in Timothy L. Smith, *Revivalism and Social Reform: American Protestantism on the Eve of the Civil War* (New York, 1965), chaps. 8, 9 and 11.

35. D. C. Bloomer, *Life and Writings of Amelia Bloomer* (New York, 1975), and Mary Earhart, *Frances Willard: From Prayers to Politics* (Chicago, 1944).

36. The animus is evident throughout Stanton, Anthony and Gage, *History of Woman Suffrage*, vol. I.

ELEVEN

American Women in Ministry: A History of Protestant Beginning Points

VIRGINIA LIESON BRERETON AND
CHRISTA RESSMEYER KLEIN

In 1970 the Lutheran Church in America and the American Lutheran Church voted to ordain women. In 1976 the Episcopalians followed. By these actions the ministry had become a possible life's work for women in all the "mainline" Protestant churches.* The general acceptance of women's ordination appeared to be a high point in a long history of expanding female leadership in the American Protestant churches.

A glance back to antebellum America reveals that the church has indeed come a long way in accepting women in roles of authority. Until the Civil War social prohibitions bolstered by certain Biblical injunctions kept churchwomen from speaking or praying aloud in religious assemblies. Literal interpretation of such passages as 1 Timothy 2:11–12 made most women uneasy even about speaking before their

---

* This chapter treats the issue of women's ordination in the context of the Christian (Disciples of Christ), Baptist, Congregational and Reformed, Methodist, Presbyterian, and Lutheran denominations. For the Disciples, at one end of this spectrum, ordination is a matter of practicality and not doctrine. For Lutherans, at the other end of the spectrum, ministry is a mediating agency for the imparting of faith through the Gospel and the sacraments. Chapter 13 will treat the Episcopalians and the Roman Catholics, for whom the priest is a representative of Christ.

sisters in women's church societies—or leading them in prayer, if indeed they were permitted to at all. Women seldom appeared at congregational or denominational deliberations, and could neither vote nor speak. Nor could they venture forth as missionaries except under the protection and counsel of their husbands. Most colleges and theological seminaries were closed to them.

By taking the initiative in home and foreign missions and in religious education, to mention two arenas of female activity in the latter part of the nineteenth century, women proved that they could serve the church in significant ways. Slowly ordination opened up to them. Yet women's victory has somehow been a hollow one. Equal access to the ordained ministry has not resulted in equal access to positions of leadership traditionally available to the clergy. Everywhere women ministers face longer periods of unemployment, lower salaries, less opportunity to shoulder full responsibility for parishes—especially larger ones—and less likelihood of appointment or election to leadership positions within ecclesiastical structures. As a result, feminist groups have emerged within most denominations to expose these inequities and to propose solutions whose minimum demands are for affirmative-action goals in the churches. Not infrequently these groups question a denomination's entire heritage for insensitivity to women in its polity, theology and piety.

Hence, the unfulfilled possibilities of women's ministry have served to keep the basic question of women's status and service in the churches in the forefront. Ordination, far from being the culmination of women's expanding participation, is another beginning point in a history of beginning points. Here we attempt to consider women's ordination within the broad historical context of women's quest for leadership in service within the American Protestant denominations, highlighting outstanding movements and eras and perhaps prodding others to explore them more carefully.

In putting together this essay we have encountered still

another kind of beginning which needs mention: the task of reconstructing the history of women in the church has gotten under way only in the last few years. Our attempt to take a broad view across denominational lines has therefore been hindered at many points by the dearth of writing on women by denominational chroniclers. Historians of American Methodism almost alone have turned their attention to the story of women in that denomination.[1] In some of the otherwise thorough histories women hardly appear at all. Fine work has appeared on women in the foreign missions movement.[2] Historian Elizabeth H. Verdesi has completed a valuable thesis on Northern Presbyterian women, focusing on the missions and the religious education movement.[3] Short historical sketches have appeared in denominational periodicals and reports.[4] Since the 1920s, periodic denominational and interdenominational surveys have explored the status of women in the church.[5] Otherwise, we have had to rely on commemorative histories of various women's societies and of the deaconess movement, and on scattered biographies and autobiographies of churchwomen.[6]

Women Alongside the Churches: The Great Missionary Societies, 1861–1925

Despite the many obstacles to full participation in their churches before the Civil War, women organized themselves into numerous local missionary societies, financing their efforts out of their household budgets. One early interdenominational attempt by women in 1834 to organize more broadly and systematically collapsed before opposition from the secretary of the American Board of Commissioners for Foreign Missions.[7]

Nevertheless, by the 1860s and 1870s, neither the fears of men on the general missionary boards nor the misgivings of the women themselves could halt the momentum of women's entry into large-scale and well-coordinated missionary activity. Women widely separated geographically joined forces to forge regional and national societies, beginning with the interdenominational Woman's Union Missionary Society of America in 1861. The principal early groups and their founding dates were:

Woman's Board of Missions (Congregational), 1868.

Woman's Foreign Missionary Society (Methodist Episcopal), 1869.

Woman's Foreign Missionary Societies of the Presbyterian Church, U.S.A., 1870.

Woman's Auxiliary (Protestant Episcopal), 1871.

Woman's Baptist Foreign Missionary Society, 1873.

Woman's Parent Mite Missionary Society of the African Methodist Episcopal Church, 1874.

Christian Woman's Board of Missions (Disciples), 1874.

Woman's Board of Foreign Missions of the Reformed Church in America, 1875.

Woman's American Baptist Home Missionary Society, 1877.

Woman's Executive Committee for Home Missions (Presbyterian), 1878.

Woman's Missionary Society of the Evangelical Lutheran Church, 1879.

Congregational Women's Home Missionary Association, 1880.

Woman's Home Missionary Society (Methodist Episcopal), 1884.

Southern women, despite being hindered by conservative ideas about the place of the "Southern lady" and by the general devastation resulting from the war, followed suit shortly after: Woman's Board of Foreign Missions, Methodist Episcopal Church South, 1878; Woman's Missionary

Union, Auxiliary to the Southern Baptist Convention, 1888; and Woman's Auxiliary, Presbyterian Church in the U.S., 1912.[8]

By 1882 the sixteen existing women's missionary societies had raised almost six million dollars and had sent out 694 single women missionaries. By 1900 the women's societies were supporting 389 wives, 856 single women missionaries, and 96 doctors. They were responsible for numerous orphanages, hospitals, schools and dispensaries around the world.[9] In home missions, the accomplishments of the women were impressive also, although we do not possess the summary statistics we have for foreign missions. In 1889 and 1890, for instance, the Woman's Executive Committee for Home Missions of the Presbyterian Church in the U.S.A. raised more money than did the main home missions board of that denomination.[10]

Such remarkable efforts and achievements call for an explanation which must begin with an understanding of the deep sense of Christian responsibility for the unconverted in an age of millennial fervor. American Protestant women were also responding to the social condition of women and children—particularly in the Far East, but also among the immigrants in American cities—in other cultures. Reports from missionaries in the Orient, which documented such religiously sanctioned practices as the binding of Chinese women's feet and the confinement of Indian women in close dark zenanas, deeply unsettled prosperous American women. Surely, they thought, Christianity would transform mores even as it made converts.[11] In addition, two generations of missionaries reported little progress in their work with men; perhaps Oriental women provided the key to opening foreign cultures to Christianization. American Protestants took the idealized Victorian view of women to heart, believing that female converts might wield all manner of moral and religious influence. But clearly male missionaries could not approach Eastern women; rather, this was uniquely a task for Western women.

Women's initiative in mission work, ripening in the post-war era, bore the marks of the emerging social order. In building their work on a national scale, women were paralleling similar developments in the rest of the church and also, of course, in American industry.[12] If Theodore Agnew's findings on the Woman's Foreign Missionary Society of the Methodist Episcopal Church hold true for other societies—and we believe that they will—women missionary leaders represented an emerging elite within the denominations.[13] Since these women were frequently the wives and relatives of male denominational leaders, the missionary societies created a virtual "interlocking directorate" of prosperous families. Such women could engage in travel and other time-consuming activities outside their homes, and frequented such Protestant watering holes as Chautauqua Lake, Ocean Grove and Martha's Vineyard. They shared the assurances of cultural and racial superiority characteristic of the age, amply illustrated in the Methodist Episcopal Society's periodical *The Heathen Woman's Friend*.

But firm belief in the goals of late-nineteenth-century American Protestantism and ties to the emerging social and religious leadership do not in themselves explain the accomplishments of the women's missionary societies. Above all, those societies must be credited with recognizing the existence and value of huge reserves of untapped volunteer labor among women of the middle and upper classes. Missionary leader Helen Barrett Montgomery noted in 1911 that women "have one tenth of the work in the home that their grandmothers bore. We must work for the life of the world."[14] Women missionary leaders displayed ingenuity in channeling the energy of these women, encouraging the multiplication of auxiliary and branch missionary societies. They further perceived that women would become most deeply involved if each of these local societies took special responsibility for a particular project or missionary field or the support of a certain missionary. Fund-raising followed this pattern of massive involvement also. Since church policies generally prohibited women from raising money in congregational or other general church meetings (lest they compete with the general missionary boards), the societies had to be well enough organized to collect "large sums in small gifts."[15]

Behind the success of the fund-raising lay broad efforts to disseminate missions information, activities in which the women had no peers. According to missions historian R. Pierce Beaver, the women's societies taught the general missionary boards the value of publicity.[16] Women provided the first easily readable and widely available missions information—"the light infantry of missionary literature."[17] Besides holding regular conventions, women developed summer schools for missions which served as opportunities for vacationing as well as learning. At other times of the year, institutes, study conferences, missionary exhibits and jubilees enlarged women's familiarity with missions. Not content with educating adult women only, the female societies cultivated enthusiasm in the next generations through societies for young people and children and through their contributions to Sunday school curricula.

By enabling single women to work in the mission fields at home and abroad, these societies freed an extremely valuable resource for the missionary cause. Until the women's societies showed the way, the general denominational boards had resisted appointing single women, unless they agreed to live safely in the household of married missionaries and to confine themselves to roles which would not expose them to danger or undue exertion.[18] But single women were eager to perform the same tasks as male missionaries. At a time when American society offered few vocational opportunities for women besides teaching, the mission fields promised exciting challenges for single women. Many restless, ambitious and devout women from small American towns and farms escaped the tedium of a confined existence by sailing to the mission fields or by venturing to the American frontiers, both Western and urban.[19] A Methodist missionary to India, Isabella Thoburn, spoke for all her sister missionaries when she said:

We have found sickness and poverty to relieve, widows to protect, advice to be given in every possible difficulty or emergency, teachers and Bible women to be trained, houses to be built, horses and cattle to be bought, gardens to be planted, and accounts to be kept and rendered. We have found use for every faculty, natural and acquired, that we possessed, and have coveted all that we lacked.[20]

The desire for "all the faculties that we lacked"—on the part of the women missionaries and their sponsors alike—helped nurture a new educational form, the religious or missionary training school.[21] This school, while not exclusively for women, was particularly attractive to prospective female missionaries and other female religious workers because most of the theological seminaries were closed to them (and did not in any case offer many "practical" courses in missions). The earliest training school, the Woman's Baptist Missionary Training School in Chicago, was established in 1881 by the Woman's American Baptist Home Mission Society. By 1916 a survey listed about sixty religious training schools, the majority of which were for women or primarily for women.[22] Like the Chicago school, many of the women's missionary training schools were started by denominational women's missionary societies or by deaconess organizations or had a close connection with such bodies. In the early years, the only educational prerequisite of most of the training schools for women was the possession of a basic literacy. The intensely practical curriculum, generally spanning one or two years and taught mostly by women, consisted of such subjects as the Bible, religious pedagogy, the history of missions, and practical work in city missions or other agencies. Supplementing the formal curriculum was a schooling in piety, with frequent meetings for prayer, visits and letters from missionaries, and the inspiring example of women like Lucy Rider Meyer at the Methodist women's Chicago Training School.[23]

Women involved in missions shared in that "respectable" or pragmatic feminism emerging at the end of the nineteenth century. Eagerness to espouse the missionary cause may have prompted them to avoid confrontation over women's-rights issues in their own denominations.[24] Nevertheless, more "radical" feminist concerns were inherently close to the surface. The missionary societies served as a training ground for lay leadership, and the women's cause and the leaders' developing skills were bound to make them seek out regular denominational forums. The few lay and clergy delegates who dissented from the 1880 refusal of the Methodist Episcopal General Conference to sanction the admission of women to the office of deacon (or elder) were aware of a certain irony in the fact that women were unofficially performing some of the functions of these offices in their missionary societies anyway. In their minority report these delegates called for the application of all offices of the laity to women "in the same sense and to the same extent as men" precisely because missionary society leaders were already engaged in "hortatory and didactic practices" and "official duties."[25]

The diaconate was another form of organization for channeling women's service in the nineteenth century, but it did not have the same critical importance as the missionary movement in the development of female leadership. The American deaconess movement grew out of the German effort to reintroduce an early Christian practice at Kaiserswerth, in 1883. Although the concept of consecrating Protestant women for church work was imported to the United States by Lutherans in 1849, it failed to take hold among them until 1884. The Methodist General Conference recognized its own order of deaconesses in 1888, shortly after Lucy Rider Meyer opened the Chicago Training School. Episcopalians also established orders. American deaconesses served the church primarily as nurses, but also pioneered as social workers.

Nevertheless, the movement never flourished in America

as it had in Europe. The Kaiserswerth Conference in Europe in 1910 drew twenty thousand deaconesses.[26] There were never more than two thousand deaconesses among all the American denominations at any one time.[27] Few American women found deaconess work a satisfying option, perhaps because other forms of lay activity were available, which was not the case in Europe. The strain of anti-Catholicism among American Protestants also worked against a concept which set women apart by special garb, living stipends instead of salaries, and, for Lutherans, highly disciplined life within motherhouses. Among the Methodists, after the initial period of organization, women who chose the work failed to emerge as leaders, deferring instead to the oversight of ministers and district superintendents.[28] Among the Lutherans, the movement rarely appealed to middle-class women interested in higher education, because of the minimal educational requirements and the close association with tedious work in hospitals.[29] Clearly, the movement failed to attract enough women of talent or to employ the full talents of women. After World War I up through the 1970s there were attempts to upgrade the image, the status and the educational requirements of the position, sure evidence that the consecration and sacrifice associated with it had all too easily led to subordination and subservience.[30]

Those few women who were not content to accept "supplementary" leadership roles in home and foreign missions or in deaconess work but hoped instead for ordination faced a lonely and often futile struggle.[31] Unlike women in the mission movement or the diaconates, they did not benefit from the buffer of supportive organizations. Unlike male seminarians, they could not receive scholarship aid or free room and board in those seminaries which did accept them. Moreover, the academic credentials which they painstakingly earned—and which were not considered essential for most male ministerial candidates of the day—were insufficient to assure either ordination or a parish position.

Such years of effort took their toll, as illustrated by the

careers of two Methodist seminary graduates. Anna Oliver and Anna Howard Shaw both sought permission for ordination from the Methodist Episcopal Church Conference in 1880. After the conference refused to act on the issue, only Oliver continued her struggle. By the time her financially weak congregation collapsed in 1883, her health was broken, and she died nine years later.[32] Shaw, who had successfully sought ordination in the smaller Methodist Protestant Church, was so embittered that she soon ceased to care about the churches and turned her attention to the suffrage movement.[33] The founding of the interdenominational Women's Ministerial Conference in 1882 (after annual meetings since 1873) reflected the effort of women to create a supportive—if powerless—agency where none existed.[34]

Women Within the Churches:
Organizational Mergers, Lay Status
and Professional Church Workers, 1920–1945

"Our place and contribution seem to be at this moment in question," wrote Lucy Waterbury Peabody, a leader of the Woman's American Baptist Missionary Society, speaking in 1927 of the women's missionary movement.[35] What threw the women into confusion about their place and contribution were several events that took place in the first quarter of the twentieth century. In 1906 the Methodist Episcopal Church South reorganized the women's missionary societies under the control of the denominational Board of Missions.[36] In 1919 the Christian (Disciples) Woman's Board of Missions and the American Christian Missionary Society were united.[37] The Presbyterian Church in the U.S.A. merged its women's missionary societies into the main missionary boards in 1923, after little consultation with the women.[38] In 1925 the Congregational Women's Home Missionary Federation disappeared into one vast denominational missionary organization.[39] As early as 1927 (if not before) some leaders in Peabody's own denomination, the Northern Baptist Convention, were suggesting that the women's missionary organizations be combined with the main ones.[40] (This was not actually accomplished until 1955.)

On the face of it, the consolidations seemed to herald a new era of "full cooperation between men and women," and many women accepted it in that spirit.[41] After all, women received positions of leadership on the new combined missionary boards, and some provision was usually made to preserve the integrity of the women's work, though budgets were no longer separate. Moreover, the popular wisdom of the time advocated greater "efficiency" and less waste through combined societies, and the women's organizations were not the only ones affected by the enthusiasm for consolidation.

In a parallel development, almost every one of the women's missionary training schools closed or was absorbed into a denominational theological seminary in the decades after World War I. There were many reasons for this. In an educational world that was increasingly moving toward a system of four-year colleges, followed by graduate study, the training schools became an anomaly. The Great Depression dried up extra educational funds and lessened the demand for graduates of the training schools. But also the theological seminaries had learned from the example of the training schools and had begun to incorporate their emphases on religious pedagogy (which became religious education), on missions and on practical experience (which turned into field education). At long last they admitted women, primarily to nonministerial programs. But in so doing they deprived the missionary training schools of their formerly unique function. And seminaries never allowed women theological educators a place among the trustees, the faculty and the student body comparable to the one they had enjoyed in the training schools.

Despite certain gains from the mergers, some women

were uneasy, and not a few grew angry over the new developments. Helen Barrett Montgomery predicted in 1911 that consolidation would work only if women truly received equal status in the integrated bodies, but she doubted that men would be "emancipated from the caste of sex so that they [could] work easily with women, unless they be head and women clearly subordinate." [42] While hoping for the best, Lucy Peabody wondered whether a new generation of women leaders would be able to develop out of the consolidated boards. [43] The disaffection of Presbyterian women was so apparent, partly in reduced female contributions to missions, that alarmed denominational leaders asked Katharine Bennett and Margaret Hodge to do a study of "Causes of Unrest Among Women of the Church." Not surprisingly, Bennett and Hodge noted that

among thinking women there arose a serious question as to whether their place of service could longer be found in the church when a great organization which they had built could be autocratically destroyed by vote of male members of the church without there seeming to arise in the mind of the latter any question as to the justice, wisdom and fairness of their actions. [44]

The supposition that women gave up power in each denomination as a result of such mergers is strong but awaits further documentation. [45] Though these mergers apparently destroyed much that missionary women had created, it is possible that they also conferred an indirect and unexpected side benefit. Out of the anger and turmoil which resulted, some women (and men) of the church were jolted into greater awareness of the issue of women's place in the church. Bennett and Hodge declared firmly that

So long as there was a service into which they could put their strength and affection, the women were willing to ignore the disabilities that faced them in general church work . . . But when the church, by action taken by the men of the church with but the slightest consultation with the women . . . decided to absorb these agencies which had been built up by the women, the by-product of such a decision was to open the whole question of the status of women in the church.[46]

It is even conceivable that, upset by the reaction of some of their loyal women, male denominational leaders settled on a half-conscious "trade-off." If women were to be deprived of their independent organizations, they would have to be granted some enhanced status in the regular denominational organization.

Other factors encouraged the reevaluation of women's position in the churches. A triumphant feminism which had just accomplished the passage of the Nineteenth Amendment had simultaneously served to educate church people. Women's success in staffing critical institutions on the home front during World War I convinced the skeptical of their ability to take on larger responsibility outside the home. The widespread acceptance of higher criticism in many denominations made it possible to interpret the Biblical "prohibitions" against women's speaking in the churches as culturally conditioned and as having limited authority for the present.[47]

Thus, the number of women who were ordained during the twenties and thirties increased by a slight but significant amount. An American Association of Women Preachers, organized in 1919 by two Methodist women, was a hopeful omen for the twenties, as was the publication of the Association's organ, *Woman's Pulpit*, beginning in 1921.[48] In another sign of the times the Congregational Hartford Theological Seminary declared in 1920: "In view of the changed attitude toward the ordination of women, we no longer require women to state on entering the seminary that they do not expect to enter the ministry."[49] Ordination had long been a theoretical possibility for Congregational, Baptist and Disciples women if they could only convince a local congregation to accede. Few congregations had proved willing in the past; in the new climate, however, ordination of women took place with slightly greater frequency. Congregationalists counted one hundred women ministers by 1927, whereas they had listed fewer than forty in 1900.[50] The Methodist Episcopal Church in 1924 began allowing ordination of women as local preachers, but without granting them full membership in the General Conference.[51] Despite the admonitions in the document "Causes of Unrest Among Women of the Church," the presbyteries constituting the Presbyterian Church in the U.S.A. voted down ordination of women as ministers in 1930, but in the same ballot allowed them to become ordained elders.

Even denominations which did not ordain women were becoming more tolerant of women speaking, and in some instances preaching, in church assemblies. In 1918 two Baptist laywomen, advocates for the Woman's Baptist Missionary Union Training School, were the first women to address the Southern Baptist Convention.[52] There were also advances in lay status. In 1920 the Methodist Episcopal Church South granted women lay rights.[53] Southern Presbyterian women began serving on national boards in 1924.[54] And, for the first time, in the 1930s some Lutheran synods allowed women to speak at synodical meetings and in some cases to hold church offices.[55]

Only a handful of women were able to take advantage of the right to ordination, and even those few had to endure attempts to discourage them. One seminarian, Margaret Blair Johnstone, was examined before the Chicago Congregational Advisory Board in the early 1930s. After attempting to persuade her to become a pastor's assistant or a religious educator, the board admonished:

We are your friends. It is because we know so well the frustration awaiting any woman in the ministry that we are urging you to enter related work. We are trying to protect you not only from heartbreak, but also ridicule. Think of the sensationalism of women evangelists. No matter how earnest you would be, no one would believe your sincerity. And consider our obligation to protect the dignity of the profession. . . . There's only a slight chance you'd get a church and little promotion or professional advancement for you if you did.[56]

One of the very few ways for a woman to acquire a parish was to succeed to the pulpit upon the death of her minister husband.[57]

If women still did not find numerous positions as ordained ministers and denominational leaders in this period, the creation of new professional positions in the church in the teens and the twenties gave them new opportunities to serve the church full time in exchange for a salary and a degree of dignity. These roles grew out of a society which was becoming increasingly preoccupied by the idea of professionalization and also out of an enlarged conception of the church as "the social center of the community."[58] To perform in this way, the church, it was argued, needed paid and specially trained religious educators, social workers, youth workers and others—no longer lay volunteers as in the past. The "expert," the specialist, the "professional" appeared in the church as in most areas of American social, economic and educational life.

Church leaders who observed that other professional roles for women were opening up in society warned that gifted women would desert the church if not given proper recognition for their talents. They called for certain minimal levels of training; for professional associations—denominational, national and local; and for standard hours, clearly defined functions, and salaries commensurate with those for similar roles in the society at large.[59]

Doubtless women gained increased recognition through their participation in the emerging corps of paid, specialized church workers. But theirs was very much a limited victory. Professionalization cut two ways: it was just as likely to exclude women as to give them access to positions in the church world. First, the number of churches which could afford to hire an expert in education or youth work or social work was limited. The new positions doubtless caught on in the church press much sooner than in the local churches. Second, women almost universally received lower salaries than men in the same positions. Third, precise delineation of roles was difficult, and it varied from church to church. The title "church assistant," for instance, seemed to have a number of other rough equivalents: director of religious education, director of young people's work, church secretary, church visitor, church missionary, deaconess, social worker, and pastor's assistant. Church journalists tried gropingly but without success to define precisely the functions of various positions.[60] Many women "professionals" became merely glorified errand girls who found themselves saddled with the detail work of the parish. Fourth, often when "professional" associations were attempted, men came to dominate them. For instance, the Association of Church Directors of Religious Education, organized in the early teens, required college graduation plus two years of specialized training in graduate school for membership at a time when many women workers in religious education could not claim this kind of background.[61] Finally, job security was not high; these new specialists were the first to go when budgets grew tight, as they did with the onset of the Depression.

Women in the Pulpit: Ordination, 1945–1970

If the social ferment of the twenties and the thirties helped women to gain new positions and rights in the churches, the events of World War II helped to consolidate these advances. Wartime disruptions in gender roles especially affected the European churches. There women with university theological training were ordained and assumed pastoral office in the absence of men. Moreover, the attempt by the Nazis to exploit the traditional arenas of women's work—

Kinder, Kirche und Küche—for the benefit of the state had provoked an adverse reaction.[62] For the first time, events in the international church prompted advances in status in the American churches. The first meeting of the World Council of Churches in Amsterdam in 1948 provided the forum for an international discussion of the "Life and Work of Women in the Church."

Events surrounding that meeting evoked a self-consciousness about the role of women at a time when secular feminism was quiescent. In preparation for the meeting, Inez Cavert of the Federal Council of Churches in America compiled the study "Women in American Church life."[63] Following the meeting, Kathleen Bliss interpreted the various national reports prepared for the conference in a volume entitled *The Service and Status of Women in the Churches*, which appeared in 1952.[64] In the same year *The Christian Century*, editorializing on Bliss's work and the 1948 meeting, called for women's ordination and produced a series of articles "intended to make better known to the American public women who are playing conspicuous parts in the church life of this country."[65] In 1952 also the United Church Women of the National Council of Churches urged member denominations to continue to study the role of women.[66]

Indeed, the ferment produced new wine. In 1953 the Disciples Committee on the Service and Status of Women in the Churches published a report calling for full and equal participation of women in all leadership positions at all levels of the denomination.[67] The Presbyterian Church in the U.S.A. voted to ordain women in 1956, and the Methodist Church granted full Conference privileges to ordained women in the same year. Interdenominational seminaries were also impelled to action. Harvard Divinity School, long inhospitable to women, began to accept them on equal terms with men in a new divinity program, while Yale Divinity School built a new dormitory for women.[68]

There were other pressures on the American churches

which contributed to these changes. Church bodies which had granted women lay status earlier were increasingly aware of their dependence on women's leadership. In addition, there were shortages of clergy and professional church workers in a period of growing church membership. Theological seminaries began admitting women to their Bachelor (now Master) of Divinity programs. Ordination of women came as a natural outgrowth of these developments. No major struggle accompanied discussion of the issue; no fanfare greeted the outcome.[69] Apparently, clergymen did not imagine that many women would seek ordination, nor did they expect them to alter the office in any significant way.

Ordination of women did not come as easily in American Lutheranism as in the other denominations. While some Lutheran bodies participated in the World Council of Churches from its founding, the Lutheran churches, as immigrant churches bound to orthodoxy, were generally isolated from the broad front of American Protestantism. They were also separated from the wartime experiences of their sister churches in Germany and Scandinavia. The question of women's ordination for Lutherans at midcentury was different from the question of equal access, the core issue by then among most other Protestants. Until the seventies most Lutherans would have found women in the pastorate an inconceivable breach of the Biblical "orders of creation" as interpreted in Lutheran doctrine. In addition, American Lutherans still revered the authority of the clergy in ways corresponding more to European than to American practice. When most European Lutheran churches adopted the practice in the sixties—after nearly two decades of study— American Lutherans were suddenly in the minority among world Lutherans.[70] The action of the European churches, based as it was on new hermeneutical principles and acceptance of the changing role of women in society, probably had as much to do with the breakup of traditional opposition in America as did American feminism.

Nevertheless, vestiges of the earlier viewpoint still remain in American Lutheranism. The Missouri Synod, long recognized for its concern with orthodoxy, has balked on the issue entirely, although some member synods of its breakaway body, the Association of Evangelical Lutheran Churches, have voted to ordain women. The Synod opposed national lay organizations for men or women until well into the twentieth century, refused to grant women teachers equal status with men in its parochial-school system, and advised congregations to grant only limited lay rights to women in 1969.[71]

Epilogue

In the process of reaching a decision for ordination, Lutherans had joined with other denominations in the late sixties and early seventies in examining anew the question of the place and status of women in the churches. Spurred on by the secular women's movement, church leaders and others marshaled a host of disappointing statistics. They found that women's participation in the church at almost all levels had declined in the decade of the sixties. For instance, among the United Presbyterians women constituted only sixteen percent of all the elders in 1974.[72] In 1967 only one quarter of American Baptist Convention directors of religious education were women, although religious education was traditionally a feminine field.[73] The proportion of single women foreign missionaries in that denomination had also declined.[74] Almost all denominational reports noted an erosion of the participation of women in all church agencies in the decade of the sixties, even in those which had customarily been associated with women, such as the mission boards.

The number of women in the ordained ministry gave the greatest reason for concern. In 1972 less than one percent of

the clergy in the American Baptist Convention, the United
Methodist Church and the Presbyterian and Disciples of
Christ denominations were women.[75] The number serving
parishes was even smaller, and smaller yet the number serving as sole or senior pastor.

In response, advocates for women in almost every denomination set up task forces and committees, surveys and news-
letters, all designed to produce a new awareness of women
in the church. Biblical arguments were rehearsed once
again. Feminists urged quotas or goals upon denominational
agencies and deliberative bodies, and denominations began
to monitor the number of women in lay and ordained positions.

To all appearances this concentrated focus on women
bore fruit. By 1976 there were about 240 ordained women in
the United Presbyterian Church, an increase of nearly
eighty percent over the 1973 figure of 131.[76] Among the
United Methodists, there were 373 women in 1970 and 620
in 1975 in all ministerial categories (deacons and elders).[77]
In most denominations the number of women employed in
denominational agencies began to rise. And the enrollment
of women in seminary ministerial-degree programs had
sharply increased.[78]

For the first time in the history of each of the major denominations, the number of ordained women is large
enough for them to project a "presence." As women in every
denomination assess their experiences, common themes surface.[79] There is a quest for jobs. At a time when church
bodies and their budgets are contracting, insufficient job opportunities plague both women and men. Many advocate
new styles of ministry such as shared positions and alternative sources of income. There is a quest for collegiality.
Women feel excluded from established modes of interaction
among the male clergy and seek to alter these patterns and
also create new networks of support for themselves. Such
networks may have their drawbacks. Some women may fear
that they cause a diminution of independence, leadership

and assertiveness that may hamper their work. There is a quest to make the churches more responsive to the experience and outlook of women in general by arguing that ordained women bring unique gifts to ministry that will enhance the churches' sensitivity to all their members. This argument is reminiscent of the overly optimistic one advanced by suffragists claiming the moral superiority of women and their potential reforming effect on the nation. Finally, there is a quest to redefine the exercise of authority in the churches. As with those other questions, this is not a "women's issue" alone. It is part of a more generalized discomfort with "directive" leadership and a preference for nondirective styles. A decisive move toward nondirective styles of thought and leadership would doubtless have radical effects on theology and ethics.

Emerging feminist groups in all denominations will continue to pose answers to these and other questions. They occupy center stage in current discussions of women in the church because they often comprise the most articulate, well-organized and politically minded of church women and because many denominational leaders, having experienced a certain measure of guilt because of their past stance toward women, are eager to redress grievances quickly. Yet, even the most ardent of their supporters will admit that the feminists wield an influence that is out of proportion to their numbers in the churches and that introduces viewpoints from outside denominational traditions.

Denominational and feminist leaders face an awesome responsibility. Together they are in a position to reshape the conception of ministry in all its manifestations—pastoral, theological, liturgical, educational. Agendas and programs will have to be weighed critically in this fluid situation. It needs to be asked whether the cultural viewpoint of the feminists in the seventies is large enough and mature enough to do justice both to centuries of Christian tradition and to the need to integrate women more fully into the life of the church. Decisions that would be unmindful of the history of the church or of the diversity of its membership might well diminish the richness of Christian life and mute the witness of women who worked so energetically alongside of and within the churches for more than a century.

NOTES

1. E.g., Theodore Agnew, "Reflections on the Woman's Foreign Missionary Movement in Late 19th Century American Methodism," *Methodist History*, vol. VI, January 1968, pp. 3–14; Norma Taylor Mitchell, "From Social to Radical Feminism: A Survey of Emerging Diversity in Methodist Women's Organizations, 1869–1974," *ibid.*, vol. XIII, April 1975, pp. 21–44; Kenneth E. Rowe (ed.), "Discovery. My Ordination: Anna Howard Shaw," by Nancy N. Bahmueller, *ibid.*, vol. XIV, January 1976, pp. 125–31; Elaine Magalis, *Conduct Becoming to a Woman* (Women's Division, Board of Global Ministries, United Methodist Church, 1973).

2. R. Pierce Beaver, *All Loves Excelling: American Protestant Women in World Missions* (Grand Rapids, Mich.: Eerdmans, 1968); Irwin T. Hyatt, Jr., *Our Ordered Lives Confess: Three Nineteenth-Century American Missionaries in East Shantung* (Cambridge, Mass.: Harvard University, 1976); also very helpful is Helen Barrett Montgomery, *Western Women in Eastern Lands* (New York: Macmillan, 1911).

3. Elizabeth Howell Verdesi, "The Professionally-Trained Woman in the Presbyterian Church: The Role of Power in the Achievement of Status and Equality," Ed.D. dissertation, Teachers College, Columbia University, 1975; also published as *In But Still Out: Women in the Church* (Philadelphia: Westminster Press, 1976).

4. E.g., "Two Goodly Heritages; Presbyterian Women: How Does Our Past Inform Our Future?," *Concern*, vol. XIX, no. 3 (February 1977). The popular histories of women in the church also provided some leads for historical scholarship: Elsie Culver, *Women in the World of Religion* (Garden City, N.Y.: Doubleday, 1967); Georgia Harkness, *Women in Church and Society* (Nashville, Tenn.: Abingdon Press, 1972).

5. M. Katharine Bennett, "Status of Women in the Presbyterian Church in the U.S.A., with References to Other Denominations" (Philadelphia: General Council of the Presbyterian Church in the U.S.A., 1929); Conference on Women's Status and Service in the Church, "Reports Relating to the Status of Women in the Church" (Philadelphia: Office of the General Assembly, 1929); Joint Committee to Study the Place of Women's Organized Work in the Church, "The Relative Place of Women in the Church," New York City, 1927; Inez Cavert, "Women in American Church Life," mimeographed, Federal Council of Churches of Christ in America, 1948; Kathleen Bliss, *The Service and Status of Women in the Churches* (London: SCM Press Ltd., 1952); Elsie Gibson, *When the Minister Is a Woman* (New York: Holt, Rinehart & Winston, 1970).

6. Margaret Gibson Hummel, *The Amazing Heritage* (Philadelphia: Geneva Press, 1970); Alma Hunt, *History of Woman's Missionary Union* (Nashville, Tenn.: Convention Press, 1964); Lorraine Lollis, *The Shape of Adam's Rib: A Lively History of Woman's Work in the Christian Church* (St. Louis: Bethany Press, 1970); Ruth Esther Meeker, *Six Decades of Service, 1880–1940: A History of the Woman's Home Missionary Society of the Methodist Episcopal Church* (1969); Ruth Fritz Meyer, *Women on a Mission: The Role of Women in the Church . . . Including a History of the LWML During Its First Twenty-five Years* (St. Louis: Concordia Publishing House, 1967); Audrie E. Reber, *Women United for Mission: A History of the Women's Society of World Service of the Evangelical United Brethren Church, 1946–1968* (1969); Patricia Houck Sprinkle, *The Birthday Book* (Atlanta: Board of Women's Work, Presbyterian Church in the U.S., 1972); Noreen Dunn Tatum, *A Crown of Service: A Story of Woman's Work in the Methodist Episcopal Church South, 1878–1940* (1960); *These Fifty Years* (Chicago: Woman's Missionary Society, 1942)—Augustana Lutheran Church; Robert G. Torbet, *Venture of Faith: The Story of the American Baptist Foreign Mission Society and the Woman's American Baptist Foreign Mission Society* (Philadelphia: Judson Press, 1955); Elizabeth Meredith Lee, *As Among the Methodists: Deaconesses Yesterday, Today, and Tomorrow* (New York: Woman's Division of Christian Service, Board of Missions, Methodist Church, 1963); Frederick S. Weiser, *Love's Response: A Story of Lutheran Deaconesses in America* (Philadelphia: Board of Pub-

lication of the United Lutheran Church in America, 1962); Lucy Rider Meyer, *Deaconesses, Biblical, Early Church, European, American* (Chicago: Message Publishing Co., 1889); Margaret Blair Johnstone, *When God Says "No": Faith's Starting Point* (New York: Simon and Schuster, 1954); Margaret Henrichsen, *Seven Steeples* (Boston: Houghton Mifflin, 1953); Hilda Libby Ives, *All in One Day* (Portland, Me.: Bond Wheelwright, 1955).

7. Beaver, *All Loves Excelling*, p. 88.

8. For a complete and helpful list of women's foreign missionary societies organized before 1911, see Montgomery, *Western Women in Eastern Lands*, foldout page following p. 286. National missionary societies developed among immigrant Lutheran women somewhat later. One of the first, the Women's Missionary Society of the Augustana (Swedish) Lutheran Church, was founded in 1892 (Burnice Fjellmen, "Women in the Church," *Centennial Essays* [Rock Island, Ill.: Augustana Press, 1960], pp. 210–12). One of the last, the Lutheran Women's Missionary League of the Missouri Synod, was not founded until 1941 (Alan Graebner, *Uncertain Saints: The Laity in the Lutheran Church—Missouri Synod* [Westport, Conn.: Greenwood Press, 1975], pp. 133–40).

9. Beaver, *All Loves Excelling*, pp. 107–8.

10. Verdesi, *In But Still Out*, p. 61.

11. See Montgomery, *Western Women in Eastern Lands*, pp. 45–75.

12. Allen R. Bartholomew, "Mission Boards Fifty Years Ago: A Half Century of Changes in Missionary Administration and Organization in the Home Boards," *The Missionary Review of the World*, vol. L, December 1927, pp. 899–905.

13. Theodore Agnew, "Reflections on the Woman's Foreign Missionary Movement in Late 19th Century American Methodism," *loc. cit.*, pp. 3–14. We know, for instance, that Helen Barrett Montgomery, a leader in Baptist women's missionary societies and first woman to be president of the Northern Baptist Convention, graduated from one of the early classes at Wellesley College and later became a trustee of the college. Her husband, a Rochester, N.Y., businessman, made a fortune supplying the new automobile industry and was also chairman of the board of Colgate Rochester Divinity School. Lucy Waterbury Peabody, another Baptist missionary leader, was related to Andrew Jackson and Grover Cleveland. Her second husband, a rich businessman, was a member and

president of the Board of Managers of the Baptist Missionary Union. See Louise Armstrong Cattan, *Lamps Are for Lighting: The Story of Helen Barrett Montgomery and Lucy Waterbury Peabody* (Grand Rapids, Mich.: Eerdmans, 1972).

14. Cattan, *Lamps Are for Lighting*, pp. 57–58.

15. Lucy W. Peabody, "Woman's Place in Missions Fifty Years Ago and Now," *The Missionary Review of the World*, vol. L, no. 12 (December 1927), p. 907.

16. Beaver, *All Loves Excelling*, p. 177.

17. Montgomery, *Western Women in Eastern Lands*, p. 38.

18. R. Pierce Beaver, "Pioneer Single Women Missionaries," *Occasional Bulletin of the Missionary Research Library*, vol. IV, no. 2 (Sept. 30, 1953), pp. 1–7; and Beaver, *All Loves Excelling*.

19. One of these adventurous women was Lottie Moon, a Southern Baptist from Virginia who arrived in north China in 1873. Overeducated by Southern standards, Moon did not see many prospects in the war-torn South of the late sixties, and the schoolteaching which she tried for a time did not wholly satisfy her. In China she was not content only with a town life of sedate teaching; she embarked upon extensive preaching tours in the back country and settled for a number of years in one of the interior towns by herself, living a style of life as close to that of the Chinese as any Western woman up to that time. See Hyatt, *Our Ordered Lives Confess*, pp. 65–136.

20. Montgomery, *Western Women in Eastern Lands*, p. 175.

21. The first, mostly informal preparation of women for missions had taken place in new women's colleges like Mount Holyoke. Hardly any woman who came under the tutelage of Mary Lyon at Holyoke graduated unconverted, and many of her alumnae became missionaries and wives of missionaries or were prominent in the organization of the missionary societies of the 1860s and '70s. See, e.g., Montgomery, *Western Women in Eastern Lands*, p. 8.

22. Walter Palmer Behan, "An Introductory Survey of the Lay Training School Field," *Religious Education*, vol. XI (1916), pp. 47–52.

23. The writers of this chapter are currently engaged with others in a study of Protestant theological education in America, which will include a section on women's missionary training schools.

24. See Norma Taylor Mitchell, "From Social to Radical Fem-

inism: A Survey of Emerging Diversity in Methodist Women's Organizations, 1869–1974," pp. 21–44.

25. "Minority Report on the Status of Women," quoted by Kenneth E. Rowe (ed.), "The Ordination of Women: Round One: Anna Oliver and the General Conference of 1880," *Methodist History*, vol. XII, April 1974, pp. 70–71. Anna Howard Shaw and Anna Oliver were the two seminary graduates seeking ordination.

26. Emilie G. Briggs, "The Restoration of the Order of Deaconesses," *Biblical World*, vol. XLI, June 1913, p. 382.

27. This 2,000 figure is an educated guess. The highest total reached in American Lutheranism, one of the denominations in which the deaconess movement succeeded best, was only 487 in 1938 (see Weiser, *Love's Response*, p. 70). In 1950, the first time for which we have clear figures, the Methodist Church had 488 active and 261 retired deaconesses (Lee, *As Among the Methodists*, p. 76).

28. Amy Blanche Greene, "Woman's Work in the Church," *Labors of Love*, vol. XXV, January 1924, p. 15.

29. Weiser, *Love's Response*, pp. 74–92.

30. *Ibid.*, pp. 67–92; Margaret Sittler Ermath, *Adam's Fractured Rib* (Philadelphia: Fortress Press, 1970), pp. 142–46.

31. Dorothy Bass Fraser, "Women with a Past: A New Look at the History of Theological Education," *Theological Education*, Summer 1972, pp. 213–24.

32. Rowe, "Anna Oliver and the General Conference," pp. 60–72.

33. Kenneth E. Rowe (ed.), "Discovery. My Ordination: Anna Howard Shaw," *loc. cit.*, pp. 126–31; Ralph W. Spencer, "Anna Howard Shaw," *Methodist History*, vol. XIII, January 1975, pp. 41–45.

34. Harkness, *Women in Church and Society*, p. 127.

35. Lucy W. Peabody, "Woman's Place in Missions Fifty Years Ago and Now," *loc. cit.*, p. 909.

36. Anne Firor Scott, *The Southern Lady: From Pedestal to Politics 1830–1930* (Chicago/London: University of Chicago, 1970), p. 141.

37. Lollis, *The Shape of Adam's Rib*, pp. 99–124.

38. Verdesi, *In But Still Out*, pp. 70–78.

39. Horton, *The United Church of Christ*, p. 227. The writers

have found no information on the circumstances of this consolidation.

40. "Report of the Committee of Nine of the Northern Baptist Convention," *The Baptist*, vol. VIII, April 2, 1927, p. 436.

41. Mrs. W. C. Winnsborough, "Woman's Part in Home Missions," *The Missionary Review of the World*, vol. L, February 1927, p. 97.

42. Montgomery, *Western Women in Eastern Lands*, p. 269.

43. Peabody, "Woman's Place," *loc. cit.*, p. 909.

44. Report of the Special Committee to the General Council of the Presbyterian Church in the U.S.A., "Causes of Unrest Among the Women of the Church," 1927, p. 11.

45. Elizabeth J. Miller has documented the loss which occurred for Baptist women after the 1955 integration of the women's foreign and home missionary societies into the American Baptist Foreign Mission Society and the American Baptist Home Mission Society. She argues that upon merger of the women's societies into the larger bodies the women received significant positions of leadership in the new societies. However, as each of these women retired or resigned, her place was filled by a man. The number of women in executive positions, never large, declined steadily to 1970. Miller's study might serve as a model for studies of the results of earlier consolidations. (Elizabeth J. Miller, "Retreat to Tokenism: A Study of the Status of Women on the Executive Staff of the American Baptist Convention," mimeographed, October 1970, pp. 10–11.)

46. "Causes of Unrest," p. 10.

47. Aileen S. Kraditor, *The Ideas of the Woman Suffrage Movement, 1890–1920* (Garden City, N.Y.: Anchor Books, 1971), pp. 64–81.

48. Gibson, *When the Minister Is a Woman*, p. 21.

49. *Ibid.*

50. Charles E. Raven, *Women and the Ministry* (Garden City, N.Y.: Doubleday, Doran, 1929), p. 22; and *Congregational Year-Book 1900* (Boston: Congregational Sunday School and Publishing Co., 1900), pp. 489–524. See also Joint Committee, "The Relative Place of Women in the Church," p. 52.

51. Magalis, *Conduct Becoming*, p. 138.

52. Juliette Mather, "Women, Convention Privileges of," *En-*

cyclopedia of Southern Baptists (Nashville, Tenn.: Broadman Press, 1958), p. 1543.

53. Magalis, *Conduct Becoming*, p. 120.

54. Bliss, *Service and Status of Women*, p. 173.

55. Augustana (Swedish Synod) allowed women delegates at synodical meetings in 1930. In 1934 the United Lutheran Church granted women rights to elected lay offices. Many other Lutheran bodies did not act until after World War II. (*The Ordination of Women*, condensed by Raymond Tiemeyer, a report distributed by authorization of the church body presidents as a contribution to further study, based on materials produced through the division of theological studies of the Lutheran Council in the U.S. [Minneapolis: Augsburg, 1970], p. 36.)

56. Margaret Blair Johnstone, *When God Says "No,"* p. 37.

57. Hazel E. Foster, "The Ecclesiastical Status of Women," *The Woman's Pulpit*, vol. XXX, January–February–March 1952, p. 2.

58. Mrs. Henry W. Hunter, "The Work of the Church Assistant," *Religious Education*, vol. XII, February 1917, p. 26.

59. See, e.g., *ibid.*; also, Agnes Mabel Taylor, "Standards of Preparation of Women Church Assistants," *Religious Education*, vol. XII, December 1917, pp. 438–46; Henry F. Cope, "The Professional Organization of Workers in Religious Education," *Religious Education*, vol. XVI (1921), pp. 162–67.

60. See, e.g., Taylor, "Standards of Preparation of Women Church Assistants," *loc. cit.*

61. E.g., most of the membership appointments announced in 1920 for this association were male. See *Religious Education*, vol. XV, October 1920, p. 293.

62. First Assembly of the World Council of Churches, "Interim Report of the Study on the Life and Work of Women in the Church," Amsterdam, 1948, pp. 5–6.

63. Mimeographed report, Dept. of Research and Education, Federal Council of Churches of Christ in America, 1948.

64. London: SCM Press, 1952.

65. "Women in the Churches," *The Christian Century*, vol. LXIX, May 21, 1952, pp. 606–7.

66. An account of one such denominational study can be found in "Women in the Church: A Symposium on the Service and Status of Women Among the Disciples of Christ" (Lexington, Ky.: College of the Bible, 1953), pp. 23–32. Apparently in reaction to

such positive responses, the official publishing house of the Lutheran Church—Missouri Synod (not a member of the WCC) published a translation of a German work opposing ordination for women (Fritz Zerbst, *The Office of Woman in the Church*, transl. Albert G. Merkens [St. Louis: Concordia Publishing House, 1955]).

67. Howard Elmo Short, "The Service and Status of Women Among the Disciples of Christ," in "Women in the Church."

68. Hazel E. Foster, "The Ecclesiastical Status of Women," *The Woman's Pulpit*, vol. XXIII (1955), p. 3; XXV (1957), p. 8.

69. Doris Moreland Jones of the Board of Higher Education and Ministry, United Methodist Church, noted these reactions in the Methodist Church General Conference in 1956 (telephone interview with Rev. Jones, June 29, 1977).

70. Christine Bourbeck, "Women as Clergymen in Germany," *Lutheran Quarterly*, vol. XVIII, May 1966, pp. 168–72; Erika Reichle, "The Ordained Woman in the Parish and in Other Ministries," *Lutheran World*, vol. XXII (1975), pp. 49–53; *The Ordination of Women*, condensed by Raymond Tiemeyer, pp. 34–35.

71. Graebner, *Uncertain Saints*, pp. 129–40, 184–86.

72. Sarah Frances Anders, "The Role of Women in American Religion," *Southwestern Journal of Theology*, vol. XVII, Spring 1976, p. 56.

73. American Baptist Executive Staff Women, "Fact or Fallacy: Equal Employment Opportunity in the American Baptist Convention," n.d.

74. Board of Managers, American Baptist Women, "Women in Church-Related Vocations," mimeographed, 1968. Comments of Richard Beers during symposium on "Opportunities for Women in Church-Related Vocations," p. 17.

75. Anders, "The Role of Women in American Religion," *loc. cit.*, p. 55.

76. "Forces Affecting the Employment of Women in the Church," n.d., mimeographed (United Presbyterian Church in the U.S.A.).

77. "Commission on the Status and Role of Women in the United Methodist Church" (pamphlet issued for the General Conference, 1976), figure 5.

78. Marvin J. Taylor (ed.), *Fact Book on Theological Education 1976–1977* (Association of Theological Schools, 1977), p. 8. For

the most recent statistics on women ministers see Constant H. Jacquet, Jr., "Woman Ministers in 1977" (study issued by Office of Research, Evaluation and Planning, National Council of Churches, 1978).

79. For a review of some of these issues, see Linda J. Hanson, "A Survey of Interests and Agendas of Women in U.S. Church Denominations," *Theological Education*, vol. XI, Winter 1975, pp. 82–95.

TWELVE

Women in Judaism: From the Reform Movement to Contemporary Jewish Religious Feminism

ELLEN M. UMANSKY

Throughout most of Jewish history, women have been excluded from positions of religious leadership. Although a handful of women did achieve recognition as scholars, as authorities in matters of Jewish law, and, if rarely, as social-spiritual heads of their communities, they were viewed as exceptions and did not significantly affect the "preferred" family-centered role of the Jewish woman as wife and mother.[1]

Steps to increase the participation of women within public religious life were first undertaken by the leaders of the Reform movement in nineteenth-century Germany. In their efforts to reinterpret the principles of Judaism in accordance with the spirit of modernity, they maintained that "it is a sacred duty to express most emphatically the complete religious equality of the female sex."[2] Although a number of liberalizing measures were undertaken, it was not until 1972 that a woman was first ordained from a Reform rabbinical seminary. While the Reconstructionist Rabbinical College ordained its first woman in 1974, the other two major branches of Judaism—Orthodoxy and Conservatism—have yet to grant women ordination. In order to understand *why* women have been denied access to the rabbinate, it is important to look not only at the evolving nature of the rabbinate, but also at the traditional position of women within Jewish religious life. Such an examination will help clarify the kinds of restrictions that the Reform movement sought to overcome, the barriers that still exist to female ordination, and the contemporary responses to the traditional role of the Jewish woman that have led to a serious reflection, reevaluation and, directly or indirectly, to a commitment for change.

The traditional exclusion of women from the rabbinate must be viewed within the more general context of the position of women in Jewish life. Although the Talmud declared that every individual possessed absolute equality, dignity, and worth,[3] this equality was conceived of within a clearly delineated, sex-role-differentiated society. Since women were regarded essentially as wives and mothers, the rabbis maintained that the home was the natural domain of women, the public sphere the domain of men. They insisted that these two spheres were separate but equal, but in reality the position of women within Jewish life was always secondary to that of men. Women were expected to be enablers. While their husbands and sons occupied themselves in study and prayer, women were to fulfill their numerous household and family obligations, provide a loving and supportive atmosphere within the home, and realize their spiritual potential through the merits of their fathers or husbands without any real "independent spiritual life to counterbalance the materialism" of their own existence.[4]

Psychologically, it became difficult for women to think of themselves as leaders. Socially, legally and religiously, they were inferior to men. They were always dependent, first on their fathers and later on their husbands. In marriage, divorce, matters of inheritance and within the courts, women's rights were severely limited. Family responsibilities exempted them from many of the 613 commandments that Jews were obligated to fulfill (including the obligations to study and to pray three times a day). Women were revered and honored as long as they did what was expected of them.

They could be strong and aggressive, but only when Jewish survival was at stake.[5] Had women attempted to create new roles for themselves, they would have been met with derision and disdain. It was Rabbi Akiva's wife, patiently waiting at home while her husband went off to study Torah, who was held up to Jewish women as an ideal; Beruria, the wife of Rabbi Meir, who became a scholar in her own right, was always viewed as an exception.

Originally, the term "rabbi" designated an officially authorized teacher and interpreter of Jewish law. While women were not explicitly forbidden to serve as legal experts, their lack of formal education actively discouraged any such aspirations. Just as the obligation to study Torah was incumbent only upon males, the commandment to teach one's children required only that a father instruct his son. Some rabbis questioned the advisability of teaching girls altogether, while others, such as the first-century scholar Ben Azzai, advocated giving girls a limited education. In either case, it was agreed that since a woman's proper role was played out within family life, there was no need to raise girls to as high an intellectual level as boys, no matter what their ability. Theoretically, women *could* become scholars, but, not surprisingly, few did.[6]

According to the traditional form of ordination (*semikha*), the rabbi was designated not only as an interpreter of Jewish law, but also as a judge. While it appears that women were not explicitly prohibited from acting as judges, in reality no woman attained that position. This can be explained by the clearly stated prohibition against women acting as witnesses, the general relegation of women to the private sphere of religious life, and the rabbinic injunction that *all* offices were to be filled by men.[7]

By the Middle Ages, the original concept of the rabbi as sage had both changed and expanded. Although rabbis were still empowered to interpret Jewish law, only the most advanced students could serve as judges in legal (as opposed to merely ritual) matters.[8] In addition, the rabbinate became a full-time occupation, with the rabbi serving as teacher, preacher and spiritual head of a congregation or community. While rabbinic enactments continued to improve the status of Jewish women, the question of a woman acting not only as a religious authority but also as a social-spiritual head of a Jewish community was never seriously considered. Again, we can cite the few exceptional women who did assume positions of leadership. The daughter of the twelfth-century Gaon of Baghdad, Samuel ben Ali, became a religious authority because her father had no sons to educate and succeed him. Later, in the nineteenth century, Hannah Rachel, known as the "Maid of Ludomir," earned a reputation as a Hasidic *rebbe*. However, neither was an ordained religious figure, nor did their accomplishments offer any real challenge to the position of women in Jewish religious life.

Both the modern concept of a rabbi, as one who primarily functions as the social-spiritual head of a congregation, and the reexamination of the position of women within public religious life can be seen as responses to Jewish emancipation. By the eighteenth century, as Jews started to participate in the economic, cultural and political life of the non-Jewish world, the mind-set of the traditional, semiautonomous Jewish community began to disintegrate. The historical consciousness which had fused medieval Jewish communities together gave way to new visions of "enlightenment" which inevitably weakened the centrality of religious life.[9] Once the all-embracing nature of religion was denied and the importance of change accepted, Jewish institutional and educational beliefs necessarily had to be adjusted in order to conform to the spirit of the modern world.

The extent to which changes were made varied. However, as the process of emancipation began, and as Jews eventually attained citizenship, the rabbi no longer functioned as the judge of a self-contained community, but as the teacher, preacher and social-spiritual head of a specific religious group. Today, a Reform rabbi receives the designation "judge" only as a formality, and most modern Orthodox rabbis have only limited jurisdiction in matters of Jewish law.[10] The form of ordination granted by the Conservative movement does not even formally empower the rabbi to serve as a judicial authority. Legally, then, a major barrier to women's ordination has been relaxed, if not lifted. As the rabbi's activities have become "increasingly restricted to administrative and pastoral functions,"[11] it has become much more difficult to deny that the continued exclusion of women from the Orthodox and Conservative rabbinate is based *primarily* on social attitudes and tradition.

Once Jews began to recognize the importance of secular education, educational opportunities for Jewish women increased significantly. While secular learning threatened men's total absorption in Torah study, providing one's daughters with a secular education became a visible symbol of Jewish adaptability within the non-Jewish world. Thus, as Jacob Katz writes, well-to-do families in the ghetto encouraged their daughters "to learn the language of their neighbors [and] to acquire a familiarity with foreign languages and literature."[12] By the end of the nineteenth century, when traditional Jewish communities in Western and Central Europe had ceased to exist, the exclusion of women from study, community life and participation in public worship contrasted sharply with the opportunities open to women within "secular" society. As Abraham Geiger, the major philosophical spokesman of German Reform, maintained, the traditional position of women could no longer be upheld. Rather, he said, the spirit of the age demanded that the subordinate status of women be overthrown; that whenever possible women and men assume the same religious obligations; that the ability of women to grasp the depths of religious belief be acknowledged and acted upon; and that no worship service either in form or in content exclude women from participation. He added that adoption of these measures would not only enrich the religion as a whole but also would make accessible to women the intimate and fervent attachment to Judaism which springs from a knowledge of its beliefs.[13]

Geiger subsequently helped to organize a number of rabbinical conferences in which "like-thinking, progressive rabbis"[14] examined Jewish traditions and beliefs in light of the outlook and spirit of the modern age. The religious status of women was one issue that received serious consideration. In 1846, at the Breslau Conference, members of the committee which had been organized to study the legal position of women stated that in order for women to be truly emancipated, their position within Jewish religious life had to be altered significantly. The committee maintained that to declare "the equality of religious privileges and obligations of women insofar as this is possible"[15] was in accordance with their "religious consciousness, which grants all humans an equal degree of natural holiness."[16]

A number of steps were taken to ensure this equality. Women were included in the quorum necessary for worship; the benediction recited by Jewish males expressing thanks for not having been created a woman was abolished; formal religious instruction for girls was introduced; and in the Reform synagogue in Berlin women and men were seated on the same floor during the worship service.[17] By the end of the nineteenth century, the major focus of Reform had shifted to the United States, and in 1875 Rabbi Isaac Mayer Wise established the Hebrew Union College in Cincinnati as a Reform theological seminary. Wise was one of the first Jews in America to champion the cause of women's rights. In 1846, at his congregation in Albany, he admitted girls into the synagogue choir, and in 1851 he introduced family pews. During the twenty-five years in which he served as president of HUC, women were encouraged to attend.[18] However, none of Wise's female students sought ordination, and it was not until 1921 that the issue of women as rabbis was formally raised.

In the late spring of that year, seventeen-year-old Martha Neumark, a student at the college since 1919 and the daughter of David Neumark, professor of Jewish Philosophy at HUC, petitioned the faculty to be assigned to lead High

Holy Day services in the fall, should a pulpit be available. The faculty's vote ended in a tie, and it was left to Kaufman Kohler, then president of the college, to resolve the matter. Kohler voted to approve the petition subject to subsequent approval by the congregation in question. He also resolved to form a joint faculty/Board of Governors committee to consider the larger issue which Martha Neumark's petition had indirectly raised—namely, given the Reform movement's commitment to women's religious equality, why should qualified women not be granted rabbinic ordination? [19]

The report adopted by the joint committee maintained that its members saw "no logical reason why women should not be entitled to receive a rabbinical degree." The report went on, however, to state: "Because of practical considerations, your committee is of the opinion that the admission of women to the Hebrew Union College with the aim of becoming rabbis, should not be encouraged." [20] The Board of Governors received copies of both the majority report and a dissenting report submitted by two of the six committee members. [21] Unable to make a decision, the board asked for a faculty opinion as to whether Jewish law prohibited the ordination of women. A number of faculty members felt that it did, but nonetheless they adopted the following resolution unanimously: "In view of the fact that Reform Judaism has in many other instances departed from traditional practice, it cannot logically and consistently refuse the ordination of women." [22] The board then referred the matter to the Central Conference of American (Reform) Rabbis (CCAR). By a vote of 56–11, it too affirmed that women could not "justly be denied the privilege of ordination." [23] However, when the Board of Governors met to reach a final decision in February 1923, it voted "that no change should be made in the present practice of limiting to males the right to matriculate for the purpose of entering the rabbinate." [24]

While Martha Neumark failed to realize her ambition of becoming "America's first woman rabbi," [25] she continued to

study at the college until shortly after the death of her father
in December of 1924. Later, she received the first "Certificate of Sunday School Superintendentship" issued by the
newly established Hebrew Union College School of Teachers in New York.[26] In an autobiographical sketch written in
1925, Martha Neumark reiterated her belief that women
were capable of becoming rabbis. She even asserted that
since more women than men attended Reform services, and
since women experience similar "paths of spiritual storm,"[27]
a woman might be *better* suited than a man to meet the
demands of the contemporary rabbinate. She also suggested
that male and female rabbis serve together, appropriately
reflecting the composition of their congregations.

In 1939, approximately ten years before Stephen Wise's
Progressive rabbinical seminary, the Jewish Institute of Religion, merged with Hebrew Union College, a woman
named Helen Hadassah Levinthal completed the entire rabbinic course at JIR. The faculty seriously debated the issue
of ordination, but decided that the time was not yet right to
ordain a woman as rabbi. As a compromise, she was given a
Master of Hebrew Literature degree and a certificate, in Hebrew, which did not designate her a "Teacher in Israel" but
stated that she had finished the curriculum. Following
HUC-JIR's more recent decision to ordain women, Helen
Levinthal's family petitioned for a posthumous award of rabbinic ordination.[28] The petition was considered but not
acted upon.

The issue was again raised in 1956. A committee of the
CCAR, formed to consider the matter, affirmed the 1922
resolution supporting the ordination of women and recom-
mended that women completing the rabbinic program at
HUC-JIR be admitted as CCAR members. Nelson Glueck,
then president of the college, supported this proposal and
maintained that HUC-JIR was prepared to ordain any
woman who passed the required courses.[29] Yet it was not
until 1972 that a woman, Sally Priesand, was admitted to the
rabbinate by HUC-JIR. Two more women, Michal Seser-

man Bernstein and Laura Geller, have since been ordained. In addition, the Leo Baeck College, the Progressive rabbinical seminary of England, recently ordained Julia Neuberger and Jacqueline Acker Tabick. Thus, over a hundred years after the rabbis assembled at the Breslau Conference had affirmed women's religious equality, Reform women have finally gained access to ordained positions of leadership.[30]

While Sally Priesand was the first woman ordained from any Jewish theological seminary, she was not actually the first woman to achieve rabbinic ordination. Regina Jonas completed rabbinical studies at the Berlin Academy for the Science of Judaism in the late 1930s. When ordination was denied because of her sex, Rabbi Max Dienemann of Offenbach[31] took the unusual step of privately granting her a Hebrew rabbinical diploma. She functioned briefly as a rabbi, but was imprisoned at the Theresienstadt concentration camp in 1940 and died shortly thereafter.[32]

Besides Reform, Reconstructionism is the only branch of Judaism which currently grants women rabbinic ordination. From the inception of the Reconstructionist movement in 1935, Mordecai Kaplan, its founder and leader, affirmed the complete religious equality of women. Conceiving of Judaism as a religious civilization, he maintained that to be a *modern civilization* Judaism had to abolish the legal disadvantages under which women suffered. He still believed that Judaism should find expression through law, but saw Judaism as a "living social process"[33] and insisted that traditional Jewish law could and should be amended.

As a Conservative rabbi in the 1920s, Kaplan instituted Bat Mitzvah as a counterpart to the Bar Mitzvah ceremony for boys and advocated calling girls up to the Torah (*aliyah*) and counting them in the quorum necessary for public worship (*minyan*). He exhorted Jewish women to demand "an equal share in the responsibilities for the social and spiritual well being of their people,"[34] and in 1968, when the Reconstructionist Rabbinical College opened in Philadelphia, it both "accepted and encouraged the ordination of women."[35] In

1974, Sandy Eisenberg Sasso became the first woman ordained as a Reconstructionist rabbi. Two other women, Rebecca Trachtenberg Alpert and Ilene Schneider, have since been ordained, and at present a little over one fourth of those studying to become Reconstructionist rabbis are women.[36] In keeping with Kaplan's vision of Judaism as a living civilization, Reconstructionism has afforded women religious equality. Only after this step was taken, claimed Kaplan, could the Jewish woman "contribute her share to the regeneration of Jewish life."[37]

Although acceptance to the rabbinate has been a recent development, as the entrance of women into public religious life gained greater approval a number of women succeeded in functioning as unordained spiritual leaders. Ray Frank, for example, was a preacher, lecturer and journalist who worked to form Jewish congregations along the Pacific Coast in the 1890s. She first came to prominence in 1890 when her Day of Atonement sermon to a group of Jews in Spokane Falls, Washington, inspired them to form a permanent congregation and build a house of worship.[38] She was offered several positions as a "spiritual leader," but declined all invitations. Early in 1893 she went to Cincinnati to study Jewish ethics and philosophy at the Hebrew Union College. Despite the fact that she never matriculated and actually attended classes for only one semester,[39] newspaper reports claimed that she had been ordained as the first woman rabbi.[40] In September 1893, five years before her public career ended, Ray Frank delivered a paper on "Women in the Synagogue" at the Jewish Women's Congress held in Chicago. She said that ordination for women was inconsequential as long as they recognized their capabilities for holding such an office. Presenting what she felt women's proper sphere of activity should be, Ray Frank maintained: "Every woman should aspire to make of her home a temple, of herself a high priestess, of her children disciples; then will she best occupy the pulpit, and her work run parallel with man's."[41]

The Honorable Lily H. Montagu, who lived in England

from 1873 to 1963, similarly felt that creating a spiritual atmosphere within the home demanded of the married
woman much time and effort. Unlike Ray Frank, Lily Montagu remained single and devoted herself to the revitaliza-
tion of Judaism as a living faith. In 1899 her article in the
Jewish Quarterly Review on the "Spiritual Possibilities of Judaism Today" sparked interest in creating a new religious
movement aimed at combating materialism and indiffer-
ence, while deepening the individual's religious spirit,
through services, publications and lectures. Enlisting the
help of Claude G. Montefiore, whose theological ideas had
given direction to her search for a "living Judaism," she
called together a group of men and women who shared her
concerns. Consequently, in 1902, the Jewish Religious
Union was established.

In 1918, six years after the Union had opened its Liberal
Jewish Synagogue in London, Lily Montagu preached her
first sermon. From 1928 until her death, she served as chairman and spiritual leader of the London West Central Liberal
Jewish Congregation and became the first Jewish woman to
gain formal recognition as a "lay minister." [42] When, with
the assistance of Claude Montefiore and Israel Mattuck, the
World Union for Progressive Judaism was formed in 1926,
her dream of a worldwide union of liberal Jewish organizations was realized. As its honorary secretary and later as its
president, she planned conferences and meetings, chaired
sessions and delivered papers, regularly corresponded with
World Union members, and continually encouraged and actively supported the formation of new liberal Jewish groups.

During the 1928 World Union Conference, Lily Montagu
preached at the Reform Synagogue in Berlin. The first Jewish woman to occupy a pulpit in Germany, she later wrote
that "German women must come down from the galleries
and take part literally and in a real sense in the construction
of and struggle for a living religion for the entire community." [43] Although she might not have labeled herself a feminist, she strongly defended the equality of women on moral

and human grounds. Within the West Central Jewish Girls Club which she and her sister Marian founded in 1893, in the juvenile courts where she served as magistrate, in the numerous organizations and congregations in which she took an active part—in every aspect of her life, Lily Montagu sought to share with others, chiefly through example, her conviction that there is only one morality, one humanity and one God. Believing that Judaism and, in particular, liberal Judaism, contained the purest conception of the divine, she maintained that every Jew could bring the world closer to the kingdom of God. As a witness to the one God of justice, love, goodness and truth, each Jew, she said, has the responsibility to reveal God through everyday conduct and to serve Him by serving others.

Paula Ackerman of Meridian, Mississippi, was the first woman to serve as spiritual leader of a Jewish congregation in the United States. Following the death of her husband, Rabbi William Ackerman, in November 1950, she successfully replaced him as head of the Reform congregation Beth Israel from 1951 to 1954.[44] While insisting that she would lead the congregation only until a suitable rabbi could be found, Paula Ackerman nevertheless realized the "revolutionary" aspect of her position. She wrote: "If I can just plant a seed for the Jewish woman's larger participation, if perhaps it will open a way for women students to train for congregational leadership, then my life would have some meaning." [45]

Since 1973, Lynn Gottlieb has served as "student rabbi" of Temple Beth Or of the Deaf in New York. Now spiritual leader of the Hebrew Association of the Deaf as well, she leads services, conducts educational programs, prepares girls and boys for Bat and Bar Mitzvah, and performs life-cycle ceremonies, through the use of sign language and voice. Although not enrolled in a formal rabbinical program, she has been studying privately since 1973 and hopes eventually to be ordained. It is not yet clear whether this will happen. Because her ordination committee is composed largely of Conservative rabbis, no further steps will be taken until 1979,

when the study group appointed by Conservatism's Rabbinical Assembly in May 1977 to look into the question of female ordination presents its report.

At present, efforts to effect change in the status of Jewish
women have been grouped under the amorphous title of
"Jewish feminism." Some see the goals of Jewish feminism
as granting equal educational opportunities to women, while
others are demanding nothing less than the full participation
of women in Jewish religious life. Similarly, Jewish feminism
began, not as a unified movement with a clearly outlined
platform of beliefs, but rather "as a series of isolated ques-
tionings in the shadow of the women's movement" [46] during
the early 1970s. Ann Lerner lists the proliferation of consciousness-raising groups, a "self-styled revolutionary Jewish
newspaper" [47] named the *Brooklyn Bridge*, friendships established during the anti-Vietnam War movement and the general impact of the secular movement for women's rights as
among those forces lending impetus to the reevaluation of
the position of the Jewish woman.

In September 1971 a small group of women calling themselves "Ezrat Nashim" began to meet as an ongoing consciousness-raising and study group. Although they saw themselves only secondarily as an activist organization, their
"Call for Change" presented at the Rabbinical Assembly's
convention in March 1972 was instrumental in bringing
about the Conservative movement's more recent reexamination of the status of women in Jewish life. Among the
changes demanded by Ezrat Nashim were the full participation of women in religious observance, synagogue worship
and decision-making bodies within synagogues and the general Jewish community. They also called for the recognition
of women as witnesses in Jewish law, the right of women to
initiate divorce, and the admission of women to rabbinical
and cantorial schools. [48]

Although the group's appearance at the convention
was not sanctioned by the Rabbinical Assembly itself, the
media attention which Ezrat Nashim received made its

members "small scale celebrities within the Conservative movement." [49] Consequently, their proposals, which had been submitted to the Rabbinical Assembly's Committee on Jewish Law and Standards, received a good deal of consideration. Early in 1973, the committee voted to count women in the worship quorum. In addition, its little-known 1955 decision allowing women to be called to the Torah received new attention, and the number of Conservative synagogues granting women aliyah increased enormously. [50]

While continuing to hold regular meetings, Ezrat Nashim has largely ceased to exert public pressure for change. Retreating "into a more introspective existence," [51] it mainly functions as a consciousness-raising group. Recently, however, its members issued a booklet on birth ceremonies for Jewish girls, and it still maintains a limited speakers' bureau. In 1973, in recognition of the growing interest in a larger, more activist organization, the members of Ezrat Nashim helped plan and lead the first national conference on "The Role of Women in Jewish Life." At the second conference, in 1974, the Jewish Feminist Organization was created "to struggle for the liberation of the Jewish woman." [52]

Seeking "nothing else than the full, direct and equal participation of women at all levels of Jewish life," [53] the JFO served as an umbrella organization for numerous regional committees. Through consciousness-raising groups, seminars, bibliographical publications and other, specifically action-oriented proposals, the JFO worked to become a force for "creative change in the Jewish community." [54] While the national Jewish Feminist Organization no longer exists, subregional chapters have continued to function, and other, often informal groups have arisen which similarly attempt to bring traditional concepts of the Jewish woman into question.

At Brown University, for example, a number of Jewish women regularly hold their own Sabbath worship service. Naomi Janowitz and Maggie Wenig, two members of the group, have recently written a prayer book for women that refers to God as "She" and includes not only various services for the Sabbath but also Sabbath home rituals and a prayer to be said on the first day of menstruation.[55] Although still in an experimental draft form, the prayer book seeks to "offer encouragement to women, as they look around and inside themselves for God, to write prayers, to pray together and to renew the meaning of all that has been passed down to us."[56]

Lilith, a new magazine devoted to Jewish feminism, presents articles that explore "the world of the Jewish woman"[57] and offers a listing of resources that include bibliographical references, local Jewish feminist organizations, religious services for women, and information on the development of new rituals and life-cycle ceremonies. Dramatic presentations, such as *Reflections of a China Doll*, Susan Merson's play about her own experiences as a Jewish woman in America, and performances by the Bat Kol players, Lynn Gottlieb's theater group which presents the lives of Jewish women through music, mime and dance, represent other, more personal responses to a growing awareness of what it means to be a Jewish woman.

This new awareness has forced Orthodoxy, Conservatism and Reform to acknowledge the increasing demands for change. In September 1975, representatives of the Reform movement's Central Conference of American Rabbis and the Union of American Hebrew Congregations agreed to initiate a series of programs and projects which would help gain acceptance for women rabbis. They also voted to pass resolutions supporting the equality of women and the right of women to receive rabbinic ordination.[58]

While Orthodoxy has neither formally considered the question of female ordination nor brought about significant changes in religious attitudes,[59] the number of Orthodox women working outside the home has grown, and steps to enlarge the scope of female religious education have been taken. It may be true that the majority of Orthodox women are currently accepting "more fully all the traditional demands made on them" [60]; but women's prayer services, support from a number of highly respected Orthodox rabbis, and articles and lectures by Orthodox women who feel that contemporary women's concerns *can* be integrated with Jewish traditional values [61] have led to a growing dissatisfaction with the position of women within Orthodox Jewish life.

Although some Conservative rabbis maintain that Jewish feminism represents nothing more than a "passing fad," [62] the issue of female ordination has been seriously raised both by the Rabbinical Assembly's Committee on Jewish Law and Standards and by the organizational arm of the Conservative movement, the United Synagogue of America. At the United Synagogue's biennial convention in 1973, a series of resolutions were adopted which (1) called on congregations to take measures ensuring the opportunity for female congregants to "assume positions of leadership, authority and responsibility in all phases of Jewish congregational activity"; (2) advocated the full ritual participation of women within the synagogue service; and (3) looked "with favor on the admission of qualified women to the Rabbinical School of the Jewish Theological Seminary of America." [63]

Despite these resolutions, the Committee on Jewish Law and Standards voted overwhelmingly against the ordination of women as rabbis in June of 1974. It also voted against the investiture of women as cantors. Similarly, Gerson Cohen, chancellor of the seminary, has expressed his own opposition to the ordination of women. He maintains that such a move would not "reflect the consensus of the Conservative movement, whether of its laity or its professional leadership" [64] and thus declares that "for the present and foreseeable future," [65] the Jewish Theological Seminary will continue to admit only men into its rabbinical program. The Rabbinical Assembly's May 1977 decision to form a study group to "produce a definitive judgment within two years on the question of ordaining women"[66] can be regarded either as a hopeful sign for change or as another attempt to delay what many feel is an inevitable step toward the recognition of women's religious equality.

As more women begin to assume positions of leadership outside the synagogue, demands for female ordination will both increase and eventually gain wider acceptance. The force of tradition weighs heavily against the future ordination of women within Conservative and, even more so, Orthodox Judaism. Yet recent reappraisals of the position of the Jewish woman, largely because of the growth of feminist consciousness and activity, have already produced concrete results. New rituals for women have been created; women's prayer services have helped to deepen religious sensibilities and commitment; plays, poems, articles and books have enriched historical as well as personal awareness of what it means to be both female and Jewish; and the issue of female ordination has paved the way for a new and broader concept of the rabbinate.

NOTES

1. Saul Berman, "The Status of Women in Halakhic Judaism," *The Jewish Woman*, ed. Elizabeth Koltun (New York: Schocken Books, 1976), p. 125.

2. Report to the Breslau Conference, 1846, quoted in W. Gunther Plaut, *The Rise of Reform Judaism* (New York: World Union for Progressive Judaism, Ltd., 1963), p. 254.

3. Mishnah Sanhedrin 4:5.

4. Rachel Adler, "The Jew Who Wasn't There: Halacha and the Jewish Woman," *The Jewish Woman: An Anthology. Response*, vol. VII, no. 2 (Summer 1973), p. 80.

5. Aviva Cantor Zuckoff, "The Oppression of the Jewish Woman," *The Jewish Woman: An Anthology. Response*, vol. VII, no. 2 (Summer 1973), p. 49.

6. For a fuller discussion of rabbinic attitudes concerning the education of women, see Leonard Swidler, *Women in Judaism*

(Metuchen, N.J.: Scarecrow Press, 1976), especially chap. 4, "Women in Relation to Cult and Torah."

7. See Maimonides' *Mishneh Torah*, Hilchot Melachim 1:5.

8. The evolution of the rabbinate and changes made in the traditional form of ordination are discussed in "Semikha," *Encyclopedia Judaica*, vol. XIV (Jerusalem: Macmillan, 1971), pp. 1140f.

9. Jacob Katz, *Tradition and Crisis* (New York: Schocken Books, 1961), pp. 270f.

10. There are two types of ordination which modern Orthodoxy recognizes. The first empowers the rabbi to make decisions on ritual matters and is the only type of *semikha* granted by the major Orthodox rabbinical seminary in America, the Rabbi Isaac El-chanan Theological Seminary of Yeshiva University. The second type additionally empowers the Orthodox rabbi to be a judge in nonritual areas, e.g., concerning financial disputes, but necessitates further study and formal recognition from an individual authorized to grant this type of *semikha*.

11. Joseph L. Blau, *Judaism in America* (Chicago: University of Chicago, 1976), p. 132.

12. Jacob Katz, *Out of the Ghetto* (Cambridge: Harvard University, 1973), p. 84.

13. Abraham Geiger, "Die Stellung des weiblichen Geschlechtes in dem Judenthume Unserer Zeit," *Wissenschaft Zeitschrift für jüdische Theologie*, Dritter Band (Stuttgart, 1837), pp. 13, 14.

14. David Philipson, *The Reform Movement in Judaism* (New York: Ktav, 1967), p. 140.

15. Plaut, *Rise of Reform Judaism*, p. 254.

16. *Ibid*.

17. Philipson, *Reform Movement*, p. 219. It should be noted that nearly thirty years after the Breslau Conference, confirmation was introduced within progressive European congregations as a ceremony which formally recognized the entrance of both boys and girls into Jewish communal life.

18. Jacob Marcus, "An 11-Year-Old Girl in 1875 Paved Way for Women Studying for Rabbinate Today," Philadelphia *Jewish Exponent*, 1972. Copy in "Women Rabbis," *Miscellaneous File*, American Jewish Archives, Cincinnati, Ohio.

19. It was a matter of "simple logic," Kohler said, that if a "girl"

was permitted to officiate as a reader and preacher, she later should be entitled to function as a rabbi ("Note to Board of Governors," HUC Correspondence and Resolution Regarding Women Rabbis, 1921–22, *Miscellaneous File*, American Jewish Archives).

20. "Majority Report of the Committee on the Question of Graduating Women as Rabbis," HUC Correspondence . . . , *Miscellaneous File*, American Jewish Archives.

21. "Minority Report of the Committee on the Question of Graduating Women as Rabbis," *ibid*. Oscar Berman and Jacob Z. Lauterbach submitted a minority report recommending "that women should not be graduated nor ordained as rabbis." Included as reasons were the opposition to female ordination expressed in Jewish tradition and religious teachings; the fact that to most Jews "such an innovation would seem absurd and ridiculous"; the belief that the ordination of women would be a "bad investment," since once a woman rabbi married "she would very likely leave the rabbinate"; and the fear that female students would distract "some of the students from their work."

22. Michael A. Meyer, "A Centennial History," *Hebrew Union College—Jewish Institute of Religion: At One Hundred Years* (Cincinnati: Hebrew Union College, 1976), p. 99.

23. *Central Conference of American Rabbis Yearbook*, vol. XXXII (1922), p. 51.

24. Meyer, "Centennial History," *loc. cit.*, p. 99.

25. *Jewish Tribune and Hebrew Standard*, April 17, 1925.

26. Martha (Neumark) Montor, letter, May 25, 1925, to Maurice Schapiro, *Correspondence File*, American Jewish Archives.

27. *Jewish Tribune and Hebrew Standard*, April 17, 1925.

28. Rabbi Israel Levinthal, letter, April 14, 1972, to Prof. Jacob Marcus, *Correspondence File*, American Jewish Archives.

29. *New York Times*, Nov. 21, 1963.

30. Despite the small number of women·who are currently ordained, by the beginning of the 1976–77 academic year 34 of the 214 students preparing for the rabbinate at HUC-JIR were women. It may well be that by 1979 six or seven women will be ordained from the Rabbinical School each year. What's more, since 1975 HUC-JIR has officially invested women as cantors, and in 1976–77 eighteen of the 45 cantorial students in the School of Sacred Music were women. (Conversation with Rabbi Larry Raphael, assistant dean, New York campus, HUC-JIR, June 3, 1977.)

31. Max Dienemann was a German Reform rabbi who helped found the World Union for Progressive Judaism and later helped develop pioneer Progressive Jewish communities in Palestine. He died in Palestine in 1939, at the age of 64. (Lily H. Montagu, introduction, *Max Dienemann: Ein Gedenkbuch, 1875–1939*, by Mally Dienemann; privately printed, 1946.)

32. *Aufbau*, Dec. 11, 1970, letter from Dr. Alexander Guttmann.

33. Mordecai Kaplan, *The Future of the American Jew* (New York: Macmillan, 1948), p. 411.

34. *Ibid.*, p. 412.

35. Sandy Eisenberg Sasso, "B'rit B'not Israel: Observations on Women and Reconstructionism," *The Jewish Woman: An Anthology. Response*, vol. VII, no. 2 (Summer 1973), p. 102.

36. Figures from Jewish Reconstructionist Foundation, New York City, June 1977.

37. Kaplan, *Future of the American Jew*, p. 402.

38. Simon Litman, *Ray Frank Litman: A Memoir*, Studies in American Jewish History, no. 3 (New York: American Jewish Historical Society, 1957), p. 8.

39. *Proceedings of the Union of American Hebrew Congregations*, vol. IV (1891–97) (Cincinnati: Bloch Publishing and Printing Co.), p. 3150. Cf. *Programme of the Hebrew Union College*, years 1890–1900.

40. Rudolph Glanz, *The Jewish Woman in America: Two Female Immigrant Generations, 1820–1929* (New York: Ktav and National Council of Jewish Women, 1976), vol. II, *The German Jewish Woman*, p. 125.

41. Ray Frank, "Women in the Synagogue," *Papers of the Jewish Women's Congress, 1893* (Philadelphia: Jewish Publication Society, 1894), p. 63.

42. Anne Sayle, "The Service of the Institution of Lay Ministers," *The World Union for Progressive Judaism Bulletin*, no. 16 (March 1945), pp. 14f.

43. Quoted in Philipson, *Reform Movement*, p. 411.

44. Meridian, Miss., *Star*, May 8, 1960.

45. Paula Ackerman, letter to Jacob D. Schwarz, Dec. 12, 1950, Box 2400, American Jewish Archives.

46. Anne Lapidus Lerner, " 'Who Hast Not Made Me a Man': The Movement for Equal Rights for Women in American Jewry,"

American Jewish Yearbook, 1977 (New York: American Jewish Committee, 1976), p. 5.

47. *Ibid.*

48. Alan Silverstein, "The Evolution of Ezrat Nashim," *Conservative Judaism*, vol. XXX, no. 1 (Fall 1975), p. 44.

49. *Ibid.*, p. 45.

50. Lerner, " 'Who Hast Not . . . ,' " *loc. cit.*, p. 22.

51. Silverstein, "Evolution of Ezrat Nashim," *loc. cit.*, p. 50.

52. Quoted in Lerner, " 'Who Hast Not . . . ,' " *loc. cit.*, p. 7.

53. *Ibid.*

54. *Ibid.*

55. A more traditional women's prayer service is offered monthly by the New York Jewish Women's Center, an organization founded in 1976 to work for the education, self-growth and awareness of all Jewish women. Of the 30–50 women who regularly attend, a large proportion consider themselves Orthodox. The services therefore provide them with the unique opportunity to fully participate in communal worship (as Torah readers, leaders in prayer, etc.).

56. Naomi Janowitz and Maggie Wenig, "Siddur Nashim: A Sabbath Prayer Book for Women," experimental draft, p. iv.

57. Cover, *Lilith*, premiere issue, vol. I, no. 1 (Fall 1976).

58. Memo from Dr. Eugene Mihaly to Dean Barth, Dean Ehrlich and Dean Spicehandler, Hebrew Union College ("Women Rabbis," *Miscellaneous File*, American Jewish Archives).

59. Lerner, " 'Who Hast Not . . . ,' " *loc. cit.*, p. 11.

60. *Ibid.*, p. 15.

61. Blu Greenberg, "Judaism and Feminism," *The Jewish Woman*, ed. Elizabeth Koltun (New York: Schocken Books, 1976), p. 185.

62. Summary of Committee on Jewish Law and Standards meeting, Aug. 29, 1973 (re: counting women for a minyan), sent to members of the Rabbinical Assembly.

63. Lerner, " 'Who Hast Not . . . ,' " *loc. cit.*, pp. 25, 26.

64. *Ibid.*, p. 23.

65. Amy Stone, "Gentlemen's Agreement at the Seminary," *Lilith*, vol. I, no. 3 (1977), p. 16.

66. *New York Times*, May 4, 1977.

THIRTEEN

Entering the Sanctuary:
The Struggle for Priesthood
in Contemporary Episcopalian
and Roman Catholic Experience

1. The Episcopalian Story

NORENE CARTER

—————◦◦◦◦—————

In this section I want to set forth a brief history of the women's ordination movement in the American Episcopal Church and in addition discuss certain limited aspects of the debate on this issue. As one who has had considerable involvement in these events, I do not speak as an impartial observer, but rather as one who *witnesses* from a particular point of view.

Emily Hewitt and Suzanne Hiatt, in their book *Women Priests: Yes or No?*, point out that in the century of Anglican debate on the ordination of women the churches of this communion have engaged in a kind of "Alphonse–Gaston minuet" over questions of authority and jurisdiction.[1] From the first published study in 1919 up to the 1976 decision of the American Episcopal Church to approve the ordination of women, the Anglican churches studied, debated and vacillated, but little action resulted. The discussion bounced from study group to commission, back and forth among the various consultative bodies of the Anglican communion. Episcopal leadership perhaps believed itself to be acting in the best Anglican tradition of discretionary caution and conservatism. Without the pressure of liberating movements in church and society, the committed and prophetic witnesses of both men and women, and the active leadership of women, the issue might well have been debated indefinitely. Fortunately, the Holy Spirit does not always move with Anglican prudence.

Hewitt and Hiatt mark the beginning of the ordination debate with the restoration of the order of deaconesses by the Bishop of London in 1862, when he ordered a deaconess by the laying on of hands.[2] Deaconesses were similarly ordered by the Bishop of Alabama in 1885 and the Bishop of New York in 1887. In 1889 the General Convention of the American church authorized the setting apart of deaconesses. The resulting controversy over the ordained status of deaconesses brought about the first of many commissions on the ministry of women. This commission, appointed by the Archbishop of Canterbury, published its report in 1919. The Lambeth Conference of 1920 resolved that the ordination of deaconesses conferred on them holy orders, and then reversed itself ten years later, revoking the earlier claim. One senses that the tone of future discussion was established in 1935 when a joint commission of Canterbury and York found no compelling reason either for or against ordaining women and proceeded with Anglican caution to affirm the "male priesthood for the church today." However, in the midst of World War II, in 1944, Bishop R. O. Hall of Hong Kong, faced with a serious shortage of priests, ordained the Reverend Li Tim Oi to the priesthood with the permission of his local synod. She was well qualified, but her ordination was rejected by York and Canterbury, and she resigned from holy orders.[3] In 1948 the Lambeth Conference rejected a proposal by Bishop Hall to ordain women deacons to the priesthood for an experimental period of twenty years.[4] From 1945 until 1965 there was little activity, though in 1958 the Episcopal Theological School in Cambridge, Massachusetts, made a little-noticed but crucial decision to institute a policy of full regular admission of women to standard degree programs that trained candidates for the ordained ministry. Thus there appeared a body of fully qualified women, many of whom soon found themselves doing a ministry which it seemed could attain its fullness only in the ordained, sacramental priesthood. It was this group of women who from 1970 on provided the grass-roots leadership for the ordination movement. In 1964 the General Convention in St. Louis changed the wording of the canon on deaconesses to read "ordered" rather than "appointed."

If little seemed to be happening to forward women's ordination in the fifties and early sixties, much was brewing just under the surface. In 1955 Rosa Parks, a black woman bearing a cross for many, refused to sit at the back of a Montgomery, Alabama, bus, and the civil-rights movement was born. In 1963 Betty Friedan, rebelling against the banal oppressiveness of women's lives, wrote *The Feminine Mystique* and initiated a new wave of feminism. In 1965 Bishop James Pike, in an action based on the 1964 canonical change pertaining to deaconesses, conferred upon Phyliss Edwards the New Testament and the stole—historic marks of the diaconate. With this action Pike became the center of a storm of controversy.

As a result of the Pike furor the American House of Bishops initiated a new study on ordination of women. In 1966 the body received a favorable preliminary report and referred the matter to Lambeth, scheduled to meet in 1968. Lambeth turned the matter back to the national churches with the notation that the Conference had returned to its original 1920 decision and now regarded deaconesses as part of the diaconate. Anglican churches in Hong Kong, Kenya, Korea and Canada, with little fanfare or notice, began to ordain women to the diaconate.

In the United States the 1970 convention in Houston, Texas, received a favorable report from the Joint Commission on Ordained and Licensed Ministries.[5] The convention voted down priesthood for women, which had passed in the lay order but lost by a narrow margin in the clerical order. However, the Houston convention did vote to ordain women to the diaconate. The triennial meeting of Episcopal women, meeting concurrently with the convention, voted

222–45 in favor of the same report that was defeated by the all-male clergy.

In 1971, the international Anglican Consultative Council, by a narrow vote, declared the ordination of women to the priesthood acceptable. Meanwhile, the American House of Bishops struck a familiar note by once again referring the matter to a study committee (apparently without reference to its own recently completed blue-ribbon study). That year marked the beginning of an intensive campaign, led primarily by women, to secure the possibility of ordination. The seminaries had done their job well, and the opening of the diaconate found a number of women "ready and desirous" of such ordination. In the spring of 1971, Suzanne Hiatt became the first woman in the United States of America to be ordained to the diaconate under the new canon. It was largely under her leadership that an identifiable movement for ordination actually emerged.

Shortly thereafter the Episcopal Women's Caucus was formed "to actualize the full participation of women at all levels of ministry and decision-making in the church."[6] The Caucus, composed of lay women, deacons and seminarians, chose to focus immediate attention on priesthood for women. The advent of E.W.C. revealed abundant support among lay women for the ordained ministry of their sisters.

At a meeting in May 1972, the caucus agreed to concentrate on the 1973 convention in Louisville and began the work of organizing. In the spring of 1973 the steering committee of the caucus joined with a group called Priests for the Ministry of the Church and became the National Committee for the Ordination of Women to the Priesthood.[7] The committee aimed at canonical change rather than constitutional change, since the latter requires legislative action at two consecutive conventions.[8] Women had been admitted as lay deputies to General Convention through the constitutional process only in 1970, after a twenty-five-year struggle, and were virtually unrepresented. Two other major concerns arose. One was the need to find political support among the men of the official church structures. The other was the voting procedure of the House of Deputies. Its rule is a conservative one which may effectively disenfranchise all but an overwhelming majority on the convention floor. In the House of Deputies a vote by orders requires a separation into lay and clerical units, which must agree among themselves in order for a measure to pass. Within any four-member lay or clerical voting unit, the failure to reach agreement pro or con—as represented by 2–2 vote—is recorded as a no. This means that as few as twenty-five percent of either order, or twelve and a half percent of the House of Deputies as a whole, can—if appropriately spread to divide the vote in half of the dioceses—thwart the will of the majority.

The Anglican Consultative Council met again in July 1973, and this time it voted 50–3 that individual synods favoring ordination of women could proceed.

In September 1973, the General Convention at Louisville defeated ordination for women to the priesthood and the episcopate, its voting procedure once again overcoming the will of the majority. On a regular one-person one-vote procedure ordination would have succeeded. Women's Triennial, powerless but faithful, voted in favor of ordaining women to the priesthood. Women deacons and laywomen expressed their pain and anger at the continued affront to the vocation of women called to priesthood. Their statement pointed to their firm conviction that the virtually all-male convention could not legislate vocations called into being and lived out in parish church and mission. Vocations are called into being by God and "are not debatable options," the statement declared.[9] Forty bishops issued a statement of conviction that "this matter of moral justice and theological justification must not rest."[10] Presiding Bishop Allin called for another study committee. Meanwhile the rest of the bishops, in an innovative mood, came upon the "principle of collegiality." Hitherto little discussed among the American House of Bishops, its purpose was to inhibit bishops from proceeding to ordain independently.[11] Such ordinations were not in fact forbidden by canon law. Traditionally ordinations had been the exclusive prerogative of a diocesan bishop with his standing committees, and many believed that it would be well within their rights to go ahead.[12] The chief argument against such ordinations was that the General Convention served as a vehicle through which the whole church could speak, but the power of this argument was somewhat diminished by the lack of representation of women in convention. (The 1976 House of Deputies was eighty-six percent male, the House of Bishops, of course, one hundred percent male. Triennial, which perhaps did speak for women, had no legislative authority.)

The next months saw several meetings and discussions between various bishops and impatient deacons who had had enough of procrastination. By the late spring of 1974, the possibility of a woman being ordained began to look more like a probability. Dr. Charles Willie, vice-president of the House of Deputies, in a sermon on June 9 in Syracuse, called for immediate ordinations. On June 15, in Philadelphia, the Very Reverend Edward Harris, dean of the Philadelphia Divinity School, repeated this demand. On July 10 a group of deacons and bishops met to plan an ordination. On July 29, in Philadelphia, eleven women [13] were ordained to the priesthood by three retired bishops, Edward Welles, Daniel Corrigan and Robert Dewitt.[14] The three had been asked by the presiding bishop, John Allin, to refrain from the ordination, but believed that good conscience required that they go ahead.

The upheaval in the life of the church caused by these ordinations has seldom been equaled in American Episcopal history. Women priests were now a reality in the church—a fact that could no longer be evaded by endless study and vacillation.

One deacon who chose not to be priested at Philadelphia, the Reverend Elsa Walberg, of the Diocese of Massachusetts, stated the matter clearly: "There may be those who say—on this Feast of Mary and Martha of Bethany—that I have chosen the 'better part' by not seeking ordination today. I know, however, that were it not for my sisters and their radical, shocking obedience to God's claim upon their lives—an obedience which gives dramatic witness to the urgency of our common vocation to priesthood and summons the whole Church to attention—there would be few to hear me or to take seriously my own deep sense of having been called to priestly ordination." [15]

On August 14 and 15 the House of Bishops gathered in Chicago for a special meeting to consider the Philadelphia ordinations. It met not as a legislative body but as a "council of bishops considering a matter of faith and order." [16] The bishops passed a resolution decrying the action of the ordaining bishops and declaring the ordinations sacramentally invalid. Procedurally there were numerous difficulties with the House of Bishops' action. In the eyes of many, the bishops acted precipitously, making a theological judgment without an adequate report from their own committee and without access to a written document of any sort. There was no discussion of the committee report. The body of the resolution itself was never discussed at all. No woman was allowed to speak on her own behalf. [17] Bishops who were apparently prepared to study endlessly the matter of women's ordination could not wait to pass their judgment on the Philadelphia ordinations. Many believed this was a necessary compromise to hold off threatened disciplinary action against the ordaining bishops. If so, it was a poor one from the point of view of the eleven women.

Aside from the procedural complications, there were serious theological problems with the substance of the Chicago resolution. The ordinations were irregular in that they did not meet the full requirements of canon law. But the bishops also claimed that the ordinations were invalid, that the service had no sacramental effect. Numerous theologians rejected the bishops' interpretation of the validity doctrine. In a very careful study done for the Diocese of Rochester, four recognized Anglican theologians stated their opinion that the ordinations were valid.[18] Frans Jozef van Beeck, S.J., compared the ordinations to baptisms administered by Donatist heretics. The church recognized these as true baptisms even though "in the very act of being incorporated into Christ's body, the church," the newly baptized separated themselves from the church. He regarded the ordinations as valid, inasmuch as the bishops had the power to ordain and the intention of doing so. He also noted that the women were capable of being ordained, i.e., proper form and matter, though this question had not been mentioned in the bishops' resolution.[19]

Perhaps the most serious charge leveled against the ordaining bishops was that in ordaining women outside their jurisdiction and without standing committee approval, they had seriously violated the integrity of the community. This was not a charge to be lightly ignored. I believe there are three implicit assumptions in this charge: first, that there is only one community in the church; second, that community is defined by jurisdiction; third, that legal processes and official channels always express the will of the community. The Rochester committee, in its report, observed that there are in the church not only different communities but different sorts of communities, some of which are by no means jurisdictional; furthermore, there are divisions and differences not only within communities but between communities. The report then noted that there were significant communities within the church (Women's Triennial, for example, and many local parishes and vestries) which desired to ordain women. Therefore, "the impulse to ordain women to the presbyterate" should be recognized as originating in community unless one assumes that "canon law and its procedures are accepted as definitive of the community mind."[20] That there was also contrary opinion in the church reflects the fact of division within it. Official processes are the means by which the life and work of community usually goes on in spite of differences and disagreements. There are times, however, when the brokenness of the church overwhelms its procedures and its compromise mechanisms. This is, I believe, the situation which prevailed in 1974. It is precisely the sort of situation which requires and calls forth prophetic action.

At any rate the question of validity seems finally to have been resolved as Anglican charity and diocesan autonomy won the day. At this writing, following the Minneapolis decision of the whole church in general convention, all the women ordained irregularly in Philadelphia (and later in Washington, D.C.) have been recognized and licensed by their dioceses as valid priests for the church.

Following the Philadelphia ordinations there were numerous celebrations of the Eucharist by women priests, two of which resulted in ecclesiastical trials for the rectors of the cooperating parishes. Meanwhile, Dr. Charles Willie, vice-president of the House of Deputies, resigned in protest against the Chicago resolutions. On September 7, 1975, Bishop George Barrett ordained four more women in Washington, D.C. Women priests had become an increasing reality on the Episcopal scene. Organizing continued for the 1976 convention in Minneapolis. The Episcopal Women's Caucus called a meeting in Dayton, Ohio, out of which grew a broadly based coalition. The National Coalition for the Ordination of Women became the primary organizing structure for the coming convention. Meanwhile, a more radical organization called Women's Ordination Now emerged out of the Philadelphia ordinations. Members of this group generally opposed pursuing the convention route any further, pressed for more independent ordinations and offered support to the recently ordained women priests.

In September 1976, the Sixty-fifth General Convention of the Episcopal Church in the United States met in Minneapolis. There a majority of both houses, deputies and bishops, voted to affirm the right of fit and qualified women to be admitted to the priesthood and the episcopacy. They did so by passing a rule of construction, instructing that hereafter the provisions of the ordination canons should be equally applicable to both women and men.

In off-the-floor discussions at the convention, the House of Bishops rejected a so-called permissive or conscience clause and encouraged the deputies to pass the canonical change without it. This clause had been designed to reassure dissident bishops that they need not in fact adhere to the new ruling. Since diocesan bishops are very nearly autonomous powers in the Episcopal Church, this was already effectively the case, but many people felt relieved that the convention had not officially endorsed such discrimination against women.

To some who had received bread and wine at the hands of sisters ordained in Philadelphia or Washington, the convention vote was in a sense anticlimactic and even painful, for along the way we had developed certain misgivings about the political process itself. Yet, even so, for those who believed that not only priestly ministry but the whole ministry of the church could come to fullness only when the vocations of women called to the priesthood were affirmed by the whole church in convention, this was a highly significant moment in the life of the church. It seemed that at last the church had spoken decisively, not only about women, or even about ordination, but about its own nature as the liberating and inclusive body of Christ. If the Episcopal Church, after spending nearly a hundred years discussing the ministry of women, could hardly be called prophetic, at last it had spoken with clarity and decision.

Unfortunately, this sense of wholeness was to be badly broken in the ensuing months, not only by the real pain of those who could not make their peace with women priests, but by the equivocal leadership of the bishops. Speaking before the House of Bishops in October 1977, Presiding Bishop John Allin expressed his belatedly formulated conviction that "Women can no more be priests than they can become husbands and fathers."[21] Immediately thereafter, in response both to Bishop Allin's comments and to threats of

schism within the church, the bishops, meeting in nonlegis-
lative session, agreed to endorse the right of dissident bishops as a matter of conscience to refuse to recognize women
in priestly orders and to refuse to ordain women candidates
for priesthood in their particular dioceses. This resurrection
of the so-called Conscience Clause amounts to a unilateral
departure from the apparent intention of General Convention with respect to the clause. It is also clearly inconsistent
with the stated intention of Convention to apply the ordination canons equally to men and women.

At one level the ordination of women is a matter of equality within the body of Christ. But it is also fundamentally a
matter of the wholeness of the church being expressed and
made incarnate at the sacramental heart of its worship, the
Eucharist. To some of us this idea seems so simple and obvious that we find it hard to comprehend the bitterness,
anxiety, pain and, finally, threatened schism that have accompanied the attempt to implement it. The first thing one
needs to realize is that what is being overthrown is not primarily a tradition, a doctrine or a Scriptural text but a world
view in which hierarchical structure and the subordination
of women are pivotal concepts. The second thing one needs
to understand is the extent to which overthrowing this world
view is experienced by many men as a direct threat to their
sexuality.

It is to these issues that I now wish to draw attention.

The arguments against ordaining women are centered on
the maleness of Christ and implicitly on maleness as normative human nature. According to E. L. Mascall, "it was
male human nature which the son of God united to his male
person . . ." [22] It follows, therefore, in George Rutler's view,
"that the priest consecrates at the head of the people because
God has singled him out in his *maleness* to be Christ for the
people." [23] Here we see a theology of the Eucharist based on
"headship" in the hierarchical order and on maleness. Compare Rutler's assertion with this statement from the Anglican–Roman Catholic agreement on the doctrine of minis-

try: "There is in the Eucharist a memorial (anamnesis) of the totality of God's reconciling action in Christ, who *through* his minister presides at the Lord's supper and gives himself sacramentally." Further on, the statement points out that ministers, when presiding at the Eucharist, are "representatives of the *whole church* in fulfillment of its priestly vocation of self offering to God as living sacrifice." [24] The emphasis here is not on headship but on symbolizing the wholeness of the church. The relevant factor is not maleness but the role of the priest as a *vehicle* to make present the reconciling action of Christ. To take such doctrine seriously, I think, one must look to the wholeness of Christ and therefore to his humanity. To focus on his maleness, as Marianne Micks says, is to "confuse the scandal of particularity with the meaning of the incarnation." [25] Robert Wright, an Anglican theologian, observed that "in Christ God redeemed humanity, not just masculinity." [26] The opponents of women's ordination not only focus on the maleness of Jesus but claim that "the maleness of Jesus cannot be separated from the masculine imagery of revelation. He is the express image of the Father." [27] It follows, according to E. L. Mascall, "that the priesthood of Christ is in no merely biological sense but in some profound and mysterious sense that lies behind and provides the ground of the biological differentiation, a male function." [28] A view of reality in which maleness is *normative* leads quite naturally to seeing women as subhuman as well as subordinate. It is also associated with the presumption of the maleness of God. This kind of anthropomorphism is rejected, of course, by the Anglican Articles of Religion, not to mention the Old Testament.[29] Such reasoning leads directly to the conclusion that women are not created in the image of God. In general, then, these arguments arise from the assumption that women are less than human in the very structures of creation. It is hard to see how women can be equal with men in any meaningful way in either a social or a theological order in which maleness is normative.

The arguments from Scripture of opponents of women's

ordination usually depend upon Pauline texts, particularly 1 Corinthians 14:34, which directs women not to speak in congregational assembly, and on 1 Timothy 2:12, which forbids women to teach. There is no serious doubt that the notion of women as subordinates is inherent in some Pauline texts.[30] When Paul speaks in this way, he gives as his theological reason the subordinate place of women in the created order. Paul's views, therefore, are not based on a particular doctrine of ministry. The limitations that he places on women's role in the church derive from a theological perspective which applies equally well to any activity of women which contravenes male "headship" or authority.

Krister Stendahl, in his excellent discussion *The Bible and the Role of Women*, points out that whenever the New Testament speaks about the role of women in the church it is always explained by reference to woman's subordinate position in the order of creation. "Nowhere is there any trace of a reference to ministry as a particular problem with a particular solution."[31] It is highly problematical, therefore, to use New Testament texts as a basis for denying women the priesthood unless one also subscribes to a doctrine of natural order in which women are seen as subordinate.

Dr. Eleanor McLaughlin, professor of church history at Andover Newton Seminary, in an unpublished paper points clearly to the fact that indeed doctrines of subordination persist. While American opponents have been understandably reluctant to push their argument to its logical conclusion, their British counterparts have been more forthright. Bruce and Duffield warn us, "It is also a Christian duty to assist women in achieving their genuine human potentialities and rights. But a duty still remains to warn them (by example as much as by precept) against the error of usurping headship over men."[32] Of women's duty to be subject and obedient to men they say that "these demands are not the remnants of an obsolete social order of antiquity but rather derived from the fact God contrived to redeem mankind by a man rather than by a woman." [33] Here we see the theology of subordination used directly to justify the male-dominated social order. Dr. McLaughlin adds that "behind such statements is the recognition that the ordination of women is a symbolic action which calls into question the hierarchical subordination of the woman in the most basic of structures, the family." And quoting again from Bruce and Duffield, "Indeed, even in a case where the wife was not herself ordained she would be sorely tempted to arrogate to herself a position in the family equal or superior to the headship over her husband exercised in the congregation by some other woman." [34]

Such an overtly sexist argument has rarely seen the light of day in American writing on the subject. But those working for the ordination of women in the last several years are well acquainted with the attitude expressed here. Surely it is just such an attitude that leads George Rutler to assert that the central job of the priest "is to be a *man* at the altar." [35] One priest has clearly stated the underlying fear. He asks us, "How would you react to the presence of a pregnant woman in the pulpit? Giving absolution? How would you, the reader—male or female—react to the sight of a beautiful long-haired woman celebrating the Eucharist? Attractive yes, but also distracting." [36]

The statement exhibits the preoccupation with sexuality that we have all experienced in our opponents' views but that has seldom been so honestly stated. The author unfortunately takes cover under a pseudonym, so that even now we do not know who it is we are dealing with. Such views might simply be counted as ludicrous and left to sink under the weight of their own absurdity except for the fact that they expose the core of sexual panic and misogyny which has been present throughout the entire lengthy struggle over ordaining women. However subtle and difficult it is to identify, women have all experienced it in practice. With respect to this issue, one cannot help but feel that it is more pervasive than we realize and is essentially linked with the intensity of the conflict, the protractedness of the debate and the final inability of some to be reconciled with women priests.

Though the tension and conflict in the church at this writing leave us uncertain as to the exact course of future events, there are things of which we may be certain. The struggle has been a painful one for many people, both those opposing and those favoring the ordination of women. Yet we know absolutely that God has been and continues to be present for all of us in the midst, indeed in the very depths, of conflict. The church is, in fact, receiving nurture not only from the growing ministry of women but through the very struggle itself. We are discovering renewed interest in theology, new ways of understanding ordination, new hopes among the laity, and new concepts of ministry. Women in the priesthood are here to stay, to celebrate the increasing wholeness of the church and to share in it. But the struggle has not been easy. Men and women have given up their futures in the church, lost their ministries, sacrificed opportunities for advancement in the hierarchy, been abandoned by their friends, been denied by their colleagues, and lost their faith. It is not easy to say yes to such things. It should *not* be easy to affirm what has been so costly, to say Amen to so much pain. It is, however, necessary, for in doing so we witness to the power of Christ to make all things new.

NOTES FOR PART I

1. Emily Hewitt and Suzanne Hiatt, *Women Priests: Yes or No?* (New York: Seabury, 1973), p. 11. For the best available survey of history and debate on the subject up to about 1970, see p. 1.

2. *Ibid*. The following chronology is based on the Appendix of Hewitt and Hiatt.

3. Hugh B. McCullum, "The Anglican Experience," in *The Ordination of Women: Pro and Con*, ed. Michael Hamilton and Nancy Montgomery (New York: Morehouse-Barlow, 1975), p. 141.

4. *Ibid*., p. 145.

5. "The Report by the Joint Commission on Ordained and Licensed Ministries," in the Appendix to Hewitt and Hiatt, *Women Priests*. An excellent, brief summary of the arguments.

6. Suzanne Hiatt, unpublished brief Caucus history.

7. *Ibid.*

8. McCullum, "The Anglican Experience," *loc. cit.*, p. 148.

9. Episcopal Women's Caucus press release, Louisville, October 1973.

10. General Convention press release no. 64, October 9, 1973.

11. Henry Rightor, "The Existing Canonical Authority for Women's Ordination," in *Toward a New Theology of Ordination*, ed. Marianne Micks and Charles Price (Somerville, Mass.: Greeno, Hadden, 1976), p. 108.

12. *Ibid.*, pp. 101–10.

13. The eleven women ordained in Philadelphia were Nancy Wittig, Betty Schiess, Merrill Bittner, Alla Bozarth-Campbell, Jeanette Piccard, Allison Cheek, Marie Moorfield, Katrina Swanson, Carter Heywood, Suzanne Hiatt and Emily Hewitt. Of these women only Suzanne Hiatt was canonically resident in the Diocese of Pennsylvania.

14. José Antonio Ramos, Bishop of Costa Rica, was a fourth bishop, present but not ordaining. Only Bishop Dewitt was canonically resident in the Diocese of Pennsylvania.

15. Rev. Elsa Walberg, press release, July 1974.

16. Harvey Guthrie, Edward G. Harris and H. Rockwell Hayes, unpublished personal report on the August 14–15 meeting of bishops, p. 1.

17. *Ibid.*, p. 6.

18. Rochester Report, written by Rev. Profs. R. A. Morris, E. R. Fairweather, J. E. Griffiss and A. Mollegen, in Hamilton and Montgomery, *Ordination of Women*, Appendix, complete version, pp. 175–95. This report was written for the Standing Committee of the Bishop of Rochester to determine the validity of Merrill Bittner's ordination.

19. Frans Jozef van Beeck, personal summary, unpublished version, written August 1974.

20. Rochester Report, pp. 192–93.

21. The four women ordained in Washington were Revs. Betty Rosenberg, Lee McGee, Alison Palmer and Diane Tichell.

22. E. L. Mascall, "The Ministry of Women," letter in *Theol-*

ogy, vol. LVII, no. 413 (November 1954), p. 428. Quoted in George Rutler, *Priest and Priestess* (Ambler, Pa.: Trinity Press, 1973), p. 35.

23. Rutler, pp. 83–84.

24. "Agreement on Doctrine of Ministry," Anglican–Roman Catholic statement, 1973, sec. 13.

25. Marianne Micks, "The Theological Case for Women's Ordination," in Hamilton and Montgomery, *Ordination of Women*.

26. Robert Wright, "Address in Favor of the Ordination of Women to the Sacred Priesthood," unpublished address given at the General Theological Seminary, New York City, 1972, p. 3.

27. Stanley Atkinson, "The Case Against Women's Ordination," in Hamilton and Montgomery, *Ordination of Women*, p. 23.

28. E. L. Mascall, quoted in Michael Bruce and G. E. Duffield, *Why Not? Priesthood and the Ministry of Women* (Appleford, Abingdon, Eng.: Marcham Manor Press, 1972), pp. 111–12. Quoted in an unpublished paper by Dr. Eleanor McLaughlin.

29. Phyllis Trible, "Depatriarchalizing the Bible," an interpretation, *Journal of the American Academy of Religion*, vol. XI, no. 1 (March 1973), p. 34. Quoted by Emily Hewitt, "Anatomy of Ministry," in *Women and Orders*, ed. Robert J. Heyer (New York: Paulist Press, 1974).

30. Haye Van der Meer, *Women Priests in the Catholic Church?* (Philadelphia: Temple University Press, 1973), pp. 36, 37. Chapter 2 of this book is a most complete and enlightening discussion of Pauline texts.

31. Krister Stendahl, *The Bible and the Role of Women* (Philadelphia: Fortress Press, 1966), p. 38.

32. Bruce and Duffield in *Why Not?* p. 139. Quoted in McLaughlin paper.

33. *Ibid.*, p. 139. Quoted in McLaughlin paper.

34. *Ibid.*, p. 136. Quoted in McLaughlin paper.

35. Rutler, *Priest and Priestess*, p. 35.

36. David Stuart (pseudonym) in Hamilton and Montgomery, *Ordination of Women*, p. 48.

II. The Roman Catholic Story

ROSEMARY RUETHER

Roman Catholic women have been late in mobilizing for the ordination of women. But once this movement begins within Roman Catholicism, its significance for world Christianity may be explosive, not only because of the large numbers and international scope of this communion but also because of the presence of a unique body, the religious sisterhoods, as an organizing force for feminism in the Church and society. Historically the sisterhoods represent both the survival and the subjugation of the original diaconal orders of ministry for women. Thus for these communities to rise as leaders of women's rights to ministry in the Church is especially appropriate. The visibility of such a movement for the ordination of women in Roman Catholicism also will make it more difficult for other denominations, such as Anglicans, to use the conservative ecumenical argument against ordination within their own bodies, i.e., "If we ordain women, we will lose the possibility of accord with Rome." Rome turns out to be as divided a camp on the subject as Canterbury.

Credit for first raising the issue of the ordination of women in the public forum of the Church goes to the original Catholic feminist organization, the St. Joan's International Alliance. Founded in 1910 in Britain by Catholic women working for women's suffrage, this group believed there was such a strong effort by the Church to make Catholic women feel that feminism was out of bounds for Catholics that Catholic women needed their own visible international organization to educate each other and the Church on the possibility of solidarity with feminist goals. The group originally called itself the Catholic Women's Suffrage Society, but changed its name in 1923 to the St. Joan's Political and Social Alliance. As the movement spread to other countries the word "International" was adopted. The Alliance continued to work on women's concerns throughout the world in the following decades.

In 1959, with the announcement of the coming ecumenical council, the Alliance began to work on a series of requests for greater participation of women in the Church. A request that the diaconate be opened to women was adopted in 1961. When the papal encyclical *Pacem in Terris* was issued, in 1963, it contained (in section 41) the following condemnation of women's subordination: "Since women are becoming ever more conscious of their human dignity, they will not tolerate being treated as mere material instruments, but demand rights befitting a human person both in domestic and public life." Earlier in the encyclical (section 15) the right to follow a vocation to the priesthood had been described as a human right that all human beings should have an option to choose freely, among other states of life. Taking these statements as its charter, the St. Joan's International Alliance submitted the following modestly worded petition to the Vatican through a Swiss attorney, Gertrud Heinzelmann: "St. Joan's International Alliance re-affirms its loyalty and filial devotion and expresses its conviction that should the Church in her wisdom and in her good time decide to extend to women the dignity of the priesthood, women would be willing and eager to respond." Petitions for the ordination of women have since been submitted yearly to the Vatican.[1] St. Joan's was, at the time of the ecumenical council, a European organization, its American section having been started only in 1965.

In the late 1960s the renewed feminist movement began to gain power and visibility in the United States. Inevitably, feminist consciousness would become an important component of the liberation thought of the renewal movement. Catholic religious were discovering that the phrase "Sisterhood is powerful" could mean them too. Feminist consciousness and a growing conviction of women's right to the ordained ministry grew hand in hand among Catholic women, specifically among women religious. Only as nuns have become conscious feminists have they also gained the confidence to declare unequivocally the injustice of women's exclusion from the ordained ministry. Moreover, feminism has not been understood "simply in secular terms." Feminism has been woven into the renewal of theology as an integral part of these women's understanding of the Gospel.

In 1972, the Leadership Conference of Women Religious, the powerful coordinating body representing ninety percent of all women's religious communities in the United States, decided to put their full authority behind the solidarity of nuns with women's liberation. This was understood in a twofold sense: that women religious would lend themselves to organizing for justice for women in society, and that women's liberation would inform the nuns' understanding of their own identity as women and as religious women. Several addresses at the 1972 assembly sounded this theme. In the 1974 assembly of the LCWR the following resolution was adopted: "1. that the LCWR supports the principle that all ministries in the Church be open to women and men as the Spirit calls them; 2. that the LCWR affirms the principle that women have active participation in all decision making bodies in the Church." [2]

Full-scale plans were put into operation to prepare high-level packets of study materials for all congregations, in order to educate them in feminist consciousness as women and to point them toward feminist praxis in society. It was decided to support and participate fully in the International Women's Year. Packets were prepared for study groups of women religious on global relations with women's liberation. Secondly, an important packet on feminist consciousness in all its aspects was prepared for study at the 1975 assembly. It was called *Focus on Women*. The study booklet *Woman as Source of Sacramental Grace* focused particularly on women as ministers. The concluding study booklet, *Nuns and the Women's Movement*, contains the following ringing charge:

—Human history has been one of constant and cumulative oppression of women on the basis of sex.

—The existence of such oppression has been gradually construed as the fact of female inferiority and has emerged as one of the major tenets of social mythology throughout the world, ironically related as it is to the possible previous myth of female power.

—Religion (as an effect rather than as an original cause of such oppression) has been a major force in its continuance, perpetuation and "canon"-ization.

—The mainstream of tradition within the Catholic Church—in significant opposition to the central revelation of human personhood, sexuality and redemptive fulfillment embodied in Christ's life and teaching—is one of the most oppressive of all religious superstructures.

—There is a growing awareness and bonding among women today who refuse to subject themselves and their sisters to such institutionalized injustice.[3]

It is characteristic of the spirit of these women that they assume a radical freedom toward the received tradition while claiming integral loyalty toward the Catholic community itself. Traditional Catholics, including most bishops, are little prepared to understand the possibility of such a union of freedom and loyalty. The theological presumption behind such a statement is that the head and Lord of the Church is Christ, not magisterium, tradition or Scripture. Scripture has a special place because it is the original written witness to Christ, but it too only partly appropriated (in the life of the early Church) his liberating message. Tradition too is an earthen vessel, both bearing and betraying Christ's message. Personal experience always remains as the primary forum to which one must turn to test the meaning of the Gospel for one's own life. But over all these stands Christ, who calls us to overcome every form of oppression, including sexism. No tradition which enshrines such oppression, therefore, can be "of him," but must stand under judgment by the liberation to which the Gospel beckons us.

With this perspective the sisters gain full confidence to be loyal dissenters, calling the Church (and themselves as Church, first of all) to true loyalty to the liberation of all persons which is the Gospel. Christ as liberator becomes the critical (and future disclosing) principle that can make relative the authority of magisterium, tradition and even Scripture, while still having full respect for these authorities when they do indeed "preach Christ." In a sense this perspective is more radical than the Reformation, since it clearly includes Scripture in its understanding of the critique of tradition. Therefore it avoids the trap of fundamentalism which has been the bane of Protestantism.

In a further study booklet published in 1976, the Committee on the Ecclesial Role of Women of the LCWR focused especially on the status and the roles of women in the Church. The following statement sums up its recognition of the radical critique of established understandings of Catholic Christianity that must flow from their new understandings of things:

There is no denying that when women argue for ordination they are calling into question hierarchical models of the Church; they are affirming that what is central to the historical Jesus is his humanity and not his maleness; they are pressing for a more adequate articulation of the notion of the *imago dei*; they are challenging inaccuracies in past formulations of theological anthropology. When we bring our experience as women to bear in theological reflection on precisely these questions, we know the urgency of the Church's call to now open its ordained ministry to women.[4]

Spurred by this kind of preparation, a major organization emerged in the American Catholic Church, dedicated to promoting the ordination of women. Plans for a conference on this theme began with a modest meeting of thirty-one women theological students and faculty at the Catholic Theological Union in Chicago in mid-December 1974. The meeting was called by a laywoman, Mary Lynch. The support for such an idea, which had already been forming, was mobilized behind the planning staff of the conference. Much of the staff consisted of leaders of religious orders who had already been active in feminism in bodies such as the LCWR. But in the selection of staff and speakers a careful effort was made to balance nuns with laywomen leaders and scholars, both married and single. This was also to be a chance to try to overcome the traditional divisions into which the Church had historically cast women: as nuns, wives and "singles."

The conference planners originally estimated a registration of about six hundred. They soon found that they had far underestimated the hunger for this forum. Registrations poured in from all over the country and were soon running over twelve hundred. Finally the official registrations were closed at twice the originally estimated number, but there were many more who attended without credentials. Even a couple of bishops showed up, sheepishly, and held a press conference to indicate their personal sympathy with the idea, although officially they had to stick to the party line that women could not (yet) be ordained. Over three fourths of the Catholic seminaries sent indications of their willingness to accept women in their student bodies and supplied information on women already studying for degrees.

The conference accomplished several things. First, it brought together a fine display of the Scriptural and theological studies already developed to support the ordination of women. This work had been unknown to the hierarchy. They now have less excuse for their ignorance, since these papers have been published in a volume by the Paulist

Press.[5] Second, it created a powerful experience of solidarity in the pursuit of priesthood for women who had previously felt isolated and unsupported. A profound moment in the conference was the liturgy of affirmation, when those who felt the call to ordination stood, and the others laid hands on them and affirmed their solidarity with their vocation. Third, the organizing staff was mandated by the conference to continue as a network center to help promote local conferences and local support groups in as many communities as possible.

In the wake of the conference, various local groups and special support groups arose. The Christian Feminist group in Washington, D.C., concentrates on appeals to Catholics to contribute funds in order to educate women in seminaries (incorporated as the Catholic Women's Seminary Fund). They do not hesitate to suggest that funds should be sent for this purpose rather than to the regular episcopal collections for the seminary education of males! At a protest rally against the recent Vatican declaration on the ordination of women, held in front of the offices of the Catholic Bishop's Conference, a check for this purpose was presented to a woman studying in a seminary. An organization of Priests for Equality has also emerged with a 2,000 membership to show the solidarity of priests with the ordination of women. This group sent a special letter to the bishops of the Episcopal Church at the Triennial Convention of that church in Minneapolis in September of 1976, expressing its strong support for ordination. Indeed, a coalition of Catholic groups made themselves visible at that convocation in prayerful vigil for the final passage of ordination for Episcopal women.

On January 27, 1977, there appeared what in an earlier era might have been the definitive termination of all these activities. The Vatican released the hastily assembled *Declaration on the Question of the Admission of Women to the Ministerial Priesthood*. The declaration states that the exclusion of women was founded on Christ's intent and is basic to the Church's understanding of priesthood, and that therefore it cannot be changed. This statement makes a rather amazing effort to separate the tradition of exclusion of women from priesthood from concepts of women's natural inferiority and status of subjection. It is clear that the latter rationale no longer works. But it is also clear that the entire tradition of the exclusion of women from priesthood has, in fact, been based on exactly these underpinnings. The declaration denies this. It asserts that, following Jesus, the Church has always believed in the equality of women with men in the natural order. Exclusion from priesthood is not based on any such concept of inferiority or subjection, but rather on some mysterious sacramental bond between Christ, maleness and priesthood.

Needless to say, such a construction of the tradition of exclusion of women from priesthood will not bear examination. A declaration that declares its hands tied, unable to change any tradition so long established, actually goes about its business by sweeping away a two-thousand-year tradition and pretending that it never existed! It asserts its fidelity to "tradition" by a sweeping denial of what has been an integral aspect of this entire tradition.

The attempt of the declaration to replace the traditional basis of exclusion with a theological construct that links maleness, Christ and priesthood astonished those who had previously had little interest in the subject. One might say that if the Vatican lost its credibility for "infallibility" in matters of morals with the birth-control controversy, it lost its credibility for "infallibility" in matters of faith with the declaration on the admission of women to the priesthood.

From far and wide came cries of dismay. Those committed to women's ordination quickly released carefully worded statements which unequivocally rejected the authority of the declaration and pointed out its historical errors and its theological untenability. But strong criticism came from quarters not previously involved in the issue. Almost the entire faculty of the Jesuit School of Theology in Berkeley (twenty-three members) sent a statement directly to the Pope pointing out the historical, Scriptural and theological untenability of the statement.[6] Even the venerable German theologian Karl Rahner issued a statement indicating the theological unacceptability of the declaration. Never has an official Vatican declaration been so roundly rejected and even ridiculed by both theological authorities and the general populace.

The Catholic liberal press took mischievous delight in reporting that according to a Gallup poll, support for the ordination of women among American Catholics actually rose, in the two months following the release of the declaration, from twenty-nine percent to forty-one percent, the sharpest upsurge of support for this idea ever to take place among Catholics. Although Gallup had been reporting a gradual rise in support for women's ordination among Catholics, the progress had been slow, a percentage point or two a year.[7] The phenomenal rise of support from mid-January to mid-March of 1977 could only have reflected the reaction to the Vatican statement. One might surmise that many Catholics were simply indifferent to the issue or supposed the Church had some good reason. But once brought face to face with the crudities of the declaration, many persons were galvanized into an opinion for the first time!

It is hard to know where this movement will go in the immediate and long-range future. One more impasse among several within recent years between public opinion in the Church and hierarchical power appears to have developed. The hierarchy loses credibility, but still holds the power. No democratic structures exist, similar to those in the American Episcopal Church, which might gradually develop a winning parliamentary battle for votes that could change a historical practice. It is likely that a long seedtime must set in. A growing practice of ministry shared by men and women will develop on local congregational levels. A certain educational process will go on between women and ordained males on the injustice of the restrictions placed on their female colleagues. Laity will become used to seeing women minister in a number of adjunct roles and wonder why not sacraments. Perhaps there will be discussions and conferences around this in local churches. House prayer groups may just go ahead and authorize women to celebrate. Struggles between bishops and liberal congregations will take place.

Eventually more bishops will be consecrated who wonder at the absurdity of the exclusion (with a growing example of women in full sacramental ministry in other churches). After that it is up to the Holy Spirit to suddenly shake the power structure anew (as in the days of John XXIII) in ways that no one can anticipate. In any case those who are committed to such a change in Roman Catholicism know that they are committed for the long haul. For it is not possible to imagine the admission of women to the Catholic priesthood without, at the same time, modifying certain fundamental notions about hierarchy, theology, Church and authority. This, even more than women, may be what the hierarchy fears.

NOTES FOR PART II

1. This material is derived from pamphlets of the American branch of the St. Joan's International Alliance, and from information supplied by letter by its long-time American leader, Frances McGillicuddy. The text of the petition to the Vatican is cited in the preface by Arlene and Leonard Swidler to Ida Raming's *The Exclusion of Women from the Priesthood: Divine Law or Sex Discrimination*, transl. Norman Adams (Metuchen, N.J.: Scarecrow Press, 1976), p. xvii.

2. The text of the 1974 statement and history was supplied me by letter by the former head of the Ecclesial Role of Women Committee of the Leadership Conference of Women Religious, Sr. Lenora Maier, O.S.F.

3. *Focus on Women* packet of the LCWR, *Stepping Stones: Conclusion*, p. 38.

4. *The Status and Roles of Women in the Church*, LCWR pamphlet, 1976, p. 23.

5. *Women and the Catholic Priesthood: An Expanded Vision. Proceedings of the Detroit Ordination Conference*, ed. Anne Marie Gardiner, S.S.N.D. (New York: Paulist Press, 1976).

6. This text has been published in a variety of places. It can be obtained by writing to the Office of Women's Affairs of the General Theological Union, 2378 Virginia Street, Berkeley, Calif. 94709.

7. This study was published in a number of newspapers. It can be obtained by writing to the Quixote Center, 3311 Chauncey Place, no. 301, Mt. Rainier, Md. 20822.

Biographical Notes About the Contributors

Rosemary Radford Ruether is Georgia Harkness Professor of Theology at Garrett-Evangelical Theological Seminary, Evanston, Illinois. She is the author of several volumes on women and theology, and edited an earlier volume published by Simon and Schuster, *Religion and Sexism* (1974).

Eleanor McLaughlin is Associate Professor, Church History, specializing in the medieval period, at Andover Newton Theological Seminary, Newton, Massachusetts. She contributed the essay on women and medieval theology to the earlier volume *Religion and Sexism*.

Elisabeth Schüssler Fiorenza is Associate Professor of Theology at the University of Notre Dame, Notre Dame, Indiana. She has published books and articles on New Testament exegesis and feminist theology.

Ruth Prelowski Liebowitz is currently an instructor in the Radcliffe College Seminars program. She is working on a book about nuns and convents in Renaissance Italy.

Elaine C. Huber, O.P., is a Ph.D. candidate at the Graduate Theological Union, Berkeley, California. She has taught at Weston School of Theology, Cambridge, Massachusetts, on Feminist Perspectives in Early Church History.

Catherine F. Smith is Assistant Professor of English at Bucknell University, Lewisburg, Pennsylvania. Her paper, "Jane Lead and Jacob Boehme, Feminism and Mysticism," was originally delivered at the Pioneers for a Century Conference at the University of Cincinnati in 1976.

Barbara Brown Zikmund is Assistant Professor of Church History and Director of Studies at the Chicago Theological Seminary, Chicago. She is also editor of *The American Religious Experiment: Piety and Practicality* (Exploration Press, 1976).

Nancy A. Hardesty is Assistant Professor of American Church History at Candler School of Theology, Emory University, Atlanta. She is also coauthor, with Letha Scanzoni, of *All We're Meant to Be: A Biblical Approach to Women's Liberation*.

Lucille Sider Dayton, a graduate student in pastoral psychology at Garrett-Evangelical Theological Seminary and Northwestern University, has been assistant director of the Urban Life Center in Chicago. She was one of the founders of *Daughters of Sarah*, a Biblical feminist newsletter.

Donald W. Dayton serves as director of Mellander Library and is Associate Professor of Theology at North Park Theological Seminary, Chicago. Author of *Discovering an Evangelical Heritage*, he is working on a Ph.D. at the University of Chicago Divinity School on the theology of Pentecostalism within the Holiness movement.

Mary Ewens, O.P., is Professor of American Studies, Rosary College, River Forest, Illinois. Her dissertation topic at the University of Minnesota was on the adaptation of Catholic women's religious orders to the United States.

Dorothy C. Bass is a Research/Resource Associate in Women's Studies and Church History at the Harvard Divinity School and a doctoral candidate in American Civilization at Brown University. Her dissertation is on the woman question in American antislavery.

Virginia Lieson Brereton, a doctoral candidate in American history and education at Teachers College, Columbia University, is coauthor of a forthcoming study of the history of Protestant theological education in America and is a member of the Institute for Research in History.

Christa Ressmeyer Klein, Assistant Professor of Church History at Lutheran Theological Seminary, Gettysburg, is co-editor of a forthcoming study, funded by the Lilly Endowment, Inc., of the history of American Protestant theological education. She recently completed her doctoral dissertation at the University of Pennsylvania on the Jesuits and Catholic boyhood in nineteenth-century New York City.

Ellen M. Umansky is a graduate student in religion at Columbia University. She is currently working on her doctoral dissertation on the life and thought of the Honorable Lily H. Montagu.

Norene Carter is a member of the Episcopal Women's Caucus, and of the Commission on Women and Ministry, Diocese of Massachusetts. She is a child development specialist and a Research Assistant in the Department of the Church, Harvard Divinity School.

Index